The New Nationalism

By LOUIS L. SNYDER

In this significant new book, a renowned interpreter of modern history ponders the recent course of nationalism—the most potent political force in the world today. To measure the impact of the nationalistic urge since 1945, Professor Snyder focuses on the meaning, development, and characteristics of nationalism in all the major areas of the globe: Europe, Africa, Asia, the Middle East, Soviet Russia, the United States, and Latin America.

Clearly and authoritatively written, this study provides the first comprehensive approach to the new nationalism. From his factual presentation, the author demonstrates the grave consequences of unrestrained nationalism and evaluates the present crucial confrontation of nationalism and internationalism. Statesmen, politicians, diplomats, historians, and informed observers will find here a convincing analysis of a powerful sentiment in contemporary society.

ism; The War: A Concise History, 1939–1945; The World in the Twentieth Century; and *The Making of Modern Man.* He edited *The Dynamics of Nationalism* and was co-editor with Richard B. Morris of the best-selling *Treasury of Great Reporting.* He is the general editor of the well-known Anvil series of original paperbacks in history published by Van Nostrand. In 1952 he received a Ford Foundation Faculty Fellowship, and in 1965 he was awarded a Rockefeller Foundation Grant for study in Amsterdam and London.

The New Nationalism

The
New Nationalism

BY LOUIS L. SNYDER

The City College of The City University of New York

Cornell University Press ❖ ITHACA, NEW YORK

Library of Congress Catalog Card Number: 68–16391

PRINTED IN THE UNITED STATES OF AMERICA
BY KINGSPORT PRESS, INC.

TO *Henry Steele Commager*

HISTORIAN AND

DISTINGUISHED REPRESENTATIVE

OF THE AMERICAN MIND

Preface

Nationalism has appeared in many guises during the last two centuries. It has changed its characteristics through time, and it has been a source of endless confusion to scholars. Yevgeny Yevtushenko, the brilliant young Russian poet, revealed this sense of disconcerting perplexity in a passage in his autobiography: "I despise nationalism. For me the world contains only two nations, the good and the bad. I am a nationalist of the nation of the good. But the love of mankind can only be reached through the love of one's country." [1] Others admit a similar befuddlement.

It is the purpose of this study to extend the pioneer work of the two most gifted scholars of modern nationalism, Carlton J. H. Hayes and Hans Kohn. In a succession of books these historians, both superb analysts and stylists, set the framework for the study of this most powerful sentiment of modern times. Not only historians but also scholars of other disciplines—political scientists, economists, anthropologists, and psychologists—owe them a debt of gratitude.

The variegated pattern of nationalism closely follows political, economic, and psychological tendencies of historical development. Since 1945 there have appeared such motivating factors as the beginning of the cold war, the emergence of new nation-states, the intensification of world-wide communication and transportation, and a new technology, including the inauguration of the atomic age and the space race. All these events influenced the nature of nationalism, which took on a

[1] Yevgeny Yevtushenko, *A Precocious Autobiography*, trans. Andrew R. MacAndrew (Harmondsworth, England, 1965), p. 20.

vii

complexion that was new, not in the Pickwickian sense, but in historical context. This new nationalism retained the basic pattern of earlier forms, but its characteristics are sufficiently different to merit the historian's consideration. Attention will be directed to the meaning, characteristics, and development of the new nationalism, with emphasis on continental and regional trends.

The new nationalism to be examined here must be distinguished from Theodore Roosevelt's "New Nationalism," which he borrowed from a phrase in Herbert D. Croly's book *The Promise of American Life* (New York, 1909). Croly warned that the policy of *laissez faire*, by giving excessive power to big industry and finance, would lead to a degradation of the masses. He urged that a program of positive and comprehensive state and federal intervention be pursued on all economic fronts. Theodore Roosevelt drew from this his conception of "New Nationalism," which meant seeking greater powers for democratic government as a means of reviving the old pioneer sense of individualism and opportunity. This followed the pattern of American tradition. But it was a limited concept, somewhat removed from the new nationalism that is the theme of this study.

I am grateful to the Rockefeller Foundation for its grant which enabled me to complete this book during a sabbatical year from my duties at The City College of The City University of New York. Responsibility for the work, of course, is my own.

I wish to thank the staffs of the New York Public Library, the British Museum in London, and the libraries of the Universities of London and Amsterdam. The assistance of these professional librarians helped smooth the way for the many daily tasks necessary for a study of this kind. For their encouragement and help I am grateful to my distinguished colleagues and friends, Hans Kohn, Sidney I. Pomerantz, Bailey W. Diffie, Michael Kraus, J. Salwyn Schapiro, and Joseph E. Wisan. My warmest thanks go to many others, including Gerald Freund of the Rockefeller Foundation; Boyd C. Shafer, Professor of History at Macalester College; Dean Leslie W. Engler of The City College of New York; Elie Kedourie, Professor of Politics and Public Administration in the London School of Economics; E. M. Crane, Jr., President, D. Van Nostrand Company, Inc., Princeton, N.J.; Miss R. E. B. Coombs of the British Imperial War Museum in London; Hyman Kublin, Associate Dean of Graduate Studies at The City University of New York; and Howard L. Adelson, Executive Officer of the Ph.D. Program in History at The City University of New York.

The final phases of this study were made in Amsterdam, a vantage point for studying European integration and contemporary nationalism. There I found a most satisfying welcome in academic and governmental circles. I am grateful to Professor A. N. J. den Hollander, Director of the Sociology Seminar and the America Institute at the University of Amsterdam, and his assistant, Dr. P. Nijhoff; Dr. Louis de Jong, Director of the Netherlands State Institute for War Documentation; Professor A. J. C. Rüter, then Director of the International Institute of Social History, Amsterdam, and his successor, Miss Maria Huninck; His Excellency Mr. Wilfred Lennon, Irish Ambassador to Holland; A. P. K. Hartog, Director-General of the European Integration Section of the Netherlands Foreign Office; and Mr. Manuel Abrams, Economic Counsellor, the United States Embassy at The Hague.

To my wife I owe, as on many other occasions, a tremendous debt as collaborator in the finest sense of the word—a source for ideas, a keen critic, and an invaluable aide in the mechanical production of this book.

LOUIS L. SNYDER

New York City
June 1968

Contents

The New Nationalism

Chapter 1

Nationalism in the Modern World

Nationalism . . . permeates every political philosophy be it national, pan-national, imperialistic or international. The sentiment of national consciousness has entered a crusading phase so powerful that every dogma of the state and of peoples in general is linked with it. It has taken as complete a hold on modern thinking and attitudes as did religion and theology on the thinking of the Middle Ages. . . . Nationalism today belongs to the people of the world.

—FELIKS GROSS

Nationalism, that state of mind in which the supreme loyalty of the individual is felt to be owed to the nation-state,[1] today remains the strongest of political emotions. Everywhere national consciousness has been molded into dogmatic philosophies and ideologies. The most important question of our time—the quest for peace—is a search for solutions to problems of conflicting nationalisms.

Nationalism is repeatedly denounced as an anachronism in the contemporary world—as an outmoded, deep-seated disease which plagues mankind and which cannot be healed by incantation.[2] Its generative element is described as egoistic: all members of a given country belong to one and the same in-group, which is distinct from the various out-groups surrounding it.[3] It is a mode of living which assures security to the in-group, requiring little or no attention to others. The accusation is made that nationalism, by dividing humanity into squabbling states, places excessive and exclusive emphasis upon the value of the nation at the expense of moral and ethical values, leading to an overestimation of one's own nation and the simultaneous denigration of others.[4] Nationalism, it is said again and again, has turned into a kind of religious faith, easily perverted into oppression and aggrandizement. Nationalism breeds imperialism, and the latter, in turn, breeds nationalism again in the people whom it subjects to its control.

In view of the juxtaposition of the strength of nationalism against denunciations of it, continued examination of the phenomenon becomes imperative. Nationalism is not a neat, fixed concept, but a varying combination of beliefs and conditions.[5] Only the prophetic scholars, such as Marx and Spengler, who used the big hypothesis to probe the mysteries of history, could judge nationalism to be tidy and ordered, a clear-cut phenomenon, like a polished apple, of definite

[1] Hans Kohn, *Nationalism: Its Meaning and History* (rev. ed.; Princeton, 1965), p. 9.

[2] Harold J. Laski, *Nationalism and the Future of Civilization* (London, 1932), p. 26.

[3] Bert F. Hoselitz, "Nationalism, Economic Development, and Democracy," *Annals of the American Academy of Political and Social Science*, CCCV (May 1956), 3.

[4] Laski, *op. cit.*, p. 26.

[5] Boyd C. Shafer, *Nationalism: Myth and Reality* (New York, 1955), pp. 7–8.

form, size, and influence. They reduced its chaos to a single order of explanation, criticized it, and confidently predicted its future development. That they did not take into account or underestimated the role of chance, contingency, and intricacy in man's development may be attributed to zeal in presenting a ready-made solution for historical problems.

Nationalism reflects the chaos of history itself. As a historical phenomenon, it is always in flux, changing according to no preconceived pattern. It is multifaceted, disheveled, murky, irreducible to common denominators. It is part actuality, part myth, intermingling both truth and error. "Myths like other errors have a way of perpetuating themselves and of becoming both true and real." [6] Functioning in a milieu of historical paradox,[7] nationalism produces strange myths which are accepted uncritically as normal and rational. It can never be reduced to a simplistic formula, for it has shades and nuances, and it encourages improvisation.

Nationalism has become a catchword with many different meanings. It is capable of generating precisely opposite reactions. To Sun Yat-sen it appeared to be a "precious possession" which enabled a state to aspire to progress, but to Jawaharlal Nehru it was "essentially an anti-feeling," feeding and fattening on hatred and anger.

We see the working of nationalism in a multiplicity of forms, some sharp and undisguised, some vague and hidden; some directed to cultural integration, others to political ends; some democratic in aspect, others veering toward authoritarianism. Its variations may be seen in the following breakdown: [8]

A force for unity. Nationalism may be a means by which politically divided nations achieve union in a single state, by which there is integration and consolidation of a country's territory (Italy, Germany).

A force for the status quo. Nationalism may reflect the effort of multinational states to prevent a breakdown into component parts of varying nationalities (the Austro-Hungarian, Russian, and German empires).

[6] *Ibid.,* p. 7.   [7] See "Paradox into Axiom" in Chapter 2.

[8] Some repetition with classifications of nationalism, discussed later, is unavoidable here. See Chapter 4. Cf. further Feliks Gross, *European Ideologies* (New York, 1948), pp. 478–479; Hoselitz, *op. cit.,* p. 1; and Hugh Seton-Watson, "Fascism, Right and Left," *Journal of Contemporary History,* I, No. 1 (1966), 188–189.

A force for independence. Nationalism may result from the desire of national minority peoples to break away from a larger entity and achieve autonomy (Poles, Ukrainians, Czechs, Slovaks, Croats, Balts, Finns).

A force for fraternity. Similarly, nationalism may represent the striving of irredentas to win union with others of the same in-group (*Italia irredenta*, Greeks, Serbs, Rumanians, Bulgarians).

A force for colonial expansion. Nationalism may be the road by which older established nations enhance their imperialist positions (Great Britain, France, Portugal, Spain, Belgium, the Netherlands).

A force for aggression. Nationalism motivates "have-not nations" to acquire greater wealth, territory, people, and power (Wilhelminian Germany, Nazi Germany, Fascist Italy, militarist Japan).

A force for economic expansion. Nationalism accompanies the attempts of more powerful nations (United States, Soviet Union) to obtain economic advantages *vis-à-vis* undeveloped nations.

A force for anticolonialism. Nationalism promotes the creation of new nation-states in the former colonies in Africa, Asia, and the Near and Middle East. It was transformed from a movement of opposition and defiance to a movement of nation-building (Ghana, Nigeria, Congo, India, Indonesia, Syria, Jordan).

In addition to the various facets of nationalism, there is further difficulty in that it is clothed with paradox and contradiction. We shall examine this tendency in more detail later, but one major paradox can be mentioned here. Essentially a product of British individualism and French egalitarianism, nationalism in its early stages stressed the libertarian formula. Refusing to recognize the claims of God and monarchy, it elevated the nation over the concepts of legitimacy and tradition. In the age of Metternich (1815–1848), reactionaries took a stand opposite to nationalism, defending instead the rights of kings and aristocracy. By the end of the nineteenth century, however, reactionaries were appropriating the fruits of nationalism for their own purposes. Liberal nationalism and totalitarian nationalism headed for a collision in World War II.

Today, in a shrunken, vulnerable world, boasting of its oversupply of atom bombs and guided missiles, nationalism would seem to be a dangerous luxury. But it still persists, and its form is even accentuated. Barbara Ward compares this modern condition to an earlier phase of Western history. The hill town of San Gimignano in Tuscany had a myriad of high towers, each attached to a family mansion and each used as a base for attack on nearby streets. The little town was hopelessly split into warring factions. The world today, with its vastly improved facilities for communication and transportation, is not much larger in effect than the city boundaries of old San Gimignano. "We, too, are building the equivalent of towers to our own houses from which to hurl atomic weapons at rivals across the frontiers which are little wider in time than a village street. . . . This is our world, as confined and vulnerable as an Italian hill city, its sovereignties almost as laughable as the old family feuds, its killings as fratricidal, its warfare as likely to destroy in one holocaust family and neighbor and town." [9]

THE OLD AND THE NEW

Boyd C. Shafer, a perceptive scholar, asks: "Are the nationalisms of the mid-twentieth century so different as to be new?" [10] The question is pertinent. Use of the term "new nationalism" is justifiable as an arbitrary device to facilitate its study. There is no such thing as a new nationalism in the same sense that there is no "ancient, medieval, or modern history"—divisions made merely for the sake of convenience. Similarly the term "First Industrial Revolution" (1750–1860) is used to describe the industrial transformation which commenced in England and used coal as a source of power, while the "New Industrial Revolution" (1860–1900), centered in the United States and Germany and using oil and eventually electricity as sources of power, was in many ways a continuation of the old, but took on different characteristics. Nationalism, too, fits this semantic pattern. Like history itself it is always subject to change, a development recognized by the pre-Socratic cosmologist Heraclitus as early as *c.* 500 B.C. ("everything is in a state of eternal flux").

The year 1945, the end of World War II, is a convenient boundary mark in the study of nationalism. Two trends are noticeable: the persistence of nationalism in its early form, and the simultaneous emergence of variations retaining basic qualities of the old but adding new and vital characteristics.

The nationalism that began in western Europe represented a rejec-

[9] Barbara Ward, *Faith and Freedom* (London, 1954), p. 209.
[10] Boyd C. Shafer in a review of William J. Bossenbrook, ed., *Mid-Twentieth Century Nationalism* (*American Historical Review*, LXXI [Apr. 1966], 916).

tion by dissatisfied peoples of the traditional sociopolitical order. It repudiated the medieval polity of Church and state; it opposed divine-right monarchy; and it denounced the hierarchical structure of privileged classes. It reflected the desire of Europeans to be governed by peoples of their own kind, to attain economic betterment, to achieve social status among peers, and to recognize a common cultural heritage. People would express their national identity to work together for the common good.

This early modern nationalism was concerned with two major ideas: the primacy of the state and the principle of sovereignty. The English Glorious Revolution of 1688, the American Revolution of 1776, and the French Revolution of 1789 solidified the concept of the modern state. The principle of sovereignty demanded that a nation be organized as a state.[11] The Glorious Revolution called for realization of "the true and ancient rights of the people of this realm." The American Declaration of Independence pronounced the equality of all men, the inalienability of such human rights as life, liberty, and the pursuit of happiness, and the duty of government to protect the rights of the sovereign people. The French Declaration of the Rights of Man and of the Citizen (August 26, 1789) held that "the source of all sovereignty is essentially in the nation; no body, no individual can exercise authority that does not proceed from it in plain terms." All these declarations were based on the principles that each national state should be distinct from all others and that its people are sovereign within it.

The pattern of early nineteenth-century nationalism was fixed to a large extent by French armies which, in response to attempts from abroad to stifle the revolutionary impetus inside France, burst beyond the borders and with missionary zeal offered the ideal of nationalism to all peoples. Napoleon was in part a prisoner of this new force and in part its champion. Throughout Europe it became the fashion for even the smallest states to imitate the French model.

Blended with patriotism ("nationalism is a fusion of patriotism with a consciousness of nationality"),[12] nationalism became the glorious banner under which men gave their lives to achieve or maintain nationhood. It was the generating power behind the revolt of South American peoples to free themselves from colonial Spain (Simón

[11] Walter Sulzbach, "The New Nationalism," *South Atlantic Quarterly*, LI (Oct. 1952), 483.

[12] Carlton J. H. Hayes, *Nationalism: A Religion* (New York, 1960), p. 2.

Bolívar, José de San Martín). It was the inspiration that brought unity to the fragmented Italies (Mazzini, Garibaldi, Cavour), and to the scattered German principalities (Bismarck). It was the motivation behind a host of drives for independence, including those of the Irish Sinn Feiners ("We Ourselves"), Bohemian Czechs, and Young Turks. Nationalism was one of the more powerful forces which led the peoples of Europe into the abyss of World War I. And in its perverted form, unleased by Hitler and the Nazi terror, it became the curse of the century.

Nationalism emerged partly tamed from the bloodbath of World War II. The real threat of a Communist takeover drove Western countries into a new sense of interdependence. Some of the old national rivalries were softened by consultation and cooperation. The British, the French, and the Dutch, faced with declining imperialism, lost their overseas colonies, and discovered to their surprise that they did not collapse in the process. But underneath the surface of the new pragmatism, nationalism retained its strength and vigor. It revealed the same variations as before, ranging from a benign cultural polish to an exaggerated tendency to stress national interests above all others. It continued to generate disputes about historical and natural frontiers. It showed itself in the concept of a so-called European Europe, which was to be independent of United States power as well as that of the Soviet Union. At the same time nationalism called for a Europe of wholly sovereign states, unlikely to speak with a common voice.

To this extended nationalism something new was added. The world in the middle of the twentieth century was far different from that of 1900. At the close of World War II came a violent awakening of the subject nations of Asia and Africa, a development that brought rapid alterations in the map of the world. Fifty-two nations established the United Nations in another attempt to break down the barriers between peoples. Since then the fight for independence has more than doubled the membership of that organization. The new nations now account for more than a third of global territory and about one-half the human race. Each is moved to express its own identity. Each boasts of its own self-interest and its own power of decision. Each seeks roots in the past. Each elevates the flag above all, refusing to surrender its national sovereignty or to allow control of its destiny by outsiders.

Nationalism has always held basically the same attitude toward the state. Nations were constituted into sovereign states; they were isolated from each other; they refused to relinquish even a part of their sovereignty. These ideas carried over from the old to the new nationalism despite the fact that the world was much too diverse for the classifications of nationalist anthropology.

Races, languages, religions, political traditions and loyalties are so inextricably intermixed that there can be no clear convincing reason why people who speak the same language, but whose history and circumstances otherwise widely diverge, should form one state, or why people who speak two different languages and whom circumstances have thrown together should not form one state. On nationalist logic, the separate existence of Britain and America, and the union of English and French Canadians within the Canadian state, are both monstrosities of Nature; and a consistent nationalist interpretation of history would reduce large parts of it to inexplicable and irritating anomalies.[13]

Despite the overlapping between the old and the new nationalisms, there are differences which merit attention. These characteristics are examined in Chapter 3.

POLITICO-ECONOMIC LAG: THE NEW NATIONALISM
AND MODERNIZATION

A puzzling element of the new nationalism is its persistence at a time when both political and economic demands seem to run in the opposite direction. In its early stages, nationalism was geared to political individualism and an agricultural, commercial economy. "Nationalism was associated with the mass mobilization of precommercial, preindustrial peasant peoples." [14] But with modernization came rapid changes in transportation and communication, interlocking relationships of industrial complexes, and world-wide techniques of the money economy. It would seem that nationalism would outlive its usefulness in this new age, when industrial and business barriers break down. Instead, the new nationalism, far from pointing the way to an international society, lags behind the process of modernization and leaves a politico-economic gap which grows wider instead of disappearing.

The problem, like all historical questions, has many facets. There are cultural repercussions. Shakespeare, Goethe, Beethoven, Michelan-

[13] Elie Kedourie, *Nationalism* (London, 1960), p. 79.
[14] Karl W. Deutsch, *Nationalism and Social Communication* (New York, 1953), p. 164.

gelo—all accepted as geniuses of humanity—still retain the status of national heroes in the lands of their birth. Modernization has seen a healthy breakdown of cultural barriers between peoples, yet, and again the paradox, the educational process has continued to emphasize national history, national traditions, national heroes, the flag, and the glory of the fatherland. On one hand, the peoples of the world have become more and more alike in cultural expression; on the other, they are separated by the wedge of an institutionalized cultural heritage.

The trend is twofold: modernization heads in the direction of internationalism, but it is held back by the centrifugal current of the new nationalism. Richard Pipes recognized this conflict:

The push and pull exerted on nationalism by the process of modernization has been the essence of the "national problem" of our time. On the one hand, modernization demands cultural levelling; on the other, it released social forces that are least prone to such levelling. Since the latter tendency is often stronger than the former, because it represents real pressures as against ideal considerations, nationalism has made remarkable headway and is likely to continue to do so.[15]

The modernization of society requires the mobilization into national life of all people without regard for class, linguistic, and religious distinctions. But instead of suppressing nationalism and national differences, the new industrialization, in a kind of inverse process, stimulates them. Both capital and labor are interested in the status of world finance and industry, but both are much more deeply involved in the condition of the *national* economy.

The process of modernization was examined brilliantly in depth by C. E. Black in his recent volume *The Dynamics of Modernization.*[16] According to Black, there has been a critical increase in the speed and sweep of change because of the extensive proliferation of knowledge in recent centuries. He defines modernization as the process by which historically evolved institutions are adapted to those changing functions accompanying the scientific revolution. Countries become modern as they learn to innovate and adapt: thus modernization must be served by different societies with different histories, institutions, and traditions.

[15] Richard Pipes, "The Forces of Nationalism," *Problems of Communism*, XIII (Jan.-Feb. 1964), 3.

[16] C. E. Black, *The Dynamics of Modernization: A Study in Comparative History* (New York, 1966).

Black sees four stages of modernization: the challenge of modernity to a hitherto traditional society; consolidation of modernizing leadership; socioeconomic transformation in a climate of rising national self-preoccupation; and sociopolitical integration of classes inside the nation-state followed by the gradual claim of its people for cultural and political integration beyond the borders.

All 130 contemporary sovereign states and the thirty or forty struggling to emerge must go through this development, each remaining at varying times in the early stages. Black divides these countries into seven basic patterns of development: original modernizing countries in the West (England and France); their interests overseas (the United States, Canada, Australia, and New Zealand); other nations in western and central Europe; the extension of these other European nations into Latin America; such autonomous non-Western countries as Russia, Japan, China, and Turkey; weak countries with adaptable traditions (Algeria, India, and Egypt); and poor, undeveloped peoples with little or no linguistic, territorial, or national sense of unity (peoples of sub-Saharan Africa and the Pacific Islands).

The advanced countries are already in the critical fourth stage of their own modernization, while the undeveloped countries are still bogged down in the early stages. The latter nations still face the choice of liberal constitutionalism, national statism, or Soviet communism: in the process they are as prone to violence and domestic strife as the developed countries were in their earlier history.

Not the least interesting aspect of the modernization of profoundly diverse societies is the recurrent theme of nationalism. The nation-state remains both fulcrum and goal: increasing modernization stays within the framework of nationalism, rather than the internationalism of the world society, as desirable as it might be. Both the advanced and the undeveloped peoples have accepted the concept of the nation-state.

MÉLANGE: THE PROBLEM OF LARGE VERSUS
SMALL NATIONS

More than a century ago, Friedrich List, a Württemberger political economist and the originator of the German customs union (*Zollverein*), made the observation that between the individual and humanity stands the nation. List's generalization made no distinction between the large and the small nation.

Nationalism from its beginning encompassed both large and small sovereign nations. Unfortunately, there are gaps in information on the differences between large and small nations and on the contrasts in their national experiences. There are unanswered questions on the distinction between old and new independent nations; between old monarchies and new republics; between unitary and federal states; between unilingual and multilingual nations; between nations of religious homogeneity and religious pluralism; and between countries that enjoyed early industrial progress and others to which it came only recently.[17]

The status of "large" or "great" is not necessarily identifiable by size alone. The small city-state of Athens dominated the ancient Greek world in the fourth century B.C. Britain, an island with a comparatively small population, held world power for centuries. Tiny Switzerland, landlocked in the heart of western Europe, still retains an important position in world finance. But, large or small, both great powers and minor nations have always insisted upon rights of political unity, independent economic policy, and cultural autonomy. Without an effective large-scale supranational organization, nations operated wholly on a power basis. The stronger nations dominated the weaker, whereupon the latter sought security as satellites of powerful neighbors. In a sense this was a kind of modernized version of the lord-vassal relationship of medieval feudalism. And just as feudalism paradoxically maintained a kind of order in its day, so did the large and small nations function in the midst of international anarchy.

Under the old nationalism England, France, the United States, Germany, and Russia furnished the models of nation-building. All had similar motivations: as nations they were responsible only to themselves; they were to be free of encroachments; they expected concessions of sovereignty from small nations—concessions which they were not prepared to make themselves. In the final analysis they always relied upon their own strength or upon treaties.

The small nations, including Austria, Italy, Norway, Sweden, Denmark, Belgium, the Netherlands, and Luxembourg, each contributed in its own way historical evidence on nation-building. Their experiences in nationalism may or may not have been significantly different from those of the great powers. However, they had one characteristic in

[17] Val R. Lorwin, "The Comparative Analysis of Historical Change: Nation-Building in the Western World," *International Social Science Journal*, XVII, No. 4 (1965), 594–606.

common with the larger nations—the desire to maintain absolute national sovereignty.

In the era of the new nationalism the problems of relationship between large and small nations have become even more conspicuous. The new nations of Africa and Asia find the experiences of the great powers unrelated to their own problems because of differences in size of electorate, nature of the elites, and natural resources. Comparatively weak, they call for national interdependence as favorable for their own existence. If there is any danger in nationalism, they say, it is certainly in the nationalism of the older great powers rather than in their own flowering sense of nationhood. Their representatives, banding together in the United Nations, attain an influence far beyond their importance, a situation which makes the great powers even more reluctant to relinquish even a part of their national sovereignty in favor of international government.

To some, including Arnold Toynbee, nationalism appears outmoded because we can no longer afford a world society in which tiny states may go to war with one another. Edward H. Carr suggests that the ideology of the small nation as the ultimate politico-economic unit seems to be losing ground: "In Europe some of the small units of the past may continue for a few generations longer to eke out a precarious independent existence; others may retain the shadow of independence when the reality has disappeared. But their military and economic insecurity has been demonstrated beyond recall. They can survive only as an anomaly and an anachronism in a world that has moved on to other forms of organization." [18]

How far the world "has moved on to other forms of organization" is still subject to debate. Anachronism or not, nationalism, be it the nationalism of the small or the large nation, retains a virulence which at the present moment gives little indication of disappearing from the world scene. One need only ask the citizen on any street anywhere whether his paramount loyalty is to his country or to the human race. Until that day comes when the automatic response is "I feel my first responsibility is to humanity!" we shall have to regard nationalism as very much alive and as a continuing threat to personal liberty and to the universality of culture.

[18] Edward H. Carr, *Nationalism and After* (London, 1945), p. 35.

Chapter 2

Paradoxes of Nationalism

*Thus far, the age of nationalism has grouped
people apart from each other, and may for a
time continue to do so. But at the same time
it is preparing them, and perhaps in part has
already prepared them, for a more thoroughgoing
worldwide unity than has ever been seen in
human history.*

— KARL W. DEUTSCH

Nationalism, in both its old and new forms, is a historical phenomenon of the utmost complexity, suffused with paradox. At once moral and immoral, human and inhuman, noble and savage, it can be either blessing or curse. In itself nationalism, like capitalism, socialism, and imperialism, has both positive and negative characteristics.[1] Circumstances so powerfully influence the feelings and opinions of men that vices can pass into virtues, and paradoxes into axioms.[2]

Historical paradox is by no means new. It may be observed in the ecclesiastical history of the Middle Ages. Medieval men were devoted to the Church as "the mother of mercy and the fountain of charity," yet they cheerfully approved the infliction of the most terrible tortures upon those who dared to hold heretical opinions. The persecution of heretics was justified morally on the ground that the Church was a law unto itself—the epitome of divine will—and that every ecclesiastical action, no matter how cruel and however repulsive to humanity, was sanctified.[3]

The rise of national states in the sixteenth and seventeenth centuries was a reaction against the rule of the Church. In some baffling way (motivation of nationalism never seems to be clear-cut), national fervor took a rigid hold on the mind of modern man. The medieval man identified himself not as a Frenchman, German, or Italian, but as a faithful son of the Roman Catholic Church. He was loyal to the ecclesiastical state. Modern man, on the other hand, saw his security in the national state. Nationalism became in political life what faith had

[1] See Hans Kohn, "A New Look at Nationalism," *Virginia Quarterly Review,* XXXII (Summer 1956), 321–332.

[2] How vices turned into virtues, and paradoxes became axioms, was the theme of Thomas Babington Macaulay's essay on Machiavelli (Thomas Babington Macaulay, "Machiavelli," in *Criticial and Historical Essays* [London, 1961], pp. 1–37).

[3] See Julius Braunthal, *The Paradox of Nationalism* (London, 1946), pp. 16–17. Braunthal quoted L. Marineo, who in his *Cosas Memorables* (1530) wrote: "The Church, who is the mother of mercy and the fountain of charity, content with the imposition of penances, generously accords life to many who do not deserve it; while those who persist obstinately in their errors, after being imprisoned on the testimony of trustworthy witnesses, she causes to be put to the torture, and condemned to the flames."

been in religion. The phenomenon was described by Lord Acton in his analysis of patriotism:

Patriotism is in political life what faith is in religion, and it stands to the domestic feelings and to home-sickness as faith to fanaticism and to superstition. It has one aspect derived from private life and nature, for it is an extension of the family affections, as the tribe is an extension of the family. But in its real political character, patriotism consists in the development of the instinct of self-preservation into a moral duty which may involve self-sacrifice. Self-preservation is both an instinct and a duty, natural and involuntary in one respect, and at the same time a moral obligation. By the first it produces the family, by the second the State. . . . The great sign of true patriotism, the development of selfishness into sacrifice, is the product of political life. . . . The love of country, like married love, stands at the same time on a material and a moral foundation.[4]

As nationalism developed it began to take on more and more contradictory aspects. Ambiguously, it became a force for both peace and war. The great masses looked upon the nation as an extension of the family, and they felt safe in its embrace. Everywhere the common people, who formed the bulk of every nation, wanted to live out their lives in peace and order. They were neither warlike nor aggressive; they were not interested in conquest, aggrandizement, colonialism, or imperialism. They wanted no slaves. They had little interest in or understanding of the diplomatic intrigues which occupied the world's statesmen.

These pacific peoples were easily transformed into crusading belligerents. Once the drumfire of propaganda began, the ordinary citizen was swept along into the path of national hatred. He was convinced that his own security and that of his family were threatened by the enemy—"the French-Corsican monster," "perfidious Albion," "the treacherous Italian," "the unspeakable Turk," "the Russian hordes," and the "Fascist beasts." Peace-loving people, trapped by suspicion and hatred, and terrified by the threat of attack, prepared to fight, always in the name of defense. Those who wanted nothing more than to be let alone were transformed overnight into warmongers.

In this way peace-loving people turn to war as a solution for their

---

[4] John Emerich Edward Dalberg-Acton, "On Nationality," in *Essays on Freedom and Power* (Boston, 1949), p. 188.

problems. They no longer see the irony of their transformation. What formerly was a simple paradox is accepted as axiomatic.

INCONGRUITY: CULTURAL INTEGRATION
VERSUS POLITICAL DIFFUSION

Its impelling thrust to both war and peace was but one of the contradictions of nationalism. Quite as perplexing was the paradox of cultural integration versus political diffusion. As always, nationalism in content and consequences accurately reflected historical circumstance. Again the paradox became axiomatic: as cultural diversities diminished, political nationalism increased.[5] Culturally, the peoples of the world were brought closer and closer together, politically they became more and more estranged.

Lord Acton pointed out that the peoples of the world are swayed by identical interests, absorbed by the same problems, and thrilled by the same emotions. Cultural barriers have gradually broken down—a consistent process since the dissolution of the medieval order, the sixteenth-century Commercial Revolution, the seventeenth- and eighteenth-century scientific and intellectual revolution of the Age of Reason, and the nineteenth- and twentieth-century Industrial Revolutions. All these historical movements contributed to the erosion of cultural diversities. The pattern was especially clear in the industrial revolutions, which brought peoples closer physically and culturally. In the words of Barbara Ward:

No rational man can deny the basic physical changes which have occurred in our universe in the last hundred years. It now takes less time to girdle the earth than it took during the eighteenth century to travel from Boston to Philadelphia or from Edinburgh to London. Even if still only a small fraction of mankind uses the new means of transport, the physical interconnectedness of those who stay at home is equally a fact. . . . However violent the effort made at various times—for instance in the thirties—to insulate national economies from the force of change or development or collapse at work in world trade, the web of commerce has grown so strongly that today the nations appear to have only two choices: either to make the intricate system function or else to strangle in its tangled skein.[6]

[5] See William G. Carlton, "The New Nationalism," *Virginia Quarterly Review,* XXVI (July 1950), 432.
[6] Barbara Ward, *Faith and Freedom* (London, 1954), pp. 208–209; courtesy of Hamish Hamilton, Ltd.

There have been many attempts—political, military, religious, psychological—to take advantage of a steadily growing cultural uniformity: the Alexandrian effort at world cosmopolitanism (*humanitas*); Roman expansion (*Pax Romana*); the medieval *sacerdotium-imperium* (Holy Roman Empire); French aggrandizement (Napoleonic Empire); German drives to world power (*Pax Germania*); the League of Nations; and the United Nations. But in each case cultural uniformity was not powerful enough to overcome the urge to political diversity.

The pattern of localized loyalty preceded the age of nationalism. In Periclean Athens as well as in Renaissance Florence, the city-state was the core of political loyalty. Each little city-state was unified on the basis of common language, customs, traditions, and ideals. Each revolved on its own axis. Each regarded the peoples on its periphery as enemies. Athenian and Spartan, Florentine and Pisan, were at each other's throats, each trying to absorb the strength and wealth of the other. Despite similar unifying features in nearby city-states, there was no sense of a greater Hellenic nationalism or of a peninsula-wide Italian community.

Modern nationalism was an extension of the city-state idea on a greater scale. The same bonds of common language, religion, customs, and heroes, the same patriotism, the same xenophobia—all these were combined to form the stuff of nationalism. Cultural barriers were broken down; technological and scientific change brought the various parts of the world closer and closer together. But while cultural diversities were disappearing, political nationalism became at the same time more and more intensified. The process continued into the middle of the twentieth century. The prophecy that the world would move toward political unification as cultural barriers were eliminated was not realized. The paradox remains.

DILEMMA: THE A-B-C PARADOX

Another incongruity of nationalism is the A-B-C paradox projected by the political scientist Hans J. Morgenthau.[7] In this self-contradiction, nation B invokes the principles of nationalism against nation A, and denies them to nation C—in each case for the sake of its own survival.

[7] Hans J. Morgenthau, "The Paradoxes of Nationalism," *Yale Review*, XLVI (June 1957), 481.

Behind this paradox lies the entire development of modern nationalism. Morgenthau sees nationalism and Marxism as the last great original contributions of the West to political thought and practice. What eventually became a threat to civilization, a scourge of political anarchy, and a mockery of political morality, the West offered as a condition of civilized life, a principle of order and freedom, and a basis for justice. Nationalism, closely connected with the idea of freedom, shared the latter's ambiguity. Nationalism sought two freedoms—collective (freedom of a nation from domination by other nations) and individual (freedom of the individual to join the nation of his choice).

According to Morgenthau, the history of nationalism is the story of the principle of national self-determination fulfilling the postulates of both democracy and nationalism. World War I was caused in part by the unfulfilled aspirations of the nationalities within the Austro-Hungarian Empire. The Allies fought the war in the name of national self-determination, and Germany turned the same weapon against Russia. The peace settlements dissolved not only the Austro-Hungarian and Russian empires, but also the German and Turkish empires, all broken down into their national components.

With the triumph of nationalism, it was assumed that the result would be a viable order in Europe. Instead, the coming of age of nationalism brought neither peace, order, nor justice. What happened was that the oppressors and the oppressed merely changed roles:

There are no inherent limits to the application of the principles of nationalism. If the peoples of Bulgaria, Greece, and Serbia could invoke these principles against Turkey, why could not the people of Macedonia invoke them against Bulgaria, Greece, and Serbia? . . . Thus yesterday's oppressed cannot help becoming the oppressors of today because they are afraid lest they be again oppressed tomorrow. Hence, the process of national liberation must stop at some point, and that point is determined not by the logic of nationalism, but by the configuration of interest and power between the rulers and the ruled and between competing nations.[8]

This was the paradox of B invoking the principles of nationalism against A and denying them to C. The process was even more involved because of the additional difficulty of applying it consistently to mixed populations. Minority problems tended to confuse the whole issue of nationalism. There were clashes between the ideas of collective and

---

[8] *Ibid.*, p. 485.

individual freedoms: the individual's rights to property and the pursuit of happiness turned out to be incompatible with his right to choose his own government according to his preference as a minority member. He could not enjoy both rights simultaneously: he had to sacrifice one or the other.

During the period of the Long Armistice between 1919 and 1939, a network of treaties was devised for the protection of minority nationalities. But the attempts to ensure minority rights were frustrated by national conflicts among the great powers and among the new states. The great powers jockeyed for favorable international positions; the little nations, some of them pawns of their stronger neighbors, also competed among themselves.

The nationalism which contributed much to the outbreak of World War II also utilized the old principle of self-determination, but in reverse. Before World War I, the Slavic minority in the Balkans had demanded dissolution of the Austro-Hungarian Empire in the name of national self-determination. Now the Germans began to use the German minorities in Czechoslovakia and Poland in an effort to destroy those nations. Russia turned to her western neighbors with similar designs. Both Nazi Germany and Soviet Russia dropped the libertarian formula typical of nineteenth-century nationalism.

It is a demonstration of the adaptability of nationalist slogans that they could be used in a twisted version for the purpose of aggrandizement. Nazi and Soviet Russian imperialism developed from the aims of dictators who concentrated an ever-increasing proportion of the forces of society in their own hands. Both Hitler and Stalin used the instruments of power over the masses toward the making of empires. Their own nations served merely as the instruments and the bases of attack.[9]

The Morgenthau A-B-C paradox indicates a self-contradictory strain in nationalism. Nevertheless, there is a certain logic in it. Fragmentation was prevented from degenerating into anarchy by political power which halted the process at a convenient point. There are hundreds of regional areas all over Europe and throughout the world, each with distinctive cultural qualities. Each possesses characteristics of a national state. But instead of thousands of nations there are relatively few, composed of diverse cultural groups herded around fixed political centers. The successful national states are those which have absorbed

[9] W. Friedman, *Crisis of the National State* (London, 1943), pp. 163–164.

diverse minority groups within their borders, though each minority considered itself to deserve national self-determination. The basis was might-makes-right.[10] The centralized power in each national state might allow national disintegration up to a certain point, but the process almost always was halted just short of chaos.

Thus the existence of every national state is paradoxically a denial of the very right of nationalism to others. National states often include particularistic cultural groups, each longing for its own national identity. The universalism of the Middle Ages was succeeded by a collection of national states, each of which was a universe in microcosm. And some were proficient in the task of denying to minor nationalities that very same nationalism which they demanded for themselves.

CONTRADICTION: COLLECTIVISM VERSUS NATIONALISM

Still another paradox associated with nationalism is the universal tendency of collectivism to become nationalistic. In the Marxist analysis of history, the coming world revolution inevitably will destroy capitalistic society, obliterate the whole system of nation-states, and bring into existence a supranational world society under the triumphant control of the working class.[11] Of all the prognostications of Marx, this belief in the ultimate international proletarian order turned out to be the most incorrect. When the long-awaited revolution occurred, it took place not in highly industrialized Britain or Germany, but in a Russia still burdened by feudal restrictions. The international Communist community of nations, far from uniting in a world supranational society, broke down into blocs of quarreling national states. Communist ideology, like other universalist concepts of the past, seems incapable of surmounting the limits of the nation-state system.[12]

The tendency of collectivism to become nationalistic applies to socialists of every timbre. According to Friedrich A. Hayek, collectiv-

[10] George Bernard Shaw: "The world is to the big and powerful states by necessity; and the little ones must come within their border or be crushed out of existence" (quoted by Elie Halévy, in *L'Ere des tyrannies* [Paris, 1938], p. 217).

[11] See Edward H. Carr, *The Bolshevik Revolution* (New York, 1951), I, 410–428, for the views of Marx and Engels on the national question.

[12] Paul Shoup, "Communism, Nationalism and the Growth of the Communist Community of Nations after World War II," *American Political Science Review*, LVI (Oct. 1962), 886. See also "Socialist Supranationalism versus Communist Nationalism" in Chapter 11.

ism on a world scale is unthinkable—except in the service of a small ruling elite. "It may, indeed, be questioned whether anyone can realistically conceive of a collectivist program other than in the service of a limited group, whether collectivism can exist in any form other than some kind of particularism, be it nationalism, racialism, or classism." [13] As long as it remains theoretical, socialism is internationalist, but in some cases, as soon as it is put into practice, it becomes violently nationalist. Hayek sees this as one of the reasons why "liberal socialism," as most people in the Western world imagine it, is purely theoretical, while the practice of socialism is everywhere totalitarian. "Collectivism has no room for the wide humanitarianism of liberalism but only for the narrow particularism of the totalitarian." [14] In theory the workers of the world have common needs and aspirations and they are supposed to be united in their opposition to their exploiters. But the practice, as so often in history, is quite different from the theory.

Collectivists have consistently underestimated the impact of nationalism. Regarding it as a temporary historical phenomenon, they repeatedly announce its demise, only to see it re-emerge more powerful than ever. Loyalty to the cultural in-group and identification of individual interests with the larger, more powerful in-group are as old as recorded history. This sentiment of belonging existed in prehistoric times, throughout the ancient era, and in the Middle Ages. In modern times, in the form of nationalism, it was intensified by every major historical movement.

It is for this reason that historians are skeptical of claims for the international character of socialism and communism. They have seen every great movement of modern times, no matter what its universalist tinge, identify itself with an in-group and work for the intensification of nationalism. Why should socialism and communism be exceptions? Is there anything inherently internationalist in the collectivist movements?

Indeed, a persuasive argument may be made that socialist and Communist states can turn out even more nationalist than the bourgeois states they are supplanting. For modern collectivist states provide education and work and jobs and promotions and insurance and increasing social services for the mass of their citizens, and anything which appears to enrich the

---

[13] Friedrich A. Hayek, *The Road to Serfdom* (Chicago, 1944), p. 140.
[14] *Ibid.*, p. 141.

collectivist state will appear to enrich the mass of its citizens. The old middle-class states provided direct benefits to many in the upper and middle classes; the modern collectivist states provide direct benefits to all. When the mass of men more and more look to the national governments for their very livelihoods, will they not become more fervently patriotic than they have been in the past? [15]

Historically, collectivism has not been able to shatter the strength of the national idea. Marxists speak confidently of the equality of workers over the world, but they tend to regard capital as belonging not to humanity but to the nation. Apparently the pull of egalitarianism extends only to the borders of the national state. When World War I began in 1914, socialists in nearly all the belligerent countries offered their services to their national governments. William II, the German emperor, was astonished by the prompt decision of the Social Democrats to serve the fatherland at a critical moment. Orthodox Marxists were disillusioned by this experience. They did not believe it possible that proletarian leaders on occasion could be more nation-conscious than class-conscious.

The universal tendency of collectivism to become nationalistic is illustrated by the history of the Soviet Union.[16] After their triumph in the revolution of November 1917, the Bolsheviks in a flush of enthusiasm called for the formation of a world society under proletarian control. Every component of the state apparatus—political, economic, social, cultural, psychological—was to be collectivized as a step in the formation of a world society. Included in this effort to create instant history was an attempt to break down the nation-state by organizing a World Federation of Soviet Socialist Republics.[17] The project disappeared almost immediately in the solvent of *Realpolitik*.

With the triumph of Joseph Stalin, Soviet nationalism grew along with Soviet totalitarianism. Stalin forced the international Communist movement to a place subordinate to the national interests of the Soviet Union. The deadly clash between Stalin and Trotsky, although stimulated primarily by a personal power drive, was fought out on the issue of Stalin's "successful-nationalist state" versus Trotsky's "immediate

---

[15] Carlton, *op. cit.*, p. 430.
[16] See "Stalin's Option for Nationalism" in Chapter 11.
[17] See Elliot Goodman, *The Soviet Design for a World State* (New York, 1960), ch. ii.

world revolution." Stalin's reward was dictatorial power; Trotsky's ultimate destiny was assassination in Mexico.

The impact of World War II brought Soviet nationalism into even clearer focus. After Hitler's Nazis invaded the Soviet Union, Stalin was all the more certain that he had to exploit Russian nationalism as a shield against dangers emanating from the capitalist world. He set up negative symbols for the current enemy, Nazi Germany, calculated almost entirely to arouse hatred for Germans as a nation rather than as representatives of the capitalist social order.[18]

After the victory of Russian arms over Nazi Germany, the Communists began to extend their rule beyond the borders of the Soviet Union. But Stalin was not successful in reaching the goal of international communism. Despite rule-by-terror, effective on the domestic scene, Stalin was never able to overcome the centrifugal pressures which emerged inside the Communist bloc. The rift between Soviet Russia and Yugoslavia in Stalin's day and between Soviet Russia and Soviet China after Stalin's death reflected nationalistic as well as ideological differences.

THE PARADOX OF IDEOLOGY

Among the varying antinational movements may be included, in addition to international socialism, such differing concepts as the Fascist International, the Commonwealth ideal, the United Nations, and European Union. The common bond between all these movements is a desire for the elimination of the national state as the determining unit in modern society. All, in one form or another, tend to denigrate the symbol of the national state. All appear to regard the national state as outworn or archaic.

Here is the paradox of ideology. While these varied movements look beyond the national state, they seem incapable of shedding themselves of its character and complexities. While casting aside the paraphernalia of national government and while seeking greater international interdependence, they paradoxically gravitate toward still greater independence of outside influence. It is an irrepressible trend.

The conflict of ideology may be observed in the experience of the

[18] Frederick C. Barghoorn, *Soviet Russian Nationalism* (New York, 1956), p. 264.

European Common Market.[19] The breakdown of economic barriers was followed by a highly satisfying increase in prosperity. But, despite high-sounding speeches, the members were gripped by a persistent refusal to allow economic union to pass over the line into political unity. The average Frenchman, Italian, or German, delighted with his newly found prosperity, continued to regard it as a French, Italian, or German miracle, not as a European accomplishment. Each Common Market country thought of its own welfare first. Efforts to transform economic into political unity were invariably obscured by the unfurling of the national flag.

NATIONALISM AND INTERNATIONAL LAW:
THE ROCK OF SOVEREIGNTY

Still another paradox of nationalism is its continuing strength when measured against the traditions of international law. The age of technology, with its necessity for closer communication between peoples, requires compounding regulations between nations, yet the new nationalism, like the old, reveals a stubborn resistance to encroachment. The nation-state refuses to leave the rock of sovereignty.

The first comprehensive formulation of international law was made by Hugo Grotius in his *De jure belli et pacis* (1625), in which he spoke of an international authority and rules of universal validity. The term "international law" itself was first used in the nineteenth century by Jeremy Bentham. It was customarily used interchangeably with "law of nations" and as an equivalent to the French *droit des gens* and the German *Völkerrecht*. As nation-states were bound closer and closer together by cross-frontier relationships in trade, communication, and culture, there were more and more calls for regulation of such relations. In this way a body of "international law" was set up and extended.[20] By the middle of the twentieth century, international law was developing on two levels, one to meet the increasing needs of the

[19] See "Economic Integration: Common Market" in Chapter 12.
[20] According to Robert Yewdall Jennings, Whewell Professor of International Relations at Cambridge University, a series of lectures by Sir Henry Maine, delivered at Cambridge in the 1880's, was sufficient in printed form of 100 pages to cover the entire field of international law at that time. On the other hand, a recent basic text required some 2,000 pages to cover the ground (L. F. L. Oppenheim, *International Law*, ed. H. Lauterpacht, [8th ed.; London, 1955], II [7th ed.; London, 1952]).

world community and another to operate while avoiding encroachment on the continuing concept of state sovereignty. There were new problems which called for legal intercession: international technology (such as civil aviation and the merchant marine), increasing concern for the protection of individual human rights all over the world, and the development of new international organizations. To these may be added the even more recent necessity for laws to control and inspect nuclear weapons, to govern international satellite communications, and to settle conflicting claims in outer space.

The question to what extent an international, or rather an interstate, code of morality can be designated "international law" is still being debated. On one side are the optimists who see a lessening of the nationalist urge, leading to the rise of an international community. They believe that the idea of a set of moral principles limiting the state's freedom of action has a long and honorable tradition in European experience. Certain principles, they say, have always been binding morally on states and governments in their relations with one another. Plato appealed to interstate unity to justify acceptance of restraint in wartime. The Alexandrian Empire and its principle of *humanitas* proposed an international system of morality, which was later extended by Roman jurists and adopted by the medieval Christian church. In the sixteenth century Jean Bodin, while admitting the sovereign power of the state, insisted that it was limited by the law of God. Rationalists of the Enlightenment held that, although the state was governed by natural law, it had to accept moral principles to be observed in international relations.

Defenders of international law, while admitting the lack of supranational authority, assert that laws are not necessarily sanctioned by force as much as by public opinion. They say that the want of actual authority to enforce observance will not deprive of their legal character rules which human beings traditionally and conscientiously obey. "This international community, which is far from having attained any political or moral unity and is always liable to be torn asunder by disruptive forces, continues to be organized on the basis of states, but its law has long since ceased merely, and is rapidly ceasing to be primarily, a law between states." [21]

Even more, say the defenders of international law, it serves a strictly

[21] C. W. Jenks, *The Common Law of Mankind* (New York, 1958), p. 17.

utilitarian purpose to the advantage of the nation-state: "The regular observance of the international law of peace is explained only too easily: it is generally observed largely because there is little temptation to violate it, because its yoke lies easily—too easily—upon the states— and also because to violate it habitually would invite reprisals and would not be in the interests of the state." [22] Behind this thinking is the feeling that international law is legal and practical because there are penalties for failure to comply, running all the way from the force of public opinion, intervention by third parties, and decisions by international organizations, to the last resort—war.

Opposite these views are those of the pessimists. Some legalists, on the ground that there is no sovereign supranational body to enforce its decisions, deny altogether the existence of international law. Several older theorists (Hobbes, Pufendorf, John Austin) claimed that it could not possibly be true law, for all law must be enforced. More recent critics admit the rapid development of a body of international law, but point out that nearly all of it is concerned with aspects of the separateness and independence of states rather than with problems of international society. They say that despite the proliferation of commercial, industrial, and military relations between nation-states there has been no profound transformation from the idea of national exclusiveness to the sentiment of international humanity. They point to the global wars of the twentieth century, the failure of the League of Nations, and the frustrations of the United Nations as indications of a decreasing faith in a common law for mankind.

The more disillusioned pessimists say that there is no such thing as international morality, that sovereign states cannot be judged by moral standards. To these observers, who consider themselves realists, there is but one formula in the relations between nations—might is right. International law might be a body of principles, they admit, but adherence to those principles by individual nations is brought about and conditioned only by fear of war.

The debate continues but the paradox remains: the greater the need for international law, the greater the trend toward nationalism. Despite their increasing interdependence, most nation-states of the contemporary world tend to maintain their sense of national identity. In most cases they adhere to the principles of state separation, state independ-

[22] J. L. Brierly, *The Basis of Obligation in International Law* (London, 1958), p. 54.

ence, state sovereignty. They show little interest in problems of international society other than those which are of direct concern to their own security—political, military, and financial. They appear to be little influenced by prophecies of danger and predictions that a world holocaust will be the inevitable result of continuing nationalism. Only time can reveal the effects of this paradox.

THE PARADOX OF NUCLEAR POWER

In the revised edition of his pioneer work *Nationalism and Social Communication*,[23] Karl W. Deutsch presented what may be the ultimate paradox—that associated with nuclear power. According to Deutsch, it had become obviously suicidal by the mid-1960's for the two chief powers, the United States and the U.S.S.R., to engage in an all-out nuclear war. Even a limited nuclear war might quickly turn into mutual suicide. With experts on both sides aware of the possibility of devastating retaliation, it became a vital interest of both the United States and the U.S.S.R. never to initiate any chain of events that might lead to a nuclear confrontation.

In this situation Deutsch sees a paradox. Nations with little or no nuclear power, he believes, can afford to act recklessly in international affairs, using threats, mobilizing their manpower for conventional warfare, resorting to limited wars, and using their communication media to inflame domestic public opinion. The United States and Soviet Russia, the real nuclear powers, cannot use such tactics. The Deutsch analysis concludes:

With the chief nuclear powers deadlocked by mutual deterrence, their remaining capabilities for limited warfare and for coping with the age of nationalism—and with its revolutions, civil wars, and provocative acts of non-nuclear powers—became limited indeed. Where a local situation could be controlled by the limited intervention of one of the superpowers, short of the mass mobilization of its conscripts, the superpower could still stay in control. But where military manpower requirements would run into the hundreds of thousands, there even local and military situations might prove to be beyond outside control by large nuclear powers, unless the active support of the local populations were secured.[24]

[23] Karl W. Deutsch, *Nationalism and Social Communication* (2nd ed.; Cambridge, Mass., 1966). The original edition appeared in 1953.

[24] *Ibid.*, p. 6.

The two great nuclear powers believe that, by cultivating a reputation for strength and moderation, they can ward off nuclear attack. Meanwhile, weaker nations have begun to regard atomic power as an equalizer in international politics. Communist China started on the nuclear road and produced atomic explosions far greater in strength than that of Hiroshima. Chinese Communist leaders have suggested that in strike and retaliation the preponderance of Chinese population would enable millions of its people to survive in a world destroyed by nuclear war. The danger of inflamed nationalism is most clearly shown by this paradox of nuclear power.

Despite its paradoxes and contradictions, nationalism is still a major guideline for human association. Repeatedly relegated to the category of fossilized historical phenomena, it shows a surprising capacity for life.

Chapter 3

Characteristics of the New Nationalism

*Nationalism, the exaggerated and unjustified
tendency to emphasize national interests,
has produced in our time the abominable
fruit of hypernationalism, the curse of
this century.*

—J. HUIZINGA

Nationalism accurately reflects the times in which it exists. The older form of nationalism came of age at the turn of the nineteenth century. The era since 1945 has been the first in which the whole of mankind accepted nationalism as its dominant political credo.

The most critical problem at the opening of the twentieth century was the threat of war. There was little sense of moral power among nations, nor was there any effective international organization capable of resolving disputes between nations. The cumulative achievements of science had brought not only swift changes in living, but also terrible and destructive weapons. The perfection of scientific techniques had been energetically pursued, but it was a feverish activity, not a healthful one. The crucial problem was how to utilize such techniques. Man had learned to control everything except the savageries of his own nature and the confusions of his government. The nations of the world competed with one another to make applied science an instrument of national policy.

In addition to the threat of war there were also such problems as class conflict, poverty, and social injustice. There was great wealth, but there was also a gap between its production and its distribution. Class warfare was intensified inside industrialized nations.

These were the twin challenges of the new century—how to resolve animosities on both the international and the domestic scenes. The world of 1900 was supposed to be progressive and rich in accomplishment, but it was on the verge of tragedy. "Everybody's nerves are tense," said Colonel Edward M. House, special adviser to President Wilson, in the spring of 1914.

This was the age of nationalism, the culmination of a century and a half of uneven development. Nationalism differed in each country according to special historic conditions and the social structure. Although the United States and Japan had entered the world scene as great powers, nationalism in the era of 1900 received its impetus in the capitals of Europe. From there it penetrated to lands where political ideas were less advanced than on the continent.[1]

[1] On the pattern of the twentieth century, see Hajo Holborn, *The Political Collapse of Europe* (New York, 1951); Hans Kohn, *The Twentieth Century:*

After 1945 nationalism changed along with the historical milieu. The world of Pitt and Palmerston, of Disraeli and Gladstone, of Lloyd George, even of Churchill and Roosevelt, no longer existed. With an empire vanished, the days of British supremacy were over. The United States and the Soviet Union had become the world's two leading powers. China emerged from centuries of lethargy and its new leaders pursued the course of a status-conscious, aggressive nationalism. The world was no longer the same as it was at the turn of the century. The new age was one of industrial and technological expansion, of population explosion. It was an era of nuclear weapons, which if used, could make a large part of the earth uninhabitable. It was the scene of a race to the moon.

In view of the internationalization of ideas and the great improvements in transportation and communication, nationalism might have been expected to become obsolescent along with the customs, traditions, and revolutionary ideologies of the nineteenth century. Such was not the case. Nationalism spread all over the globe until the whole of mankind accepted its general political attitudes. The peoples of the new states saw in nationalism the best and most convenient means of ensuring their security. To them it appeared to be an extension of family or tribal loyalty on a larger scale. In setting up the apparatus of state, they imitated the older countries. Consciously or unconsciously, they recapitulated the experiences of two centuries of European history as they sought bonds of language and traditions.

The design varied in different eras, but fundamentally it was the same. Everywhere there was a deep regard for flag, anthem, and fatherland, and everywhere countries accepted the strictures of national sentiment. Everywhere there was an accentuation of what Henry Steele Commager calls "the critical stigmata of nationalism"—language, culture, traditions, heroes.

POPULISM: THE NEW NATIONALISM AND SOCIALISM

The new nationalism displayed a characteristic tendency to become socialist. Not only the older governments but also those of the newly

---

Midway Account of the Western World (New York, 1949); and J. Salwyn Schapiro, *The World in Crisis* (New York, 1950).

emergent nations were forced to admit their obligation to promote the welfare of the masses. Here again nationalism took on the overtones of historical experience.

Modern nationalism was initially a bourgeois phenomenon, created of, by, and primarily for the middle class, which was very much aware of its politico-economic aims and strongly determined to achieve them. Up to this time the vast rural population of Europe had owed its loyalty to the Church, the hereditary princes, and the privileged nobility. The new bourgeoisie snatched power for itself and controlled the nation-state in its own interest. This middle class was strong enough to maintain its power despite revolutionary agitation directed against it in the revolutions of 1830 and 1848 and the Paris Commune of 1871. The nineteenth century was pre-eminently the age of the bourgeoisie.

The new century became, in the words of Franklin D. Roosevelt, the "century of the common man." Despite the inferior position it occupied at first, the populist movement for greater control by the masses gained strength over the century. What the workingman regarded as unattainable during the early decades of the nineteenth century became within reach by the end of the century.[2] From 1900 on, the worker began to demand more rights. Although he had to fight to obtain them, he was moderately successful in achieving a new freedom. At one time he had been burdened by an accumulation of impedimenta which he had to suffer without any other solution than resignation or adaptation. Now he was to find fewer social barriers and limitations. "Estates" and "castes" were going out of style, and the idea that ordinary men were equal before the law gathered strength.

This new status for the common man was realized in a variety of social patterns ranging all the way from the Scandinavian welfare state

[2] An example of this populist trend was the Chartist movement. On May 13, 1839, a giant petition, or charter, was presented to the English Parliament. It made six demands: universal manhood suffrage; equal electoral districts; salaries for members of Parliament; abolition of property qualifications for members of Parliament; secret ballot; and annual elections of Parliament. Although the Chartists presented gigantic petitions to Parliament (1839, 1842, 1848), they were not successful in stirring the British people to revolt. Yet, by the end of the century, all the Chartist demands, with the exception of annual elections of Parliament, had became a part of the British constitution. Thus, the workers eventually won those rights which earlier, in the form of the Chartist demands, had reduced Queen Victoria to tears of frustration and fear (see Elizabeth Longford, *Queen Victoria* [New York, 1966], pp. 195–197).

and the British Labor government to the Communist society of Soviet Russia.[3] The new nations, too, combined their sense of nationalism with socialism. Nationalism grew among undeveloped peoples not only because it was an instrument to drive out colonial powers but also because centralized state machinery could satisfy mass demand for modern technology, heavy industry, and the consequent rise in the standard of living.[4] A small minority which had been educated in Europe usually seized control in these new nations, but this did not mean that the masses were excluded altogether. Nationalism was on the march, but it was not bourgeois nationalism. It was rather a populist form, under compulsion to increase and socialize national power.[5]

This association of nationalism with socialism was one of the most significant trends of the twentieth century. Marxists, adhering to scientific determinism and the concept of inevitability, see the union of nationalism and socialism as the realization of predictions made a century ago by Karl Marx. According to this theory, evolved from Hegelian dialectic, nationalism and socialism are two conflicting elements (thesis and antithesis) in recent historical development. From this point of view, nationalism is a sentiment sponsored and controlled by bourgeois capitalists, while socialism is the province of the proletariat. The opposing trends unite in a synthesis called national socialism or fascism.

The theory is monistic, and on the surface at least, impressive. But the formula is open to challenge. The blending of nationalism and socialism has taken place in democratic countries as well as in Fascist or Communist dictatorships. It has appeared in the newly emergent nations as well as in the older, established countries. Every vital revolutionary movement of the twentieth century has been both national and social. This has been true whether the national leader was Sun Yat-sen in China, Mustafa Kemal in Turkey, Nasser in Egypt, or Nehru in India. All regarded socialism of varying degrees as in natural combination with nationalism. All set up the flag as a symbol of nationalism and at the same time pointed to the welfare of the masses as their socialist concern. All cannot be relegated to the category of national socialist

[3] See José Ortega y Gasset, *The Revolt of the Masses* (New York, 1932), pp. 53–63.

[4] William G. Carlton, *Political Thought since World War II* (New York, 1964), p. 424.

[5] *Ibid.*, p. 425.

fascists. It is more appropriate to say that the mixture of nationalism
and socialism merely reflects the spirit of the day, an era in which the
common man has reached political maturity.

THE CHARISMATIC LEADER

In the new nationalism, even more than in the old, the charismatic
leader plays an important role. The word "charisma," of Greek origin,
means "gift," and was initially meant as a "gift of grace," or a divinely
inspired call to leadership. Max Weber described charisma as "a certain
quality of an individual personality by which he is set apart from
ordinary men and treated as endowed with supernatural, superhuman
or at least specifically exceptional powers or qualities." [6] He can inspire
and sustain personal loyalty apart from his office or status. He is
supposed to possess supernatural or extraordinary powers given to few.
He is always larger than life in skill, ability, and courage. He communi-
cates his sense of mission to his followers. He does not live as other
men, nor is he motivated by ordinary rules. A revolutionary in times of
trouble, he breaks precedents and creates new ones. Above all, he is said
to be selected by fate for a role of leadership.[7]

The mystic aura which surrounds the sentiment of nationalism is
made to order for the charismatic leader. He is certain that he himself
embodies the character of the nation. He utilizes nationalism not only
as a prop for his own status but also to generate the "mission" of his
people in the world. From their viewpoint the people see in the
charismatic leader the total expression of their own traits and character.
Always the power of the leader depends largely upon the image he is
able to maintain in the perceptions of his people. He may be of any
persuasion—dictator or democrat, theorist or activist. Many are mili-
tary-minded men who appeal to national pride and xenophobic fears to
extend their own power.

As the older nationalism blossomed in the nineteenth century, it
presented a series of leaders all touched with charisma—Napoleon
Bonaparte, Metternich, Louis Philippe, Bismarck, Napoleon III, Disraeli, Kossuth, and Garibaldi. Each had extraordinary gifts of leader-

---

[6] Max Weber, *The Theory of Social and Economic Organization*, ed. Talcott
Parsons (New York, 1947), p. 358.

[7] *Ibid.*, pp. 358–362.

ship; each used nationalism for his own purposes; each became the spear point for the mission of his people. The pattern was repeated in the first half of the twentieth century with Gandhi and Nehru in India, Mussolini in Italy, Hitler in Germany, Stalin in Russia, Churchill in England, and Franklin D. Roosevelt in the United States. Each followed the star of his own destiny, and each was a fervent nationalist.

Charismatic leaders flourished in the new states formerly under colonial rule. "Their very attainment of independence generally signified that the old order had broken down and the supports that sustained it had disappeared or were rapidly being weakened."[8] With the breakdown of the old traditional legal authority in a climate of uncertainty and unpredictability, there came a need for leadership that would bridge the discredited past and the mysterious future. The "inspired" leader stepped to center stage—Nkrumah in Ghana, Kenyatta in Kenya, Sukarno in Indonesia, Ben Gurion in Israel, Mao Tse-tung in Communist China, Ho Chi Minh in North Vietnam. Many were men of military mind—Boumedienne in Algeria, Mohammed Ayub Khan in Pakistan, Ne Win in Burma, Thanom Kittikachorn in Thailand, Nguyen Cao Ky in South Vietnam. All claimed to epitomize the national will; all aroused awe and devotion in their followers; all spoke of "the nation's rightful place in world society"; all were men gripped by a sense of mission.

A similar trend may be noted in the cases of Nasser in Egypt, Peron in Argentina, and Castro in Cuba. Among the more interesting examples is General Charles de Gaulle, president of the Fifth French Republic.[9] Advised by his "ancestral memory" that Europe (equated with Christendom) ought naturally to fall under the leadership of France, he looked upon Paris as the center of the world. His formula was simple: de Gaulle plus France equals Europe. He presented himself as an indispensable man. He was confident that the future of the French Republic would be assured only if the citizens gave him open and massive support. But he was equally certain that the Republic would collapse and that France would suffer disastrous confusion if her people turned from his leadership. It was a classic case of charismatic autointoxication.

[8] See the excellent study by Ann Ruth Willner and Dorothy Willner, "The Rise and Role of Charismatic Leadership," in *Annals of the American Academy of Political and Social Science*, CCCLVIII (Mar. 1965), 77–88.
[9] See "France: De Gaulle and National Grandeur" in Chapter 5.

RELATIONSHIP OF NATIONALISM TO DEMOCRACY:
INDIVIDUALISM AND THE STATE

A distinction between the old nationalism and the new may be found in their differing attitudes toward individualism, popular sovereignty, and the state. The earlier form of nationalism arose within the framework of the Age of Reason, with its accent on the natural rights of man, parliamentarianism, liberalism, and democracy. This was the era of flowering individualism. Confined in the eighteenth century to the shores of the Atlantic, nationalism then expressed the humanitarian character of the Enlightenment.[10] The new and growing order of liberty and tolerance became firmly rooted in the national life and character. The formative period of early modern nationalism took place in a milieu of discussion, compromise, and reconciliation. In England, John Locke presented the theses that the liberty and the dignity of the individual were the basic elements of national life and that government was based on the consent of the governed. These ideas were to be expressed in the American Declaration of Independence. In France, Jean-Jacques Rousseau advocated the idea of personal liberty, claiming that the ideal community was based on the virtue of its free citizens and their deep love for the fatherland. The streets of Paris reverberated with the famous cry: "Liberty, Equality, Fraternity!"

In its subsequent development, the mainstream of nationalism took two directions. One course retained the earlier accent on individualism. It held sovereignty to be centered in the people united by a "general will." This view was bourgeois in origin, conterminous with the transition from rural to urban economy, and reflected the impact of capitalism. This form of nationalism continued to be grounded on the rights of man.

The second stream of nineteenth-century nationalism originated in the era of post-Napoleonic disillusionment and continued through the Bismarckian period of "iron-and-blood" to the era of imperialism and to the world wars of the twentieth century. This kind of nationalism encouraged a romantic revival of the past, worship of national heroes, and a belief in military force. All these tenets ran counter to the virtuous ideals of individualism and liberty. As peoples implemented their national goals, less and less emphasis was placed on their own

[10] Hans Kohn, *Nationalism: Its Meaning and History* (rev. ed.; Princeton, 1965), p. 17.

rights as individuals and on moral values, while more and more attention was directed to the state. This development culminated in the rise
of dictatorships in Russia, Spain, Germany, Italy, and smaller countries.
The leader (Generalissimo, Caudillo, Fuehrer, Duce) identified himself
with the state, and demanded sheeplike obedience from his followers.

The new nationalism revealed the influence of both these strains. The
Western democratic nations still retained the skeletal framework of
individualism, but even these countries tended toward limitation of
personal freedom in favor of a more powerful state apparatus. Both
form and spirit of the shift could be observed in the experience of the
welfare state in England and in the Scandinavian countries, in
the "authoritarian democracy" of the Fifth French Republic, in the
preference of the people in the democratic West German Republic
for a powerful father-figure, and in the increasing encroachment of
federal power against the states in the United States. In each case the
democratic base was retained but with a considerably enhanced regard
for the role of state power as against the individual.

The trend was even more emphatic among the new nations of Africa
and Asia. Neither Africa nor Asia ever produced its own Renaissance,
Reformation, or Enlightenment, and hence they have no sense of
rebellion against past conditions. The African or Asian, relying on
ancient traditions, often subjected himself and his destiny to an immense power far above his comprehension. People lived in villages and
belonged to tribes. They bowed before power as before a natural
force: they paid their taxes and held fast to the *status quo* by totem and
taboo. In such societies, Western individualism had no meaning. The
idea of the individual's holding sovereign power was foreign to peoples
molded by tradition, custom, and propriety.

It is understandable, therefore, that in the newly emergent nations
the leviathan of the state became the repository of the national will.
The tendency was to exalt the state, produce a strong leader, and keep
the individual in a secondary position.

INVERSE NATIONALISM: THE FRAGMENTATION OF
COMPETITIVE SUBSOCIETIES

The older form of European nationalism was both unifying in nature
(nineteenth-century Germany and Italy) and disintegrative (early
twentieth-century Austria-Hungary and Turkey). As national states

solidified, they resisted the formation of subsocieties as detrimental. The existing fragmentation was directed against such larger European unifying schemes as the "pan" movements and the United States of Europe.

After 1945 the new nationalism in Europe retained a divisive character, manifested in such nationalistic drives as that for French glory, the German call for reunification, and Albanian particularism. At the same time most European states continued to oppose further interregional rivalries or additional fragmentation into linguistic or minority groupings. These existed on a minor scale, such as the Flemish-Walloon rivalry in Belgium, Welsh nationalism in Britain, and Catalan and Basque calls for regional autonomy in Spain. But by far the greater tendency was to retain the *status quo* by resisting European integration on the one side and subsocietal fragmentation on the other.

Quite different was the experience of the new nations of Asia and Africa. The new nationalism brought national unity as well as a kind of inverse nationalism, expressed in societal and tribal fragmentation. The development of new states followed a similar historical pattern. In each case national morale and energy surged to a high point in the struggle for independence. In working together to break the bonds of colonial control, both leaders and masses achieved a sense of national dignity. Local antagonisms were forgotten for the moment. The elixir of nationhood at first proved to be a strong solvent for animosities and rivalries.

The new nations were handicapped because they had inherited territories whose borders had been created artificially by the colonial powers as convenient and desirable. But these borders set lines of division among peoples who spoke the same language and often included minorities who themselves wanted independence. Thus the divisive force was built in. The colonial governments had not been concerned with creating a sense of nationalism among the peoples they controlled. Quite to the contrary, they deliberately fostered fragmentation on the general principle of divide-and-rule. They encouraged limited education facilities, but deliberately maintained political education at a low level and seldom granted local participation in important decisions.

Despite this unfavorable climate for national unity, the new nations were born in a flurry of political activism and dynamism. Afro-Asian nationalist leaders, educated in Western universities, were dashing and heroic in the days of struggle for liberation. But when the time came for the positive tasks of constructing the national state, they found the task unexciting and boring. The revolutionary *élan* quickly subsided. In the words of Rupert Emerson: "The fine bright flame of revolution inevitably burns itself out before long, and the more humdrum tasks of peaceful reconstruction and advance, so slow to show results, may seem a shabby substitute for the stirring days of violent and heroic action." [11]

Afro-Asian nationalist leaders believed the fallacy that independence would automatically bring unity, centralization, and efficient government. Their first concern after independence was national integration of the many social orders and minorities that had been inspired by the colonial regimes. Here they faced a task greater than they had expected.[12] The Afro-Asian minority problems were fully as complicated as those in the Balkans. Nationalist zeal was replaced by ethnic, linguistic, and regional group sentiment. National unity quickly disappeared as subsocieties and subgroups contended for advantageous positions in the new nations. Each competitive society regarded independence merely as a mandate for its right to dominate other groups. The variety of subsocieties was bewildering: varying ethnic groups, different economic strata, competing classes. Each group reasserted its traditional heritages and jockeyed for position of greater power. The spirit of national mobilization broke down in a welter of conflicting loyalties.

In Africa there were dozens of tribes cut by international boundaries.[13] The example of the Congo demonstrates the pressure of interregional rivalries. Given its independence suddenly by Belgium in 1960, the Congo Republic almost immediately began to disintegrate as subgroups clashed in a power struggle. Patrice Lumumba was murdered in 1961; Katanga seceded in 1962–1963; full-scale civil war in 1964 led to intercession by the United Nations. In 1960, Nigeria came to nationhood with high expectations as Africa's most powerful and democratic nation. But within a few years Nigeria had to face the possibility of

[11] Rupert Emerson, "The Progress of Nationalism," in *Nationalism and Progress in Free Asia*, ed. Philip W. Thayer (Baltimore, 1956), p. 75.

[12] See Clifford Geertz, "The Integrative Revolution: Primordial Sentiments and Civil Politics in the New States," in *Old Societies and New Nations*, ed. Clifford Geertz (New York, 1963).

[13] "A tribesman's relation to his tribe is usually regulated in minute detail by custom which is followed unquestioningly and considered part of the natural or the divine order. Tribal custom is neither a decree of the General Will, nor an edict of legislative Reason. The tribesman is such by virtue of his birth, not by virtue of self-determination. He is usually unaware that the destiny of man is progressive, and that he can fulfil this destiny by merging his will into the will of the tribe" (Elie Kedourian, *Nationalism* [London, 1960], pp. 74–75).

being split into a series of *de facto* nations based on common tribe, common language, common religion, and common culture. Traditionally torn by tribal rivalries, Nigeria went through further violent tribal uprisings, and the nation seemed dangerously close to disintegration.

Similar difficulties inhibited intraregional cooperation in Asia. Most of those states which had fallen to European conquest had had an "imperialist" period of their own, and the old rivalries reappeared after the breakdown of Western colonialism. The leaders of Southeast Asian independence were more at home in dealing with their former colonial masters than with each other. Unforgotten were the traditional rivalries between the Theravada Buddhist Burmese and the Theravada Buddhist Thai; between the similarly Buddhist Thai and Cambodians; between the Cambodians and the Buddhist Vietnamese; and between the Muslim peoples of the Malaysian-Indonesian archipelago.[14] The rivalries were sometimes geographic as well as religious: those, for example, between the valley and hill peoples in Laos, Burma, Vietnam, and Thailand. The new governments were as little disposed to recognize such competitive groups as were the old colonial masters.

Every vital revolutionary movement among the undeveloped nations envisaged a great increase in centralized national power.[15] But nationhood brought only a superficial unity. In a recent study, I. R. Sinai decried the "great revolution" that had supposedly been brought about in the populous new nations and criticized it as a colorful masquerade, a sort of superior political orgy, superficially exciting but essentially undermining and leading only to a process of dissolution. In their days of control, Sinai wrote, the Western imperialists, too easygoing, had sentimentalized the alien cultures over which they had ruled and failed to overhaul the social structures of the subject nations. They gave the non-Western peoples a taste for Western-style living without supplying them with the economic base or the management training to provide it. The result was that proud new nations became worse off than they had been under colonialism. Lacking the assertive individualism of the West, believing their own propaganda about the spiritual superiority of their way of life, the new nations broke down into conglomerations of squabbling competitive subsocieties.[16]

[14] Frank Trager, at Symposium on United States Foreign Policy held at Racine, Wisconsin, in September 1965 (quoted in *Saturday Review*, Oct. 30, 1965, p. 100).

[15] William G. Carlton, "The New Nationalism," *Virginia Quarterly Review*, XXVI (July 1950), 432.

[16] See I. R. Sinai, *The Challenge of Modernisation* (New York, 1964).

PSYCHOLOGICAL MOTIVATION

Among the factors in the structure of nationalism are common language, race, religion, and traditions. Each is important in its own way, although none is sufficient standing alone or in combination with the others to explain the flourishing vigor of nationalism. Added to these factors is psychological motivation. Because nationalism is a sentiment, it has psychological overtones. The psychological drive plays a most significant role in the meaning and development of nationalism.[17] Arnold Toynbee argued that nationalism is an anachronism because the paramount loyalty of the individual is to the human race, but he overlooked the human impulse which finds satisfaction in a nation of common institutions and creeds.

Psychological motivation, always at work in the older nationalism, carried over into the new nationalism in intensified form. It was especially strong among those Afro-Asian peoples who had undergone the ignominy of subservience to colonial powers. The colonial peoples had been the objects, not the wielders, of power. Rigidly maintained in low status, they were suppressed, oppressed, insecure, and frustrated. They lost so much face in the power struggle that they became convinced of their inferiority. How could one explain otherwise that only a handful of colonial masters could control vast masses of peoples?

World War II was scarcely over when the great recessional of the colonial powers began, followed by the power drives of the subjugated peoples. Nationalist liberator heroes spoke the language of freedom and equality. For people who had known the despair of frustration, nationalism provided a feeling of compensation. They would identify themselves vicariously with the nation. Congolese no longer listened to orders from their Belgian overlords; Indonesians stopped the custom of bowing low and touching their foreheads to the floor in the presence of Dutch masters; the Chinese knew that the days of the Opium Wars and the Boxer Rebellion were past. The inferiority complex began to dissolve in the solvent of a new national consciousness.

The process was by no means sudden and clear-cut. The non-Western personality took on ambivalent characteristics. Most of the new nations stood with one foot in each world—the old and the new. The experience of India is an example. Nationalist leader Jawaharlal Nehru on the one hand urged rapid industrialization of his country and on the

[17] See Louis L. Snyder, *The Meaning of Nationalism* (New Brunswick, N.J., 1954), pp. 40-54, 69-72, 89-109, 127-128, 155-160.

other bespoke his reverence for the Gandhian ideal of small, self-sufficient communities still in the hand-spinning stage. But whether or not they adopted Western ways, the newly independent peoples were intrigued by the sense of nationhood. Psychologically, they could walk with heads up instead of down. This in itself was a revolutionary development.

THE NEW NATIONALISM AND MORALITY

The new nationalism was tinged with the odium and odor of amorality that had been developing since the inception of the nation-state. Behind it was a process of transformation from positive to negative force, from inspirational to ignoble quality, from blessing to curse.

Born in the Age of Reason, modern nationalism was tempered by rationalists who believed in the perfectibility of mankind. In his *Outline for an Historical Picture of the Human Mind* (1795), Condorcet theorized that the human race was advancing continuously toward perfection. He divided the history of mankind into nine epochs, from the opening era of hunters and fishermen, to the time of Descartes and the French Revolution, including the discoveries of Locke, Newton, and Rousseau, when reason, tolerance, and humanitarianism became the watchwords of man. Condorcet predicted confidently that in the tenth epoch—that of the future—man would progress to the point when all inequalities of opportunity would disappear and when individual human nature would reach perfection.

After its crusading Jacobin phase, nationalism took on characteristics of that moral tone advocated by the rationalists: it was suffused with individualism, tolerance, liberalism, and democracy. This brighter side was reflected in Herder's cultural nationalism which granted to every people the right to enjoy its special folkways and historical traditions. Herder's nationalism, essentially nonaggressive and humanitarian in nature, was built around the principle of the unity of mankind. It regarded the culture of each nationality as an organism and each branch of culture as an organic part of the larger organism. It called on each people to develop its own peculiar gifts and propensities and projected the idea that the perfection of the various nationalities was requisite to the perfection of mankind. For Herder the final justification of national existence lay in the contribution of the national group to humanity at large.[18] This view was advocated by such apostles of liberal nationalism as Mazzini: "Each nationality has its special mission of humanity. The mission constitutes a nationality. Nationality is sacred." [19]

During the course of the nineteenth century, liberal nationalism gradually deteriorated until it lost most, if not all, of its earlier moral character. Tolerance was often replaced by a hardening intolerance. Nationalism sometimes became violent and exclusive, as people began to show an absolute faith in their superiority over other nationalities. The tone was set by interpretations of Hegel, who found the highest expression of objective morality in the state. In the Hegelian view, ideal morality was the union of the subjective (conscience) with the objective (law and tradition): the individual was supposed to uphold and conform to rational political institutions and laws from a sense of duty. Just as Machiavelli in the early sixteenth century excluded morality from politics, so did Hegel in the early nineteenth century place the nation-state above morality:

In the history of the World, only those peoples can come under our notice which form a state. For it must be understood that this latter is the realization of Freedom, *i.e.* of the absolute final aim, and that it exists for its own sake. It must be further understood that all the worth which the human being possesses, he possesses only through the State. For his spiritual reality consists in this, that his own essence—Reason—is objectively present to him, that it possesses objective immediate existence for him. Thus only is he fully conscious; thus only is he a partaker of morality—of a just and moral social and political life. For Truth is the Unity of the universal and subjective Will; and the Universal is to be found in the State, in its laws, its universal and rational arrangements. The State is the Divine Idea as it exists on Earth. We have in it, therefore, the object of History in a more definite shape than before; that in which Freedom obtains objectivity, and lives in the enjoyment of that objectivity. . . . The morality [*Sittlichkeit*] of the State is not of that ethical [*moralische*] reflective kind, in which one's own conviction bears sway; this latter is rather the peculiarity of the modern time, while the true antique morality is based on the principle of abiding by one's duty (to the state at large). . . .

[18] See Robert R. Ergang, *Herder and the Foundations of German Nationalism* (New York, 1931), pp. 248–253, and Hans Kohn, *The Idea of Nationalism* (New York, 1944), pp. 427–451.
[19] *Life and Writings of Joseph Mazzini* (London, 1891), III, 33.

Morality is Duty—the substantial Right—a 'second nature' as it has been called; for the first nature of man is his primary merely animal existence.[20]

Hegel's conception of the nation-state as a superpersonality, as the source of all law and ethics, and as the expression of the divine idea on earth, was used to mobilize national enthusiasm in Bismarck's drive to unify the conglomerate Germanies. Residues of Hegelianism also appeared in national fabrics elsewhere. There was no Kantian categorical imperative to limit state action, no international parliament to restrict aggression. In vain did such advocates of international justice as John Stuart Mill plead that the doctrine of nonintervention, "to be a great principle of morality," must be accepted by all governments. The fact was that all governments acted as they pleased in their own interest and were limited only by superior strength. National egoism, becoming more and more intensified, came to be accepted as moral, and therefore desirable. In aggressive form it helped pave the way for the bloodbaths of 1914–1918 and 1939–1945.

This deficiency of moral tone, which was carried over into the new nationalism after 1945, infected both great powers and little states alike. The great powers identified their own standards with general humanitarian principles. In the cold war, the United States and the Soviet Union oppose each other as the champion of moral systems, each operating on a national scale and each proclaiming standards which it recommends for all nations. The two giants challenge each other, not only along political and economic lines, but as bearers of universal moral standards. This has made of the new nationalism a kind of secular religion, as described by Hans J. Morgenthau in a discerning passage:

The new nationalism is in truth a political religion, a nationalistic universalism which identifies the standards and goals of a particular nation with the principles that govern the universe. The few remaining nations of the first rank no longer oppose each other within a framework of shared beliefs and common values which impose effective limitations upon the means and ends of their policies. Rather they oppose each other now as the standard-bearers of moral systems, each of them of national origin and each of them claiming to provide universal moral standards which all

---

[20] Georg Wilhelm Friedrich Hegel, *Lectures on the Philosophy of History,* trans. J. Sibree (London, 1890), pp. 40 ff.

other nations ought to accept. The moral code of one nation flings the challenge of its universal claim into the face of another, which reciprocated in kind.[21]

Lesser powers are not in a position to make such extravagant claims, but they similarly believe their nation to be on a high moral plane, and regard their national character as superior and their prestige as precious and unchallengeable. The smaller states, like the great powers, also think the new nationalism has only one thing in common with the old: the nation is always the fulcrum of politics. All are inclined to dismiss the idea of gratitude among nations for past favors: "Let us forget what you did for us yesterday. What can you do for us today?" There is one dominating principle: national sovereignty is not to be infringed upon.

This bending of national morality infects the new states as well as the old. Quickly forgetting their birth pangs, the new nations of Africa and Asia have adopted the way of national egoism. Undeveloped nations accept aid from the great powers as their natural right, with no *quid pro quo* basis. They either threaten to go over to the camp of the other side in the cold war if assistance is halted, or urge their benefactors to "Go to hell!" or to "Go jump into the Nile!" The new nation-states reject absolute moral principles and use their newly found nationalism as a tool of political power. They have little inclination to measure nationalism in terms of justice, order, and peace; they utilize it for the sake of self-interest. In this respect the new nationalism imitates the worst features of the old.

[21] Hans J. Morgenthau, "The Paradoxes of Nationalism," *Yale Review*, XLVI (June 1957), 488.

Chapter 4

Classification: Projection of a Typology

The sentiment of nationality, that most simple of all ideals which appeals to the largest quantity of brute force, has in its nature no political affinity either with liberty on the one hand or with tyranny on the other; it can be turned by some chance current of events, or by cunning or clumsiness of statesmen, to run in any channel and to work any wheel.

—GEORGE MACAULAY TREVELYAN

Attempts have been made to unravel the complexities of nationalism by classifying its varying forms. Although all kinds of nationalism have certain characteristics in common, they can be divided logically into distinct categories. All the disciplines concerned with nationalism have devoted attention to classification.[1] Historians favor these chronological lines as generally applicable (there are always exceptions):

Integrative nationalism (1815–1871). In this period nationalism was a unifying force which helped consolidate states that had outgrown their feudal divisions, and united others that had been split into factions. Both the Germanies and the Italies, once geographical expressions, were unified on the basis of nationalism.

Disruptive nationalism (1871–1890). The success of nationalism as a factor molding the unification of Germany and Italy aroused the enthusiasm of subject nationalities in other countries. Minority nationalities in the Ottoman Empire, Austria-Hungary, and other conglomerate states sought to break out of oppression.

Aggressive nationalism (1900–1945). The first half of the twentieth century saw a collision of opposing national interests and the explosive impact of two world wars. During this time nationalism became almost identical with imperialism.

Contemporary nationalism (1945–). In its most recent form the new nationalism asserted itself partly in colonial revolts against European masters. This period of colonial emancipation and nation-building saw the extension of nationalism into a broad, global framework.

THE CLASSIC HAYES FORMULA

The pioneer work of Carlton J. H. Hayes did much to dispel the fog surrounding the nature of nationalism. Hayes was the first to suggest a distinction between original and derived nationalism.[2] The difference

---

[1] For a discussion of classifications of nationalism by various disciplines, see Louis L. Snyder, *The Meaning of Nationalism* (New Brunswick, N.J., 1954), pp. 112–132.

[2] Carlton J. H. Hayes, "Two Varieties of Nationalism, Original and Derived," *Proceedings of the Association of History Teachers of the Middle States and Maryland*, XXVI (1928), 70–83.

involved a moral judgment. In Hayes's view, every subject or oppressed nationality began its nineteenth-century agitation for national liberty and union in the spirit of Mazzini, Condorcet, or Herder. People sought an ideal of justice through self-sacrifice, a revolutionary trend. A nationality which had once been oppressed, but which had obtained its freedom, then transformed its "original" nationalism into a "derived" nationalism which made it reactionary, militarist, and imperalist.

Hayes added to his general moral evaluation of nationalism a breakdown of the different major types which have evolved in Europe within the last two centuries. In this typology of theoretical aspects, each form corresponded generally to the historical temper of the times. The Hayes formula became the standard treatise on the subject.[3]

Humanitarian nationalism. The first systematic doctrines of nationalism were expounded in the eighteenth century. While they differed from each other in certain details, they were all infused with the spirit of the Enlightenment. Based on natural law, they were evolved by more or less pure reason. They were presented as inevitable and therefore desirable steps in progress. In object they were strictly humanitarian. They were so much infused with this motive that they may be described as variant specimens of a single humanitarian nationalism.

Humanitarian nationalism had three main advocates. Henry St. John Bolingbroke, a conservative Englishman, projected an aristocratic form of nationalism tinged with humanitarianism. Jean-Jacques Rousseau, the French *philosophe*, advocated a democratic form of nationalism, humanitarian in spirit. Johann Gottfried von Herder, the German philosopher, unlike Rousseau and Bolingbroke, saw nationalism as a cultural rather than as a political phenomenon. As a group the humanitarian nationalists believed that every nationality was entitled to unhampered development consonant with its own genius.

At the end of the eighteenth century the theories of nationalism reached a point at which they were either aristocratic or democratic, or neither one. Democratic nationalism became Jacobin. Aristocratic nationalism became traditional. The nationalism which was neither democratic nor aristocratic became "liberal."

Out of the cry, "Liberty, Equality, Fraternity!" there emerged a new French national fervor, which spread through all Europe. From

[3] The précis here is based on Carlton J. H. Hayes, *The Historical Evolution of Modern Nationalism* (New York, 1931), *passim.*

that day on, the development of nationalism became constant and uninterrupted.

Jacobin nationalism. Jacobin nationalism was based in theory on the humanitarian democratic nationalism of Rousseau and was developed by revolutionary leaders for the purpose of safeguarding and extending the ideas that had been asserted and partially established in the early days of the French Revolution. Developing in the midst of domestic rebellion and foreign intrigue, Jacobin nationalism acquired four characteristics: it was suspicious and intolerant of internal dissent; it relied eventually on force and militarism to attain its ends; it became fanatically religious; and it was infused with missionary zeal.

Jacobin nationalism was more religious than rational. It was political as well as cultural, and it appropriately produced political instruments. It was both democratic and republican. Because it was intolerant, its apostles felt the need to employ every conceivable means to obtain popular conformity. At home it created numerous novel agencies of popular propaganda; abroad its missionary zeal was evidenced by its armies and war.

Jacobin nationalism was the prototype of the later national conscript armies, public schools, public instruction, controlled journalism, and lip service to freedom. Napoleon's use of the *levée en masse*, the nation in arms, followed Jacobin nationalist ideology. Jacobin nationalism, with its suspicion and intolerance, set the pattern for the twentieth-century nationalism of Russian communism, Italian fascism, and German national socialism.

Traditional nationalism. Those intellectuals who most vigorously opposed the French Revolution and Napoleon championed nationalism and dressed it in distinctive clothes. The clothing was not "reason" or "revolution" but history and tradition. Thus, the aristocratic, humanitarian nationalism of Bolingbroke emerged as traditional nationalism. At its root was the idea that the quiet happiness of humanity could be ensured less by the masses than by the classes. The traditionalists held that nationality and the state had just evolved; it was idle to discuss how they began—perhaps by contract. From this point of view the state was no mere partnership to be made or suddenly dissolved at pleasure. It was a combination not only between those who are living, but between the living and the dead and those yet to be born as well. The people, or the nationality, were not to be considered distinct from their government; they had no right to dissolve the social tie which linked them to their forefathers.

In effect, traditional nationalism was a countermovement to the forces set in motion by the French Revolution, even though it claimed the same humanitarian motives as had the Jacobins. Yet, it was no less warlike than Jacobinism. It was the motivating force of growing resistance on the Continent, exemplified by nationalistic awakenings in Germany, Holland, Portugal, Spain, and Russia. The Battle of Waterloo was a struggle between Jacobinism and traditionalism, resulting in victory for traditional nationalism.

Among the earlier apostles of traditional nationalism was Edmund Burke, who glorified the aristocrats, flaunted the genius of English lords, feared the despotism of the multitudes, and preached loyalty to family, locality, and region. In France, Burke's theories attracted support from the Vicomte de Bonald, and in Germany, from Friedrich von Schlegel. While Napoleon and his marshals were the product of Jacobin nationalism, Castlereagh, Nelson, Wellington, Archduke Charles, and Alexander I represented traditional nationalism.

Liberal nationalism. Midway between Jacobin and traditional nationalism was liberal nationalism. Like the others, this type originated in the eighteenth century. It began in England, the country of perpetual compromise and of acute national consciousness. The earliest apostle was Jeremy Bentham, who in his *Fragment of Government* (1776), proposed the theory that states should respect economic liberty, including freedom of the individual to engage in any profession or industry, to enter any contract at will with the employer and employee, and to trade with anyone freely. War was evil, and it ought to be eliminated. Bentham proposed a program of universal peace which included a world organization, disarmament, and an international court.

Bentham's liberal nationalism and his concept of internationalism spread to the Continent, where advocates appeared in Germany (Humboldt, Theodor Welcker, Baron vom Stein), France (Guizot, Victor Hugo, Casimir-Périer), and Italy (Mazzini, Garibaldi, Cavour). It was Giuseppe Mazzini in Italy who gave the final wording to describe this type of nationalism. The nation, he said, was an instrument appointed by God and charged with the welfare of the human race. Fatherlands were the workshops of humanity. The state must educate and train its members in the light of moral law; it must arrange and direct its activities in behalf of humanity at large.

Liberal nationalism was mainly evolutionary. It was certainly not reactionary. While tending to be revolutionary in practice, it was not so in theory. It was not aristocratic, and, although it paid lip service to democracy, it tended to be middle-class. It emphasized the absolute sovereignty of the national state but sought to limit the implications of this principle by stressing individual liberties—political, economic, and religious—within each national state. In general, liberal nationalism stood for an independent constitutional government to end despotism, aristocracy, and ecclesiastical influence, and thus to assure every citizen that he could exercise personal liberty.

Liberal nationalism survived World War I. It was against this liberal nationalism that Communists, Fascists, and National Socialists fought regardless of the sides on which the belligerents happened to be.

Integral nationalism. With the sharpening of rivalries between national states, nationalism assumed a form decidedly hostile to humanitarianism and liberalism. In the journal *L'Action Française*, Charles Maurras defined integral nationalism as "the exclusive pursuit of national policies, the absolute maintenance of national integrity, and the steady increase of national power—for a nation declines when it loses military might." Integral nationalism made the nation not a means to humanity but an end in itself. It placed national interests above those of the individual and above humanity. It refused cooperation with other nations.

In domestic affairs integral nationalism was highly illiberal and tyrannical because it required all citizens to conform to a common standard of manners and morals and to share the same unreasoning enthusiasm. All personal liberties were subordinated to nationalism. If the common people should complain, democracy would simply be abridged in the name of national interests.

Integral nationalism flowered in the first half of the twentieth century. In Russia it began as an economic and social reform with protests against militarism, imperialism, and nationalism. As it discovered that the nations of the world were not ready for its messianic mission, Russia ended by converting its own peculiar brand of integrated nationalism into a nationalism of the Union of Soviet Socialist Republics. Integral nationalism could be observed similarly in the pre–Second World War dictatorships in Hungary, Poland, Turkey, and Yugoslavia, as well as in Hitler's Germany.

The theorists of integral nationalism look back to Auguste Comte, the founder of positivism and an early sociologist. Comte based his political organization not on metaphysical concepts like the general will, but on the positive fact of force, material force, as a permanently dominating thing. In the same way Hippolyte Taine, a misanthrope, defended aristocracy and monarchy.

Thus, during the time from the French Revolution to the early twentieth century, the ideas and theories of two centuries changed from praise of man to enhancement of national egoism. Loyalty to the national state was elevated above all other loyalties, and all social, cultural, economic, and even religious considerations were subordinated to the ends of nationalism.

Economic nationalism. Superimposed upon these developing theories was continuing economic nationalism. In the early stages, political considerations lay behind nationalism, but a tendency developed to regard the state as an economic as well as a political unit. Modern nations erected tariffs against each other in their intense preoccupation with economic self-sufficiency. The resultant struggle for markets, raw materials, and fields for the investment of capital came during the rise of integral nationalism. Economic nationalism merged with imperialism to become one of the driving forces of contemporary history.

THE KOHN DICHOTOMY

Equally challenging is the theme developed by Hans Kohn on the dichotomy between Western and non-Western nationalism.[4] Kohn sees nationalism as the fruit of a long historical process. One nationalism may not be the same thing as another, depending always on the historical traditions and the political climate in which each arises. Kohn contrasts two sociopolitical environments in which nationalism had to grow and develop: the Western world (England, the British colonies, the Netherlands, and Switzerland); and the non-Western world (central and eastern Europe and Asia). These two areas provide the poles around which the new age, with its multiplicity of shadings and transitions, evolves. Kohn's dichotomy may be understood best by breaking it down into categories of origins, characteristics, and development of nationalism in the two areas.

[4] The précis of the Kohn dichotomy is based on Hans Kohn, *The Idea of Nationalism: A Study in its Origin and Background* (New York, 1944), pp. 329 ff., 349 ff., 573 ff.; *Prophets and Peoples* (New York, 1946), *passim;* and *The Twentieth Century* (New York, 1949), pp. 19–32. See also his paper, "Nationalism and Internationalism in the Nineteenth and Twentieth Centuries," presented to the International Congress of Historical Sciences, Vienna, 1965, and his *Prelude to Nation-States: The French and German Experience, 1789–1815* (Princeton, 1967).

Origins. In the Western world the rise of nationalism was a predominantly political occurrence; it was preceded by the formation of the future national state or coincided with it.

Outside the Western world nationalism arose not only later, but also at a more backward stage of social and political development. It grew in protest against and in conflict with the existing state pattern and found its first expression in the cultural field. The frontiers of an existing state and of a rising nationality rarely coincided. Each new nationalism received its original stimulus from cultural contracts with some older nationalism, and then began to extol the heritage of its own past.

There is also a contrast in historical motivation. In the Western world the Renaissance and the Reformation saw the creation of a new society in which the secularized bourgeoisie, gaining political power, abandoned in fact and in theory the universal, imperial concept of the medieval world. Vital changes took place in the social order. Nationalism in this area was a product of indigenous forces.

Historical motivation was quite different in central and eastern Europe and in Asia. The Renaissance and Reformation did not result in profound changes in the Germanies, where the two great historical movements were essentially scholarly and theological in nature. Russia and the Near East remained untouched, thus deepening the old cleavage between Western and Eastern empire. Universalism in politically ephemeral form persisted. Nationalism here was a product of cultural contact and of a mistaken interpretation of the past.

Characteristics. Western nationalism was born out of spirit of the Enlightenment and the struggle for liberty, constitutionalism, tolerance, and a society of free citizens based on laws. Here was the pluralistic and open society.

In the non-Western world the spirit of the Enlightenment was rejected or belittled; the tendency was toward an authoritarian uniformity of state and faith. Nationalism meant either collective power and national unity; independence from foreign domination, rather than liberty at home; or the necessity for expansion by the superior nation. Here was the authoritarian, closed society.

Western nationalism was closely connected with and influenced by the ideas of civil liberty and rational cosmopolitanism current in the eighteenth-century Age of Reason.

Non-Western nationalism, on the other hand, was opposed to outside influences. Originally influenced by the West as teacher and model, non-Western classes began to develop their own form of nationalism, ending in opposition to the "alien" example of rationalism and liberalism. The goals were narrow, self-centered, antagonistic.

There were differences, too, between reality and ideality. Nationalism in the West stressed the political reality. Here it was a response to the challenge of building a nation in the midst of current struggles without too much regard for the past. The nation was accepted as a vital, existing, real thing. Political integration was sought around a rational goal, as well as a belief in rational political ends.

The non-Western world, in contrast, became absorbed in a search for the ideal fatherland. Nationalism here was concerned often with myths and dreams of the future, without any immediate connection with the present. The nascent nation held a wistful image of itself and its mission. It looked to the past, to nonpolitical and history-conditioned factors.

Western and non-Western nationalism had different concepts of what the nation meant. The Western idea was that nations emerged as unions of citizens, by the will of individuals expressed in contracts, covenants, and plebiscites. Integration was almost always centered around a political idea, a common future achieved by common effort. Emphasis was put on universal similarities of nations.

In the non-Western view the nation was a political unit centering around the irrational, precivilized folk concept. Unable to find a rallying point in society or in the free and rational order, nationalism found it in the folk community, which was elevated to the dignity of an ideal or a mystery. Emphasis was placed on the diversity and self-sufficiency of nations.

The West accepted a legal and rational concept of citizenship. It appealed to individual rights. It thought all men to be fundamentally alike as individuals, regardless of social class or historical nationality.

In the non-Western world the appeal was to collective rights, to peculiarities of race or class. The entire idea of citizenship here was infinitely vague, lending itself easily to the exaggerations of imagination and the excitations of emotion.

Western nationalism, reflecting the optimism of the rationalists on the possibilities of natural law, was self-assured.

Non-Western nationalism, on the other hand, without roots in sociopolitical reality, lacked self-assurance. Often its inferiority complex was compensated by overemphasis and overconfidence. It regarded itself as deeper, richer, and more valuable than Western nationalism.

Western nationalism obtained its chief support from the politically and economically powerful and educated middle class, and, with a shift in emphasis, from the organized labor movements which were oriented on a social-democratic basis.

Non-Western nationalism gained its main support from the aristocracy and the masses.

Development. Western nationalism, relying on the autonomy of the individual and on voluntary association, and believing that one must hold a rationalistic and humanitarian regard for one's fellow man, gradually asserted itself as an outgrowth of the Enlightenment. The secularized Stoic-Christian tradition lived on in Protestant England and in Catholic France. The growth of nationhood was to a large extent the process of internal forces.

Non-Western nationalism, originally impelled by and dependent upon outside forces, developed in two opposing branches. One accepted the Western form, with its implications (British Parliamentary institutions; the French middle-class republic; the Industrial Revolution).[5] The second branch stressed national peculiarities and uniqueness and set itself outside the influence of cultural contact with alien civilizations. Spellbound by the past, fascinated by the mysteries of ancient times, re-creating tribal solidarity, and tending toward isolation, non-Western nationalism utilized history for national ends.

The Kohn structure clarifies many inconsistencies and contradictions surrounding the meaning of nationalism. It directs attention to opinion at certain times and in places where nationalism functions. It takes into consideration many advantages of the multidisciplinary approach, with emphasis on political, social, cultural, economic, and psychological factors, and is especially valuable in its treatment of the process of cultural influence and resistance in non-European areas. For many years the appearance of nationalism in non-European areas was regarded as a kind of spasmodic occurrence. Kohn reveals how the idea

[5] There has been some criticism of Kohn's geographical typology on the ground that it tended to discount the manifestations of democratic (Western) nationalism among the nations which he places in the non-Western category. Yet, Kohn spoke specifically of a non-Western branch of nationalism which accepted the Western form. See the review of Kohn's *The Idea of Nationalism* by H. H. Gerth, in *American Journal of Sociology,* LI (Jan. 1946), 341.

of nationalism could be communicated by cultural diffusion, while at the same time its meaning and form could take on characteristics dictated by the aims and aspirations of the peoples concerned. Thus, in India nationalism as a dominantly Western idea has been transformed into a moral obligation to protect the nation from foreign and alien influence. A new mission, grounded in legends and dreams of the past and guaranteeing heavenly bliss and redemption, is discovered and hailed as a beacon for a darkened world.

Critics of Kohn contend that his classification is far too favorable to the Western world, that he cleanses Western nationalism of tribal impurities, and that he disregards any manifestations of antidemocratic or non-Western nationalism in the West. The criticism is unjust: in his writings Kohn has demonstrated again and again his understanding of nationalism as a curse as well as a blessing. He sees its deleterious effects in the West as well as in non-Western nations. His formula takes into account gradations of light and shadow: the open, pluralistic society is never perfect. Kohn's work is a major contribution to the study of nationalism.

STATE-NATION, NATION-STATE, AND HYBRID FORMS

Another broad classification of nationalism was stimulated by the debate among historians following the unification of Germany in 1871. German historians, justifying the acquisition of Alsace-Lorraine, insisted that Bismarck was merely recovering land that had hitherto belonged to Germans. French historians, on the other hand, objected that the most important component of a nation was neither race nor language, but the will of its people, as expressed by Ernest Renan in his famous definition:

A nation is a grand solidarity constituted by the sentiment of sacrifices which one has made and those that one is disposed to make again. It supposes a past, it renews itself especially in the present by a tangible deed: the approval, the desire, clearly expressed, to continue the communal life. The existence of a nation is an everyday plebiscite.[6]

This debate, reflecting opposing opinions on either side of the Rhine, continued on well into the twentieth century. Friedrich Meinecke

[6] Ernest Renan, *"Qu'est-ce qu'une nation?"* (Paris, 1882), p. 27.

described the differences while projecting the concepts of state-nation and nation-state.[7]

The western Atlantic world, including America, accepted the idea of a "state-nation," the concept that the nation developed within the chrysalis of the state.[8] A common sovereignty provided common institutions: the new sense of nationhood transcended cultural differences. Here the state-nation represented a new cultural synthesis which rose above ethnic differences and in which nationality was usually regarded as a matter of individual choice. The key idea was Rousseau's "general will." The national spirit was a sense of community arising from a common past and hope for a common future. Politically, the idea was expressed in the concept of popular sovereignty.

On the other side, central and eastern Europe developed the "nation-state," the concept that the nation could grow only within the chrysalis of the individual culture. Here ethnic and political frontiers coincided, and nationality was regarded as reflecting ethnic identity. The nation was originally defined as a cultural rather than a political entity: the growth of national consciousness created a demand for the "nation-state." Instead of accepting Rousseau's general will, Germans preferred the idea of the *Volksgeist*, or "national soul" or "national spirit." This national spirit was supposed to be an objective force whose increasing motion produced the unique culture of each nation.

Thus, the Western "state-nations" (nations formed by states) and "nation-states" (states formed from nations) represented a dichotomy in European development, based on varying historical experiences east and west of the Rhine.

Utilizing this formula projected by Meinecke, Pflanze describes how the unification of Italy and Germany in the nineteenth century shows striking variations of the bifurcation.[9] Both drives for national unity produced what Pflanze calls hybrid types. Through the leadership of Cavour, Italy developed a nation-state on the central European model, but at the same time based on the western European tradition of popular sovereignty. The Italian movement for unification was

[7] See Friedrich Meinecke, *Werke*, V: *Weltbürgertum und Nationalstaat* (Munich, 1962), 9 ff.

[8] The analysis here is based on that of Otto Pflanze, "Characteristics of Nationalism in Europe, 1848–1871," *Review of Politics*, XXVIII (Apr. 1966), 139–143. See also Hans Rothfels, "Grundsätzliches zum Problem der Nationalität," *Historische Zeitschrift*, CLXXIV (1952), 339–358.

[9] Pflanze, *op. cit.*

grounded on a union of ethnic nationalism and popular sovereignty. Mazzini supported a European state of unitary nation-states based on popular sovereignty and republican constitutions.

Pflanze also shows how Germany strayed from the formula and evolved a hybrid type. Through the activities of Bismarck, Germany achieved a state-nation on the European model, while at the same time rejecting the western European tradition of popular sovereignty. The Second German Reich formed in 1871 was a state-nation in the sense that it included ethnic aliens and excluded millions of ethnic Germans (Austrians and Bohemians). This was the *Kleindeutschland* of 1848 under Prussian leadership and excluding Austria and other German enclaves. The German nation-state was unable to assimilate the aliens within its borders (Alsatians, Lorrainers, Danes, Poles, and the like) despite a rigid program of Germanization. The emergence of a strong German nationalism revived the idea of ethnic nationalism. Following the defeat of 1918, this was perverted into Hitlerian racialism.

Pflanze's distinction between the state-nation and the nation-state of nineteenth-century Europe has already been applied to the study of the new nationalism. For example, Philip D. Curtin sees the dominant force in recent African politics as the desire to build nations of the state-nation type. While Africa presented a number of possible nationalisms, in the first two decades of the African revolution there was a clean sweep of the state-nation type: the state was to create the nation, not the reverse. African leaders did not claim national self-determination, but rather an independent political life so that they could become nations.[10]

CLASSIFICATION IN OTHER DISCIPLINES

To these typologies of nationalism projected by Hayes, Kohn, and Pflanze may be added those suggested by scholars in other disciplines, including political scientists, sociologists, and psychologists.[11] Max Sylvius Handman, political scientist, emphasized the political nature of nationalism in the following classification: oppression nationalism, prevalent among people exposed to a regime of disabilities and special subordination (Poles, Jews, Irish); irredentist nationalism, common

[10] See Philip D. Curtin, "Nationalism in Africa, 1945–1965," *Review of Politics*, XXVIII (Apr. 1966), 143–153.
[11] See Snyder, *op. cit.*, pp. 122–132.

among such peoples as Italians, Rumanians, Serbs, and Bulgars, demanding liberation from domination, and almost identical with imperialism; and prestige nationalism, depending on reaction to contempt or insufficient esteem and demanding respect for the glorious past (Action Française in France; Mosley's Fascists in Britain). Handman stressed the predominantly negative qualities of nationalism and also neglected its social and cultural aspects.[12]

To sociologists nationality is a conflict group, and the various types of nationalism reflect the types of opposition and conflict which characterize the relations between conflict groups. To Louis Wirth, the forms of nationalism were distinguished by group power-struggles.[13] His four basic types all stressed profound social conditioning reflecting the aims and aspirations of groups as a vital factor: hegemony nationalism, an expansionist variety typical of the nineteenth century in which the national group is motivated by the urge to consolidate smaller principalities into larger and more dynamic units (the best examples are the unification of Italy and Germany); particularistic nationalism, a separatist variety based on the secessionist demand for national autonomy (potential nationalities in the Austro-Hungarian Empire before World War I); marginal nationalism, a virulent borderland variety (Alsace-Lorraine, Silesia, Schleswig, the Saar, Rhineland, the Italo-Austrian border); and the nationalism of minorities, in which minorities strive for recognition of their own traditional nationality and seek to maintain their own culture within another nationality.[14]

Similarly, psychologists place emphasis upon the group mind when classifying the types of nationalism. The point of departure is always the working of the mind and group acceptance of ideas, ideals, and

[12] Max Sylvius Handman, "The Sentiment of Nationalism," *Political Science Quarterly*, XXXVI (1921), 107–114.

[13] Louis Wirth, "Types of Nationalism," *American Journal of Sociology*, XLI (1936), 723–737.

[14] Wirth later discussed this fourth basic type, the nationalism of minorities, which he broke down further into three orientations: pluralistic, concerning the search for cultural autonomy and civic equality; secessionist, in which freedom is sought from the dominant majority; and militant, in which domination over the majority is sought with assistance from militant conationals across the border. Wirth spoke of another minority group which desired to be assimilated in the majority group (for example, the American Negro), but this was not in any real sense a "national" movement. See Louis Wirth, "The Problem of Minority Groups," in *The Science of Man in the World Crisis*, ed. R. Linton (New York, 1945), pp. 347–372.

symbols. Thus, Gustav Ichheiser projected two basic major forms: conscious nationalism, when members of a certain national group vociferously profess national values, consciously and with awareness strive toward national goals, glorify the real or imaginary peculiarities of their own community, and reject positively any feeling of hostility to other peoples; and subconscious (or unconscious) nationalism, attributable to members of a national group, who, even though they do not formulate or pronounce in any articulate way their special national ideas and beliefs, are nevertheless so influenced by prejudiced ideas that, without being aware of it, they see and judge everything from their own national point of view.[15]

THE SYMMONS-SYMONOLEWICZ FORMULA:
COMPARATIVE TYPOLOGY OF NATIONALIST MOVEMENTS

The most recent attempt at classification which would include the new nationalism is that projected by sociologist Konstantin Symmons-Symonolewicz in 1965. Suggested as a typology somewhat narrower than that proposed by Wirth and others, Symmons-Symonolewicz does not attempt to classify all the varieties of nationalism as a sentiment, an ideology, or a political program, but instead limits his attention to nationalist movements.[16] He does not include the nationalism of the majorities or the dynamics of their development.

Following in part the pattern of definition set by Florian Znaniecki,[17] Symmons-Symonolewicz defines nationalism as "the active solidarity of a group claiming to be a nation and aspiring to be a state." He uses the term in an ethically neutral sense: nationalism is neither good nor bad, neither liberal nor illiberal, neither democratic nor undemocratic. "When seen as a movement, nationalism represents a series of stages in the struggle of a given solidary group to achieve its basic aims of unity and self-direction." [18]

[15] Gustav Ichheiser, "Some Psychological Obstacles to an Understanding between Nations," *Journal of Abnormal and Social Psychology*, XXXVI (1941), 427–432.

[16] Konstantin Symmons-Symonolewicz, "Nationalist Movements: An Attempt at a Comparative Typology," *Comparative Studies in Society and History*, VII (Jan. 1965), 221–230.

[17] Florian Znaniecki, *Modern Nationalities* (Chicago, 1952), see especially pp. xiii, xvi, 10, 21.

[18] Symmons-Symonolewicz, *op. cit.*, p. 227.

This suggested classification distinguishes between two major kinds of nationalist movements: minority and liberation. Symmons-Symonolewicz sees minority movements as aiming at self-preservation; they are "real minorities," groups which are so weak, or so territorially located, that the aim of liberation from the majority group is for them inconceivable. The liberation movements, on the other hand, are those which are able to achieve independence, or believe that they can do so.

Category of minority movements. Here a basic distinction is drawn between the perpetuative-segregative and perpetuative-pluralistic types. Both tend to preserve their cultural identity, but the pluralistic type seeks also for full civic equality for its members, while the other wants only to be left alone. Examples of the perpetuative-segregative type are the medieval Jewish ghettos or the imperial Ottoman millet system. Minority rights, as in the minority treaties of post-Versailles Europe, would be a solution satisfactory to the perpetuative-pluralistic type.

The third type, the irredentist, is limited to those border groups which seek to secede, even though they are only a minority and cannot hope to be successful on their own. They can win their goal only when their desires are shared and supported by an expansionist neighboring state which claims them as conationals.

Category of liberation movements. In this category Symmons-Symonolewicz draws distinctions in terms of historical development and the nature of unity. He defines the restorative movements as those which involve nations whose independent existence was interrupted recently and which were successful in retaining their social structures in a relatively intact form (Poland or Hungary in the nineteenth century).

The revivalist movements refer to those ethnic communities which lost their political identities some centuries ago and which have to rebuild both their historical traditions and social structure. With their leading classes lost, they become reduced socially and intellectually to the level of the lower social strata (Flemish, Catalan, Finnish, or Lithuanian nationalities in the nineteenth century).

The ethnic movements are those which have no tangible historical tradition but whose sense of solidarity has been activated by such ideologies as democracy and self-determination (Latvians, Estonians, or the Somalis and Kikuyu in Africa).

By the autonomist-secessionist type Symmons-Symonolewicz means those regional entities which, despite their ties to the mother group, develop a certain distinctiveness that is expressed in their demand for some degree of autonomy. On rejection of this demand, separation rather than autonomy becomes the goal. "These movements are rather nationalisms *in statu nascendi* than true nationalisms, but they evolve rapidly in this direction, once their aim of separation is achieved." [19] Successful examples are those movements which created the United States of America and many Latin-American states. Unsuccessful movements of the same type may be seen in the attempted secession of the Confederate States, or the movements aiming at autonomy of such ethnically Russian territories as Siberia.

In the anticolonial type Symmons-Symonolewicz sees "national" movements behind which there are still no nations, nor even cultural or ideological unities from which such nations could easily develop. This type is far removed from genuine national movements. Its unity is mostly of a negative type, resting on opposition to, and rejection of, colonial rule. "Notorious" examples are Congolese "nationalism," as well as the internal dissension in Indonesia, Burma, even India and Pakistan.

The final category, nativist movements, does not represent modern nationalism at all, but rather one of nationalism's most primitive components—xenophobic tribalism, "or in Toynbeean terms, a reaction of the 'zealots' to conquest and disruption of the old order." [20] Examples can be found in the various millenarian movements, but also in such movements as the struggle of the Caucasian mountaineers under Shamyl against Russia in the nineteenth century or that of the Riff mountaineers under Abd-el-Krim against Spain and France in the twentieth century.

The Symmons-Symonolewicz formula, sociological in concept, is based on the assumption that the aims of all movements concerned with exclusive loyalty to a given group are essentially similar.[21] It does take

---

[19] *Ibid.*, p. 229.   [20] *Ibid.*

[21] Sociologists have conflicting views about the nature of the nation, but they seem to agree that a nation is formed only when, in addition to economic and ecological juxtaposition, there are cooperation and association. R. L. Sutherland and J. L. Woodward say that not until the "we-sentiment," or "the feeling of oneness" (conviction of a group superiority and the awareness and willingness to work toward a common objective) has appeared, does a nation really exist (Robert L. Sutherland and Julian L. Woodward, *Sociology* [New York, 1940], p. 351). Admitting that such traits as common language, religion, government, and

into consideration the effects of historical development, geographic location, cultural development, economic advancement, and current political situation. The liberation movements include several types of modern nationalism as well as at least one archaic variety. The final two types of liberation movements, the anticolonialist and nativist (the first negative and the second xenophobic and tribalistic), are accurately named, and certainly may well be the best terms to be used to describe the developing nationalism in contemporary Africa.

There is no rivalry between historians and sociologists in the matter of classifying types of nationalism. Both disciplines are handicapped by the tendency to place too much emphasis upon their special views—historians tend to be preoccupied with moral evaluations of nationalism and regard it primarily as a state of mind, while sociologists almost automatically search for the social movement as basic in nationalism. Symmons-Symonolewicz is aware of these difficulties and quite rightly urges a blending of both approaches.

A PROPOSED CONTINENTAL
OR REGIONAL CLASSIFICATION

All classifications of nationalism are arbitrary and suffer from much the same weakness as does the practice of dividing history into varying epochs. Such distinctions are made merely for the sake of convenience. Any typology of nationalism tends to set sharper divisions than exist in reality. In tracing the development of the new nationalism it becomes necessary to set up some guide for interpretation. The new blends of nationalism which appear on the postcolonial scene do not fit snugly into past classifications.

If we are to project a new classification from the historian's point of view, we must distinguish between vertical and horizontal conceptualizations. The Hayes formula is distinguished by two characteristics: it stresses a chronological, or vertical, approach, treating nationalism from its origins in modern form in the French Revolution; and its area is limited mainly to the European continent. Nationalism came of age at a time when the French experience was critical in European history. In the nineteenth and early twentieth centuries came the solidification of

---

traditions all contribute to the development of a nation, they hold, nevertheless, that the "we-sentiment" is the only indispensable factor.

national spirit in individual European states and the Europeanization of the world. What happened in the rest of the world seemed secondary to the European experience.

During the first half of the twentieth century, nationalism began to escape its European bonds and penetrate into all continents. This is not to say that elements of nationalism had previously been altogether lacking in those areas. They were there in latent form. There was an intensification of a sentiment already in existence, but forms differed according to the historical experience of each area.

The Kohn dichotomy, on the other hand, is horizontal in essence. It contrasts two sociopolitical environments in which nationalism grew and developed. It connects the origin of Western nationalism with concepts of individual liberty and rational cosmopolitanism current in the eighteenth century, while the later nationalism in central and eastern Europe and in Asia and elsewhere tended toward a contrary development. The latter form of nationalism not only arose later, but also at a more backward stage of social and political development, growing in protest against and in conflict with the existing state pattern and finding its first expression in a national culture.

Because the new nationalism covers the relatively brief period since 1945, the vertical or chronological conceptualization has little meaning. It would be best then to stay with the horizontal approach and to seek special characteristics that exist in large areas. One of the most predictable qualities of nationalism is that it is almost always influenced by the historical process in any given area.

The various forms of the new nationalism seem to follow a continental pattern. The distinctions are never absolutely clear, but they seem to coincide with continental or regional lines. The classification proposed here is based on general area characteristics: it is not assumed that the pattern is wholly distinctive. Secondly, it should not be confused with regional or continental nationalisms in the sense of such movements as Pan-Africanism, Pan-Arabism, Pan-Asianism, or Pan-Americanism. The "pan" movements as a whole go beyond the limits of a nationality or a nation. The earlier forms, Pan-Germanism and Pan-Slavism, were not only cultural in origin but were also associated with national aggression. The later types were supranational.

The following classification is presented as a framework for study of the new nationalism:

Europe: Fissiparous nationalism. In Europe the new nationalism tends to recapitulate the experience of the old; that is, it remains fragmented, split, and particularistic. Fissiparous nationalism reflects the ideology of the small nations as the ultimate politico-economic units. Perhaps they can survive only as an anachronism. But for the time being they exist. There is much talk about a United States of Europe, about Europe as a "third force" (along with the United States and Soviet Russia), but despite the earnest attempts to integrate all of western Europe, nationalism remains strong and unbending.

Africa: Black nationalism. African nationalism emerged with explosive impact. In the variegated pattern one state after another established its independence. An important element was the appearance of a dominant ethnic motif. This was the predictable response of peoples who rebelled in anger at decades of white imperialism. The outer coating of African nationalism is in some respects imitative of Western forms, but deep within the new structure is a racial core of hostility to white domination. The term "nationalism" is applied indiscriminately throughout the vast continent to every show of resistance against the old colonial rule. It is an almost impossible task to separate the African desire for self-government from the deep opposition to European control. This is by no means a new phenomenon in history: Toynbee speaks of xenophobic reaction against foreign encroachment as an almost universal antecedent of modern nationalism.[22] In the case of Africa, however, the process has taken on racial overtones which have become decisive.

The Middle East: Politico-religious nationalism. The Middle East, too, experienced this process of liberation, independence, and building the nation-state. Here nationalism is affected by the area's close proximity to Western civilizations. The religious element has long been of importance in this cradleland of three great faiths. Christianity shifted its center westward and its influence spread throughout the world, but Islam and Judaism retained their fulcrums in the Middle East. Many factors have been important in the rise of Arab nationalism, in the reconstruction of Israel, and in the appearance of state nationalism in Turkey and Egypt, but in all these cases religious nationalism, tinged with political overtones, is a kind of common denominator.

Asia: Anticolonial nationalism. Among the generalizations used to compare Africans and Asians, it is often said that Asians are more

[22] See Arnold Toynbee, *The World and the West* (New York, 1953).

sophisticated, their civilization has deeper roots, their concept of democracy is older, and change is more integrated in their society. It would seem then that nationalism would develop in Asia along more compact and stable lines, but such is not the case. The pattern is mercurial and unpredictable. While it varies from area to area, from country to country, it is distinguished generally by an anti-Western tone. It is responsive most of all to the demands of oriental "face"—a sensitive national pride which rebels spontaneously and almost automatically against domination from the outside. In Asian nationalism the psychological motivations of anti-imperialism and anticolonialism appear to be of even greater import than economic drives.

Latin America: Populist nationalism. In Latin America nationalism has taken on a revolutionary tinge, reflecting generations of political change affected by rebellion against established but "temporary" authority. The form of democracy is utilized, but not its spirit and deeper meaning: all power is reserved for the strongest group, for the most powerful military junta. This process, somewhat removed from that of British parliamentary rationalism, is a combination of Spanish pride, fickleness, and fierce sense of independence. The party in power usually wraps itself in the mantle of patriotism and claims exclusive monopoly of the national image. A common factor is lesser or greater devotion to the idea of opposing "Yankee domination." Here, too, there are many variations of nationalism.

The United States: Melting-pot nationalism. The United States was built by people who were driven out of the safe and settled corners of the earth and came to a strange and hostile land. These people became Americans, a new breed. In a comparatively short time Americans became more alike than they were different. Their nationalism was an amalgam of spiritual idealism (libertarianism and egalitarianism) and materialism (business and industry). Stimulated by the Puritan heritage, American nationalism took on a moralistic quality, a desire to convince the peoples of the world that the American government was the best on earth and that all other peoples should imitate American virtues and ideals. When the United States took on the role of world leadership in the global age, the mélange of qualities distinguishing the old form of nationalism was retained, while added to them were such characteristics as transition from provincialism to regionalism to nationalism, retreat from autarchic isolationism, and anticommunism. As neophyte nations emerged to take their place in the world order, most of them were influenced, at least on the surface, by the prototype of American nationalism.

The Soviet Union: Messianic nationalism. In the great land mass of contemporary Russia, Marxist-Leninist-Stalinist communism was supposed to give an overwhelming example of the desirability and efficacy of an international world society. Its aim was to destroy the archaic Czarist society cursed by capitalistic, bourgeois nationalism. It was to be a great experiment—the end of obsolescent nationalism. But, ironically, instead of becoming the homeland of a new world society, Soviet Russia revived Czarist messianic nationalism in another form. Earlier Czarist nationalism had confined itself to enforced Russification of contiguous areas. The new Soviet nationalism sought expansion not only in neighboring countries but in any vacuum or weak area of the capitalistic world. The Soviet urge for expansion took on all the fervor of the Islamic *jihad* against unbelievers. It was a truly remarkable feat—while denouncing the curse of aggressive bourgeois capitalist nationalism, Moscow pursued its own messianic nationalism as a blessing, "unselfish in motivation, liberating in effect."

Once again it should be stated that these geographical configurations of the new nationalism are presented merely as a convenient framework for study. Despite the variations in design, the basic mold of nationalism remains the same wherever it appears. Idioms, traits, and characteristics peculiar to any nation will generally reflect the historical development of that nation. Neither history nor nationalism conforms to scientific laws or to rigid, precise categories.

Chapter 5

Fissiparous Nationalism: European Phases

For the European of our age nationalism is the most important thing in the world, more important than civilization, humanity, decency, pity; more important than life itself.

—NORMAN ANGELL

The continent of Europe, homeland of modern nationalism, has been subjected to the impact of historical homogeneity and geographical heterogeneity. The first may be seen in the persistent drive for integration, the second in the equally enduring and more effective urge for fragmentation.

Factors encouraging integration. The European states have a common spiritual heritage. There is a common language tradition: with the exception of Magyar, Finnish, and Basque, of vague origins, the root language is Indo-European (father, pater, Vater, padre, père, papa, patar). The religious tradition is Christian: the Muslim flood from North Africa was contained at the Battle of Tours in A.D. 732, and Europe remained Christian. Economic interrelations between the European peoples were strengthened over the course of centuries. Similarly, in such areas as art, music, literature, philosophy, law, science, and technology, the European trend was toward integration.

The tradition of integration survived the fall of the Roman Empire. Under the systems of feudalism and manorialism, medieval Europe split into multifarious fragments, but the idea of a universal state in a universal Church was retained. While it remained vague and shadowy, the concept of a Holy Roman Empire persisted throughout the Middle Age and even into modern times. The idea of European integration never died.

Factors encouraging fragmentation. Against this pattern of general historical homogeneity is the divisive force of geography. The picture of Europe as one unified land mass is somewhat exaggerated. A French geographer defines it as follows:

Between the heavy land masses of Asia and Africa, there is a sort of puzzle of mingling lands and seas called Europe. Between the Arctic Ocean, the North Atlantic, the Mediterranean Sea, and the widening forests and shrublands of Soviet Asia, the European lands consist of peninsula and isthmian areas, plus a scattering of islands all around. It scarcely deserves to be called a continent. However, it is and always has been an exceedingly important part of the globe.[1]

[1] Jean Gottmann, *A Geography of Europe* (rev. ed.; New York, 1954), p. 1.

This geographical diversity had some effect in the artificial creation of the modern national sovereign state. Some European countries, notably England and France, achieved early unification. Others, especially the Germanies and Italies, remained collections of particularistic units (in the late eighteenth century there were almost eighteen hundred German sovereign states, principalities, and free cities). Europe was engulfed in international anarchy. Instead of working together, the nations of Europe waged war against one another. The fourteenth-century rivalry between Florence and Pisa was recapitulated on a larger scale in the nineteenth-century conflicts between France and Prussia. Instead of a European patriotism, there developed national loyalties replete with localized codes of conduct, national flags and anthems, national currencies and tolls. Differences inside Europe were on occasion greater than those between some countries inside and some of those outside. For example, Britain was closer to Australia than to Greece; Sweden was closer to the United States than to France.[2] Under this increasing sense of nationalism, disloyalty to the state became the ultimate crime. Where the worst medieval crime was heresy, punished by excommunication, the most detested violation of law in the modern era was treason, punishable by execution.

Thus, the trend toward fragmentation (geographical and political) was stronger than the urge to integration (economic and cultural). Instead of concerting their politics and combining their strengths, the countries of Europe reasserted an inward-looking nationalism.

European nationalism was a major force in the origins of both world wars of the twentieth century. The peoples of Europe went to war in 1914 in an outburst of nationalistic fervor—the French "à Berlin," the Germans "nach Paris." Only under the realization of rising casualty lists did this exaltation subside. Nationalistic tendencies endured throughout the war. For example, General Pershing stoutly resisted the idea of distributing American troops among French units, and demanded that Americans fight as a national force. After the war the defeated Hohenzollern, Hapsburg, Romanov, and Turkish empires were split under the banner of national self-determination. The nation, even the small nation, still was regarded as the ultimate political unit.

European nationalism was also an important contributing cause of World War II. During the Long Armistice from 1919 to 1939, the

[2] Max Beloff, *Europe and the European* (London, 1957), p. 14.

nations of Europe reverted to the old system of national combinations by treaty. There was, however, a modicum of restraint on the arrogance of national sovereignty, expressed in the first faltering steps of the League of Nations. Then Adolf Hitler appeared on the scene "to work out in extreme institutional form and with the total logic of the lunatic the unlimited pretensions of Western nationalism." [3] Hitler carried the exclusiveness of nationalism to its ultimate absurdity, to its violent, paranoiac stage. "Hitler's broom, sweeping across the frontiers of Europe, instead of destroying, intensified national sentiment; for the Nazi doctrine of the *Herrenvolk*, ruling over inferior races, was a direct provocation to national resistance." [4]

Napoleon at St. Helena spoke sadly of his frustrated mission to unite the squabbling countries of Europe into a compact United States of Europe (under control, of course, of himself and his family). Hitler, Germany's version of the French conqueror, pursued a similar goal. In his self-appointed task of guarding western Europe against the inroads of communism, Hitler drew upon the arrogance, the unlimited pretensions, and the unbridled assertiveness of Western nationalism.[5] To these he added German nationalism, which was suffused with the added bitterness of defeat in World War I. The end result was nationalism stripped to its bare and vicious form—revolutionary, extreme, irrational. Instead of helping to unify Europe, Hitler aggravated its centrifugal tendencies.

European peoples went to war in 1939 with melancholy resignation but with determination to remove the Hitler cancer. A host of diverse nationalities joined in a common task. The goal was achieved: Hitler was smashed.

The hope that nationalism would recede from its high watermark was based on a combination of several factors:

Status of small states. The smaller states of Europe seemed to have outlived their usefulness after 1945. Mention has already been made of Edward H. Carr's judgment that in Europe small national states had demonstrated their military and economic insecurity beyond recall and that they could survive only as an anomaly and an anachronism in a world that had moved on to other forms of organization.[6]

[3] Barbara Ward, *Faith and Freedom* (London, 1954), p. 190.

[4] G. D. H. Cole, *The Intelligent Man's Guide to the Post-War World* (London, 1947), p. 1077.

[5] Ward, *op. cit.*, p. 190.

[6] Edward H. Carr, *Nationalism and After* (London, 1945), p. 35. See also Chapter 1.

Promise of the United Nations. There was faith in the germinating United Nations, which would avoid the pitfalls which had destroyed the value of the old League of Nations. Now at last, it was thought, a more effective international tribunal would function as an agency for peace.

Recession of colonialism. Those European nations which had taken the lead in nineteenth-century imperialistic expansion lost their overseas colonies as well as foreign investments. Was it not obvious that the strong European national state of the past, boasting heavy commitments overseas, was weakening?

Shifting bases of nationalism. Nationalism was moving from its European center to the Middle East, Africa, Asia, and Latin America. Just as the Industrial Revolution of the late eighteenth and nineteenth centuries had stimulated nationalism in England and western Europe, so now the spread of industrialization to the undeveloped areas of the world was followed by growing nationalism elsewhere than in Europe.

Role of Russian communism. The success of the November 1917 Revolution in Russia inspired revolutionary activity elsewhere on the European continent. Perhaps Marxian internationalism in one form or another would supersede an outmoded nationalism.

To the Eurocrats these intermingled factors indicated a progressive weakening of nationalism. Some even claimed that for Europe "nationalism is dead." But the report was very much exaggerated. The European unity that had been forged in a common hatred for Hitler soon disintegrated. European nationalism became even more insistent, despite talk of European entity, united fronts, and Atlantic alliances. Today Europe has reached a plateau of prosperity, due in part to economic integration.[7] But politically and financially, European nations preserved their strong sense of nationalism.[8]

At the same time, while the fragmented new nationalism of the post-1945 era in Europe retained many characteristics of the old, it cast off that belligerent, blatant quality that had contributed much to European problems in the twentieth century. The slow but patient drift to economic union, even if it did halt at the line of an effective

[7] See Chapter 12.

[8] "Still intensely nationalistic in financial matters, European governments discourage outsiders from entering their bond markets by imposing coupon taxes ranging up to 25% on alien bond purchases. American bonds, on the other hand, being tax-free and easily transferable, are snapped up in $10,000 and $20,000 lots by zip-lipped Swiss bankers representing unmentioned clients" (*Time*, Jan. 14, 1966, p. 64).

international parliament, indicated a political maturation. Europe began to experience a diminution of aggressive nationalism, but the strong urge for national sovereignty and fragmentation was still present.

The strength of contemporary nationalism in Europe is revealed in the fact that Britain's devolution of her empire was not matched by a conterminous liquidation of nationalism. One early manifestation of modern nationalism came in seventeenth-century England, the European leader in political thought and activity, economic enterprise, and scientific spirit. The hope of present-day Eurocrats that Britain would undertake a similarly vital role, this time putting an end to the strictures and prejudices of nationalism, was not fulfilled.

As the great imperial power and colonizing agent of modern times, Britain recognized the futility of seeking to maintain its old position in a world of altered conditions. The new order brought her several difficult problems: how to relinquish what remained of the old imperial status and at the same time retain as much as possible of her former position of strength and prestige; how to continue amicable and useful relationships with new nations; how to open the way for modernization not only of political institutions but also of the social order; and how to maintain the population of an already overcrowded island. In all these aims, political and economic, the British were not successful in casting off the old nationalism.

Britain's political relations with Europe had long been characterized by that sense of "splendid isolation" so conducive to nationalism. The phrase, "going to Europe," expressed a greater consciousness of distinctions than "going to America" contained for the American island of Martha's Vineyard.[9] The basic tenet of British policy *vis-à-vis* the European mainland was to prevent the emergence of any dominant power there. For this Britain fought with determination against Philip II, Napoleon, and Hitler, all equals in the British pantheon of arch villains because they tried to dominate Europe.

In World War II, Britain emerged again as one of the great powers.

[9] René Albecht-Carrié, "To a British Friend: Are You in Europe?" *Journal of International Affairs*, XVI, No. 1 (1962), 18.

In 1945, as Europe lay in ruins with her people frustrated, distraught, and chastened, Britain had a splendid opportunity to assume the political leadership of a United States of Europe.

Europe . . . begged for Britain to give it a lead. But so concerned were we with our own problems . . . and so afraid were we of hitching onto our own ankles the ball and chain of Europe's chaos and destruction, that we turned a deaf ear to these cries. So the Europeans, with the help of American aid, went ahead with their own plans, first the pooling of coal and steel, then the plan for a European army, but still hoping we would join and lead these movements and inviting us to do so.[10]

Impelled by fears of losing even a small part of her sovereignty, Britain returned to the comfort of splendid isolation. The old suspicion of Continentals, their politics, conspiracies, and traditions, was retained. When the idea of a European army failed, British cynics reacted with "I told you so!" and insisted that the idea of a European political federation was a pipe dream.

The retreat to political nationalism was open and clear-cut, but economic nationalism brought with it some problems. As the movement for European economic integration gathered momentum with the formation of the European Coal and Steel Community and the Common Market of the Six, the British at first refused to take part. Rather than be trapped in Continental economic entanglements, Britain would earn her living and pay her way by depending primarily on the Commonwealth for preferential trade arrangements. The British government argued at first that for Britain to join the Common Market would betray her obligations to the Commonwealth. In this ingenious way, what was clearly a case of economic nationalism was placed on a plane of political loyalty and integrity. The fact was that imperial preference was no longer the effective instrument of promoting Commonwealth trade that it had been in the nineteen thirties. Not more than 30 per cent of Commonwealth exports went to the United Kingdom. Moreover, after the formation of the European Economic Community (EEC), there was a noticeable rise in trade between the Commonwealth and the Common Market countries.[11]

[10] Anthony Nutting, "Britain's Imperative," *Journal of International Affairs*, XVI, No. 1 (1962), 28–29.
[11] *Ibid.*, p. 32.

The unexpected success of the Common Market impelled the British government to re-examine its position.[12] It partly relinquished economic sovereignty by associating with the European Free Trade Area (EFTA), or the Outer Seven.[13] Yet there was hesitation and doubt: even as a member of the Outer Seven, Britain still barred Common Market products if they were in competition with British farmers or Commonwealth suppliers. To Common Market members this was suspiciously similar to a case of "Heads I win, tails you lose!" The Outer Seven gave Britain a market of 40,000,000 people as compared with 170,000,000 in EEC. But the tariff walls of the Common Market remained too high.

Britain continued to lag behind and failed to earn her share of Europe's economic boom.[14] British leaders began to see that, even though continental Europe was still forced apart politically by nationalistic pressures, it was growing ever more firmly locked economically. They were appalled when American industrialists began to invest heavily in Common Market areas and to build factories there in preference to Britain. The British applied for membership in the Common Market, only to be rejected brusquely by de Gaulle's veto.[15]

FRANCE: DE GAULLE AND NATIONAL GRANDEUR

If the British attitude toward the new nationalism remained hesitant and fluctuating, that of the French was clear-cut and unyielding. France put her faith in the permanence of sovereign states and the durability of national interests. By emphasizing national rather than supranational cooperation, she profoundly influenced the entire Continent. One by one, in domino pattern, the bastions of European federalism fell in response to moves by Paris.

The new French nationalism was primarily the work of a charis-

---

[12] See Chapter 12.   [13] See Chapter 12.

[14] Among the reasons given for Britain's failure to share in Europe's prosperity were the following: a weak export-import ratio leading to critical balance-of-payment deficits; inability of the British to make their economy sufficiently competitive in world markets; rigid union rules; unwillingness of both British labor and management to extend themselves; inflation of prices for goods and services; wage increases unaccompanied by rising productivity; welfare expenditures without adequate fiscal backing; and general misfortune. The freeze on prices and wages by the Wilson government in 1966 and the devaluation of the pound in late 1967 were designed to prevent an economic collapse.

[15] See Chapter 12.

matic leader, President Charles de Gaulle.[16] De Gaulle's mind was like the Louvre, filled with battle pictures in which the French were always winning. An enthusiastic apostle of French nationalism, he expressed such sentiments as these:

Our country, with her tinted sky, her varied contours, her fertile soil, our fields full of fine corn and vines and livestock, our industry, our gifts of initiative, adaptation and self-respect, make us, above all others, a race created for brilliant deeds.

The sword is the axis of the world, and greatness cannot be shared. (1934)

The emotional side of me tends to imagine France, like the princess in the stories or the Madonnas in the frescoes, as dedicated to an exalted and exceptional destiny. But the positive side of my mind also assures me that France is not really herself unless in the front rank; that only vast enterprises are capable of counterbalancing the divisive ferments which are inherent in her people. In short, to my mind, France cannot be France—without greatness. (1955) [17]

This was the same de Gaulle who in 1940, by example and forceful action, had staked his career on his own ability to create unity among a highly individualistic people who had undergone an ignominious defeat by the Germans.[18] In extravagant tones he insisted that he not only spoke for France, he was France—a designation that made little impression upon wartime leaders Franklin D. Roosevelt and Winston Churchill. In his *War Memoirs*, in which he spoke of himself both in the first and third persons, de Gaulle identified the nation with himself:

And today I was at the head of a ruined, decimated, lacerated nation, surrounded by ill-will. Hearing my voice, France had been able to unite and march to her liberation. . . .

The immediate dismemberment of Charles de Gaulle's government did not, of course, escape the notice of the various foreign offices.[19]

[16] See Chapter 12 for further treatment of de Gaulle and supranationalism. Some overlapping is unavoidable here. On de Gaulle's career, see also David Schoenbrun, *As France Goes* (New York, 1957); Philip Williams, *Politics in Postwar France* (New York, 1954); Alexander Werth, *France, 1940–1955* (New York, 1956); and David Thomson, *Democracy in France* (New York, 1958).

[17] Quoted in *Time*, Feb. 8, 1963, p. 23.

[18] Edgar S. Furniss, Jr., *France under de Gaulle* ("Foreign Policy Association Headline Series," No. 139 [New York, Jan.–Feb. 1960]), p. 4.

[19] *The War Memoirs of Charles de Gaulle; Salvation, 1944–1946*, trans. Richard Howard (New York, 1960), pp. 269, 320. When he retired temporarily in 1946, de Gaulle was certain that with him went the wind from the heights, the hope of

For France, de Gaulle had a special kind of sentiment, compounded of mysticism and romanticism. France to him was not merely a *patrie*—it was a mystique. His goal was to restore dignity to a country that had been beset by humiliation, despair, and debilitation. He was certain that a call from the depths of history, as well as the instinct of the nation itself, had led him to assume French sovereignty. He would impose order, law, and justice, and demand from the world respect for the rights of France. He would bend to the common interest the various elements of the nation in order to lead it to salvation. In this task he would not compromise to the slightest degree.

De Gaulle did, indeed, have an important political role in the country for which he held such deep regard. The postwar Fourth French Republic had a dismal record. The French people were thoroughly tired of the traditional political instability which had prevented recovery from the war. In May 1958 they turned to General de Gaulle. Once in power he moved swiftly to consolidate his position. He supervised the drafting of a new constitution which set up the Fifth French Republic and chose for himself an Olympian role as president ("above the battle").[20] Acknowledged by his supporters as the national leader, he brought strength and prestige to his office by using a system of executive decrees. It was to be an ironfisted democracy.

De Gaulle succeeded in creating the illusion that he carried more weight than his country. A master of political maneuver, shock tactics, and sleight-of-hand performances, he managed to lift France by her bootstraps, made her appear much more powerful than she actually was, and won world attention for her. It was an extraordinary achievement.

De Gaulle recognized only three possibilities for France: communism, which claimed to establish scientifically the foundations for a just and efficient society; European federalism, which aimed to reduce

---

achievement and ambition for France which upheld "the national soul." This concept of the French "national soul" recalls the devotion of nineteenth-century German nationalists to that evanescent ideal (see Louis L. Snyder, *From Bismarck to Hitler* [Williamsport, Pa., 1935], pp. 19–20; and Louis L. Snyder, *German Nationalism: The Tragedy of a People* [Harrisburg, Pa., 1952], pp. 189–190).

[20] See Carl J. Friedrich, "The French Constitution in Political and Historical Perspective," *Harvard Law Review*, LXXII (Mar. 1955), 801–837, and Stanley Hoffmann and Nicholas Wahl, "The French Constitution of 1958," *American Political Science Review*, LIII, (June 1959), 332–382.

national identity and thereby eliminate the rivalry which for centuries had divided European peoples; or Gaullism, which emphasized the national grandeur of a revived France. De Gaulle regarded the third way simply as a necessity. Gaullism was "a rejection of decadence, an act of faith in the possibility of France continuing to exercise in this second half of the twentieth century the major role she had played for a thousand years." [21]

France's democratic strong man regarded himself as the inheritor not only of French but also of European legitimacy. He wanted the same kind of Europe as had Napoleon, although he would impose unity by the force of his own personality instead of by arms.[22] His grand design was a confederated "L'Europe des patries," a "Europe of the Nations" which would defend national independence by avoiding any decisions imposed from outside national boundaries. In de Gaulle's estimation, Paris was not only the center of Europe, it was also the center of the world. His preoccupation was to preserve national identity. He would not under any circumstances accept any element of supra-nationality.

Above all, de Gaulle was dissatisfied with American influence in Europe.[23] He would construct, along with Britain and Germany, a "second pillar" capable of maintaining an equilibrium with the Americans, and he would make the interests of Europe prevail over those of America where they did not coincide. He advocated the end of the "direct, visible, and permanent" presence of American power in Europe. Everything must be subordinated to French independence, even those close bonds that united France with her allies. France would not be bound eternally to Washington by gratitude for past favors.

---

[21] André Fontaine, "De Gaulle's Grand Design," *Weekend Telegraph* (London), No. 54 (Oct. 1, 1965), p. 29.

[22] J. H. Huizinga, "Which Way Europe?" *Foreign Affairs*, XLIII (Apr. 1965), 490.

[23] See Donald McKay, *The United States and France* (Cambridge, Mass., 1951); and Raymond Aron and August Heckscher, *Diversity of World: France and the United States Look at Their Common Problems* (New York, 1957). "The paradox is that whereas de Gaulle indignantly rejects an Atlantic system in which one state, America, has a leading role by virtue of her possession of great nuclear and indeed economic superiority, he proposes for Europe, a similar situation in which one nation, namely France, has a leading role, and this in spite of the fact that she is less important both economically and numerically than either Western Germany or Britain, or indeed (if numbers only should count) even Italy" (Lord Gladwyn, *The European Idea* [London, 1966], p. 77).

Because he held no office when the European Economic Community was formed in 1958, de Gaulle was unable to influence the shape of the organization. The framers of the Treaty of Rome, the bloc's basic charter, had more than economy in mind when they set up the community. They intended that eventually economic integration would lead to political integration. France and Germany would no longer be enemies: there would be a wedding of France's farms with Germany's factories, and each would enjoy a larger market stripped of national frontier barriers. The terms of the treaty designated three formal stages for the evolution of the community from 1958 to 1970. There would be a unanimous decision to pass from the first stage to the second (a step taken in 1962): members were bound by the treaty not to turn back. The third stage came automatically at the end of 1965, shifting the community from control by outright veto to control by majority.

On December 28, 1958, shortly after he came to power, de Gaulle made an abrupt decision allowing France to participate in the Common Market on an equal basis with the other members.[24] From the beginning, however, he refused to accept the idea that this implied a step toward European political integration. From his viewpoint each country should retain control over its own economic life. It was precisely because of this lack of federative aspects that de Gaulle felt he could bring France into the Common Market without sacrificing his principle of national grandeur.

De Gaulle's attitude toward the Common Market gradually hardened when it became obvious that there was, indeed, a danger that its members were working toward a common government. His sense of nationalism was so overpowering that when it was threatened he could dismiss as inconsequential the economic gains made by France as a member of the Six. He began to place barriers in the way of the Common Market's expansion. In January 1963 he resolutely opposed British entry into the community. In July 1965 he boycotted the meetings of the organization in Brussels. Soon he was attacking the architects of the Common Market as "a technocratic, stateless, and

[24] On French relations with the Common Market, see Warren C. Baum, *The French Economy and the State* (Princeton, 1958); Henry W. Ehrmann, *Organized Business in France* (Princeton, 1957); William Diebold, Jr., *The Schuman Plan: A Study in Economic Cooperation in 1950–1959* (New York, 1959); J. Hasbrouck, "Will the Common Market Succeed?" *Foreign Policy Bulletin*, Oct. 1, 1959; and H. I. Macdonald, "European Common Market," *Behind the Headlines*, XVIII, No. 4 (1958).

irresponsible clique," and their plans as "a project removed from reality." [25] He would not allow decisions affecting the superior interests of France to be imposed by a "stateless bureaucracy," with its "supranational pretensions." Above all, he would not allow France to lose automatically her power to veto Common Market decisions, though this stage was reached in January 1966.

Their differences came to a head over the issue of financing agricultural subsidies. The Community tried to formulate a Market-wide policy to support farm prices, a plan which actually would aid French farmers. But de Gaulle refused to accept it because he believed it would hasten the political integration of western Europe. He declined further cooperation. The other members demanded that, in exchange for their approval of de Gaulle's system of national farm financing, France should support the Community's institutional framework, such as its executive commission and its parliament. To de Gaulle this was unacceptable. He would not allow use of the Common Market as a vehicle for supranational European political integration. He opposed the European Commission and its German head, Walter Hallstein. He would not accept decisions made by majority vote. His real objective remained a European political union on his own terms—that is, based on agreements between sovereign governments.[26]

German, Italian, and Dutch comembers of the Common Market criticized de Gaulle's increasingly nationalistic attitude. Even his countryman, Jean Monnet, "father of Europe," said: "The most striking thing about General de Gaulle's is his nationalistic view of world affairs." [27] None of this made the slightest impression on the French president. He continued to insist that he was not really opposed to European unity, but that France must remain sovereign inside any such federal organization. He had expressed this view in 1962: "Who in good faith can dispute the fact that France must help to build Western Europe into an organized union of states so that gradually there may be established the most powerful, prosperous, and influential political, economic, and military complex in the world?" [28]

De Gaulle's stiff nationalism set him into conflict not only with the Common Market but also most violently with the partnership of the

---

[25] *Time*, international ed., Sept. 17, 1965, p. 66.
[26] William Millinship, in *The Observer* (London), Oct. 24, 1965.
[27] New York *Herald-Tribune*, Paris ed., Sept. 11–12, 1965.
[28] Quoted in *Time*, Feb. 8, 1963, p. 23.

North Atlantic Treaty Organization.[29] Organized in 1949 among fifteen allies, NATO was perhaps the most highly integrated voluntary alliance in history. It was a product of the bitter experience during the Long Armistice of 1919–1939, when Hitler had become powerful precisely because of the division among Western nations. NATO was designed to resist aggression before it occurred. It involved joint planning and training in peacetime for instant, coordinated use of combined Allied armed forces in war. One of its functions was to remove the threat of another aggressive Germany by integrating West Germany into a defensive coalition with other European countries and the United States.[30] NATO was especially valuable for France, which has been made militarily virtually impregnable since 1949. In the absence of such an integrated system France was attacked three times in the last hundred years, despite her faith in mutual defense systems.

In a press conference held on September 5, 1960, de Gaulle expressed a theoretical justification for his opposition to European integration: "The states . . . are the only entities which have the right to give orders and the power to act. To imagine that something can be built up which can act effectively and be approved by the peoples outside or over and above the states is an illusion." [31] This attitude eventually crystallized into the view that NATO integration meant "vassalage" and "subordination to the United States." In a press conference held on September 9, 1965, de Gaulle described France as "a nation which keeps its hands free." "At the expiration of our present commitments, that is 1969 at the latest, we shall end the subordination which is being described as integration and which puts our destiny into the hands of foreigners." [32] France would make no sacrifice of national sovereignty.

In de Gaulle's view, World War II had been fought to establish

[29] On NATO, see Gardner Patterson and Edgar S. Furniss, Jr., *NATO: A Critical Appraisal* (Princeton, 1957); Ben T. Moore, *NATO and the Future of Europe* (New York, 1958); and Marshal Juin and Henri Massis, *The Choice before Europe* (London, 1958). On de Gaulle's relations with NATO, see René Pleven, "France in the Atlantic Community," *Foreign Affairs* XXXVIII (Oct. 1959), 19–30.

[30] In addition, NATO enveloped West Germany's twelve army divisions and 650 combat aircraft in a command-and-supply structure so effective that never again could a German general staff plot or wage war against Germany's neighbors. See Benjamin Welles, in *The New York Times*, Mar. 22, 1966.

[31] Quoted in John Pinder, *Europe against de Gaulle* (London, 1963), p. 35.

[32] *The New York Times*, international ed., Sept. 10, 1965.

French sovereignty, not only against Hitler and his Vichy confederates, but against France's main allies. He was adamant in his views:

There is France's will to be responsible for herself, which is indispensable if she is to believe in her own role and be useful to others. The will of France is incompatible with a defense organization in which she is subordinate. . . .

The question is to restore a normal situation of sovereignty in which everything that is French, on the ground, in the air and on the seas and every foreign element stationed in France, must be under the sole control of French authorities.[33]

This meant that NATO's political headquarters in Paris as well as SHAPE's military headquarters would have to be relocated outside France.[34]

To a great extent de Gaulle's opposition to NATO was a result of his suspicion of the United States. He bluntly termed NATO a "cover" for an "American protectorate" in Europe. Since World War II, he said, Washington, backed by London, had made mistake after mistake and had gone from one diplomatic defeat to another. The Americans, he charged, had set up in NATO a shaky barrier against Soviet Russian imperialism, but they had been unable to prevent further Western retreats before Asian and African nationalism. Worst of all, said de Gaulle, the United States controlled 95 per cent of the West's nuclear strength, and its statesmen and commanders were in a position to dictate Allied strategy. This was objectionable because United States leadership was so unpredictable that it might lead to a nuclear holocaust, engulfing Europe. France, said de Gaulle, must participate in any decision involving military conflict and must have full equality in the standing group—the tripartite body charged with planning NATO's military strategy.

Thus, NATO became the test of Gaullist grandeur. In de Gaulle's

[33] *The New York Times*, Feb. 22, 1966.
[34] SHAPE (Supreme Headquarters Allied Powers Europe) had been set up in 1951 by General Eisenhower and had been commanded by a series of American generals named by a series of American presidents. Reconstructing NATO's military infrastructure outside France would be a costly process. There still remained the problem of what to do with fourteen U.S. air bases and some forty U.S. supply depots scattered around France, as well as what to do with the 550-mile-long NATO fuel pipeline stretching from St. Nazaire to Germany.

opinion, it had been formed to meet conditions that no longer existed, and hence was obsolete.

De Gaulle's attack on the integrated defense structure of the Western alliance met with the unanimous opposition of France's allies. His critics denounced him as a person motivated by past rancors and arrogant individualism. It had been said that his preoccupation with French glory was legitimate as long as he did not revert to the fatal narrow nationalism of the nineteenth century. But now he was accused of being the "wrecker" of Allied defense. In the nuclear age, his pursuit of national independence and sovereignty was chimerical. He was offering not "L'Europe des états" but "L'Europe de l'état c'est moi." His nuclear policy was engulfed in self-contradiction: calling for a strategy of maximum deterrence, he demanded instantaneous use of nuclear power while at the same time asking for withdrawal of France from the NATO command. "On the one hand, his provocative diplomacy has cost him the indispensable confidence even of such a uniquely generous and long-suffering protector as America has shown itself to be these many years past, while at the same time it has frightened off the European bride he woos with offers of nuclear protection of derisory value." [35] It was charged that de Gaulle's "reckless" rebuffs to the power on which Europe depended for its defense were due to envy: "De Gaulle's evident hostility to America is fed by his envy of American power. His own nature cannot brook a rival in authority; nor is it tolerable to him that France should be weaker than America." [36]

In the NATO capitals it was feared that de Gaulle's action would engender a return of German nationalism.[37] The departure of France from NATO would make West Germany, militarily and politically, the biggest and most powerful Continental member of the organization. Bonn's bargaining power would be multiplied. And the smaller European nations, once more left alone, would occupy the fringe of a

---

[35] Huizinga, *op. cit.* p. 491.   [36] Pinder, *op. cit.,* p. 36.

[37] "The overriding danger of de Gaullist doctrine and the French nationalism it exalts has always been that it could help stoke a resurgence of nationalism inside Germany. . . . Bonn set off with enthusiasm on this integration route as offering the best prospects for protecting the Federal Republic's integrity and territory, for containing any recrudescence of nationalism and, over the long run, for bringing the reunification of Germany in freedom" (editorial in *The New York Times,* Apr. 12, 1966).

continent dominated by the Germans.[38] Already the contagion of French nationalism had stimulated an extreme right-wing party in the Bavarian and Hamburg state elections, and there was a rise in neo-Nazi activity.

None of this criticism had the slightest effect on de Gaulle. For the remaining fourteen members of NATO, efforts to explain the mistakes and paradoxes of de Gaulle's logic became a despairing ritual. Frustrated Eurocrats blamed him and his "outmoded nationalism" for extinguishing the flame of European integration. Meanwhile, de Gaulle sought to rebuild his frequently mentioned "Europe from the Atlantic to the Urals" by stepping across West Germany (with its too-dangerous economic dynamism and military potential) and clasping hands with the Soviet Union.

In early December 1967, at the sixteenth press conference of his nine-year rule, de Gaulle addressed 1,100 newsmen. In a hundred minutes he called in the name of France for secession of French-speaking Quebec from Canada, threw England out of Europe, threatened the Common Market with destruction, called the United States the principal enemy, and denounced Israel for going to war in June 1967 against his admonition. His speech invoked outrage around the globe.[39] To critics it was a scintillating example of bootstrap nationalism in action: when a country slips to a second-rate position among nations, lift it by its bootstraps through oral shock treatment. "Talk the country back to glory." De Gaulle was described as a master of this special form of nationalism.

THE NEW GERMAN NATIONALISM

German nationalism was born in the darkness of Napoleonic despotism.[40] Napoleon's attempt to spread the ideas of the French Revolution into the Germanies by force of arms stimulated the rise of German

[38] Henry Tanner, in *The New York Times*, Apr. 3, 1966.

[39] *Time*, Dec. 8, 1967, p. 30.

[40] On the older German nationalism, see Hans Kohn, "Romanticism and the Rise of German Nationalism," *Review of Politics*, XII (Oct. 1950), 443–447; Koppel S. Pinson, *Pietism as a Factor in the Rise of German Nationalism* (New York, 1934); Robert R. Ergang, *Herder and the Foundations of German Nationalism* (New York, 1931); and Snyder, *German Nationalism: The Tragedy of a People*.

nationalism. He abolished the hodgepodge of particularistic states and gave them a boost toward unity by eliminating most of the small principalities. Significantly, the first impulse for German nationalism came from the outside.

As a means of overcoming their humiliation and despair, the Germans turned to their past, when the first German Empire had been the cockpit of Europe. An unsubtle people, they adopted romanticism, with its accent on imagination instead of reason, as a bulwark against the principles of 1789 and the machinations of Napoleon. In their glorious past they rediscovered the "medieval freedom" which had little in common with the Anglo-French rationalistic concept of liberty. They would think with the blood and give free rein to all that was German. An anti-French sentiment, combined with romanticism, culminated in the War of Liberation against Napoleon. The germs of nationalism multiplied under the stimulus of the *Freikorps* (patriotic volunteers), Turnvater Jahn's *Turnerschaften* (gymnastic societies), and the *Burschenschaften* (student fraternities). The German professors at the Frankfurt Assembly in 1848–1849 sought to achieve national unity on the basis of a lukewarm liberalism, but they failed. Liberalism was effectively throttled.

Otto von Bismarck—Junker, monarchist, conservative—shrewdly utilized a combination of diplomacy and wars (1864, 1866, 1870–1871) for the purpose of Prussian aggrandizement and glory. But the Iron-and-Blood Chancellor was responsible for sending his country into the twentieth century clothed with the relics of feudalism and with only the outer trappings of Western democracy. Germany's sense of nationhood remained fragile and insecure. Her people had never experienced a nationalist, bourgeois, democratic revolution comparable to those in Britain or France.

Germany's nationalism contributed to both world wars. After her collapse in 1918, she was forced to accept the onus of war guilt expressed in the Treaty of Versailles. German nationalism, instead of coming of age along cultural lines, went berserk under Adolf Hitler. Hitler perverted the entire German heritage: he grasped German romanticism and extended it into an extreme, irrational worship of the Wagnerian concept of life and death. The Germans, accustomed to obedience, responded to Nazi appeals for service to false ideals. A supposedly civilized people remained mute in the presence of crimes unparalleled in history.

It is a law of life that everything has its cost. Germans paid heavily for the cancerous spread of Hitlerism. In 1945 their country lay in ruins, its cities destroyed, its youth wounded, its people stunned by destruction, economic breakdown, mass expulsion, occupation, and partition. The old nationalism seemed to be dead.

Then came one of the most remarkable recoveries in history. Within two decades the German phoenix rose from the ashes. Politically, West Germany emerged as a viable democracy, with a smoothly functioning government oriented to the Western free world.[41] Economically, West Germany underwent a striking period of growth, called by the Germans themselves a *Wirtschaftswunder*, an economic wonder.[42] Whereas the Weimar Republic was associated in the German mind with a disastrous economy, the Bonn Republic was noted for economic progress. Devastated cities were rebuilt; several million new homes were constructed; old factories were replaced by modern units. More than thirteen million refugees from the East were incorporated into the economy. Average living standards rose more than 50 per cent above pre-World War II levels.[43] West Germany emerged as Europe's most dynamic industrial state—after the United States she became the largest exporter of manufactured goods in the world. Although no longer the world power she had been in the early twentieth century, the new Germany became one of the most active nations on the European scene.

Along with West Germany's recovery came a revival of national consciousness. This new German nationalism maintained a level inside the mainstream of the established democratic parties.[44] It bore none of the ugly marks of the fanatical Nazi era, but it could be recognized as a

[41] On the political development of West Germany, see Gordon A. Craig, *From Bismarck to Adenauer: Aspects of German Statecraft* (Baltimore, 1958); Arnold J. Heidenheimer, *The Governments of Germany* (New York, 1961); Richard Hiscocks, *Democracy in Western Germany* (New York, 1957); Elmer Plischke, *Contemporary Government of Germany* (Boston, 1961); and Edgar Alexander, *Adenauer and the New Germany: The Chancellor of the Vanquished* (New York, 1957).

[42] On the new German economy, see Wolfgang F. Stolper, *Germany between East and West* (Washington, D.C., 1960); Henry C. Wallich, *Mainsprings of the German Revival* (New Haven, 1955); and Ludwig Ehrhard, *Prosperity through Competition* (New York, 1958).

[43] Klaus Epstein, *Germany after Adenauer* ("Foreign Policy Association Headline Series," No. 164 [New York, Apr. 1964]), pp. 5–6.

[44] C. L. Sulzberger, in *The New York Times*, Feb. 21, 1965.

revived nationalism. "Our reason," wrote Hans Christ, "tells us that we are Europeans, but our feelings waver, for we cannot quite be both a nation and European." [45] German politicians spoke increasingly of "national identity," "national pride," "national substance," and "national achievement."

Germany after 1945 was fundamentally changed. The mysticism and irrationalism which had caused Germany so much trouble in 1871 and 1918 was now outmoded, at least for the time being. The new Germany was protected against the dangers of overcentralization. The key to this change was the disappearance of Prussia: the center of gravity shifted from east of the Elbe to the west and southwest, to areas where the political climate was more susceptible to Western conditions. The anti-Western sentiment of the past began to disappear as the new Germany tried to take on a liberal and democratic complexion.

There were four major ingredients in the new German nationalism: the urge to reunification; the attitude of the younger generation; the influence of de Gaulle: and the emergence of neo-Nazism. In combination these trends produced a changing national character.

Urge to reunification. In 1919 the peacemakers at Versailles split the defeated Germany into two parts by setting up the Polish Corridor. This move, calculated to punish Germany for her guilt in "starting the war," was certain to provoke the revival of German nationalism. It did just that: Danzig and the Polish Corridor became Nazi tools for whipping the German masses into a nationalistic frenzy. In 1945 the victorious Allies once again promoted the schizophrenia of a divided Germany, which produced the Federal Republic of West Germany and the Soviet-dominated Democratic Republic of East Germany. West Germany went on to become Western-oriented, affluent, and self-satisfied; East Germany, lean and dissatisfied, became a satellite state resting on Moscow's bayonets. The new Germany was split into four parts. Earlier conquerors, including the Romans, the Swedes in the Thirty Years' War, and the Napoleonic French, had dropped their iron curtains between north and south. Over the years there developed the cold Protestant North and the affable, beer-drinking Catholic South. The new East-West split cut this historical Germany into quarters and generated an "Athens versus Sparta" complex.[46]

[45] Hans Christ, *Die Rolle der Nationen in Europa, Gestern-Heute-Morgen* (Stuttgart, 1962), p. 65.

[46] On divided Germany, see Rudolf Walter Leonhardt, *This Germany: The Story since the Third Reich* (New York, 1964).

The issue of reunification led to an intensification of the new German nationalism. Historically, few nations have ever been able to stand such division for long. The prosperous West Germans, who took pride in their economic achievements, were impatient with their nation's international status as a political cripple. The most zealous advocates of reunification felt that the opposite of unity had been achieved and that the two Germanys were more divided than ever. They pointed to the existence of the Berlin Wall as a mark of permanent division.[47]

The most strident calls for reunification came from the thirteen million refugees and expellees from East Germany. These refugees escaped from the German Democratic Republic, which West Germans called "Mitteldeutschland" to remind the world that there was still a portion of Germany in the East. The expellees came from that eastern section beyond the Oder-Neisse line, lands now held by Poland. Today, one out of every five West Germans has his homeland in the East. The desire of these people to return to their homes is a powerful factor in the solidification of the new nationalism.

Konrad Adenauer, who retired from the chancellorship of the West German Federal Republic on October 15, 1963, after holding power for fourteen years, was successful in creating a democratic state and in integrating the Bonn Republic into western Europe and NATO. His one great failure was his inability to achieve the reunification of Germany.

There has been continuous and bitter argument since the early 1950's as to whether this failure has been inevitable—in other words, whether reunification has been "objectively" unattainable—or whether it has been the price of Adenauer's clear-cut option for the West [an option which precluded bargaining with the Russians over reunification]. Adenauer always asserted that the policy of building up Western strength was not only desirable in itself, but was also likely to lead to reunification: he believed that a strong West could sooner or later impose terms upon the Russians and that these terms would include the reunification of Germany. It is clear now that this policy erred in exaggerating the possibilities of both Western strength and Russian weakness.[48]

---

[47] From the Communist viewpoint, the Berlin Wall stopped the loss of East Germany's labor force, as a result of which its economy has steadily improved. In Western eyes, the Berlin Wall was an admission of ideological bankruptcy. On the Berlin Wall, see Eleanor Lansing Dulles, *Berlin: The Wall Is Not Forever* (New York, 1967).

[48] Epstein, *op. cit.*, p. 7.

The failure of this policy embittered Adenauer, who suspected the "Anglo-Saxons"—British and Americans—of softness toward the Russians. In the final years of his chancellorship, he initiated a policy of reconciliation with de Gaulle and France, while maintaining a rigid attitude toward Russia. This hard line was revised by his successor, Ludwig Erhard, who saw dangers in the shadow of the new nationalism: "I will fight nationalism with all my strength. My Government is very clear on this and the U.S. Government and public opinion should support me more." [49]

Attitude of the younger generation. In the immediate post–World War II years most German youth wanted to relinquish its heritage of nationalism and become "European." "Ohne mich!" ("Without me!") was the watchword. This cynicism was grounded in a distrust of the elders who had allowed themselves to descend to Nazi barbarism. Young Germans became tired of the anti-German prejudice they encountered on trips abroad. At Speakers' Corner in Hyde Park they could be observed talking animatedly to groups of Englishmen about the unfairness of it all. It was a strange dual role: at home they bitterly accused their parents, but abroad they argued that it was unreasonable to punish Germany forever for past crimes. It was futile and masochistic, they insisted, to dwell on an admittedly horrible past.

The new young Germans were rebellious, pragmatic, and skeptical. They believed in *Gelassenheit* (playing it cool). They would not be trapped by the old slogans. The youthful German poet Hans Magnus Enzensberger deprecated the worship of national sovereignty: "The beer hall is the only place left in which it is still taken seriously." [50] This was, perhaps, a minority opinion, for paradoxically, German youth resented the dismemberment of their country. The older nationalism had exerted a strong effect on the youthful mind (Young Turks, Young Italy, Young Germany). The new German nationalism similarly attracted the support of young people in search of a cause. They listened impatiently as the whole world talked of self-determination, a precious right denied to their own country. The younger generation feels itself a part of German history. [51]

---

[49] *The New York Times,* Feb. 21, 1965.

[50] Quoted in *Time,* June 4, 1965, p. 23.

[51] "Those [German students] who were born after World War II think they owe little to the past; in a sense, they are people without parents. They are intense in their desire for freedom, and they take a position that is designed to prevent a

Influence of de Gaulle. A major factor in the reawakening of German nationalism was the killing of the myth of western European unity by General Charles de Gaulle. The Germans were attracted by de Gaulle's "Europe of the Fatherlands." "True, the very concept was a reminder to the Germans that their own Fatherland was only partly involved in the scheme; moreover, the looser the union the more starkly the question would pose itself: Which nation was to lead it?" [52] Attachment to de Gaulle would satisfy German ambition for an acceptable role in the world. In the late years of his chancellorship, Konrad Adenauer was influenced by de Gaulle's nationalistic evangelism, an attitude shared by former Defense Minister Franz Josef Strauss. There was an unmistakable development of a "Gaullist foreign policy" within the dominant German party, the Christian Democratic Union (CDU), in the summer of 1963. The leader of this faction was Adenauer himself, who regarded reconciliation with France as his greatest achievement.[53]

For a time Adenauer and de Gaulle worked together to achieve Franco-German cooperation. Adenauer agreed to support de Gaulle within the Common Market, and de Gaulle, in turn, adopted the West German attitude of intransigence on Berlin.[54] But the honeymoon ended when it became evident that de Gaulle rejected the nation of Europe as a supranational organization. The French president insisted that France alone would be the next nuclear power and tried to maintain controls on Germany's military equipment, especially nuclear weapons. Finally, de Gaulle's action in closing the door of the Common Market on Britain convinced the Germans that the French president remained, above all, a French nationalist. European integration was a difficult task because of de Gaulle's unbending attitude. "It was this profound swing in German opinion that made the Franco-German treaty a dead letter even before it was ratified; what Dr. Adenauer had seen as his crowning achievement thus became the prelude to his forced retirement in 1963." [55] Chancellor Erhard, Adenauer's successor, and Foreign Minister Gerhard Schröder both retreated from the Gaullist

new authoritarianism. There must be no second Hitler. The new type of nationalist feeling, which they do not clearly recognize, can become a strong political force unless they are kept in tune with internationalism" (Dulles, *op. cit.,* p. 172).

[52] Richard Lowenthal, "The Germans Feel Like Germans Again," *The New York Times Magazine,* Mar. 6, 1966, p. 39.

[53] Epstein, *op. cit.,* p. 57.   [54] Furniss, *France under de Gaulle,* p. 49.

[55] Lowenthal, *op. cit.*

position. Under Chancellor Kurt Kiesinger, West Germany saw her "grand design" not in companionship with de Gaulle but in the reshaping of relations with the East-bloc nations.

Rise of neo-Nazism. The German public was profoundly shocked by the revelations in 1945 which showed the full extent of the Nazi terror, especially the policy of genocide. The West German government enacted a series of stringent laws against the revival of anti-Semitism and paid a billion dollars in reparations to Israel, the symbolic home of world Jewry. At the same time, the vast majority of older Germans, most of whom willingly or unwillingly had been drawn into the all-embracing Nazi state, wanted to forget the past. Most Germans wanted to allow the statute of limitations against further trials of Nazi criminals to expire in the spring of 1965, but the angry reaction of world public opinion forced Chancellor Erhard and the Bundestag to extend the statute.

In this atmosphere there was a revival, slight but nevertheless obvious, of neo-Nazism. An amalgam of several right-wing movements appeared in the formation of the National Democratic Party (NPD), despite the strict laws banning neo-Nazi organizations. Young people were attracted by the party's nationalistic demands for an end to the war-crimes trials, for Germany's withdrawal from NATO, for banishment of foreign workers, and for the return of the Oder-Neisse territories annexed by Poland after World War II. The party promoted drum-and-bugle rallies and parades in the same Nuremberg square where the Nazis had held their huge annual reviews. The NPD rolled up small successes in local elections in Bavaria (8 per cent of the total vote in Bayreuth; 7.3 per cent in Nuremberg), Schleswig-Holstein, and the city of Hamburg. Party leaders claimed 16,298 members in 1965.

The NPD disclaimed any connection with Nazism. But a dozen of the eighteen members of the party's executive board were former card-holding Nazis; half held high SS rank and were entitled to the golden badge of the Nazi party. The party flag was flame red, centered with an empty white circle ready for a new, or old, symbol. For the first time in the history of the West German Federal Republic, right-wing extremist nationalism became something more than a specter. Although currently weak, neo-Nazism may well play an increasingly important role in the event of an economic reversal or a political vacuum. Most dangerous of all, the absence at this time of any significant neo-Nazism does not necessarily mean that there is an overriding enthusiasm for the existing democratic structure of the West German Republic.[56]

Changing national character. Using the concept of national character in a cautious and limited sense, it is reasonable to say that the over-all temper of the German people has changed from romantic idealism to a more prosaic materialism. We see here evidence that national character is not permanent. Even if such traits be considered stereotypes, the fact that they attract widespread credence make them worthy of attention.

The older form of German nationalism which appeared during the era of Napoleonic despotism was clothed in romanticism. The young Germans who took part in the War of Liberation were dreamers willing to sacrifice their lives for the fatherland. The German nationalism which crystallized out of this romanticism drew the attention of apostles who despised the Western community. They were contemptuous of French "bourgeois decadence" and British "constitutional chaos." They had faith in German *Kultur*, in the German "soul," and in the German mission to save the world.

The German national character was molded in the Prussian image. Prussian ideals became widely known as German. This occurred despite the dichotomy between the Prussian Protestant North and the Bavarian Catholic South, between the stern Prussian and the good-natured Bavarian. Prusso-German traits included thoroughness, discipline,

---

[56] The electoral success of the NPD touched off a lively debate on the possibility of a rebirth of Nazism. Some saw a trend toward a revival of Nazism, while others denied it and pointed out that Nazism of the older type was associated with racialism, terrorism, and abandonment of democracy. On December 30, 1966, the American Council on Germany, Inc., issued a statement doubting the rebirth of Nazism and warning against the danger of "condemning an entire people for the views of a small minority." The statement was signed by twenty-nine American authorities on Germany, including Karl Brandt, Henry C. Wallich, George N. Shuster, Hans J. Morgenthau, Henry A. Kissinger, Robert Strausz-Hupé, Hajo Holborn, and Harry D. Gideonse (*The New York Times*, Dec. 30, 1966, p. 4).

Skeptics, unimpressed by these distinguished names, referred to the early days of Nazism, when the movement was comparatively weak and unimpressive. These observers say that any resurgence of German nationalism, which in the past was accompanied by militarism and brutality, is made even more dangerous by the psychological imbalance produced by partition. They say that if German nationalism produces a revisionist threat, neo-Nazi or non-Nazi, both Europe and the world would face new dangers.

obedience, pedantry, punctuality, love of decorations and titles,[57] deference to the constituted authority (*Obrigkeit*), and respect for the military. Balanced against German romanticism was a contradictory literal-mindedness which led Germans to confuse nonsense with fact. Germans turned to "thinking-with-the-blood." This was dangerous irrationalism.

In the recovery-and-reconstruction era after 1945, German attitudes underwent a significant change. In a kind of stock-taking Germans asked themselves how they could possibly have followed a barbaric Fuehrer. Many tried to expiate the disgrace of the Nazi past. Some, in a flurry of self-exculpation, tried to balance the slaughter of Jews with the expulsion of Germans from the East. Others answered charges of atrocity by pointing to the Allied bombing of Hamburg, Dresden, and other German cities. Weary of masochistic attitudes toward the past, many Germans shoved the Nazi experience into the dark recesses of their minds. Hitler, the arch culprit, was dead. Let Germans get to work.

The escape to materialism became a kind of national occupational therapy. There was less interest in traditional philosophical speculation and in the old idealism of the past. This was accompanied by a pragmatic approach to German problems. The new German became more cautious than romantic, more skeptical than literal-minded. He began an energetic pursuit of private profit. The trend was deplored by the older generation (West Germany became a youthful nation; half of its 58,000,000 citizens were born or grew up after the Nazi era). Simultaneously, class lines became more fluid as careers were opened to talent and as young people went into business instead of the bureaucracy and military service. Along with the *Wirtschaftswunder* came the *Hängebauch*, the drooping belly of prosperity.

Actually, Germany's changing character has benefited from a psychological climate geared by and suited to the new democracy. The extent of change will depend upon the continuing strength of democracy in the Bonn Republic, a new government in a nation without meaningful democratic traditions. Most important of all will be the reaction to the rise of neo-Nazism, for here is the crucial test of

[57] For example, addressing a man with three degrees as "Herr Doktor, Doktor, Doktor!" or a deputy general manager's spouse as "Frau Generaldirektorstellvertreter," or a servant girl as "Fräulein Dienstmädchen."

whether or not the Germans have learned anything from their immediate past.

URGE TO SEPARATION: OTHER EUROPEAN COUNTRIES

The pattern of nationalistic fragmentation extends to other European countries from the comparatively large (Italy and Spain) to the postage-stamp sovereignties (Monaco, Luxembourg, Liechtenstein, Andorra, and San Marino). Italian nationalism retains its strength, despite the observation that the Italians' family loyalty is their true patriotism.[58] Although Spain and Portugal on March 17, 1939, two weeks before the end of the Spanish Civil War, signed a treaty of friendship and nonagression known as the Iberian Pact,[59] and although both peoples have a common origin, speak languages which derive from the same roots, and have many other similarities, each chose the way of strict national sovereignty.[60]

It would seem that the Scandinavian bloc—Sweden, Denmark, Norway, and Finland—linked by similar parliamentary systems, laws, education, a Lutheran background, and a passion for social reform, might draw closer together and relinquish national sovereignty in a common cause. Indeed, a trend toward common citizenship is indicated by the fact that today all citizens of the Nordic bloc may live, work, and draw welfare benefits almost anywhere in Scandinavia. Yet, despite this unifying aspect, the Scandinavian peoples remain separated not only by formidable physical barriers but also by distinctive national characteristics, the result of differing environment and traditions. In the Scandinavian countries, as elsewhere in Europe, nationalism has proven to be a hardy sentiment. The national flag still exerts a greater attraction than ethnic, religious, or cultural similarities.

Linguistic rivalries often play a major role in the clash of European nationalisms. In Great Britain, Welsh nationalists retain their own tongue and refuse to grant that the English flag may rightfully be

[58] See Luigi Barzini, *The Italians* (New York, 1964), an entertaining and provocative dissertation on the delights and deficiencies of the Italian national character.

[59] Text in G. de Martens, *Nouveau recueil général des traités*, 3ème Série, XXXVII (Leipzig, 1939), 339–341.

[60] See John Davis Lodge, "The Iberian Peninsula and Western Europe," in *Journal of International Affairs*, XVI, No. 1 (1962), 77–88.

flown in Wales alongside the Welsh Dragon.[61] But by far the most interesting case history of linguistic nationalism in contemporary Europe is found in Belgium. The roots go back to the partition of 1830, when Flemings and Walloons broke away from Holland to form a new country. At first there was no real language problem, because the franchise was restricted to members of the educated class, who normally spoke French no matter what their origin. Belgian society was at first dominated by the Walloons, who lived in the southern industrial areas and regarded the Flemings to the north as poor relations. The balance began to shift as rivalry was intensified after World War II. The Flemish-speaking people began to outnumber those who spoke French (4,500,000 Dutch-speaking Flemings; 3,500,000 French-speaking Walloons; 1,000,000 bilinguals). Flemings began to protest that although Dutch and French had official parity, French was still the language for those Flemings who wanted to get ahead in Belgian society.

Walloon and Flemish rioters clashed in Brussels. The government tried to end the dispute by authorizing French in the south, Dutch in the north, and both languages in Brussels, a French-speaking island in the north. Neither side was satisfied by the plan. The Walloons preferred the *status quo,* while the Flemish nationalists began to call for a semiautonomous Flemish state. Police broke up running fights between Flemish nationalists and French-speaking Walloons. On August 22, 1965, nearly a hundred Flemings ostentatiously walked out of a church in Ostend when the priest began the mass in French for vacationing Walloons. The gendarmery were forced to drive through the streets in armored vehicles to halt the ensuing riots.[62] The next December there were riots in the Dutch-Belgian border region. The Fourons is an area of six predominantly French-speaking villages which were transferred in 1962 under new linguistic laws from the French-speaking Liége province to the Flemish province of Limburg. On December 19, 1965, two hundred Flemish demonstrators who had motored from the Antwerp region toured the villages of Fourons carrying flags with the emblem of the Flemish lion. Fifty persons, including a village burgomaster, were injured in the riots.[63]

[61] *Daily Telegraph* (London), Aug. 17, 1965.

[62] *Daily Telegraph* (London), Aug. 23, 1965.

[63] *The New York Times,* international ed., Dec. 20, 1965. Similarly, on May 20, 1966, a two-day riot broke out in Louvain, Belgium, when Flemish students at

The quarrel was based on linguistic, not ethnic, differences. Families of Flemish stock have been intermarrying with Walloons for centuries: perhaps 30 per cent of Belgian marriages today cross the linguistic frontier.[64] Yet, paradoxically, the language barriers survive in a country which has taken a leading role in plans for political and economic integration of Europe. The Belgians recovered rapidly from World War II, and later from their hasty disengagement from the Congo. They were enthusiastic supporters first of Benelux and then of the Common Market. But so strong were language rivalries that Flemish nationalists became committted to splitting the nation. They called their country the "Congo of Europe."

That language need not be necessarily a divisive factor in nations is indicated by the Swiss experience. Until the mid-nineteenth century the Swiss Confederation was politically a loose union of virtually autonomous cantons. Because each canton enjoyed a large measure of self-government, Switzerland was able to avoid the difficulties of fragmentation which had been experienced by the Balkan states. The people spoke German, French, and Italian, all recognized officially in 1874 as national languages. Romansch, a dialect of the Alpine regions, was added as a fourth national (but not official) language in 1937. The population varied around these figures: the German Swiss constituted approximately 71.9 per cent of the total population; the French Swiss 20.4 per cent; and the Italian Swiss 6 per cent. To what might have been linguistic barriers were added religious differences. Protestantism was dominant in more than half the cantons and Catholicism in the others.

French revolutionary troops occupied Switzerland in 1798 and named it the Helvetic Republic, "one and indivisible," but Napoleon restored its federal government in 1803. At that time and again in 1815 the French- and Italian-speaking peoples of Switzerland were made equal to each other. In 1815 the Congress of Vienna neutralized Switzerland and recognized its independence. In 1847, seven Roman Catholic cantons seceded and organized a separate union called the Sonderbund. In 1848 the new Swiss constitution established a federal state modeled upon that of the United States, with powers shared between central

Louvain University demonstrated in protest against a decision to maintain the French-language section of the university (*The Observer* [London] May 22, 1966).

[64] H. D. Ziman, in *Daily Telegraph* (London), May 9, 1966, p. 16.

government and individual cantons. The revised Federal Constitution of 1874 established a strong central government but still retained large powers of local control in each canton. Switzerland was the first European state to make such experiments in political democracy as the referendum and the popular initiative.

Switzerland thus provides an excellent case history of a cultural community and a political idea which hold together above diversity of language and race. Nationalism here rests on a spiritual decision. In December 1938 the Swiss Federal Council addressed a message to the nation summing up the principles of nationalism and liberty as they had developed in Switzerland in the past one hundred and fifty years:

For the very reason that we reject the concept of race or common descent as the basis of a state and as the factor determining political frontiers, we gain the liberty and the strength to remain conscious of our cultural ties with the three great civilizations. The Swiss national idea is not based upon race or biological factors. . . .

The Swiss federal state is an association of free republics; it does not swallow them, it federates them. The cantonal republics maintain their individuality, and thereby they are the sources and pillars of our intellectual wealth, the strongest bulwark against intellectual uniformity. Our Swiss democracy has been built up organically from the smaller units to the larger units, from the township to the canton, and from the canton to the federal state. Next to federalism and democracy, Switzerland is based upon respect for the dignity of the individual. The respect for the right and liberty of human personality is so deeply anchored in the Swiss idea, that we can regard it as its basic concept and can proclaim its defence as an essential task of the nation. . . .

We recognize the individual human personality as the strongest creative force in the life of the spirit, and the State has accordingly limited its own sphere of power.[65]

It is an indication of the pervading nature of nationalism that it could stimulate rivalry between Flemish nationalists and French-speaking Walloons in Belgium and at the same time encourage close cooperation among German-, French-, and Italian-speaking Swiss. While other European peoples called for the precedence of the community—nation,

[65] *Neue Zürcher Zeitung*, Dec. 12, 1938, quoted in Hans Kohn, *Nationalism and Liberty: The Swiss Example* (London, 1956), p. 129. The author of the official address of the Federal Council was Federal Councillor Philipp Etter, a representative of the Catholic canton of Zug.

race, class, or language group—over the individual, the Swiss government's respect for the individual and his rights brought peace among the varied linguistic, religious, and ethnic groups in the conglomerate country. Nationalism remained a double-edged sword, responsible at once for both divisive and federating tendencies.

The recrudescence of nationalism in the countries of western Europe was accompanied by its revival in the eastern Communist satellite states, where it showed surprising strength.[66] The monolithic, supranational Communist state set up in Moscow was challenged by the satellites which wanted to follow their own "road to socialism." This feeling was especially strong among the peoples of the Balkans, who were once dismissed by Karl Marx as "ethnic trash." Yet, nationalism in that area remained a powerful force that could shape even abstract ideologies. History was recapitulated in the Balkans: Christianity there had broken up into national churches; similarly, communism in the region became increasingly nationalistic. The minorities in the Balkans were durable: they tended to become more and more nationalistic as they gained privileges. The international Communist society which Moscow hoped would develop in the Balkans foundered on the rock of nationalism.

Marshal Tito of Yugoslavia was influenced by old-fashioned ideas of nationalism and declared his neutrality between Russia and the capitalistic nations.[67] He survived Moscow's wrath. The process of disintegration was halted temporarily in 1956 by Premier Nikita Khrushchev, who sent Russian tanks into the streets of Budapest to quell the Hungarian Revolution. In the long run this sort of action could not prevent the satellite countries from pursuing their purely national interests. In mid-May of 1966, Moscow was astonished by a four-hour speech given in Bucharest by Communist Party leader Nicolae Ceauşescu on the occasion of the forty-fifth anniversary of the Rumanian Communist Party. In an unexpected manner Ceauşescu made a bitter attack on the Soviet Union which ran from the Lenin era through the Stalin period to the Russian dispute with Communist China. In the midst of his speech Ceauşescu spoke favorably of "nationalistic communism" and emphasized "the nation as a form of human community." He also denounced military blocs as "incompatible with the national independence and sovereignty of peoples," a scarcely hidden attack on the Warsaw Pact, which had been initiated as a counterbalance to

[66] See Chapter 11.   [67] See Chapter 11.

NATO.[68] Significantly, the Kremlin did not respond this time with tanks, but instead sent Leonid I. Brezhnev, Soviet Russia's Communist Party chieftain, to Bucharest to discuss "subjects of mutual interest." Clearly Moscow was not in a mood to stifle the new Communist nationalism so popular among the satellites in eastern Europe. It was understandable that Russia would seek to avoid trouble at her back when confrontation with Communist China was coming closer and closer.

Stephen Borsody regarded national sentiment as fostering the forces of opposition to Communist dictatorship and Soviet Russian imperialism:

Nationalism, in these circumstances, was a force working for freedom. Not even the brutal Soviet suppression of the Hungarian Revolution, in 1956, discouraged the spirit of national resistance. It discredited only the liberation propaganda addressed to the "captive nations." In an unexpected way, the Hungarian Revolution and the Polish October helped to convert Russia to the wisdom of allowing greater independence to the "people's democracies." [69]

FEDERALISM VERSUS NATIONALISM IN EUROPE

Western Europe recovered rapidly from the effects of the two world wars. Again it radiated economic and technological power, as well as cultural, literary, and scientific energy. In politics Europeans began to seek new ways to make their influence felt more effectively.[70] By comparison with western Europe's wealth of talent and its will to innovate, the Communist satellite countries were timid and halting in their experimentation. Most of the developing countries had few energies left beyond those they devoted to building political, social, and economic foundations for their natioanl life and livelihood.[71]

[68] *Time*, May 20, 1966, p. 29. At the same time Ceaucescu tried to avoid a real break with the Soviet Union or with the Communist credo. While encouraging nationalist themes at home, he preferred to mute them abroad (C. L. Sulzberger, in *The New York Times*, Oct. 14, 1966).

[69] Stephen Borsody, "Division and Reunion: Problems of Peace and Federalism in Central Europe," *Central European Federalist*, XII (Dec. 1964), 10.

[70] Philip E. Moseley, "New Trends and Needs in the Study of Contemporary Western Europe," *American Council of Learned Societies Newsletter*, Oct. 1965, p. 1.

[71] See Walter Adams, *A Report on the Strategic Importance of Western Europe* (Sept. 1964), a report to the United States Advisory Commission of International Education and Cultural Affairs.

One of western Europe's most perplexing problems was the clash between integration and the new nationalism. On the one side were the Eurocrats, who advocated federalism and spoke hopefully of a new western Europe successfully united. They were certain that no single European nation would ever again play the great power, and that the only true power on the Continent would be a united Europe. Under the shield of the United Nations and the protective Atlantic partnership with the United States, a new United States of Europe was supposed to halt the march of nationalism. The Eurocrats regarded the Common Market as the beginning of a free, united, and supranational Europe.

This supranational thrust of the Eurocrats collided head on with the new nationalism, a much stronger affirmation of national personality than the old-fashioned nationalism of the nineteenth century. The new nationalism called for independence, although not necessarily complete separation from the mainstream of European politics. In contemporary Europe both large and small units continue to eke out a precarious independent existence. In the older nationalism the urge was always toward the goal of complete independence. In the new nationalism many European nations persist in retaining the shadow of independence when the reality has all but disappeared.

The new nationalism in Europe was epitomized by General de Gaulle, who adamantly refused the "technocratic, stateless, and irresponsible Areopagus destined to fringe on French democracy," and maintained that only through a loose aggregation of sovereign nations could "the true Europe evolve." But at the same time the new nationalism repeated the rough pattern of the old. There were the old familiar terms of "balance of power," "second-rate nations," "the world's two superpowers," "cracks in the Western alliance," and "fissures in the Soviet bloc."

In the struggle between federalism and nationalism, the latter was obviously in ascendancy. Indeed, it might be said that federalism itself was but a form of national and not international government, for federalism depends on the existence of nationalism in the first place. In a sense federalism reflected the triumph of nationalism. The outcome is not clear. Max Beloff has expressed this uncertainty:

Whether as a result of the progress of "union" and "integration" . . . the present temper of the European nations will alter to such an extent that the pressure from their peoples for particular ends will be directed to the

European rather than the national institutions, so that a new political community will in fact have come into existence, with all the institutional consequences that this implies, is something about which only speculation is possible. It may be that some quite different combination is preparing itself in the wings of history; we cannot know.[72]

[72] Beloff, *Europe and the European*, p. 276.

Chapter 6

Black Nationalism:
The African Experience

FLY HIGHER AND HIGHER THE UGANDA FLAG

Our fight for land will never cease.
It was ours and it will be ours,
   forever and forever.
We do not fear those who speak
   behind our backs.
If they scorn us, they will not be
   here forever.
We look for the day to arrive
When great jubilation will reign
   everywhere.
And the children of black men
   throughout the world
Will know happiness in the
   return of their rights.

—*Uganda Renaissance,* January 1961

The continent of Africa, more than 11,530,000 square miles in extent, three times the size of Europe, only recently became an active partner in world history. With the exception of Egypt, one of the cradlelands of Western civilization, Africa has remained—alone among the great continents—silent and passive through the course of history. Its coastline was explored and settled by small European groups in the fifteenth-century Age of Exploration, but not until the third quarter of the nineteenth century was Africa south of the Sahara integrated into modern world society.

European conquerors carved up the giant continent into colonies and protectorates. They exploited its natural resources. At the same time they halted tribal wars, reduced the toll of disease, improved transportation and communication, and constructed roads, power plants, plantations, and mines. Even so, comparatively few Europeans came to Africa. By the middle of the twentieth century, of a total population of two hundred million, only six million, or approximately 3 per cent, were of European background. As late as 1945 there were only four independent states in Africa (Ethiopia, Liberia, Egypt, and South Africa); 90 per cent of the continent was still under colonial control.

World War II marked the beginning of the end of colonialism in Africa. During the war, Allied leaders, anxious for African support, hinted at eventual self-government. But the global prestige of the white man began to decline when reverses were inflicted by the Japanese. African troops who had served overseas and who had learned new skills returned home to demand more political power. In what has been called "a revolution of rising expectations," all Africa exploded in a drive for emancipation that turned into a wild scramble. The process began in the north in the relatively progressive Arab-Muslim states, which were geographically associated with the Mediterranean world and better prepared for self-rule.

The cry "Uhuru" ("Freedom!" in Swahili) was heard south of the Sahara. The white minority was overwhelmed, as one new independent state after another appeared. The colonial powers began to leave Africa, sometimes in haste. The older map with its colored outlines of European possessions was supplanted by one that depicted a patchwork of independent states. By 1964 there were thirty-four independent

African states, surpassing Europe (thirty-one) and Asia (twenty-nine).

During the rapid liquidation of European rule, the receding colonialism took on a variegated pattern.[1] Although the British were not altogether aware of the pace of nationalism in Africa,[2] they wisely predicted developments there. From the beginning they based their African policy on eventual self-rule. They trained Africans for the responsibilities of government; they placed African chiefs in charge of local affairs under the guidance of British officials in a kind of indirect rule. They gave more power to African leaders, and more voting privileges to the people. Eventually, the British were able to withdraw from most of their African colonies without the ignominy of being pushed out.[3]

The French colonial policy was "assimilation": the colonies were to be absorbed into a national French framework. France still dominated her African possessions at the end of World War II, but liquidation was soon inaugurated. Between 1958 and 1960, some twelve million people in the hinterland of the Sahara were given their independence, although they remained loosely joined to France in the French Union.

The fever of independence appeared in the Belgian Congo in the late 1950's. After an uprising in January 1959, the Belgians, on June 30, 1960, suddenly granted full independence to the Congo. With no preparation for this unexpected concession, the Congolese descended to chaos. The Italians lost their African possessions as a consequence of the war, but retained administration of Somaliland through the United Nations.

Only Portugal and Spain remained outside the periphery. Both continued to designate their African possessions as "overseas provinces," in theory holding the same rights as metropolitan provinces but in fact

[1] For the process of decolonization see Gwendolen Carter, *Independence for Africa* (New York, 1960); Charles G. Haines, ed., *Africa Today* (Baltimore, 1955); Thomas Hodgkin, *Nationalism in Colonial Africa* (New York, 1957); Roland Oliver and J. D. Fage, *A Short History of Africa* (Baltimore, 1962); Alex Quaison-Sackey, *Africa Unbound* (New York, 1963); Calvin W. Stillman, ed., *Africa in the Modern World* (Chicago, 1955); and George W. Shepherd, Jr., *The Politics of African Nationalism* (New York, 1962). In October 1966 the British protectorate of Bechuanaland became the independent state of Botswana—the world's one hundred thirtieth sovereign state.

[2] Lord William M. Hailey's classic study *An African Survey: A Study of Problems Arising in Africa South of the Sahara* scarcely alluded to African nationalism in the first edition (London, 1938). This was corrected in the 1957 edition.

[3] For background material see Rupert Emerson, *From Empire to Nation: The Rise of Self-Assertion of Asian and African Peoples* (Cambridge, Mass., 1962).

remaining colonies. Both tried to resist the pressures that had brought freedom to some two hundred million Africans. Although the Portuguese in Angola on the Atlantic coast and Mozambique on the Indian Ocean were outnumbered by about fifty to one, Portugal refused to grant independence to her colonies. Spain gave up her protectorate in Morocco but not the rest of her African possessions.

Africa was the last continent to enter the age of nationalism, and thereby, the modern era.[4] This marked the culmination of a long historical process whereby society was transformed after the English and French revolutions.

In this transformation which is fundamentally one and the same everywhere, the unity of mankind, long postulated by universal religions by the Stoics, by the rational humanism of the age of Enlightenment, is for the first time becoming a reality. The rise of nationalism, the quest for equality and human dignity, which now transform ancient and primitive tribal societies in sub-Saharan Africa, put the capstone to the growing edifice of humanity. We are at the beginning of a new era of history, in which all formerly isolated and secluded parts of the globe are entering into communication and intercourse on a footing of legal equality.[5]

The process had been accelerated by the time it reached Africa, the last great home of empire. Rapid liquidation took place. But the Africans had much less experience and training in self-government than had the peoples of such former colonial dependencies as India and the Philippines.[6] The transition was beset with perplexities and filled with critical tensions, though they were not much more severe than the bitter struggles which took place in Europe and the Americas before their peoples were able to achieve and maintain nationhood.

Africa presented a unique situation because both the nation and the state had to be created. African nationalism, stemming from Negro-African resentment of white colonialism, was promoted by a small elite of leaders whose job it was to create nations in areas where nations, as we know them, seldom existed. It was not an easy task, for controversy marked the path of development.

[4] Hans Kohn, "Changing Africa in a Changing World," *Current History*, XLI (Oct. 1961), 194.

[5] Hans Kohn and Wallace Sokolsky, *African Nationalism in the Twentieth Century* (Princeton, 1965), pp. 15–16.

[6] T. Walter Wallbank, *Contemporary Africa: Continent in Transition* (rev. ed.; Princeton, 1964), p. 11.

Nationalism was both blessing and curse for the new African nations—a blessing because it won their hotly desired freedom. But independence did not automatically bring with it either efficient government, social equality, or economic prosperity. Africans learned, as had others in the past, that the road to justice was a thorny one.

CHARACTERISTICS OF ETHNIC NATIONALISM

To those Westerners who forget the development of their own nations, African nationalism seems baffling, paradoxical, and crude. Its outstanding characteristic was its ethnic or racial quality.[7] Dominant racial overtones reflected hatred for the white man—a residue of colonialism. Each new state was affected by antiwhite sentiment. African nationalists denounced the white man as a demagogue who tried to maintain the *status quo*. Mbonu Ojike, a Nigerian, put it plainly: "They [the European imperialists] employ their hush-hush policy of gradualism and of the you-will-never-get-there technique to retard progress in Africa. They speak of democracy but act imperialistically. They say 'we fight for freedom,' but they give Africa political servitude and ignoble tutelage. They proclaim religious tolerance, but are themselves the worst example of religious bigotry and proselytism." [8]

The euphoria produced by independence could not obliterate the feeling of resentment against the white man. At the ceremony marking the independence of the Congo, Patrice Lumumba spoke of

the mockery, the insults, the blows submitted to morning, noon, and night because we were "*Nègres.*" We have known the law was never the same, whether dealing with a white or a Negro; that it was accommodating for one, cruel and inhuman to the other. . . . We have known that in the cities there were magnificent houses for the whites and crumbling hovels for the Negroes, that a Negro was not admitted to movie theaters or restaurants, that he was not allowed to enter so-called "European" stores, that when the Negro traveled, it was on the lowest level of a boat, at the feet of the white man in his de luxe cabin.[9]

[7] Some observers use the designation "black nationalism" to refer to the African states. As used here it is to be distinguished from the extremist sense it has taken on in the United States (Black Muslims).

[8] Mbonu Ojike, in *Africa, Today and Tomorrow* (New York, 1945), pp. 45–46; courtesy of African Academy of Arts and Research.

[9] Patrice Lumumba, in *Africa Speaks,* ed. James Duffy and Robert Manners (Princeton, 1961), pp. 90–91.

The retained anger was expressed in this poem:

Young Africa's Plea

Don't preserve my customs
As some fine curios
To suit some white historian's tastes.
There's nothing artificial
That beats the natural way,
In culture and ideals of life.
Let me play with the white man's ways,
Let me work with the black man's brains,
Let my affairs themselves sort out.
Then in sweet re-birth
I'll rise a better man,
Not ashamed to face the world.
Those who doubt my talents
In secret fear my strength;
They know I am no less a man.
Let them bury their prejudice,
Let them show their noble sides,
Let me have untrammelled growth.
My friends will never know regret
And I, I will never forget.[10]

The thinking was essentially xenophobic—an angry protest against foreign encroachment and interference by the white man. Most African nationalists pointed to the continent as the black man's land. The black man would do with it what he wanted, and he would no longer allow the white man to profit exclusively from it. No matter what the argument, it eventually boiled down to the basic issue, black versus white man.

All Africa was gripped by the acute problem of the plural society ("a society comprising two or more elements of social orders which live side by side, yet without mingling, in one political unit").[11] People of different color had to learn to live in the same society. Africa

[10] *An Anthology of West African Verse*, compiled by Olembe Bassir (Ibadan, Nigeria, 1957), p. 57.

[11] Cf. John S. Furnivall, *Colonial Policy and Practice: A Comparative Study of Burma and Netherlands India* (Cambridge, England, 1948), p. 446.

became a laboratory for one of the world's most disturbing problems, that of race relations.[12]

To the white man, reduced from his superior status or even expelled, nationalism in Africa meant simply a return to primitivism. The black man, it was said, was constitutionally incapable of industrializing or modernizing his society. The white man's favorite question was: "What would have happened in North America had the rich land been left to the backward, lazy Indian?" The European minority was worried about its future. Predictions were made both inside and outside Africa that there would be a mass slaughter of whites in the new nations. Skeptics pointed to the Mau Mau uprising in Kenya, disorders in Uganda and Tanganyika, and violence in the Congo as precedents for the outbreak of racial war.

Despite the angry tone of nationalist leaders, there was no mass slaughter. Once they had achieved their independence, black Africans were inclined to accept social differences. Relations between the races became even easier in some areas than they had been under colonial regimes. For example, white settlers in Kenya, who had given way to despair and had sold their homes, eventually returned to live side by side with the four other ethnic groups—Bantu, Nilotic, Nilot-Hamitic, and Hamitic.[13]

It is not yet clear what direction nationalism and racialism will take in the new Africa. The peoples there have been subjected to the power and efficiency of Western culture, and they are impressed. It remains to be seen whether or not they will surrender to the ways of the white man. The assimilative process may be cultural, but almost certainly it will not be biological. Racial barriers will remain. Moreover, it is unlikely that the new African will reject altogether his tribal loyalty, his old gods, and his traditional family customs in the process of cementing national ties.

RECAPITULATION: IMITATIVE ASPECTS

National sentiments reflect the historical experiences and cultural images of peoples. Such attitudes may differ in detail, but in their essence they represent the same state of mind whether in Europe,

---

[12] Wallbank, *op. cit.*, p. 12.   [13] See Chapter 6.

Africa, Asia, or Latin America. People everywhere have a sense of community with their fellow nationals. Through education and environmental conditions they learn to think of themselves as agents of their own tradition and history.

The transformation of ancient and primitive societies in sub-Saharan Africa into modern states took place within the framework of nationalism. At one time this area had been a hunting ground for slaves, who were gathered by traders and sold in the open market place for transportation to "civilized" areas of the globe. African societies contributed no Kants, no Beethovens, no Michelangelos. Intellectually and politically this was virgin soil. Suddenly the whole area was opened to the civilizing process—to European laws, customs, traditions, and business. And along with European ideas and ideologies came the flags of nationalism.

There was a unity of slavery and illiteracy on the African scene, but there were no common customs, language, or religion. Interests differed from region to region. As the newly independent states took on national identity, they applied local distinctions to a larger scale. Africans began to imitate Europeans. This does not necessarily imply inferiority of the African organism, even if the white man sought to impose on the black man a condition of subservience. The latter was overwhelmed by what seemed to him to be the success of white enterprises, great or small. African students who flocked to Europe and America returned to their homelands as leaders in the drive for nationhood but also as agents for Western civilization. They had become familiar with European and American ways. Now they used tested means of communication to make nations out of their largely illiterate countrymen.

Nation-building in Africa recapitulated European experience with such nationalist symbols as flags, anthems, stamps, and coins. African parliaments imitated the British form, judges wore the traditional wigs, African soldiers marched in British stride. Africans had won liberation from colonial control, but not necessarily from European civilization. Almost overnight peoples untrained in democracy were called upon to vote, form political parties, and decide issues of national policy. Clerks became presidents; they lived in palatial quarters and rode in luxurious limousines. The European veneer was there even if deep inside himself the African harbored resentment against his former colonial masters.

African leaders were sensitive about the imitative quality of their neophyte nations.[14] It was difficult to reconcile such imitativeness with self-respect. This sensitivity became one of the more obvious qualities of the new nationalism in Africa. Proud Africans, stigmatized by slavery and colonial oppressiveness, sought self-respect through freedom and equality. This was a dominating factor in the drive for political independence.

NEGATIVE AND POSITIVE FACETS

Despite the imitative quality of African nationalism, it would be wrong to equate it completely with European experience, to comprehend it in European instead of African terms, or to regard Africa merely as an extension of Europe. It would be more accurate to say that European civilization for the last several centuries, and in concentrated form in the latter half of the nineteenth century, penetrated into an area with a vastly different social and cultural framework. The method was imperialistic: an advanced civilization imposed its will on an undeveloped continent.

After 1945 the expansion receded as European control was forced out and the outposts of European colonialism eliminated. The process was hastened by the rise of African nationalism, a force that spread throughout the continent, primarily as a reaction against the white man. The process here differed from that in Europe: at no time was European nationalism a continent-wide force operating as a unit against external enemies.

African nationalism also differed from European in social basis. European nationalism was nurtured in an age of mass education: patriotism—love for the fatherland—was instilled among a literate people in home and school. African nationalism, on the other hand, arose in a vastly different society. Most Africans, imbued with tribalism and traditionalism and addicted to ancient taboos, had no conception of a nation. The African illiteracy rate hovered around the 90 per cent mark; relatively few people had access to higher education. In this milieu African nationalism was captured and controlled by a tiny minority, that familiar elite trained in Western colleges and universities and exposed to Western ideas. These nationalist leaders had an ambiva-

[14] Cf. Frank Moraes, *The Importance of Being Black: An Asian Looks at Africa* (New York, 1965).

lent feeling toward Europe, a kind of love-hate relationship. They wanted independence, but at the same time they were willing to work together with their former colonial rulers in the task of modernization.

The result was that African nationalism operated at two levels: negatively and externally, in response to European imperialism, it asserted and won the right of Black Africa to achieve independence from white rule; positively and internally, it represented the aspiration of the new African states to obtain the benefits of modernization.

On the first, or negative, level, African nationalism was a reaction against alien rule. The revolt finally came when Africans refused to accept the idea that all the world revolved around western Europe. They opposed both imperialism and white supremacy. They were sure that national independence would bring equality.

On the second, or positive, level, African nationalism revealed the desire of the African to propel himself into the twentieth century. Both the educated elite and the illiterate masses were convinced by contact with the white man that European customs were highly desirable. But the African wanted reform on his own terms, without subservience, without imposition from the outside, without patronizing gifts from another world. In this sense African nationalism represented the dignity of the black man as a human being. He wanted to be relieved of the colonial mentality instilled in him by Europeans, those selfish white men attracted not by humanitarian ideals but by gold, diamonds, copra, and mahogany. He would regenerate the best of his own cultural past and combine it with the technological knowledge of his former masters to achieve his own modern society.

PERSISTENCE OF TRIBALISM

Although Africans possessed a strong sense of community, they did not relish the task of nation-building. Nationalism was a European invention, geared to European needs. For the African it could appeal to a heterogeneous collection of groups on the basis of racial solidarity against the white man, but it could not heal the fragmentation of African society. Among most African peoples the first attraction of loyalty was not the nation but the clan and then the tribe. Each clan considered itself autonomous both socially and politically. The larger unit—the tribe—was far closer to the clan than to the new artificial nation.

Despite his urge for modernization, the African was handicapped by the continued existence of tribalism as a way of life. African tribalism turned out to be a serious obstacle to national unity.[15] The tribe, closely knit and exclusive, like the family writ large in the social order, remained the unit of society. The African personality was built around it. Elspeth Huxley described its core:

It is a personality that puts manners above principle, family above self, race above humanity. Responsive to nuances of relationship, it is often blind to the consequences of acts. There is at the heart of it a profound cynicism, derived partly from a religion based on fear of the supernatural rather than a trust in the divine, and partly, perhaps, on the multiplicity of termites.[16]

When white colonists swarmed into Africa in the late nineteenth century, they Balkanized much of the continent along tribal lines. They were the protectors and the African tribes were their protégés. But after 1945 tribal society began to disintegrate under the impetus of independence. The tribal components of many African states found it difficult if not impossible to join in collective action. Nationalist leaders spoke of unity while pandering to tribal sensitiveness. Boundaries of new states were often set up without any regard to ethnic groupings, resulting in tribal convulsions. New boundary lines imposed artificial divisions on an already complicated pattern of tribal and subtribal groupings.

For the African desertion by his colonial masters was a profound psychological shock. With his bonds of dependence loosened, he began to feel insecure and abandoned. He turned on his one-time protector and reverted to his earlier tribalism. An unconscious feeling of resentment lay at the root of his race hatred. Whether he turned to the mystical formulas of his tribalism or accepted the flag of nationalism, he still held the white man in contempt.

No matter where it existed, tribalism ran counter to the course of nationalism. Sometimes nationalism was a unifying force, while tribalism was divisive; on other occasions the opposite was true.

[15] William R. Bascom, "Tribalism, Nationalism, and Pan-Africanism," *Annals of the American Academy of Political and Social Science*, CCCXLII (July 1962), 21–29.
[16] Elspeth Huxley, "Clues to the African Personality," *The New York Times Magazine*, May 31, 1964, pp. 18, 34.

Several examples may be cited to illustrate the rivalry between nationalism and tribalism. The Republic of the Ivory Coast, with an area of 125,000 square miles and about three million people divided into sixty tribes, came into existence on August 7, 1960. President Félix Houphouet-Boigny, a member of the Baoulé tribe, called for the maintenance of cultural ties with Europe, but frankly admitted, "The Ivorian nation doesn't yet exist. France left the Ivory Coast a mass of tribes unaware of each other's existence. We are only gradually breaking down tribal barriers." Although many adopted the Roman Catholic or Muslim religion, most Ivorians still placed great faith in fetishes. Houphouet-Boigny himself continued to consult witch doctors. "Africa is animist," he said. "We have no right to be ashamed of our animism. It is the basis of our lives." [17]

An even more intense tribalism existed in Burundi. After World War I, Belgium assumed a mandate over a part of German East Africa—Ruanda-Urundi. This small territory (approximately 21,000 square miles) had the greatest population density (214 per square mile) on the continent.[18] After World War II, the Belgians gradually disengaged themselves. The United Nations trusteeship was terminated on July 1, 1962, and Ruanda-Urundi became two independent states with their traditional names, Rwanda and Burundi. Carving out new states could not eliminate the old feudal society. For generations there had been tribal rivalry between the towering Watusi and the shorter but far more numerous Bahutu (84 per cent of the population). Enraged, machete-wielding Bahutus chopped down Watusi and burned villages. In three years, three heads of government died at the hands of assassins.[19]

Tribal hostilities and antagonisms even split Nigeria, which since its independence in 1960 was widely hailed as the exemplar of functioning democracy. With the largest population of any African nation, some thirty-six million inhabitants, the country was split into these major ethnic groups: Hausa and Fulani, Ibo, Yoruba, and other smaller components.[20] Through the nineteenth century the area was torn by tribal warfare. Regional friction did not disappear with the formation of a federation of four self-governing regions drawn up according to reli-

[17] *Newsweek*, international ed., Aug. 9, 1965, pp. 36–37.
[18] Robert D. Hodgson and Elvyn A. Stoneman, *The Changing Map of Africa* (Princeton, 1963), p. 108.
[19] *Time*, Oct. 29, 1965.   [20] Bascom, *op. cit.*, p. 25.

gious and tribal lines.[21] Tribalism and nationalism clashed. Although Nigeria's leaders tried to unify the country on a national basis, the tripartite division could lead to a disintegration into three or more separate states.

The problem of developing national unity and a sense of national identification stronger than tribal loyalty faced most new African nations. Thousands of tribes, each with its own traditions, taboos, and prejudices, each suspicious of and hostile to its neighbors, were asked to accept the artificial boundary lines set up by nationalist leaders. Few had expressed any desire for unity in the past, and few wanted it even now.

Despite the obstacle of tribalism, nationalism took strong hold on the continent. Bascom described the pattern as follows:

Where tribalism is not exacerbated by open conflict, . . . it is being eroded by increasing mobility and urbanization, by increasing inter-tribal contact and intermarriage, by education, and by nationalism. The nationalist movements have united peoples of different cultural and linguistic backgrounds in the effort to end colonial rule, and the longer their struggle for independence, the stronger these bonds have become. National identification and pride received a great lift when independence was actually achieved, and, since independence, the familiar forces of nationalism have been at work, with participation in the United Nations and in international affairs, national anthems and flags, national heroes and statues, new embassies and public buildings, and other symbols and functions of sovereignty.[22]

TWO FACES: EUROPEAN PARADIGM VERSUS NEGRITUDE

African nationalism took on a two-faced quality. Under the aegis of the Western world, one face looked toward the future. This was

[21] The northern region is held by the Muslims, the eastern region by the Ibo tribe, and the western and midwestern regions by the Yoruba. Since independence, the Muslims have dominated the Federal government. Voter-intimidation, ballot-box stuffing, and political assassinations made a mockery of Nigeria's reputation as a democratic state.

The seeds of tribal hatred were deeply planted in Nigeria. Independence from Great Britain left her divided into mutually suspicious regions, separated tribally and religiously. Regional passions boiled. Worst of all was the reversion to tribalism. In the army tribalism among both officers and men virtually eliminated any chance of creating a disciplined, truly national force. The nation remained perilously near disintegration.

[22] Bascom, *op. cit.*, p. 26.

epitomized in the bright-eyed African child with his attention riveted to the blackboard, by the barrister studying the intricacies of Roman law, by the surgeon at the operating table, and by enthusiastic adults seeking painfully to understand the miracle of the written word. This view rejected colonialism and all its evils, yet was willing to accept the technology of Western civilization as highly desirable.

The second face of African nationalism looked longingly at the almost vanished past. Here was a conscious attempt to revive the old traditions, to restore self-confidence and dignity, and to find a philosophical basis for the state. Attempts were made to seek new values in the African personality. There was pride in the untamed Africa— chiefs in bizarre raiment, strong-limbed warriors wearing plumes and carrying rattles, tribesmen screeching eerie war cries, witch doctors, and drums.

This face has been given the name "Negritude," a word intended to describe the rediscovery or reawakening of African culture and traditions. Other terms have been used to express the same or similar meaning: "Neo-Africanism," "Africanhood," "African Renaissance," "African Personality," and "nativism." Although there may be some variations in definition, all these terms have one common denominator—the rejection of Western values.

Let us dwell for a moment on nativism and then examine the closely related concept of Negritude. From the African point of view, the peoples of the vast continent had been subjected to control by what amounted to an absentee sovereign—a ruling power that made political and economic decisions which were nearly always to its own advantage. The absentee sovereign was either tyrannical or paternalistic, but it was always alien. Freedom for the African meant freedom from the absentee ruler.

Africans used two means to challenge the absentee sovereign: nationalistic revolutions and nativistic movements. The revolutions after 1945, directed by Africans trained in Europe or America, led to the formation of political parties, parliaments, and electorates. The process was rapid, accompanied by comparatively little bloodshed. The European powers soon lost control, especially if they were weak and were paternalistic in policy.

But where the absentee sovereign retained its strength and sought to impose a tyranny, the movements of dissent emerged as nativism.

Nativistic movements represented the reaction of a people barred from achieving goals they believed to be desirable. They have been compared by anthropologist Paul Bohannon to the juxtaposition of repression and displacement in psychoanalytic theory.[23] African nativists placed emphasis upon traditional cultural traits and upon the old values.

Nationalism and nativism were different attacks on the same problem of colonialism. Africans of organizing ability used their energy in movements which led to nationalism. Nativists turned back to the old myths, morals, and culture—the essence of Negritude. There was a desperate search for an identity that had roots in many traditions. Negritude always remained closely associated with the desire for liberation from colonialism and the avowal of African culture.

Most African leaders expressed in one way or another a preference for Negritude as a basis for nationalism. Tom J. Mboya, general secretary of the Kenya African National Union, considered nationalism to be the dominating political force: "Africa is awake and is on the march to the tune of nationalism, while nationalism is dictating the tempo and rhythm of the march of the peoples of Africa to independence, freedom, order, justice, and economic dignity." What direction should African nationalism take? Under the impact of imperialism, unbridled economic and human exploitation had proceeded unchecked. "Socially, the African people found themselves uprooted and placed outside the age-old values and beliefs on which their communities had thrived for centuries." [24] As time went on, the African people rediscovered themselves. They became conscious of their own identity, yet found themselves deprived of authority over their own lives.

Mboya admitted frankly that, despite oppression, the colonialists gave Africa modern scientific methods of production and education. The new Africa, he said, would harness fully these advantages of the colonial era, but he also pointed to the deep echoes of the African past with its ideals, values, and cosmological ideas, "the past that the African has lost touch with due to the interposition of colonial rule." Admittedly, during the years of European control, the material lot of Africans had improved slightly, but "we lost our dignity, and our status

[23] See Paul Bohannon, *Africa and the Africans* (Garden City, N.Y., 1964), pp. 10–30.

[24] Tom J. Mboya, "Tensions in Economic Development," in *Restless Nations* (New York, 1962), p. 41.

among the peoples of the world went down to rock-bottom. The Europeans ruled and we obeyed them." [25]

The key word in Mboya's analysis is "dignity." The African personality, rooted in tribe and family, was inward-looking, defensive, proud, and passionate. After decades of being made to feel inferior, Africans began to think of their own dignity and pride. They had loosened the bonds of political control; now they would escape cultural suffocation by the West and revive their own enduring values.

The Mau Mau revolt was a rejection of Western civilization. Jomo Kenyatta, who was imprisoned by the British from 1953 to 1959 for his part in the Mau Mau rebellion, was angered by the suppression of African culture:

Africans are not hostile to Western civilization as such; they would gladly . . . share in the intellectual and material benefits which it has the power to give. But they are in an intolerable position when the European invasion destroys the very basis of their old tribal way of life, and yet offers them no place in the new society except as serfs doomed to labor for bare subsistence. There is not one of the boasted blessings of white civilization which has yet been made generally available to the Kenya Africans. . . . It is not in human nature . . . to submit forever to complete oppression, and the Africans make their claim for justice now, in order that a bloodier and more destructive justice may not be inevitable in time to come.[26]

As a cultural manifestation of nationalism, Negritude received literary expression in poems, articles, books and international congresses. Patrice Lumumba, first premier of the Congo, expressed the idea in this emotional poem, "A Morning in the Heart of Africa":

> For a thousand years you, Negro, suffered like a beast,
> your ashes strewn to the wind that roams the desert.
>
> Your tyrants built the lustrous, magic temples
> to preserve your soul, preserve your suffering.

[25] *Ibid.*

[26] Jomo Kenyatta, *Kenya: The Land of Conflict* (London, 1944?), pp. 22–23. The Mau Mau leaders insisted that their followers take oaths which placed them beyond the pale of society: this was nativism in its most extreme and vicious form. Ultimately, the Mau Mau movement was brought under control, chiefly by creating new rituals to cleanse the oath-taker from his primitive bonds. But the conditions which led to Mau Mau violence have not changed to any significant degree.

Barbaric right of fist and the white right to a whip,
  you had the right to die, you also could weep. . . .

The dawn is here, my brother, dawn! Look in our faces,
  a new morning breaks in our old Africa.

Ours only will now be the land, the water, the mighty rivers
  which the poor Negro was surrendering for a thousand years.

And hard torches of the sun will shine for us again
  they'll dry the tears in your eyes and the spittle on your face.

The moment when you break the chains, the heavy fetters,
  the evil, cruel times will go never to come again.

A free and gallant Congo will arise from the black soil,
  a free and gallant Congo—the black blossom, the black seed! [27]

The first Conference of Negro Writers and Artists, held at the
Sorbonne, in Paris, on September 19–22, 1956, resulted in the birth of
the Society of African Culture. Its aims were to interpret "our culture
patterns by ourselves," and to build up a community of cultural "to-
tems." Leopold Senghor directed attention to Negritude:

Whether we like it or not, 1955 will mark an important date in the history
of the world, and first and foremost in the history of the coloured peoples.
Bandoeng will be from now on a rallying for these peoples. . . . How can
we believe that the Bandoeng spirit, which for us is primarily a spirit of
culture, does not also animate the Indians, and particularly the Negroes of
America? For the Negro race, more than any other, was the victim of the
great discoveries. The European Renaissance was built on the ruins of
African Negro civilisation, the force of America has waxed fat on Negro
blood and sweat. The slave trade cost Africa two hundred million dead.
But who can tell what cultural wealth was lost? By the grace of God, the
flame is not quenched, the leaven is still there in our wounded hearts and
bodies to make possible our Renaissance to-day.

But this Renaissance will be the doing not so much of the politicians, as
of the Negro writers and artists. Experience has proved it, cultural liberation is an essential condition of political liberation.[28]

[27] Patrice Lumumba, "A Morning in the Heart of Africa," *Africa Today*, VIII
(Feb. 1961), 2.

[28] Leopold Senghor, "The Spirit of Civilisation, or the Laws of African Negro
Culture," in *The First Conference of Negro Writers and Artists* (Paris, 1956), pp.
51 ff.

At this same conference an effort to place Negritude on a global basis with African roots was made by Aimé Césaire, who, although born in Martinique, inspired a West African literary movement. In a paper titled "Culture and Colonisation," Césaire spoke of the unity of African civilization:

I think it is very true that culture must be national. It is, however, self-evident that national cultures, however differentiated they may be, are grouped by affinities. Moreover, these great cultural relationships, these great cultural families, have a name: they are called *civilisations*. In other words, if it is an undoubted fact that there is a French national culture, an Italian, English, Spanish, German, Russian, etc., national culture, it is no less evident that all these cultures, alongside genuine differences, show a certain number of striking similarities so that, though we can speak of national cultures peculiar to each of the countries mentioned above, we can equally well speak of a European civilisation.

In the same way we can speak of a large family of African cultures which collectively deserve the name of Negro-African culture and which individually reveal the different cultures proper to each country of Africa. And we know that the hazards of history have caused the domain of this civilisation, the locus of this civilisation to exceed widely the boundaries of Africa. It is in this sense, therefore, that we may say that there are, if not centres, at least fringes of this Negro-African civilisation in Brazil and in the West Indies, in Haiti and the French Antilles and even in the United States.[29]

It is too early to judge the direction of Negritude as an element of African nationalism. Already there exist differences among its advocates, who may be divided into three groups. One group, believers in historical continuity, insists upon a renaissance of African traditions in their original tribal form without Western dilution. A second category, accepting the idea of sociopolitical and cultural discontinuity, calls for a clear break between the current African and his forefathers as well as the beginning of a new society. A third group, proponents like the others of Africa for the Africans but emphasizing reality instead of theory, advocates social modernization of the tribal system according to what is called "the African personality." All three agree that Negritude is the dominant emotional force in all contemporary Africa except the Arab north. All three denounce the American Negro for what they

[29] Aimé Césaire, "Culture and Colonisation," in *The First Conference of Negro Writers and Artists* (Paris, 1956), pp. 193 ff.

describe as his efforts to achieve outward conformity with the dominant white race. All three are united in the belief that the African must advance by methods of his own and by his own efforts.

CONFRONTATION OF NATIONALISM AND SOCIALISM

Once their eyes had been opened by nationalism, African peoples decided that they must attain a decent standard of living. As have-not nations, they were faced with the problem of simultaneously developing their political life while at the same time carrying out a war against poverty, illiteracy, and disease. "The seizing of political independence occurred in fourteen years, and the African people are obviously determined that their economic and social emancipation will not take much longer." [30]

The war against poverty required a dynamic ideology to bring together the former colonial states that remained patchworks of different tribal and language groups. It was necessary to rationalize governmental involvement in the process of economic growth. African leaders, boasting of their realistic pragmatism, turned to socialism in varying forms. Politically, they saw the benefits of nationalism; socially and economically, they thought of their future in terms of socialism. Above all, they wanted a more abundant life. [31]

The existence of tribal communalism throughout Africa did not mean a widespread experience in the ways of modern socialism. Traditional African societies utilized a variety of cooperation patterns, but these did not necessarily correspond with socialist techniques. African leaders soon recognized the impossibility of positing a universal and monolithic socialist form for their new nation-states.

African leaders seemed committed to socialism, but not to either Russian or Chinese communism. [32] Messianic Russian nationalism envisioned in the vast continent a happy hunting ground for extension of Soviet control, and Chinese Communists pronounced Africa as "exceedingly favorable" for revolution. Moscow and Peking labored to

[30] Thomas Patrick Melady, "The Sweep of Nationalism in Africa," *Annals of the American Academy of Political and Social Science,* CCCLIV (July 1964), 94.

[31] *Ibid.* North American whites live to an average of sixty-eight with an average annual per capita income of $2,200; African blacks, with a per capita income of less than $100, live to an average of forty years.

[32] This is the theme of the essays in William H. Friedland and Carl G. Rosberg, Jr., eds., *African Socialism* (Stanford, 1964).

influence African students, intellectuals, and officials. But because of their heavy-handed diplomacy and awkward techniques, both Russians and Chinese alienated the new African states. African leaders looked with suspicion at the contrasting economies of West Berlin and East Berlin. While they were willing to use the tools of socialism, most were more impressed by the Scandinavian variety or the restrained and planned socialism of social democracy. British justice and American enterprise attracted greater attention than Russian or Chinese totalitarian politics and subversion campaigns.

The pattern of African socialism was by no means uniform. There were diverse types, varying from Leopold Senghor's intellectual socialism in Senegal; to Julius Nyerere's *Ujamaa*, a cooperative concept of socialist development in Tanzania; to Sékou Touré's practical approach of forced labor in Guinea; to Kwame Nkrumah's national socialism in Ghana. In each case, however, there was little urge to join international Marxian society. Of the two movements—nationalism and socialism—nationalism remained much the stronger.

THE ROLE OF PAN-AFRICANISM

Concurrent with the programs of Africanization and Negritude which followed the spread of nationalism in Africa was the expansion of Pan-Africanism, or what might be called a pancontinental nationalism. Much of the impetus for Pan-Africanism in its early days came from America—from Marcus Garvey's back-to-Africa, Black Zionist movement [33] and William E. B. Du Bois's promotion of "the African personality," African independence, and Pan-Africanism.[34] Pan-Africanism was designed originally to establish a universal confraternity among the black race, from the backward tribes of Africa to the Negro intellectuals of the United States. For years the idea remained a fanciful conjecture and attracted little attention.

With the sudden blooming of nationalism in Africa in the middle of the twentieth century, Pan-Africanism was revived in a new and vigor-

[33] See Edmund D. Cronon, *Black Moses: The Story of Marcus Garvey* (Madison, Wis., 1955). Garvey, a Jamaican with extraordinary oratorical gifts and a flair for showmanship, aroused Negro racial pride, but his movement was a failure.

[34] See W. E. B. Du Bois, *The World and Africa* (New York, 1947). Du Bois, founder of the National Association for the Advancement of Colored People and a leftist intellectual, is regarded as the father of Pan-Africanism. Garvey and Du Bois had little use for each other (see Cronon, *op. cit.*, pp. 128–131, 190).

ous form. Its apostles came from the ranks of African intellectuals and political leaders. No longer was it considered an ephemeral figment of the imagination, but rather a goal attainable within the present generation. Pan-Africans pointed to the ridicule with which African nationalism had been treated even a few short decades before and insisted that federation on either a regional or pancontinental scale was entirely possible.

The new Pan-Africanism was neither anti-Western nor anticommunist; it was simply pro-African and pro-Africa. Its goals were the Africanization of the politics, economy, social system, and culture of the entire continent. It opposed any revival of the old imperialism and directed its fire against relics of colonialism in South Africa, Rhodesia, and the remaining Portuguese colonies. It took a noncommittal position in the cold war between the United States and Soviet Russia. It would allow Europeans and Asians who still lived in Africa to remain there provided that they were willing to accept the principle of equality of franchise. It looked with pride on the formation of new national states, but regarded independence as merely a temporary gain on the road to continental unity.

While the goal of Pan-Africanism was continental in scope, it had to contend with the division of Africa north and south of the Sahara. The Arab and Muslim north, motivated primarily by religious ideals, was drawn into the vortex of Middle Eastern pan-nationalism. The Pan-African idea was defended more tenaciously south of the Sahara, where even Negro Muslims were unimpressed by the process of Africanization.

The Sixth Pan-African Congress was held at Manchester in 1945. The idea of Pan-Africanism was also expressed at meetings held on African soil. The First Conference of Independent African States met in April 1958 in Accra, the capital of Ghana. Eight nations were invited: Liberia, Ghana, Ethiopia, the United Arab Republic, Sudan, Tunisia, Morocco, and South Africa (the latter refused to attend). The delegates hailed African unity ("Forward Africa, United!"), supported the Algerian rebellion, and condemned white rule in South Africa, Kenya, and the Portuguese colonies. The meeting ended with the hymn "God Bless Africa," and April 15 was designated "Freedom Day."

The Second Conference of Independent African States met at Addis Ababa in June 1960. In addition to those countries which had sent delegates to the first conference, there were representatives from Guinea, Somalia, Nigeria, Cameroon, Algeria, Mali, Madagascar, and Sierra Leone. Again there were resolutions supporting Algeria, condemning South Africa, seeking economic cooperation among African states, and calling for a United States of Africa.

Added to these gatherings were All-African People's Conferences in which African leaders and intellectuals, rather than governments, met to promote the cause of Pan-Africanism. Delegates attacked neocolonialism, assailed relics of chieftaincy, and recommended the formation of an African Legion consisting of volunteers to protect the freedom won by African nations.

Despite this activity, the road to Pan-Africanism proved to be a thorny one. The federation principle appealed to the new African leaders and stimulated the entire Pan-African movement. There were efforts at regional federations as stepping-stones. But an attempt to include all the states which had formerly been part of French West Africa soon foundered. A projected Union of Central African Republics, a federation of the four states which had comprised French Equatorial Africa, also failed. Similarly, a proposed East African federation of Uganda, Kenya, and Tanganyika was terminated almost before it began. There were too many difficulties: lack of internal unity, suspicion between nations, too many linguistic groups. Above all there was disagreement on the nature of a supra-African organization. One group favored abandonment of internal sovereignty in favor of union, while another called for a confederation of independent states.

By 1960, the critical year of liberation in Africa, the new nations polarized into rival groups, the Casablanca and the Monrovia (Brazzaville) blocs. The Casablanca states (Morocco, Ghana, Guinea, Mali, United Arab Republic, and Libya) called for nonalignment in the East-West struggle but leaned toward the Soviet side. The Casablanca bloc condemned Israel, France, and South Africa. It laid the groundwork for an African consultative assembly and a joint African military high command.[35]

The more numerous Monrovia group, composed of nations with more moderate policies, favored "community" rather than union. Included were the original twelve Brazzaville states of French West Africa and French Equatorial Africa, plus Liberia, Togo, Nigeria,

[35] On aims of the Casablanca bloc, see *The Party* (publication of the Convention People's Party Bureau of Information and Publicity, Accra), No. 19 (1962), p. 11.

Tunisia, Ethiopia, Libya, Somalia, and Sierre Leone. This bloc was neutral with leanings toward the West; it was pro-Israel; it favored the United Nations Congo operation; and generally it was less critical of French policy in Algeria.[36]

In May 1963 the heads of thirty-two African states met at Addis Ababa for another Pan-African conference. Here it was agreed to establish a new Organization of African Unity (OAU), implying that the Casablanca and Monrovia groups would disband. An attempt was made to smooth out the differences between the two blocs. This was the climax of the Pan-African movement. There were eloquent pleas for continental unity, but the basic problem remained: how much political sovereignty would the individual African states be willing to relinquish in favor of a United States of Africa?[37]

Thus, the issue of nationalism versus Pan-Africanism remained unresolved. Although both movements were manifestations of the same general urge toward independence and freedom, their goals remained separate. Nationalism in Africa was concerned with building effective national polities, while Pan-Africanism was devoted to building large political unities. The attempt to construct new states while molding Pan-African unity was handicapped from its beginnings with frustrations, paradoxes, and seemingly insurmountable difficulties. The new states had enough problems of their own without the added difficulties of suprastate political unification. If western Europe with its century-old traditions remained fragmented and far from continental unification, could one reasonably expect the African states, with much less political experience, to solve the problem within a few years? First things must come first, as recognized by George Padmore, a proponent of Pan-Africanism:

The revolution taking place in Africa is threefold. First, there is the struggle for national independence. Second is the social revolution which follows the achievement of independence and self-determination. And thirdly, Africans are seeking some form of regional unity as the forerunner of the United States of Africa. However, until the first is achieved the

---

[36] On aims of the Monrovia bloc, see Hodgson and Stoneman, *op. cit.*, p. 122. A third group was the PAFMECSA, the Pan-African Movement of East, Central, and South Africa.

[37] See David E. Apter and James S. Coleman, "Pan-Africanism or Nationalism in Africa," in *Pan-Africanism Reconsidered*, ed. American Society of African Culture (Berkeley, 1962), pp. 32 ff.

energies of the people cannot be mobilized for the attainment of the second and third stages, which are even more difficult than the first.[38]

The achievement of nationhood almost invariably brings a sense of euphoria to the people concerned. But in the African states there arose a whole set of problems which had been kept underground during the era of colonialism. The high-sounding constitutions were well and good; they brought dignity and emotional satisfaction. Considerably more important, however, was the necessity of creating workable political institutions, training the citizenry in use of the franchise, and mobilizing resources for modernization of the society and the economy. Before seeking the goal of continental unification, it was necessary that African political leaders create stable political communities.

They cannot mark time awaiting the liberation of all Africa; they must address themselves immediately to meeting those challenges they confront in that part of the continent for which they are responsible. Not the least demanding of those is the need to shift from the role of agitator against government to a government official ready and willing to control agitators.[39]

CASE HISTORY: KWAME NKRUMAH
AND GHANIAN NATIONALISM

The course of African nationalism was set by revolutionary leaders who had served their apprenticeships in the universities and streets of London, Paris, and New York. These nationalists were convinced that once independence was achieved a paradise of peace, prosperity, and happiness would follow. The task turned out to be even more difficult than they had imagined: little did they understand that the building of a nation was a highly complex process and that there was nothing automatic about it. Nor did they realize that along with political change came economic and social dislocations that had to be met. The result was continual crisis.

The case of Kwame Nkrumah and Ghana gives testimony to the almost overwhelming difficulties of nation-building. Here an African leader became successively his country's builder and then nearly its

---

[38] George Padmore, *A Guide to Pan-African Socialism: A Program for Africa* (Accra, 1957), p. 18.
[39] Apter and Coleman, *op. cit.*, p. 96.

wrecker. As a leading apostle of African national consciousness, Nkrumah symbolized Pan-African union, but he proceeded systematically to sabotage the dream by establishing a dictatorship. His career reflected the frustrations of the new African national life.

Kwame Nkrumah was born in 1909 in a village hut in the Gold Coast.[40] The son of reasonably well-to-do parents (his father was a goldsmith and his mother a trader), he began his primary schooling at the Catholic Mission School at Nkroful. From there he went to the Catholic Mission School at Sekondi, and later to Achimoto College, from which he was graduated in 1931. Here the young man fell under the influence of James Aggrey, who inspired him to study in the United States.[41] He gained admission to Lincoln University in Oxford, Pennsylvania, where he worked at various jobs. In New York City's Harlem he peddled fish and slept in subways.

In 1945, Nkrumah went to London to study at the London School of Economics. There he met George Padmore and other politically-minded Africans, with whom he attended the Sixth Pan-African Conference at Manchester in 1945. The next year he helped organize the West African National Secretariat. He then formed a group of his own called "the Circle," pledged to train for revolution in Africa. Immersed in African nationalist politics and left-wing movements, he became a Marxist, and from then on he retained an interest in socialist principles.

Returning to the Gold Coast, Nkrumah became secretary of an independent political organization known as the United Gold Coast Convention (UGCC) at Accra. He was invited to this post by his political mentor, J. B. Danquah.[42] Soon he was embroiled in strikes and boycotts. In 1946, Britain granted a new constitution which gave the Gold Coast a greater amount of self-government but reserved a veto power for the governor-general. Nkrumah coupled his secretarial du-

[40] See Kwame Nkrumah's autobiography *Ghana* (Edinburgh, 1959). Nkrumah coupled his life story with his country's destiny. See also the eulogistic sketch, "Life Story of the Prime Minister," in *The Gold Coast and the Constitution*, pamphlet of the *Daily Graphic* (Accra, 1952), pp. 3 ff.

[41] Dr. James E. Kwegyir Aggrey, after teaching for many years in North Carolina, was principal of Achimoto College. An important figure in the formative years of African nationalism, he was known for his statement, "Both black and white keys are necessary to play the piano." Aggrey presented such parables as a means of instilling self-respect among Africans.

[42] Dr. Danquah died in prison as Nkrumah's captive after an illness for which his one-time protégé was accused of refusing him medical attention.

ties with agitation against this constitution, which he said came too late and granted too little. After riots in February and March of 1948, in which twenty-nine lost their lives and 230 were badly injured, the British jailed Nkrumah, Danquah, and others and appointed a commission of inquiry to investigate the situation.[43]

Freed from prison, Nkrumah began a campaign among Gold Coast youth for "Self-Government Now." He denounced his mentor, Danquah, as hopelessly old-fashioned, criticized the UGCC as ineffectual, and demanded action. His impassioned speeches and fiery articles in his newspaper, the Accra *Evening News,* made him a popular national hero. On June 12, 1949, he addressed a huge audience of sixty thousand in Accra and announced the formation of his own Convention People's Party (CPP). He called for strikes and boycotts as a means of attaining immediate self-government. On January 8, 1950, in the same arena, he denounced the new Coussey Report and called for a general strike.[44] Once again the British imprisoned him, this time for thirteen months. While Nkrumah was in prison, general elections were held on February 8, 1951.[45] Nkrumah's party, the CPP, topped the polls. He was then released and appointed "Leader of Government Business." Britain gave the Gold Coast extended powers of self-government, but not the full degree demanded by nationalist agitators. Nkrumah, though not satisfied, decided to work from his new position for further gains.[46] Within a year he had the constitution modified to make him prime minister of the Gold Coast.[47] On March 6, 1957, the Gold Coast became Ghana,

[43] The Watson Report of 1948 recommended greater autonomy for the Gold Coast. London, intent upon bypassing the radicals, appointed another group, a "Constitutional Committee," headed by an African judge, Henley Coussey, to draft suggestions. Nkrumah attacked this committee as pro-British and far too moderate.

[44] In Nkrumah's view the Coussey Report was unsatisfactory because it fell short of full self-government.

[45] British colonial officials handled this election admirably. Trained special teams were sent to tour the country, lecturing and showing motion pictures on how the election would work. Illiterate voters were given symbols to assist them at the polls. This election has been described as the greatest single political development in the history of modern Africa (see Wallbank, *op. cit.,* p. 60).

[46] The news of Nkrumah's success projected him to the forefront of African nationalist leaders. He was invited to the United States in June 1951 to receive the LL.D. degree at Lincoln University. He then went to London to address public meetings and consult members of Parliament. He was accorded an enthusiastic reception on his return to the Gold Coast.

[47] "The elevation of an African to the office of Premiership within the Commonwealth is a challenge to Malan's racial creed. Whether Dr. Malan likes it or

the first of the African former colonies to attain freedom. With a population of 7,500,000 living in an area the size of New York State and Pennsylvania combined, and with its rich cocoa industry, Ghana seemed to have a good start toward prosperous nationhood. Nkrumah was elected to the presidency in 1960.

From the beginning of his regime Nkrumah devoted his main efforts to political problems: "Seek ye first the political kingdom, and all other things shall be added to it." On the theory that a strong state required an unassailable and indispensable national hero, he began to imitate the worst features of European political behavior. It was not long before Ghanian democracy was transformed into a dictatorship. Nkrumah ended the two-party system by installing the CPP, his own party, as the sole governmental authority.[48] Freedom of press and of assembly were denied. Many able Ghanians were thrown into prison or forced into exile. Even Komlo Gbedemah, a competent finance minister who had given years of devoted service to Nkrumah, was dismissed and forced to flee for his life.[49] Nkrumah dismissed the Supreme Court and made himself the final arbiter of legal appeal.[50]

To build the myth of his indispensability, Nkrumah had himself pronounced "Founder of the Nation," "Osagyefo" (Redeemer), "Teacher and Father," "His Messianic Majesty," "The Great Christ of Our Day," "The Savior," and "The Leader." His image in lifelike statues appeared throughout the country. His name adorned public buildings, schools, institutes, and highways. He surrounded himself with sycophants who spoke of the Ghanian Revolution "founded on the ideological principles of Nkrumaism." His controlled press sang praises to the great man:

> Our inspired leader, Osagyefo Katamanto, Oyeadieyie,
> Kwame Nkrumah, who commands the unflinching loyalty
> and support of all seven million inhabitants of
> this country, is proud to be paying at this

---

not, from now on an African Prime Minister will sit with other Dominion Prime Ministers in a Commonwealth Conference. Thus the elevation of Kwame Nkrumah means the decline and fall of Malan's Herrenvolk institution" (pamphlet of the *Daily Graphic* [Accra, 1952], pp. 3 ff).

[48] The election of 1964, probably rigged, showed a 98.5 per cent margin for the Convention People's Party.

[49] *Time*, Sept. 10, 1965, p. 31.   [50] *The New York Times*, Feb. 25, 1966.

time in his political career the price of
courageous leadership.

But we are convinced of the justness of our
Messiah's sacred mission to effectuate a United
States of Africa. And our dynamic Party, under
our time-tested leader, Teacher and Father,
has pledged itself to the remorseless prosecution
of the battle against the crafty enemy.

In this crusade, we shall use every legitimate
weapon in our armoury. We shall ask for no quarter
or give any. We shall keep ever aloft the blazing
torch of Nkrumaism until the crumbling ramparts
of imperialism, colonialism and neo-colonialism are
raked to the ground.
Nkrumaism shall triumph!
Long live Osagyefo!
Long live our Dynamic Part!
Long live Ghana! [51]

Nkrumah was not content with ruling only Ghana. As Africa's
self-appointed leader of nationalism, socialism, and African unity, he
proposed to unify the entire continent under one government. Calling
himself Africa's "Man of Destiny," he placed himself at the head of the
Pan-African movement and began to interfere in the internal affairs of
other African nations. In 1962, at the age of fifty-three, following
letters of praise pouring in after his latest published theories on African
socialism, Nkrumah made himself "Life President" of Ghana and
looked forward to an even greater role in African continental politics.

Unfortunately, Nkrumah's country was plagued by economic ills
from the first day of his rule. He understood the necessity for reform:
he tried to modernize agriculture, build local industry, extend communications, and improve the health of his people. He inaugurated the
Volta River project which called for construction of a great dam
capable of producing 500,000 kilowatts of power to facilitate manufacture of aluminum from the nation's great supply of bauxite. He built
schools and hospitals and doubled Ghana's literacy rate. He established
state-owned corporations as well as a state-owned airline and shipping
line.

[51] *The Party*, No. 25 (Sept. 1962), p. 1.

Yet, economic troubles continued to harass the dictator. His state corporations lost money. In the course of bartering with the Communist bloc, he mortgaged Ghana's valuable cocoa, gold, and timber resources in return for equipment that was often useless. All industrial contracts came through the government with a standard 10 per cent bribe known as "dash." Millions of dollars were squandered on grandiose schemes. Tiny Ghana had embassies in fifty-one foreign countries. Politicians owned huge housing estates, office buildings, and even the country's newspapers. The country which had begun its independence as the richest of African states was virtually bankrupt from mismanagement by the ninth year of Nkrumah's reign.

By early 1966 popular discontent was aroused to a point where it could no longer be restrained. There were increasing attempts on Nkrumah's life, as well as growing unrest in the army of nine thousand men. In late February 1966, several days after his departure for Peking, Nkrumah was overthrown by a military coup. He retired in exile to Guinea, where Sekou Touré, Africa's outstanding nationalist, at first greeted him enthusiastically: Nkrumah was embraced, given a villa, and made Guinea's honorary "co-President." Touré said at the time, "Nkrumah belongs to all Africa, not just Ghana. His voice and my voice are one."

Ghanians, reacting joyfully to the coup, danced in the streets and shouted: "The tyranny is over!" "No more Nkrumah—no more Russians!" Nkrumah's life-sized statue outside Parliament in Accra was hacked into a thousand pieces which were then distributed to the mob. The new military regime, launching a series of inquiries into Nkrumah's misdeeds, accused him of being the organizer of an elaborate network for African espionage and subversion. Nkrumah's "African socialism" had left behind it a trail of wreckage.

This is a classic case, not peculiar to Africa, in which the people's catalog of grievances proved weightier than a leader's feats as nation-builder. The substitution of charisma for freedom did not work. Nkrumah's fall, coming during a succession of similar coups,[52] marked the end of the first phase of postcolonial development—an era dominated by the nationalist martyr-hero who had prepared himself for liberation while in prison. Slogans and myths were not enough.

[52] Other African nations, including Algeria, Burundi, Congo (Leopoldville), the Central African Republic, Upper Volta, Dahomey, and Nigeria, also experienced military coups protesting against tyrannical or corrupt politcians.

Nkrumah's exit was an important event. It brought about a drastic change in Africa's power structure and sent diplomatic shock waves reverberating to Moscow and Peking. The Chinese and Russians lost their African foothold. And on the continent itself the overturn in Ghana indicated growing difficulties for the new nation-states.

POINT AND COUNTERPOINT:
KENYA AND SOUTH AFRICA

The effects of racial nationalism were especially severe in Kenya and South Africa. In the British colony of Kenya, before its independence in 1963, the comparatively small European community of white settlers hoped to maintain control over the indigenous population indefinitely. The African majority, angered by white domination, demanded reforms. Resentment against white settlement started a rebellion in 1948 that reached its height from 1952 to 1957 in the Mau Mau terror.

The Mau Mau, a secret society opposed to white rule, was organized among the Kikuyu tribe, which had always had a strong witchcraft tradition. The society was infected by a sense of exclusiveness, based as much on envy and hate as on racial and national pride.[53] From its beginning it was violently anti-European, as this Mau Mau hymn shows:

> You Europeans are nothing but robbers,
> though you pretend to lead us. Go away, go
> away, you Europeans; the years that are
> past have been more than enough for us. . . .
>   Come together and weep. See how the Europeans
> oppress us. . . .
>   Have no fear in your hearts; God is in heaven.
> Be brave, God's power is here, and the Europeans
> will be driven out. . . .
>   You Europeans make merry now, [but] the day is
> coming when you will weep because of the
> evil you have done. May you be destroyed in
> the sea.[54]

[53] See *Kenya—The Mau Mau: A Background Note*, Information Office, British Embassy (Washington, D.C., 1952).

[54] Josiah Mwangi Kariuki, *"Mau Mau" Detainee* (Middlesex, England, 1964), p. 85.

Jomo Kenyatta, the Kenyan nationalist leader, spoke out against European encroachment:

If Africans were left in peace in their own lands, Europeans would have to offer them the benefits of white civilization in real earnest before they could obtain the African labor which they want so much. . . . By driving him off his ancestral lands, the Europeans have robbed him of the material foundations of his culture, and reduced him to a state of serfdom incompatible with human happiness. The African is conditioned, by the cultural and social institutions of centuries, to a freedom of which Europe has little conception, and it is not in his nature to accept serfdom forever. He realizes that he must fight unceasingly for his own complete emancipation; for without this he is doomed to remain the prey of rival imperialisms, which in every successive year will drive their fangs more deeply into his vitality and strength.[55]

These were measured words, but along with them went grotesquely uncivilized behavior. Members of the Mau Mau were required to take a killing-oath which forced them to slay when called upon. The oath-takers were not allowed to hesitate or think: they murdered on instruction, admitting that they themselves were no good to anybody any more after taking the oath.[56] Gruesome orgiastic rites were devised to capture new members. The activities of the organization were directed not only against the British settlers but also against Africans considered to be pro-British.

Beginning a campaign of terrorism in 1952, the Mau Mau raided lonely farms, and attacked and killed settlers. Christian Africans who refused to take the oath were slaughtered. British troops, supported by loyal Kikuyu, put down the rebellion, killing in the process about seven thousand Mau Mau by the end of 1954. Not until 1957 was the movement crushed.

With Kenyatta jailed in the midst of the revolt, a new generation of political leaders, including Tom Mboya, took over the struggle for independence. In 1959 the British released about eighty thousand Mau Mau who had been imprisoned. London made concessions to Kenyan nationalism by lifting political restraints and ending exclusive European ownership in the Kenyan highlands. In 1961, Kenyatta, still in prison,

[55] Jomo Kenyatta, *Facing Mount Kenya: The Tribal Life of the Kikuyu* (London, 1953), p. 318.
[56] *Report by the Parliamentary Delegation to Kenya*, Cmd. 9081 (London, 1954), pp. 11–12.

was elected to assume the reins of government. In 1962 he became independent Kenya's first prime minister.

The Mau Mau crisis brought about a re-evaluation of the plural society not only in Kenya but in most of Africa. Europeans began to realize that their conception of a "white man's country" was no longer valid. Shocked British settlers in Kenya accused the British government of betraying their interests. Some concluded that black African nationalism was to be accepted as a permanent feature in Kenyan life. Others, fearing a renewal of Mau Mau barbarism, left the country. To the Kenyan leader Tom Mboya the issue was clear-cut:

> The question is not whether it is wrong to use violence, but whether nationalism can be expected to remain silent to the extent it has been in . . . countries . . . [where] there is no constitutional channel through which nationalism can achieve its objectives. . . . Had it not been for Mau Mau, perhaps these changes would never have taken place; at any rate, they would not have come as quickly as they did.[57]

Opposed to black African nationalism were the Portuguese, who wanted to maintain their position in Angola and Mozambique; the South Africans; and the Rhodesians. These three became natural allies in a white rulers' bloc in the south.

While much of the rest of Africa was convulsed in political crises, the ruling class in South Africa became even more rigidly entrenched: "No more explanations, no more apologia, no more conciliation; instead the fortress will be held, by whatever means." [58] The issue was explosive, for South Africa's 12,000,000 Africans made up 66 per cent of the population, compared to 3,800,000 ruling whites. Black-white relations were controlled by a policy called *apartheid* (separateness), aimed at total separation of each racial group—European, Asian, African, and colored (mixed blood).[59] When the white South African spoke of *apartheid*, he meant *baaskap* (white supremacy). The granite-minded prejudice often reached ludicrous proportions. By law

[57] Tom Mboya, *Freedom and After* (Boston, 1963), pp. 42–45.

[58] Colin Rhys Lovell, "The Republic of South Africa," *Current History*, XL (Apr. 1965), 226.

[59] "Any person who is in charge of or has control of any public premises . . . may, whenever he deems it expedient . . . set apart or reserve such premises . . . or any bench, seat, or other amenity on such premises . . . for the exclusive use of persons in one particular race." Fines (not exceeding 50 pounds) or imprisonment (not exceeding three months) were set for offenders. (*Separate Amenities Act*, No. 45, 1953.)

quarters for black servants had to be separated from the white man's house by at least fifteen feet. The white South African would allow Africans to prepare his food and bathe his children, but not to share a bus seat with him or stand behind him in a queue. The Nursing Act of 1957 made it an offence to employ a white nurse or student nurse under the supervision of a black nurse. A series of similarly harsh laws gave the government powers unequaled in the democratic world.

All this was part of a special problem—the clash between Bantu and Afrikaner nationalisms. The Bantus, or Africans, the largest ethnic group, constituted two-thirds of the population of South Africa. Yet, Bantu nationalism was suppressed and driven underground by the government. The African National Congress was banned, leaving secret organizations such as the National Liberation Movement to speak for Bantu nationalism. Assailed by *apartheid*, politically sterilized, economically handicapped, restricted and jailed, black Africans espoused Bantu nationalism as a solution for their problems. The movement took on strong antiwhite, anti-Western tones. Black nationalism was the reaction to white nationalism.

White nationalism was strongest among the Afrikaners: the English in South Africa showed little interest in nationhood. Because of their separate language, religious ties, common culture, and consciousness of political independence, the Afrikaners, descendants of the original Dutch settlers, had a strong sense of national identity. Afrikaner nationalism achieved its goal of independence in 1961, when the Union of South Africa became a republic and withdrew from the Commonwealth. Resisting Anglicization, opposing even fusionist policies, supporting the cohesive elements of language and religion, and stressing their own culture, Afrikaner nationalists were victorious in the clash with Bantu nationalism. This was the culmination of a century and a half of struggle. Despite the numerical superiority of the Africans, Afrikaner nationalists refused to accept a multiracial state. Having been once suppressed themselves, they now became oppressors.

Most South African whites, especially the Afrikaners, who had no homeland in Europe to which they could return, described their own attitude as "right, just, and necessary." Conscious of the stability of their country, they had no notion of the belief held by outsiders that white South Africans were living in a trap. They pointed to their ever-growing prosperity, to skyscrapers and automobiles. Faced with hostility both inside the country and throughout the world, they paid careful attention to military defense. Fortified by 250,000 trained white soldiers, with many more in reserve, a modern air force, and a huge defense budget, they considered themselves well prepared to meet any invasion. Their mood was belligerent, based on the belief that the outside world just did not understand. They pointed to the chaos in the Congo as justification for their own point of view.

African nationalists bitterly opposed South Africa's *apartheid* policy. The Organization of African Unity insisted at the Addis Ababa conference in May 1963 that the United Nations put pressure on South Africa, a move which only solidified the South Africans behind their government.[60]

A similar clash of racial nationalism in Rhodesia came to a climax. Here some 217,000 whites tried to maintain their rule over four million blacks in the face of critical world opinion. The problem started in 1895, when a small group of Britons known as the Pioneer Column pushed north from South Africa to help implement Cecil Rhodes's concept of "Africa British from Cape to Cairo." At the turn of the century Rhodesia was settled by whites as far north as the Zambesi River. Soon Rhodes's vision was changed to "Africa white from Cape to Cairo." White colonists occupied and developed the best lands of Rhodesia. By 1923, Rhodesia was a self-governing colony.

The British settlers in Rhodesia believed that their farms, industries, and livelihood, as well as their very lives, were endangered by the flood of African nationalism.[61] They were convinced that only through independence could the line be held. In November 1965, Prime Minister Ian Smith issued the "Unilateral Declaration of Independence," which severed his country's ties with the Commonwealth.[62]

African nationalists both inside Rhodesia and throughout the continent were stung into action by this new crisis. Rhodesian African

---

[60] In 1960, Liberia and Ethiopia asked the Court of International Justice for a judgment on South Africa's racial policy of *apartheid*. Six years later, after six thousand pages of evidence and a legal cost of $18,000,000, the court decided not to accept the case on a technicality. The whites in South Africa joyously greeted the verdict as a landmark decision in their favor.

[61] *Daily Express* (London), Oct. 1, 1965.

[62] The Declaration of Independence, read over the radio, began: "Whereas in the course of human events . . . it may become necessary for a people to resolve the political affiliations which have connected them with another people." The statement went on to borrow liberally from the phraseology of the American Declaration of Independence of 1776. Missing were the words: "All men are created equal."

leaders, including the two most prominent, Joshua Nkomo and Nda-baningi Sithole, were jailed. The Organization of African Unity threat-ened to invade Rhodesia, a prospect not especially feared by the strongly armed Rhodesians. Britain expelled Rhodesia from the sterling area, suspended her preferential treatment as a Commonwealth mem-ber, imposed controls on trade and currency exchange, and banned purchase of Rhodesia's main crops, tobacco and sugar. However, Prime Minister Harold Wilson barred use of military force to break the rebellion. The embarrassing issue was thrown into the lap of the United Nations.

TROUBLED AFRICA

Critics of Black Africa point again and again to its instability. It is said that the Africans cannot govern themselves, as the crises in the Congo, the bloodshed in Nigeria, and Nkrumah's tyrannical rule in Ghana have shown. There is instability, indeed, but this is due in large part to the conditions under which the Africans have been forced to govern themselves rather than any inherent inability in self-govern-ment. The new nations had artificial boundaries made in the days of imperialism by European administrators who paid no attention to the hundreds of tribal lines that made up the political map of Africa. The charge of chaos in the Congo is offset by such examples of com-paratively good government as the Ivory Coast under President Félix Houphouet-Boigny and Kenya under Jomo Kenyatta. The latter suc-ceeded in overcoming the tribal rivalries of the Luo and his own Kikuyu and brought them together in a national spirit of *harambee* (togetherness). The danger of splitting along tribal lines in Kenya was averted, at least for the time being.

Some critics see nothing but grimness and disaster in the emergence of African nationalism. A recent book by Blaine Littel, a former correspondent for the Columbia Broadcasting System, describes his five-month tour following the route carved out by Henry M. Stanley in 1874 to open the gates to colonization.[63] It is a bleak portrait of the emerging nations. Littel witnessed comic-opera politics, slapdash gov-ernments waging a downhill struggle against poverty and disease, and social chaos. The Europeans, said the author, had abandoned a child

[63] Blaine Littel, *South of the Moon: On Stanley's Trail through the Dark Continent* (New York, 1966).

that could not take care of itself. The white men, blessed by Church, state, crown, and commerce, had come on a civilizing mission, and they had failed. They departed leaving behind as a legacy for their black brothers a taste of the unattainable and a gnawing sense of inferiority. Population continued to outrace social programs on a continent that worshipped fertility as a god; agricultural projects were directed by novices; and governmental machinery was unable to break away from tribal rivalries. Littel concluded that the aspirations of the black man were blunted by the demoralizing gap between what he saw the white man enjoy and what he could achieve in a lifetime. What was happening, said Littel, was a steady inexorable return to the bush, a trail marked by abandoned cars needing only gasoline to make them run again, discarded radios requiring only batteries to bring them back to life, and vanishing roads and crumbling plantation homes— relics of the white man's occupation of the land.

It is, perhaps, too much to expect that nationalism could come to Africa in peaceful raiment. Such an ideal state of affairs had not been achieved elsewhere. In effect, the African experience was a recapitulation of that in America and Europe. The violence is a reminder of what the Americans and the nationalities of eastern Europe underwent in their time. Africans were sure that they, like the Americans, were seeking to bring forth new nations conceived in liberty and dedicated to the proposition that all men are created equal. They seemed helpless in averting the process of Balkanization that had split Europe into a mass of quarreling people. Their birth pangs were equally harsh, their problems as severe and frustrating.

It is difficult to weave a meaningful historical pattern because of the variety of conditions throughout the continent. The drives for national viability were complicated by tribal and regional antagonisms, language problems, incompetent leadership, shopworn slogans ("Africa's mystique"), hurriedly written constitutions, and such economic problems as unemployment, low wages, inflation, corruption, and decreasing foreign assistance. Nation-building, complicated even under the best circumstances, found rough passage on the African scene.

The situation remains fluid: change in Africa has always come slowly. Some observers interpret recent military coups as signs that Africa has become another South America. Others regard the times of trouble as a normal accompaniment to nation-building. Whatever the explanation, Africans seek their way between the darkness of their past and the glare of a strange, modern world.

Chapter 7

Anticolonial Nationalism: Asian Trends

Nationalism . . . [is] a terrible epidemic.
—RABINDRANATH TAGORE

*Nationalism is . . . that precious possession
which enables a state to aspire to progress.*

—SUN YAT-SEN

The vast land mass of Asia, homeland of nearly one-third of the human race, has been shaken by change in the last several decades. In the Asian revolt were three related factors: dissatisfaction with the process of Westernization; a growing belief in communism as a liberating force; and a rising nationalism intensified by resentment of European domination. In all three motivations the compulsive force was anti-imperialism—opposition to colonialism in all its forms.

In the nineteenth century the accessible areas of Asia either became colonies of European powers or were forced to submit to the "unequal treaties system." European civilization penetrated into and progressively transformed Asian societies. Indians, Chinese, and Japanese felt the impact of Western industrialism and capitalism. Asians learned much about European politics, technology, and power. But with knowledge came disenchantment. Asians began an energetic struggle to modernize their ancient cultures while simultaneously seeking independence. They were tired of European extraterritorial rights and leaseholds. They wanted freedom, but at the same time they remained dependent upon the West for scientific and technical education, without which they could not modernize their societies and regain cultural and political initiative.

The process of change was accelerated by the events of World War I. Asians grew critical of a civilization which produced such catastrophe. They saw the defeated European powers lose their territories, leaseholds, and special rights in Asia.

Asian resentment against Western intrusion stimulated the national self-consciousness which eventually led to the end of the great Western empires. The most significant development was the dissolution of the British empire in Asia. The problem facing the British there was similar to that in Africa—how to withdraw without friction and leave behind orderly governments and stable economic systems. A major step was the subdivision of India in 1947. The Dutch, too, relinquished their hold on their Far Eastern empire in the Netherlands East Indies, though they did it unwillingly. Sovereignty over nearly all of Indonesia was transferred to the United States of Indonesia. When the French tried to return to Indochina at the close of World War II, they found their way barred by guerrillas. The French offer of semi-independence was unacceptable to the nationalists. After paying a huge cost in money and lives, the French finally withdrew from Indochina, which was then split into separate governments in Laos, Cambodia, and North and South Vietnam.

The imperialism which distressed Asians was not altogether a European monopoly; the Japanese participated too. The Chinese, who entered the war against Germany in 1917, were angered after the conflict when Japan was allowed to retain the former German leasehold of Shantung. The Japanese later returned the area but they held on to the concessions and privileges which the Germans had formerly enjoyed. While the Western countries were preoccupied with European theaters of war, Japan avoided extreme actions, instead expanding her trade and industries and becoming an exporter of capital, mainly to areas on the nearby mainland.

The second factor at the root of Asian revolt was the expansion of communism. The Russian Revolutions of 1917 gave additional impetus for rebellion. Lenin's denunciation of capitalism and imperialism, especially his thesis that imperialism was but one aspect of capitalism, made a strong impression throughout Asia. Colonial peoples there had already identified imperialism with capitalism because almost all the large industrial and business enterprises were in foreign hands. Now they could understand why Marxist-Leninist ideology linked the two. The result was that new moves for independence merged into socialism of one form or another, all the way from democratic to Bolshevik varieties.

When it became obvious that the revolution predicted by Marx had not occurred in the highly industrialized countries of western Europe, Russian activists turned to Asia as a kind of ready-made substitute. It was believed that perhaps capitalism might be outflanked in a vast pincers movement with its fulcrum in the Far East. There began an intensive two-way traffic of ideologists and activists from Moscow to various points of Asia. Asian liberation leaders went to Russia to learn at first hand the techniques of revolution that might be used by the masses at home. Trained Communists were sent from Moscow to strategic cities in Asia to stir up discontent among an already dissatisfied people. This was favorable soil for Communist growth.

The third basic factor in the Asian revolt was the impact of the new nationalism. At first nationalist rebellions took the form of economic boycotts against Western products. Then came political combinations, demands for independence, propaganda campaigns, and guerrilla warfare. In the consequent transformation of the Orient, nationalism played, as elsewhere, a dominant role. It was a powerful force in an explosive situation. "In the immense area of Asia, from the eastern Mediterranean to the Sea of Japan, the new nationalism remains the strongest political impulse. The yearning for national identity and independence from foreign control is stronger here than the appeal of either American democracy or Soviet or Chinese communism." [1] The common denominator of Asian nationalism was always anti-imperialism, a sentiment expressed in the common aphorism of Asians: "We want friends, not bosses."

CHARACTERISTICS OF THE NEW ASIAN NATIONALISM

Asian nationalism is as difficult to define as its European counterpart. The concept was placed on the agenda of the Pacific Relations Conference which met at Lucknow toward the end of 1950. The inaugural address of Prime Minister Jawaharlal Nehru of India was intended as a defense of Asian nationalism. In a strange performance the speaker admitted that he could not define his subject:

So, if you meet here in India and consider problems of Asian nationalism and other problems, I wonder exactly what you mean by Asian nationalism. Is it different from the European variety, and if so, how does it differ? What exactly is nationalism? I do not know and it is extremely difficult to define, if you need to define it. In the case of a country under foreign domination it is easy to define what nationalism is. It is anti-foreign power. But, in a free country, what is nationalism?

Yet, the speaker went on to declare that "nationalism is a strong force today in every part of Asia. Any other force that may seek to function must define itself in terms of that nationalism." This led a commentator to observe: "Nationalism cannot be defined, but everything else must be defined in terms of this indefinable!" [2]

In general, nationalism in Asia was similar to the pattern elsewhere, whether in Europe, Africa, the Middle East, or the Americas. It dif-

[1] James Reston, in *The New York Times,* international ed., Sept. 9, 1965.
[2] M. N. Roy, "Asian Nationalism," *Yale Review,* XLII (Sept. 1952), 99.

fered in a way that can be explained best not by definition but by a set of characteristics. The over-all picture may be the same but the details vary.

In Asia, as elsewhere, nationalism appeared in a variety of forms. In India it took on the complexion of an ideological drive against colonial rule—a drive which was complicated by the love-hate attitude of Indians toward the British. In Indonesia it was a highly emotional demand for freedom from Dutch rule. In China it became the tool of a militant Communist leadership which appropriated what it claimed to be the orthodox Marxist-Leninist position and tried to expand its influence throughout Asia. Despite these variations in Asian nationalism, there was common ground:

Nationalism in Asia was distinguished by a mercurial, highly emotional quality. This characteristic was not unknown elsewhere, but in Asia it became a recognizable pattern. The situation was paradoxical: the stereotype of brooding Asian idols from which flowed a spirit of serenity, contemplation, and moral nobility coexisted with supercharged emotionalism, sometimes in fickle, sometimes in irrational form. But Asian nationalism was an overwhelming, on occasion uncontrollable, source of energy. Often it was difficult to recognize because it was not clearly formulated either in intellectual content or in practice. "It is, rather, a huge emotional reservoir which can be tapped for good or ill depending on the kind of leadership which captures it." [3]

This emotional quality was described by Rupert Emerson, who spoke on Asian nationalism to a group of Indian students at Benares in 1936. He opened his discussion with warm praise for the Indian nationalist movement and expressed hope that Indian independence did not lie too far in the future. This part of his talk was received with much enthusiasm:

I then moved on, however, to suggest that on the basis of European and other experience nationalism was not an unmixed blessing and that it embraced within it real sins and dangers which I hoped the leaders and the people of the new and rising India might find it possible to avoid. It was here . . . that the enthusiasm markedly cooled, perhaps because it was felt inappropriate for a Westerner to indulge in warnings to Indians concern-

[3] William L. Holland, ed., *Asian Nationalism and the West* (New York, 1953), pp. 4–5.

ing their own problems, perhaps because the nationalist movement represented so all-absorbing and sacred a cause as to make any suggestion of criticism unacceptable.[4]

This "all-absorbing and sacred" cause was deep-rooted and unpredictable. An example of its puzzling nature occurred in March 1966, when Indonesian army leaders, after a series of coups and counter-coups, and other political juggling, took over power from President Sukarno ("whom we all love"). It was a kind of indirect shadow play which bewildered most Westerners, but which to Indonesians seemed quite simple. This political intricacy may be recognized elsewhere (Kwame Nkrumah in Ghana, for example), but it reached its greatest subtlety in Asian nationalism.

The new Asian nationalism was primarily a negative concept. In country after country it started as a progressive, liberating force, only to become unhealthy and reactionary after liberation. Its positive qualities faded and became tarnished once the victory of liberation was won. Dynamic energies which had been devoted to the task of freedom began to wither away after private interests intruded upon the sense of public devotion.

In response to common need, Asian political parties united in opposition to the foreign devil. After years of subservience to foreign countries, the peoples of India, Pakistan, Ceylon, Burma, Indonesia, the Philippines, and Korea, among others, were able to achieve nationhood. But once freedom was attained, the nationalism that had won it took on a different aspect. Nationalist leaders were unable to go beyond the heady phase of anticolonialism. There were many problems to be solved, including social disunity, administrative inefficiency, and economic decline, but liberation leaders clung to the outworn slogans of the past. Asian leaders distracted attention from their own disastrous misrule by setting up false national purposes and by denouncing all political enemies as victims of neocolonialism. "From China to Indonesia, nationalism in Asia is totally negative: it expresses deep-seated hatred of anything resembling foreign control." [5]

Asian nationalism was beset by endemic communal clashes and hostilities. No continent has a monopoly of antagonisms and turmoil. The

[4] Rupert Emerson, "The Progress of Nationalism," in *Nationalism and Progress in Free Asia*, ed. Philip W. Thayer (Baltimore, 1956), p. 71.

[5] Theodore Hsi-En Chen, of the University of Southern California, quoted in *Time*, Apr. 9, 1965, p. 33.

history of most peoples includes chronicles of fighting: everywhere men of war are chosen as heroes. But the peoples of Asia, volatile and quick to anger, have been especially prone to race, class, and religious hatreds. The black-white antagonisms in Africa were mild compared to the plethora of enmities which colored Asian nationalism.

This disposition to friction made a successful Pan-Asian movement highly improbable. In 1947, Nehru, in an effort to achieve Asian solidarity, called the first Asian Relations Conference. In 1955 the Colombo powers (Pakistan, India, Ceylon, Indonesia, and Burma) convened the Asian-African Conference at Bandung. Here twenty-nine nations tried to speak in a common voice on economic and cultural cooperation, human rights, self-determination, problems of dependent peoples, and the promotion of world peace. The delegates condemned colonialism and declared their nonalignment in the cold war. But Bandung unity foundered on such issues as Sukarno's designs on Malaysia and Nasser's South Arabian Federation.

Hostility was a common condition throughout the continent. India and Pakistan were torn by ancient hatreds between Hindus and Muslims. After the British withdrew in 1947, ethnic and religious rivalries were perpetuated: the new frontiers left millions of Hindus and Muslims in the wrong countries, with the result that tens of thousands of both faiths were slaughtered. British-supported Malaysia and the former Dutch Indonesia were unfriendly neighbors. In both countries the inhabitants were locked in dangerous conflicts among themselves: Malaysia was torn by hatred between Malay and Chinese populations, and Indonesia by Communist and anti-Communist factions. Despite the centralized control in Communist China, there was friction between northern and southern Chinese, as well as discrimination against such minorities as the Tibetans. The peoples of Vietnam, Laos, and Cambodia, the former states of Indochina, all harbored ancient hatreds against each other. The Japanese took giant steps along the road to democracy, but they still showed contempt for the pariah Eta caste and for the despised immigrants from Korea. All over Asia, communal rivalries proved so bitter that nation-building became a process of the utmost complexity. Added to the accumulated antagonisms of the past were the fears and hostilities of the present.

Asian nationalism was tempered by religious feuds. Almost everywhere in Asia, with the exception of Communist China, three great religions—Hinduism, Buddhism, and Islam—had an impact on formative nationalism. The religions of Asia carried their old doctrines into the twentieth century. Hinduism retained a rigid caste system which outlawed the lower social orders.[6] High-caste Hindus sought purification if they came into accidental contact with even the shadow of an Untouchable. Legislation introduced to break down traditional prejudice against the 65,000,000 Untouchables had little effect.

Buddhism was equally divisive, despite its supposed tolerance.[7] Thousands of Buddhist monasteries throughout Southeast Asia helped keep alive their own languages, literature, and customs, and Buddhists returned hate for hate with other religions.

Similarly, India and Pakistan were torn by the old hatred between Hindus and Muslims. Pakistan was the more susceptible of the two to religious influences, for as a proselytizing religion, Islam counted retention and extension of the faith as a true element of nationhood.[8] The Islamic concept of holy war—the *jihad*—caused clashes throughout Asia because of its discrimination against infidels.

Asian nationalism took on the characteristics of linguistic rivalries. There were more than three thousand languages and dialects distributed throughout Asia. India is a nation of multiple languages. Minority groups have often made demands based on linguistic affinity, a practice which has caused the government considerable difficulty. When an attempt was made in early 1966 to pronounce Hindi the official tongue, even though it was understood by fewer than half the people, the minority groups staged bloody riots. Typical of the linguistic problem was Sikh nationalism in the Punjab, a large northwestern state on the subcontinent. The Sikhs demanded official recognition of Punjabi, the language spoken by seven million Sikhs and some Hindus in the Punjab, protesting that they were the victims of discrimination and asking that their Punjabi-speaking region be made into a separate state. Their Hindi-speaking neighbors opposed this request. The issue led to severe

[6] See B. R. Ambedkar, *The Untouchables* (New Delhi, 1949); Lewis S. S. O'Malley, *Popular Hinduism, the Religion of the Masses* (New York, 1935); and Jean A. Curran, *Militant Hinduism in Indian Politics* (New York, 1951).

[7] See Sir Charles N. E. Eliot, *Hinduism and Buddhism: An Historical Sketch* (2nd ed., 3 vols.; New York, 1954); Arthur F. Wright, *Buddhism in Chinese History* (Stanford, 1959); and Thomas David Whys, *Buddhist India* (Calcutta, 1957).

[8] See Wilfred C. Smith, *Modern Islam in India* (London, 1947); and Binyendra M. Chaudhuri, *Muslim Politics in India* (Calcutta, 1946).

clashes between Sikhs and Hindus. Three members of the ruling Congress Party who visited the Punjab were burned alive.

Asian nationalism was undemocratic. With few exceptions, notably India, the emergent nations of Asia preferred dictatorship. It was believed that only a dictator could mold the masses into a nation and prepare them for industrialization. When economic programs failed, the dictators turned to aggressive nationalism as a substitute. M. N. Roy made a distinction between Asian nationalism and democracy:

The bulk of the people throughout Asia are steeped in ignorance, which keeps them wedded to medieval prejudices. The teleological view of life, the most outstanding feature of the medieval religious culture, creates an authoritarian mentality—the psychological predisposition to cultivate submission as a virtue and to accept authority as providentially ordained. With the ignorant multitude, this cultural tradition takes the form of fatalism; it makes the politically-minded minority regard dictatorship or paternalism as more desirable than democracy.[9]

Asian nationalism should not be identified with the spirit of progress, the urge for freedom, and the preferences for constitutionalism and parliamentarianism which usually accompany the democratic way of life. Asian nationalism did not have in its background the cultural and idealist tradition with which the Enlightenment had provided the West. Asian nationalism sprang from anti-imperialism, which was but another aspect of hostility toward the white race. Added to this contempt for the foreign white devil was a series of racial hatreds that plagued Asian nations—Burmese against Indians, Japanese against Koreans, Indonesians against overseas Chinese, Indians against Tamils. The melting pot was rare in Asia. Under such circumstances Asian nationalism did not acquire freedom or constitutionalism or the other attributes of democracy.

NATIONALISM IN INDIA

British influence in India began in the early seventeenth century. The English East India Company, chartered in 1600, controlled key positions and provinces in the subcontinent until 1784, when Pitt's East

[9] M. N. Roy, "Democracy and Nationalism in Asia," *Pacific Affairs*, XXV, No. 2, p. 141.

India Bill created a board of control and placed political, financial, and military supervision in the hands of the government. In 1858, following the disaster of the Sepoy mutiny, administration was taken over by the crown. In 1876, Queen Victoria assumed the title Empress of India, and it became customary to speak of the Indian possession as "the brightest jewel in the British Crown." Most Englishmen looked upon the subjugation of India not as conquest but as a civilizing mission.

It was not easy to modernize India. The British ruled about three-fourths of the subcontinent. The 562 Indian states remaining were controlled by petty or major princes with varying degrees of autonomy under British protection. Some states were larger in area than certain European countries. The British retained control of foreign affairs, defense, and currency in the states of India.

British policy and methods in India aroused a desire for self-government and liberty—ideas unprecedented in the Orient. In 1835 the English historian Thomas Babington Macaulay, chairman of the Committee of Public Instruction in India, suggested that Indian education be based upon the study of the natural sciences and of the growth of liberty from ancient Greece to modern England.

It may be that the public mind of India may so expand under our system that it may outgrow that system and our subjects having been brought up under good government may develop a capacity for better government, that having been instructed in European learning, they may crave for European institutions. I know not whether such a day will ever come, but if it does come it will be the proudest day in the annals of England.[10]

Britain's political aims were laudatory, though they were difficult to realize. Socioeconomic difficulties were even greater. The British tried to meet the problem of population growth, for the subcontinent was overpopulated in relation to its food supply. They managed to reclaim 56,000,000 acres through irrigation. They built the great Ganges and Jumna canals with 1,200 miles of main channels and 6,500 miles of distributaries. But the industrialization process was painfully slow. There were comprehensive measures to combat epidemics, food shortages, local famine, and ravages of poverty.

Before the English came, India had been a huge battlefield for

[10] Quoted in Hans Kohn, *Nationalism: Its Meaning and History* (rev. ed.; Princeton, 1965), p. 85.

contending rulers and tribes. The British brought with them the advantages of peace and order. But to Indian nationalists British rule was progressive exploitation and manipulated division of the country. A break with orthodox traditionalism which prepared the way for Indian nationalism was made by Ram Mohan Roy, a Bengali Brahmin, who advocated social reform and a lessening of caste rigidity.[11] "The chief value of his labors, to our mind," wrote an Indian nationalist, "seems to lie in his fight against the forces of medievalism in India, and it is for this reason that we claim for him the honor of being the Father of the present Indian renaissance."[12] Indian nationalists, inspired by Ram Mohan Roy, began to insist that taxes and tariffs should be adjusted to benefit India, not Britain. Hardier souls called for independence.

At the end of 1885 the First Indian National Congress met in Bombay. Its purpose was to unify all the hostile and hitherto disparate elements in India, with its great number of principalities and its conflicting religions and castes. This was the first Asian conference to present a public platform for political aspirations. Though the membership of the Congress was overwhelmingly Hindu, in the first three decades of its existence three Muslims, four Englishmen, and one Parsee acted as its president, one Englishman twice and the Parsee three times.[13]

In the early twentieth century the leadership of the Indian National Congress shifted from liberal Westerners to the radical Indophiles. The latter were led by Bal Gandahar Tilak, who turned for inspiration to the Hindu past and called for a semireligious, fiercely xenophobic nationalism. In World War I, Indian princes and the masses remained loyal to Britain and furnished money and 1,200,000 fighting men for the war effort. In 1919 the British Parliament passed the Government of India Act, partly in recognition of India's loyalty during the war and partly as a concession to growing nationalist sentiment. The preamble described the policy of the British government "to provide for the increasing association of Indians in every branch of administration and the gradual development of self-governing institutions with a view to the progressive realization of responsible government in British India as an integral part of the British Empire." Indian civil servants

---

[11] Hans Kohn, *The Age of Nationalism: The First Era of Global History* (New York, 1962), p. 92.

[12] Bepin Chandra Pal, *The New Spirit* (Calcutta, 1907), p. 52.

[13] Kohn, *Nationalism: Its Meaning and History*, p. 86.

were allowed to take administrative positions. Most important was the establishment of a national parliament, with a Legislative Assembly and a Council of State, which met at Delhi. But only a million people in India's vast population were allowed to vote.

This act did not satisfy Indian nationalists, who wanted more responsible government both at central and at provincial levels. They continued to agitate for more basic reforms. In 1927 the British government appointed a royal commission under Sir John Simon to examine the situation. After two visits to India, the commission in 1930 presented its report, which called for greater Indian responsibility in administration, extension of suffrage, and a decentralized government. Indian nationalists condemned it "as a cup of milk for the hungry lion." More than 30,000 Indian patriots complained so loudly that they were jailed by the British.

By this time the leadership of Indian nationalists had shifted from Tilak to Mohandas Karamchand Gandhi (1869–1948), who became known to the world as a frail little man bowed down by the weight of years and by the sorrows of mankind. In 1888 he went to England, studied at London's University College, and was called to the bar at Inner Temple. He returned to India in 1891. After a visit to Pretoria, he decided to stay in South Africa to support the cause of Asiatic immigrants. Twenty-one years later he returned to India, where he began to apply the methods he had learned in South Africa.

Gandhi called for resistance to British imperialism by "soul force" and "noncooperation." This later developed into a general campaign of civil disobedience or nonviolent noncooperation. Gandhi explained his idea of passive resistance:

Passive resistance is a method of securing rights by personal suffering; it is the reverse of resistance by arms. When I refuse to do a thing that is [distasteful] to my conscience, I use soul-force. For instance, the government . . . has passed a law which is applicable to me. I do not like it. If by using violence I force the government to repeal the law, I am employing what may be termed body-force. If I do not obey the law and accept the penalty for its [violation], I use soul-force. It involves sacrifice of self. . . .

To use brute-force . . . is contrary to passive resistance, for it means that we want our opponent to do by force that which we desire but he does not. . . .

Passive resistance cannot proceed a step without fearlessness. Those alone can follow the path of passive resistance who are free from fear, whether as to their possessions, false honor, their relatives, the government, bodily injuries, or death.[14]

Preaching his concept of *satyagraha* (soul force), the little Hindu lawyer captured the imagination of the Indian people. Impressed by his ideals and saintly habits, they revered him as a *mahatma, a* "great-souled" or saintly man. Through Gandhi the nationalist movement reached India's more than half a million villages, penetrated into the urban factories and slums, and became truly a mass movement. The people scrupulously followed Gandhi's admonition to boycott all for-eign-made goods. Only in this way, Gandhi insisted, could *swaraj* (self-determination) be achieved.

Jawaharlal Nehru (1889–1964), who had been educated at Harrow and Trinity College, Cambridge, worked with Gandhi and later be-came his successor. A fervent apostle of Indian nationalism, Nehru resented Western imperialism:

Long subjection of a people and the denial of freedom bring many evils, and perhaps the greatest of these lies in the spiritual sphere—demoraliza-tion and sapping of the spirit of the people. It is hard to measure this, though it may be obvious. . . .

Nearly all our major problems . . . have grown up during British rule and as a direct result of British policy: . . . the minority problem; various [vested] interests, foreign and Indian; the lack of industry and the neglect of agriculture; the extreme backwardness in the social services; and above all, the tragic poverty of the people. . . .

The record of British rule in India during the nineteenth century must necessarily depress and anger an Indian.[15]

The policy of civil disobedience and boycott led to rioting and disorder for which both Gandhi and Nehru were jailed.[16] Meanwhile, an important role in the drive for independence was played by the Indian National Congress, which had been founded in 1885.[17] By 1935 the Congress was in reality a native parliament which represented the

[14] Mohandas K. Gandhi, *Hind Swaraj or Indian Home Rule* (Vithalnagar, India, 1938), pp. 131–136.

[15] Jawaharlal Nehru, *The Discovery of India* (New York, 1959), pp. 215, 221.

[16] In all, Nehru spent thirteen years in prison for illegal and subversive activities.

[17] On the Indian National Congress, see Hemendra N. Das Gupta, *The Indian National Congress* (Calcutta, 1946); Indian National Congress, *Congress Presiden-tial Addresses,* (2 vols.; Madras, 1934–1935); Bhogaraju Pattabhi Sitaramayya, *The History of the Indian National Congress,* (2nd ed., 2 vols.; Bombay, 1946–1947).

Hindu masses. In August 1942, in the midst of World War II, the Congress launched what was virtually a rebellion all over India against British rule. The British, refusing to yield, jailed Congress leaders for the duration of the war.

The drive for independence was made more difficult by the conflict between Hindus and Muslims. The Indian National Congress, Hindu in composition, had to contend with Muslim rivalry. In 1906 the Muslim League had been organized and for some years it had worked with the multicommunal Indian National Congress.[18] The Muslim minority, under the leadership of Mohammed Ali Jinnah (1876–1948), demanded that those parts of India where the Muslim population was most heavily concentrated should become a separate state when independence was won. To this the Indian National Congress was violently opposed, but the failure of the government to overcome friction between the Indian National Congress and the Muslim League convinced the British that no solution to the problem could be made without partition. By early 1947, London announced that there would be a one-year deadline for the transfer of power to Indian hands.

The India Independence Bill was introduced into the British Parliament in July 1947 and became law in two weeks. India became independent on August 15, 1947. Both India and Pakistan decided to remain inside the Commonwealth as separate dominions with full sovereignty. This was the most momentous step in the history of decolonization, for British India had been the most conspicuous symbol of European imperial power. Yet, the British withdrew quickly. It took less than half a century for Britain to release its hold on India.[19]

The triumph of Indian nationalism did not resolve ethnic and religious antagonisms among the peoples of the subcontinent. The new frontiers of India and Pakistan were set up in such a way that millions of Hindus and Muslims were left outside their preferred countries. In a little over a year about five million had moved from one dominion to the other, seeking security among their coreligionists.

The Republic of India, with a population of 446,000,000 (exceeded only by China's 710,000,000), struggled with enormous political, eco-

[18] On the Muslim League, see Wilfred C. Smith, *The Muslim League, 1942–1945* (Lahore, 1945); Binayendra M. Chaudhuri, *Muslim Politics in India* (Calcutta, 1946); and Walter E. Duffett, *India Today: The Background of the Indian Nationalist Movement* (Toronto, 1941).

[19] Kohn, *The Age of Nationalism*, p. 98.

nomic, and educational problems. On January 30, 1948, Gandhi was assassinated by a Hindu extremist, and was succeeded by Nehru. Pakistan, a new nation of 99,000,000, mostly Muslims, began its existence under handicaps of geographic division, backwardness, corruption, and inexperienced administrators. Under Field-Marshal Mohammed Ayub Khan, president of the republic, reforms were inaugurated.

Since the sixteenth-century Mogul invasion of India, Muslims and Hindus had fought for control of the subcontinent. The centuries-old feud had been sublimated to some extent during the long era of British rule, but with independence in 1947 it burst into flame at its old heat. Hatreds increased as nationalism solidified in both India and Pakistan. The old attacks were repeated: Muslims charged that Hindus were caste-ridden, and Hindus countered that Muslims were unclean. The Muslims ate cows; the Hindus worshipped them. The result was a communal purge with slaughter on both sides. In late 1965, India and Pakistan went to war but quickly came to terms after pressure from the United Nations and Western supporters of both countries.

Although India has had a long history, Indian nationalism was a product of only the last century. Educated Indians became the fathers of Indian nationalism. Those who studied at British universities [20] learned Western ideas of freedom, constitutionalism, parliamentarianism, and nationalism:

They have imbibed the ideas which we ourselves have set before them, and we ought to reckon it to their credit. The present intellectual and moral stir in India is no reproach but rather a tribute to our works. . . . [The educated Indian] has conceived and pursued the idea of managing his own affairs, an aim which no Englishman can fail to respect. . . . He has by speeches and in the press done much to spread the idea of a united and self-respecting India among thousands who had no such conception in their minds.[21]

The British helped to create Indian nationalism without willing it. Later, until about 1937, they found themselves more and more obliged to resist its development.

Throughout its history in the course of the last century Indian

[20] In 1923 the English universities counted among their students 1,401 from Asia (among whom 1,094 from India and Ceylon) and 1,171 from Africa (among whom 298 from Egypt); see Kohn, *The Age of Nationalism*, p. 93.

[21] *Montagu-Chelmsford Report on Constitutional Reforms in India* (London, 1918), Article 139.

nationalism has been distinguished by its nonmilitant character. This does not mean that domestic politics were peaceful. There were advocates of terrorism to achieve independence, but by far the dominant philosophy was that projected by Gandhi in the thirty years from 1917 to 1947. Gandhi's teaching that hate should be returned with love, that violence corrupted the soul, and that British laws must be greeted with nonviolence and noncooperation had a tremendous effect on the Indian masses. They understood him when he wrote to a British official: "I cannot intentionally hurt anything that lives, much less human beings, even though they may do the greatest wrong to me and mine."

Gandhian nationalism thus succeeded in attaining independence through nonviolence. There are some who say that mutual slaughter of Hindus and Muslims after partition indicated the bankruptcy of the Gandhian ideology. Yet, it left a residue. The war between India and Pakistan in late 1965 did not escalate and was soon halted.

The older form of Gandhian nationalism sought to soothe internal rivalries between Hindu nationalism and Muslim separatist nationalism. In its early stages the Indian National Congress adopted a secular policy by inviting Indians of all denominations to its meetings. But gradually the Congress took on the coloration of Hindu nationalism with scarcely concealed anti-Muslim overtones. The division of the subcontinent into India and Pakistan was the logical outcome of this process. It meant the solidification of Hindu and Muslim nationalisms in a kind of politico-biological process by which one cell was split into two. The story of these two nationalisms and their relation with one another is still unfolding.

CASE HISTORY: ACHMED SUKARNO
AND INDONESIAN NATIONALISM

Among the political difficulties of the new states in Asia and Africa [22] was the inadequacy of nationalist leaders. There were exceptions, of course, but most liberation leaders who demonstrated ability in the

[22] For recent research on the emergence of the new sovereignties, see Max F. Millikan and Donald L. L. Blackmer, eds., *The Emerging Nations: Their Growth and United States Policy* (Boston, 1961); Gabriel A. Almond and James S. Coleman, *The Politics of the Developing Areas* (Princeton, 1960); Clifford Geertz, ed., *Old Societies and New States: The Quest for Modernity in Asia and Africa* (Glencoe, Ill., 1963); and John H. Kautsky, ed., *Political Change in Underdeveloped Countries: Nationalism and Communism* (New York, 1962).

drive for independence were unequal to the task of exercising responsibility when in power. An example may be found in the decolonization of Indonesia and the career of Achmed Sukarno.[23]

The Netherlands East Indies before 1950 consisted of an area of 735,000 square miles and a population of approximately seventy million, two-thirds of whom were concentrated in the islands of Java and Sumatra. One of the world's richest areas, it had great wealth in tin, rubber, spices, oil, quinine, and copra. The Dutch gradually extended their power over the great domain from 1798, when they took over the Dutch East India Company. The mother country benefited not only from trade with her rich colony but also from investment in the islands.

The Dutch, reluctant to grant self-government to this carefully guarded society, were convinced that their paternal rule afforded the East Indies a modern administration and satisfactory progress. They tried to encourage old social and cultural traditions in the islands as a means of protecting them from the impact of Western nationalism. They favored the dominantly Chinese class of businessmen, protected the plantation-owners of European origin, and left the people largely in a position of subservience. At the turn of the century, when the Dutch parliament took over control of colonial affairs from the crown, a so-called ethical policy was introduced. A corps of highly trained experts was charged with the task of steering the wards of the Netherlands toward gradual modernization while at the same time shielding them from social disintegration. The new approach represented a genuine, if half-hearted, concern for the welfare of the people.[24]

Although the islands were spread over a distance of three thousand miles and although they were inhabited by a variety of peoples, there were some elements of unity. The people were mostly Muslim in religion, and the Malay language was understood everywhere. Gradu-

[23] On the decolonization of Indonesia see George McT. Kahin, *Nationalism and Revolution in Indonesia* (Ithaca, N.Y., 1952); David Wehl, *The Birth of Indonesia* (London, 1948); Charles Wolf, Jr., *The Indonesian Story* (New York, 1948). See also Fred Greene, "The Nationalist Revolution in Indonesia," in Andrew Gyorgy and Hubert S. Gibbs, eds., *Problems in International Relations* (New York, 1955), pp. 207–217; Hubertus J. van Mook, "Indonesia and the Problem of Southeast Asia," *Foreign Affairs*, XXVII (July 1949), 561–575; and Harry J. Benda, "Decolonization in Indonesia: The Problem of Continuity and Change," *American Historical Review*, LXX (July 1965), 1058–1073.

[24] Benda, *op. cit.*, p. 1060. See also J. J. van Klaveren, *The Dutch Colonial System in the East Indies* (The Hague, 1953), and B. H. M. Vlekke, *Nusantara: A History of the East Indian Archipelago* (Cambridge, Mass., 1943), chs. xiv, xv.

ally, a nationalist movement rose to challenge Dutch control. Added to the desire for self-government was an economic factor—the Netherlands had tried to supply all the manufactured goods required in the Indies from factories in the home country.[25] Indonesian patriots, regarding this pressure as unfair, decried the difference in standards of living in the Netherlands and in the Indies. There was also disenchantment with discrimination in education.

The emergence of an organized nationalist movement was slow, largely because of the lack of effective leadership. Shrewdly utilizing the old aristocratic elite as their agents in the islands, the Dutch were able to render ineffective the protests of budding nationalists against foreign rule. Not until politically conscious labor groups appeared in cities and on plantations did the movement obtain the leadership necessary to direct their "inchoate nationalist feeling." [26] Indonesians who had acquired a Western education were angered by policies of discrimination in both government and business employment. This growing elite provided latent Indonesian nationalism with the leadership it required to become an active movement.[27]

In 1913 the Partai Sarekat was founded and quickly took over control of the Indonesian nationalist movement. Within seven years it had a membership of 2,500,000. In the 1920's the Dutch government set up a rigid system of political control which kept the nationalist movement neutralized. Its leaders were interned. Meanwhile, in 1925, the Dutch passed the Indies Government Act, which gave some control to Indonesians but reserved final authority for Dutch officials.

After the catastrophe of Pearl Harbor, the Japanese occupied the Dutch colonial realm in the East Indies.[28] During the forty months of occupation Dutch rule evaporated. The Japanese released imprisoned Indonesian nationalists and set up a puppet government. The flourishing modern economy was milked for Japanese benefit. This turbulent

[25] See W. F. Wertheim, *Indonesian Society in Transition: A Study of Social Change* (The Hague, 1959), pp. 91–105.

[26] George McT. Kahin, "Indonesian Politics and Nationalism," in William L. Holland, ed., *Asian Nationalism and the West* (New York, 1953), p. 68.

[27] *Ibid.*

[28] On the Japanese occupation, see Willard H. Elsbree, *Japan's Role in Southeast Asian Nationalist Movements, 1940 to 1945* (Cambridge, Mass., 1953); B. R. O'G. Anderson, *Some Aspects of Indonesian Politics under the Japanese Occupation, 1944-1945* (Ithaca, N.Y., 1961); and M. A. Aziz, *Japan's Colonialism and Indonesia* (The Hague, 1955).

period acted as a kind of sociopolitical catalyst, unleashing the revolution.[29] The Dutch lost prestige by their weak defense against the invaders and by their refusal to permit Indonesians to obtain arms for defense. At the same time the Japanese started a propaganda campaign to discredit the Dutch. Even more important was Japanese support for Indonesian nationalist leaders, especially Achmed Sukarno. The Indonesian nationalist movement became stronger and was better equipped to fight the Dutch when the latter returned and tried to reassert their authority.[30]

British troops who came to the islands in 1945 found that the nationalists, now organized in strong army cadres, were in no mood to return to Dutch rule. Nor were the British, after the exhausting war, inclined to assist the Dutch in Indonesia. They advised the Dutch to negotiate some kind of settlement. The Dutch proposed that the islands become a democratic Commonwealth of Indonesia in union with the Netherlands. To the nationalists this proposal for federation was anathema; they wanted independence and a treaty between sovereign powers. The Linggadjati agreement, signed on March 25, 1947, was a compromise calling for a federated United States of Indonesia (USI) bound to the Netherlands in an indissoluble union. The pact was ratified by the Dutch and Indonesian legislatures in March 1947.

Meanwhile, the situation remained tense. Nationalist underground activity increased and the Dutch enhanced their military power. In the summer of 1947, Dutch troops invaded Java, the coast of Sumatra, and all of Madura. The United Nations intervened, but in December 1948 the Dutch started a so-called police action that was actually a war against the nationalists. After world-wide denunciations and severe criticism in United Nations debates, the Dutch international position deteriorated rapidly.

Another attempt to solve the problem was made with an agreement concluded at The Hague on November 2, 1949, providing for a Netherlands-Indonesian Union, but this, too, was unfruitful. Without international support, the Dutch were too weak to retain control of their rich colony.

The key figure in the drive for Indonesian independence was Achmed Sukarno (Soekarno), born in Surabaja, Java, the son of a schoolteacher. As a high school student he was influenced by several

[29] Benda, *op. cit.,* p. 1061.   [30] Kahin, *op. cit.,* p. 70.

nationalist leaders. After he obtained an engineer's degree from Bandung Technical College in 1925, he devoted all his energy to the nationalist cause. As a young revolutionary he called for "Marhaenism," which he described as "a type of Marxian socialism adapted to the Indonesian community and spirit." In 1928 he became one of the founders of the Indonesian Nationalist Party (PNU). Jailed repeatedly by the Dutch, he was in prison when the Japanese landed in Indonesia in 1942.

From the beginning of their occupation the Japanese allowed Sukarno and other revolutionary leaders wide latitude to build up the nationalist movement.

The direct contact which Sukarno and others were allowed with rural and urban labor and the skill of the Indonesian underground organizations, particularly those led by Sjahrir and Sjarifuddin, in supplementing their work resulted in a much greater stimulus to the nationalist movement than the Japanese had expected. By 1945 Indonesians were not only keyed to a higher pitch of nationalism than ever before, but the orientation of that nationalism was as much anti-Japanese as it was anti-Dutch; and though it was anti-Dutch, it was for the most part well disposed towards the other Allies.[31]

On December 27, 1949, after the formal transfer of sovereignty at Amsterdam, Sukarno was elected president of Indonesia. Thus began the extraordinary career of a charismatic leader in power. The former revolutionary continued to set ideological goals. Now he pointed the way to a glorious future by projecting what he called the five principles of "Pantasila"—belief in God, humanism, nationalism, democracy, and social justice.

Even more important in Sukarno's gallery of ideas was the principle which he represented by the acronym "Nasakom," a national front blending nationalist, religious, and Communist forces. This was political expediency, for Sukarno was faced with a critical power struggle inside Indonesia and he decided to use his power of persuasion to mediate between opposing factions. To accomplish this it was necessary that he walk a tight line between the right-wing nationalistic generals who controlled the army [32] and the powerful Indonesian Com-

[31] *Ibid.*, pp. 70–71.

[32] On the Indonesian army, which played a decisive role during the Sukarno regime, see Daniel S. Lev, "The Political Role of the Army in Indonesia," *Pacific Affairs*, XXXVI (Winter 1963–1964), 349–365.

munist Party (PKI) with about 3,500,000 members.[33] Sukarno would use Nasakom to settle internal conflicts by the Indonesian customs of *musjawarah* (peaceful discussion) and *mufakaat* (consensus). Above all, he would seek to retain the Communist "kom" in his beloved Nasakom, on the principle that the Indonesian revolution was left-wing. He denounced those whom he described by the acronym "Nek-olim"—neocolonialists, colonialists, and imperialists, who, he said, were seeking to push Indonesia to the right. Nekolim, he predicted, would be defeated by "Nefos" (newly emerging forces) that would destroy imperialism.

Sukarno spoke grandiloquently of discussion, consensus, and democracy, but he carefully announced that he was the originator of a "guided democracy," specifically Indonesian.[34] There was no mystery here: guided democracy was merely disguised dictatorship. Sukarno cast aside all constitutional restraints and eventually proclaimed himself president for life. He lived like an oriental potentate, moved from palace to palace, and surrounded himself with flatterers, all in the midst of accelerating poverty. A superb orator, he addressed throngs of 150,000 in the Merdeka (Independence) Square of Djakarta. Like Nkrumah in Ghana, Sukarno used the techniques of American advertising to build up his image as "Great Leader of the Revolution," "The Beloved Immortal," and "Bung [Brother] Karno." On occasion he could be suitably modest. He would appall his followers by hinting at his possible death: "Sukarno is just a man. Like you, sisters and brothers, my age is in the hands of God." [35] At the same time he could place himself on a plane with Washington, Jefferson, Garibaldi, Mazzini, and Cromwell.[36]

To the outside world Sukarno's political policy seemed erratic and paradoxical. He announced that he would re-create *majapahit*, the great Javanese empire of the tenth to the fifteenth century. He proposed himself as the authentic leader of the Afro-Asian world. He withdrew Indonesia from the United Nations and from the World

[33] On the Indonesian Communist Party, see Ewa T. Pauker, "Has the Sukarno Regime Weakened the PKI?" *Asian Survey*, IV (Sept. 1964), 1058–1070.

[34] See Harry J. Benda, "Democracy in Indonesia," *Journal of Asian Studies*, XXIII (May 1964), 448–456; and Willard A. Hanna, *Bung Karno's Indonesia* (New York, 1961).

[35] *The New York Times*, international ed., Aug. 28, 1945.

[36] Achmed Sukarno, "Address to the National Press Club," May 18, 1956, *Department of State Bulletin*, XXIV (June 4, 1956), 936–939.

Bank. He spurned assistance from the United States ("To hell with your aid!"), as well as investments from the Western world, which in Sukarno's language were "Olefos" (old established forces). He accepted assistance from both Moscow and Peking.

The veteran fighter for national liberation turned to an aggressive nationalism. He proposed "confrontation," or a "crush Malaysia" policy. Malaysia, a new nation set up by the British on September 16, 1963, consisted of four million Malays, four million Chinese, a million Indians and Pakistanis, and 700,000 Koreans, Eurasians, and British. The member states were Malaya, Singapore, and the Borneo territories of Sarawak and Sabah. The British retained a defense base in Malaysia, and the country remained a member of the Commonwealth. Sukarno interpreted the formation of the new federation as a deadly plot to "encircle Indonesia." He was especially concerned about the peoples of Sarawak and Sabah who shared the islands of Borneo with the Indonesians. He announced to the world that "by the time the cock crows on January 1, 1965," his confrontation with Malaysia would end in victory. Appealing to Indonesian patriotism, he called for destruction of the new country.

The difficulty was that Sukarno's nationalism was operating in a vacuum. Indonesia, one of the most fertile countries on earth, had a potentially productive and prosperous economy. Sukarno proclaimed that in twenty years Indonesia would be the richest nation in the world. Instead, he drove it straight toward bankruptcy. At one time a rice-surplus area, Indonesia by 1965 was reduced to importing 150,000 tons of rice a year. The price of this staple food rose tenfold from 1963 to 1965. The formerly productive tin mines and rubber plantations deteriorated until they became almost useless. Housing, education, and hygiene remained at deplorably low levels.

In this chaotic situation Sukarno's talk about "the liberating effect of nationalism" aroused little enthusiasm. His seizure of foreign properties could not stem economic disaster. Nor could his militant nationalism exercised against Malaysia, the main target, and also against every Western country which he linked to imperialism, turn the people away from their immediate problem of the increasing poverty. His popularity with the masses declined rapidly.[37] In late 1965, after an abortive

[37] The extent of friction may be gauged from the five assassination attempts on Sukarno's life from 1957 to 1965: by grenade at Djakarta (1947), by mortar fire in Makassar (1958), by air attack on two presidential palaces (1960), by grenade in

Communist coup, a group of generals seized power, relegated Sukarno to a secondary role, and tried to solve critical problems in government, foreign policy, and the economy. Whether they can establish a regime viable enough to prevent a Communist resurgence remains to be seen.[38]

The rise and fall of Indonesia's flamboyant leader illustrates the pitfalls of nation-building in the contemporary era. Charismatic leadership and nationalist slogans have not been enough to provide some emergent nations with the strength to survive at a satisfactory level. Sukarno's brand of mystic nationalism did not fulfill its glittering promises to the Indonesian people. His fall was marked by popular disenchantment with his pretensions as a national hero. What Indonesia needed, said one disappointed nationalist leader, was "not Sukarno but rice and trousers."

THE THREE FACES OF CHINESE
ANTICOLONIAL NATIONALISM

At the beginning of the nineteenth century the Manchu dynasty held nominal control over a huge empire stretching from central Asia to the Pacific and from Siberia to India.[39] Chinese society was rigid in structure, proud of its culture, contemptuous of foreigners, and devoid of national feeling. The initial attempt to open China to the West was made by the British in the Opium War (1839–1842).[40] For some time British merchants enjoyed a lucrative trade by gathering the opium poppy in India and selling it in the huge Chinese market. When the Chinese government sought to abolish the practice, the British intervened. The brief conflict ended in humiliating defeat for China. The Treaty of Nanking, signed on August 29, 1842, required China to pay a heavy indemnity, to cede the island of Hong Kong to England, and to

---

Makassar (January 1962), and by gunfire at Djakarta (May 1962). Sukarno escaped unscathed each time, but at least ten bystanders were killed in these attacks.

[38] Some 87,000 Communists were said to have been liquidated in the vengeful months following the coup that failed. In the Communists' attempt to gain power they murdered the best of the army generals. The popular reaction against communism was devastating.

[39] On the Manchu dynasty see Franz Michael, *The Origin of Manchu Rule in China* (Baltimore, 1942); John Ross, *The Manchus* (Paisley, Scotland, 1880); and Percy H. Kent, *The Passing of the Manchus* (London, 1912).

[40] See Arthur Waley, *The Opium War through Chinese Eyes* (London, 1958).

open five ports (Canton, Ningpo, Foochow, Shanghai, and Amoy), as well as other cities, to British trade.[41]

European trade increased as a result of the Treaty of Nanking and subsequent treaties (called "unequal treaties" by the Chinese) between China and other countries. The Chinese people were hostile toward European merchants and missionaries living in treaty ports. A second Anglo-Chinese war was set off in 1857, when Chinese officials boarded a ship bearing the British flag to arrest a Chinese murderer in the crew. France joined the conflict. Again the Chinese were defeated, whereupon they hastened to make peace with the Treaty of Tientsin, signed June 26, 1858.[42] Similar treaties were made with France, Russia, and the United States. China was now opened to foreign penetration on a major scale.

After the military weakness of China was revealed in the Sino-Japanese War of 1894–1895, the major powers, one after another, began to demand political and economic concessions in the form of leaseholds and spheres of influence. Germany in 1898 obtained a 99-year lease on the harbor of Kiao-chao, France leased Kwang-chao-wan, England the port of Wei-hai-wei, and Russia took the Manchurian peninsula on a 25-year lease. In this "Battle for the Concessions" the imperialist powers extracted rights from the Peking government to build railroads and mines and to lease coastal areas for naval bases. Each imperialist power sent soldiers, missionaries, merchants, and engineers into its sphere of influence. The United States, oscillating between humanitarian ideals and strategic realism, between involvement and abstention, proposed an "Open Door policy" allowing all countries to trade without hindrance in China.[43]

It was only natural that the spoliation of China should arouse opposition. Angered and humiliated Chinese nationalists pointed out that their country, unlike India, was not a colony and deserved better treatment. They denounced the leaseholds and concessions, rights of extraterritoriality, and greedy demands of the European powers for trade preference. Chinese opposition to Western colonialism took three forms:

[41] See Edward Hertslet, ed., *China Treaties between Great Britain and China*, I (London, 1908), 7–12.

[42] *Ibid.*, I, 18–35.

[43] For the step-by-step formulation of the Open Door policy see William W. Malloy, ed., *Treaties, Conventions, International Acts, Protocols, and Agreements between the United States of America and other Powers* (Washington, D.C., 1910–1923), I, 244–260.

traditionalist nationalism, Westernized nationalism, and Communist nationalism.

Traditionalist nationalism. Growing Western domination aroused resistance among all classes of Chinese. The traditionalists, active during the early stages of Western penetration, opposed European civilization and demanded that it have no contact with their own. This attitude was more a defensive reaction than a true nationalism: the Chinese would retain their own culture in the midst of imperial pressures. After it became obvious that the ancient technique of playing one barbarian off against another had failed, Chinese intellectuals for the first time began to advocate reform. They would retain ancient values but they would institute reforms to obtain an honorable place for China in the modern world.

Outstanding among these traditional nationalists were Chang Chih-tung (1837–1909) and K'ang Yu-wei (1858–1927). Chang Chih-tung, a government official and administrator, envisioned a new nation which would combine the holy teaching of Confucianism with the strength provided by modern ways and means. Confucianism combined with Western technology, he said, would save the new China:

We should here state that there are now three things necessary to be done in order to save China from revolution. The first is to maintain the reigning dynasty; the second is to conserve the holy religion; and the third is to protect the Chinese race. These are inseparably connected; in fact they constitute one; for in order to protect the Chinese race we must first conserve the religion, and if the religion is to be conserved we are bound to maintain the dynasty. But, it may be asked, how can we protect the race? We reply, by knowledge; and knowledge is religion; and religion is propagated by strength; and strength lies in troops. . . .

In order to render China powerful, and at the same time preserve our own institutions, it is absolutely necessary that we should utilize Western knowledge. But unless Chinese learning is made the basis of education, and a Chinese direction is given to thought, the strong will become anarchists, and the weak slaves. Thus, the latter end will be worse than the former.[44]

K'ang Yu-wei, historian and philologist, said that his study of Confucianism had led him to the conclusion that its ideas were being perverted by the monarchy and its obedient scholar-bureaucrat sup-

[44] Chang Chih-tung, "Learn," trans. S. I. Woodbridge (Shanghai, n.d.), pp. 8–9, 13–14.

porters. He regarded Confucianism as public spiritedness and equality
instead of the corrupt selfishness and subjective authoritarianism typical of the government of his day. K'ang's proposal for changing the
civil service examinations to cover modern knowledge was accepted by
the emperor.[45]

Other traditional nationalists were angered by mild words and called
instead for activism in the struggle against the foreign devils. The
I-ho-ch'uan (Righteous Harmony Band) came to be known as Boxers
when the Chinese word was mistaken by Westerners for a similar word
meaning "fists." The society made its appearance in northern China in
1898. Originally aimed at Roman Catholic missionaries and converted
Chinese, the movement opposed everything foreign. Both old and
young flocked to the society and formed themselves into small bands.
Every Boxer was assured that he was immune to death or injury
because his body was protected from sword cuts and bullets. "Protect
the country; destroy the foreigner," was a favorite Boxer slogan. A
typical Boxer placard read:

> The Gods assist the Boxers,
> The Patriotic Harmonious Corps,
> It is because the Foreign Devils disturb the Middle Kingdom. . . .
> Push aside the railway tracks,
> Pull out the telegraph poles,
> Immediately after this destroy the steamers.
>
> The great France
> Will grow cold and downhearted.
> The English and Russians will certainly disperse.
> Let all the Foreign Devils be killed.
> May the whole Elegant Empire of the Great Ching Dynasty be ever
>   prosperous! [46]

Unchecked, the Boxers began looting, burning, robbing, and killing
until they were beyond control. In 1900 an attack on foreigners took
242 lives. The Western powers, including the United States and Japan,
sent military expeditions to rescue their besieged nationals.[47] To atone

[45] David Nelson Rowe, *Modern China* (Princeton, 1959), p. 31.

[46] Translation by Chinese scholars in the May 5, 1900, issue of the Peking and
Tientsin *Times*.

[47] On the Boxer uprising, see Chester C. Tan, *The Boxer Catastrophe* (New
York, 1955); and George N. Steiger, *China and the Occident: The Origin and
Development of the Boxer Movement* (New Haven, 1927).

for the uprising the Chinese were required to pay an indemnity of $333,000,000.[48]

It became obvious that traditional nationalism, vague and ephemeral in intellectual content, and wild and blustering in its activist phase, was not a satisfactory response to Chinese national needs. No traditionalist was successful in taking over command of a major nationalist movement.

Westernized nationalism. Once imperialism began to weaken, control of Chinese nationalism was assumed by leaders who had been educated in the West and were familiar with Western ideologies of nationalism, democracy, and socialism. Outstanding among the revolutionary leaders was Sun Yat-sen (1866–1925), who for years worked tirelessly to reform and modernize China.[49] Along with his Western education, Sun was influenced by the ideals of the American and French revolutions. The basis of his program was what he called the "Three Principles of the People"—nationalism, political democracy, and the "people's livelihood." Nationalism meant achieving a political unity that would enable the Chinese to resist the colonial powers. Democracy was to be reached by stages—military control, education for self-government, then a democratic central government. The "people's livelihood" was a far-reaching plan for modernization of industry and agriculture. But nationalism was central to Sun's philosophy. In the struggle between nationalism and cosmopolitanism, he preferred the former:

Nationalism is a treasure, the possession of which causes a nation to aspire to greater development, and a race to seek to perpetuate itself. China today has lost that treasure. . . . Cosmopolitanism has been the cause of the decadence of China. . . . Cosmopolitanism will cause further decadence if we leave the reality, nationalism, for the shadow, cosmopolitanism. . . .

First let us practice nationalism; cosmopolitanism will follow.

If henceforth we Chinese find some way of reviving our nationalism . . . then no matter what foreign political and economic force will oppress us, our race undoubtedly will not be extinguished in a thousand or even ten thousand years.[50]

[48] Several years later the United States turned back a large share of its indemnity to China and asked that it be used to pay for the education of Chinese students in America.

[49] On Sun Yat-sen, see Paul M. W. Linebarger, *Sun Yat-sen and the Chinese Republic* (New York, 1925); Abbie M. Sharman, *Sun Yat-sen: His Life and Its Meaning* (New York, 1934); and Marius B. Jansen, *The Japanese and Sun Yat-sen* (Cambridge, Mass., 1954).

[50] *The Triple Demism of Sun Yat-sen*, trans. Paschal M. D'Elia (Wuchang, 1931), pp. 118, 130–135, 137.

Sun Yat-sen's ambition was realized in part when Manchu rule collapsed. In October 1911 the smoldering resentment against the government that had resisted modernization and reform and had allowed foreigners to seize its essential powers came to a head. On February 12, 1912, the Manchu dynasty was driven from power and the Chinese Republic established. The first decade of the Republic's life was a dangerous and depressing period in which competing war lords engaged in a confusing struggle. Sun sought to carry out his program under the Kuomintang (National People's Party) until the nation was ready for full democracy. He accepted assistance from Russian Communists, who predictably tried to swing the Kuomintang toward communism. In 1925, Sun traveled to northern China in a fruitless attempt to persuade the war lords to support the Republic. He died on March 12, 1925.

From then on the leading Kuomintang figure was Chiang Kai-shek (1887–), apostle of democratic nationalism.[51] The Kuomintang was beset with factionalism, the curse of Chinese politics. But under Chiang Kai-shek the Nationalist Party took over China and ruled it from 1926 to 1930. Chiang Kai-shek balanced the budget and won the support of foreign governments by a program of national consolidation. Progress was made toward abolishing special foreign privileges in China and regaining full self-government. This inevitably brought friction from two sources, the Communists and Japan. Chinese nationalism and Japanese imperialism were on a collision course: the impact came in 1931 with Japanese aggression in Manchuria.

Communist nationalism. The threat of communism in China came not so much from the Soviet Union, which did not wish involvement with China, but from Communists inside the country. The small intellectual elite of Westernizing nationalists, including Sun Yat-sen and Chiang Kai-shek, unfortunately had little contact with the masses. This became an insurmountable handicap as Communist propaganda took advantage of political chaos and the continued poverty of the people. Chinese Communists learned a basic lesson from Europe: they sought to combine nationalism, industrialization, and Marxism in a package irresistible to the masses.

In 1927, Chiang Kai-shek became embroiled in civil war with the

---

[51] On Chiang Kai-shek, see Hollington K. Tong, *Chiang Kai-shek, Soldier and Statesman* (Shanghai, 1937; rev. ed., Taipei, 1953); Emily Hahn, *Chiang Kai-shek* (New York, 1955); and *The Collected Wartime Messages of Generalissimo Chiang Kai-shek, 1937–1945* (2 vols.; New York, 1946).

Communists. During World War II, both Nationalists and Communists united against Japan as the common enemy, but there was little trust on either side. Expelled from the cities of eastern China, the Nationalists began to lose popular support just at the time when the Communists were gaining it by propaganda at the grass-roots level. When the Japanese surrendered in September 1945, the stage was ready for a showdown between Nationalists and Communists. The critical confrontation took place in Manchuria. Though the invading Russians had signed a treaty with Chiang pledging support, they allowed the Chinese Communists to appropriate the huge store of Japanese arms there.

Because China was split between Nationalists and Communists, the United States sent General George C. Marshall on a peace mission. It was unsuccessful. Neither side was ready for compromise. By the end of 1946, the civil war was on again in full blast. Three million Nationalist troops held the cities, while a million Communist guerrillas occupied the countryside. Chiang's government, weakened by graft, corruption, and inefficiency, made no effort to improve the lot of the peasantry—a critical mistake that worked to the advantage of the Communists. The Communists, on the other hand, exploited the weaknesses of the Kuomintang government. They won peasant support by proposing and instituting land reforms. They attracted students and intellectuals. Meanwhile, they were winning in the field, laying siege to Nationalist garrisons and cutting off communications between them. City after city in Manchuria fell to the Communists, who then turned south.

The year 1949 marked the collapse of Nationalist China. In April the Communists crossed the Yangtze River and captured Nanking, the capital. Shanghai soon fell. In October the People's Republic of China was proclaimed with its capital at Peiping, renamed Peking. Nationalist resistance ended on the mainland and Chiang Kai-shek and his defeated government fled to the island of Formosa, or Taiwan, just a hundred and ten miles off the coast of southern China. Here, supported by American aid, Chiang awaited the day of his return.

Communist China, under the leadership of Mao Tse-tung and his lieutenants, Chou En-lai, Chu Teh, and Liu Shao-chi, turned the "people's democratic state" to totalitarianism. The seventeen million members of the Communist Party were given the task of transforming the country.[52] Here the Chinese leaned heavily on Russian experience, incorporating secret police, mass arrests, executions, forced labor,

[52] See Claude A. Buss, *The People's Republic of China* (Princeton, 1962), pp. 41 ff.

brainwashing, five-year plans, and collectivization—all the familiar practices of Stalin's Russia.

An indication of the direction of the new regime was given by the "five loves" set as a standard for the Young Pioneer Corps: Fatherland, People, Labor, Science, and Public Property. Note that "Fatherland" was awarded first place in this ideology. In theory, Chinese communism was supposed to return to the Marxian orthodoxy which Soviet Russia, it charged, had violated. One might presume that letter-perfect Chinese Communist ideologists might have insisted upon a revival of Marxian internationalism, but the choice was Communist nationalism instead. Seldom has there been a more rigid nationalism in its integral form.

Chinese Communist leaders, while preaching peace, adopted a policy of nationalist expansion. They sought to increase China's influence in Asia, Africa, and Latin America. In 1951, Communist China occupied Tibet on the ground of old claims to suzerainty, and in 1959 it ruthlessly suppressed rebellion there. Border disputes with India nearly led to war on several occasions. Communist China intervened in the Korean War in late 1950. It supported North Vietnam in its struggle with South Vietnam. Again and again Peking claimed that it would "liberate" Formosa from Chiang Kai-shek's Nationalist government.

Meanwhile, the two Communist giants began to pull apart and to denounce each other in increasingly bitter terms. Peking accused Moscow of revisionism and retreat from orthodoxy; Moscow denounced Peking for reckless aggression. When Khrushchev announced that there were "different roads to socialism," Mao replied with the aphorism, "Let a hundred flowers bloom, let a hundred schools of thought contend." Clearly, Mao Tse-tung had diluted Chinese communism with a massive dose of nationalism.[53]

In early 1967, China was gripped by a confused power struggle among Communist leaders. Mao Tse-tung, elderly but holding firmly

[53] Even the Soviet Union accused the Chinese Communists of surrender to nationalism. When the Central Committee of the Chinese Communist party sent a reply to Moscow's invitation to the Soviet Communist party's 23rd Congress opening March 29, 1966, the Chinese replied in a long note of refusal which included this sentence: "Moreover, you sent an anti-Chinese letter to other parties, instigating them to join you in opposing China. You wantonly vilified the Chinese Communist party as being 'bellicose,' and 'pseudo-revolutionary,' and 'refusing to oppose imperialism,' and 'encouraging United States imperialist aggression,' and as being guilty of 'adventurism,' 'splitism,' 'Trotskyism,' 'nationalism,' 'great power chauvinism,' 'dogmatism,' and so on and so forth" (*The New York Times*, Mar. 24, 1966, p. 14).

to his role as dictator, had proclaimed a Great Proletarian Cultural Revolution with the aim of destroying the last vestiges of the old social order. Millions of teen-aged Red Guards flocked to his call. The youngsters surged through the capital of Peking, sacking ministries, arresting people, and in general creating pandemonium. Some went to Shantung province and wrecked the birthplace of Confucius, whose counsel for moderation and nonviolence had influenced the Chinese people for more than two thousand years. Chinese students in Moscow tried to place wreaths on Stalin's grave, only to be pushed away by Soviet police. Inside China the anti-Mao establishment, opposing the Red Guards, mobilized industrial workers and sent them to protest. Maoists and anti-Maoists raged aimlessly through the streets as China slid dangerously close to anarchy.

THE COURSE OF JAPANESE NATIONALISM

In the second half of the nineteenth century, Japan demonstrated to the world that an oriental nation could win equality with the Western powers. At the opening of the twentieth century she shocked the world by her military and naval victory over czarist Russia. This spark set off a great series of nationalistic movements which eventually broke over Asia and Africa after World War II and swept away almost all the colonial regimes. The success of Japan as a modern nation-state encouraged the rise of nationalistic regimes throughout Asia. Behind Japan's dynamic force was a remarkable people who absorbed ideas and ideologies from the rest of the world but at the same time maintained their own national identity.

Japan closed herself to foreigners in the early seventeenth century and remained isolated until the era of the steam engine, when she was opened by force.[54] Decisive influence came from the West in two explosive impacts. The first was initiated by U.S. Commodore Matthew C. Perry's "black ships," which forced their way into Tokyo Bay in July 1853.[55] Within a single generation Japan was transformed from a

---

[54] The saying that Japan was as closed as an oyster is a bit exaggerated. See Montague Paske-Smith, *Western Barbarians in Japan and Formosa in Tokugawa Days, 1603–1868* (Kobe, 1930), based largely on records of the British East India Company and archives of British consulates at Nagasaki and Osaka.

[55] See Matthew C. Perry, *Narrative of the Expedition of an American Squadron to the China Seas and Japan performed in the Years 1852, 1853, and 1854,* comp. Francis L. Hawks (3 vols.; Washington, D.C., 1956); Arthur Walworth, *Black*

feudal society into one of the world's leading industrial powers—an event scarcely paralleled in history.[56] The second explosion was set off by General Douglas MacArthur's "Initial Post-Surrender Policy for Japan" in August 1945.[57] Once again the pace of industrialization, this time without the aid of militarism, astonished the world.

Japanese nationalism was shaped within a framework set up by these two encounters with Western, especially American, civilization. For convenience in study and analysis we can set up three stages: *kokutai*, nationalism turned inward; ultranationalism—mission and aggression; and the new rational nationalism.

Kokutai: Traditional Japanese nationalism. Japanese feudalism was already disintegrating even before the enforced opening of the country to the West. In 1867, revolutionary leaders deposed the shogun,[58] restored the secular authority of the emperor, and brought the imperial court to Edo, renamed Tokyo. The new emperor took a "charter oath," promising that "knowledge shall be sought all over the world," and the imperial reign was named the Meiji (Enlightenment). The Meiji reformers turned Japan carefully to the road of modernization. From 1868 to 1894 the outer coating of Japanese society was Westernized.

During the era of the Meiji restoration and formation of the centralized nation, nationalism became the dominant political force in Japan. Western ideas of nationalism were superimposed on the already existing form and accelerated its growth. This amalgam of old and new was utilized by the political oligarchy, representative of the still-powerful feudal forces, for its own benefit. It industrialized and militarized the country in order to retain control of Japanese society.

Ships off Japan: The Story of Commodore Perry's Expedition (New York, 1946); Townsend Harris, *Journal* (Garden City, N.Y., 1930); and Samuel Wells Williams, "A Journal of the Perry Expedition to Japan, 1853–1854," ed. F. W. Williams, *Transactions of the Asiatic Society of Japan*, XXXVII (1910), 1–259.

[56] See Hugh Borton, *Japan's Modern Century* (New York, 1955); E. Herbert Norman, *Japan's Emergence as a Modern State* (New York, 1940); Walter W. McLaren, *A Political History of Japan during the Meiji Era, 1867–1912* (London, 1916); and John H. Gubbins, *The Progress of Japan, 1853–1871* (Oxford, 1911).

[57] See Supreme Commander for the Allied Powers, *Political Reorientation of Japan, September 1945 to September 1948* (2 vols.; Washington, D.C., 1949), the official history of General MacArthur's first three years as occupation commander in Japan.

[58] The office of shogun, which combined the duties of generalissimo and prime minister, was held by the Tokugawa family from the early seventeenth century.

Modern Japanese nationalism thus resulted from the impact of European power. That it took on another complexion was due to a different set of historical circumstances. Western nationalism arose in a framework of universalism (Roman Empire to *Corpus Christianum*—the dualism of universal Roman Catholic Church plus the Holy Roman Empire). European states during the Renaissance and Reformation represented in part a pluralistic disruption within a unified world. European national sentiment from its beginning was conscious of international society.[59] In the Asian world, and especially in Japan, there was no notion of a corporate body or international society in the European sense. A single entity—international society—confronted several more or less closed societies and forced them to "open the country." The Japanese were not aware of being within the international community: they were dragged into it. The ruling hierarchy regarded nationalism primarily as a means of defending the traditional sociopolitical order from the infiltration of European Christianity and industrialism.[60]

This early defensive form of nationalism was based on a concept of national polity called *kokutai*, which means literally "the substance, or the body of the nation," or "the national entity." The word could refer to the entire social and political fabric of the nation, or, in a restricted sense, to a basic governmental policy formed to meet internal and external problems.[61] The term could also denote a sense of "national honor." [62] According to *kokutai*, the essential national polity of Japan consisted of three elements: loyalty to the Throne, sense of mission, and belief that Japanese possessed superlative inborn qualities.

The first element of *kokutai*, veneration of the emperor, was similar to the Egyptian attitude toward the pharaoh. Until the Meiji restoration, Japanese peasants, composing by far the largest part of the popu-

[59] Hans Morgenthau, *Politics among Nations: The Struggle for Power and Peace* (New York, 1949), pp. 160–161.

[60] Masao Moruyama, *Thought and Behavior in Modern Japanese Politics*, ed. Ivan Morris (London, 1963), pp. 138–139.

[61] Richard Story, *The Double Patriots: A Study of Japanese Nationalism* (London, 1957), p. 5.

[62] "The term *kokutai* can mean many things, but it is appropriate to interpret its meaning as *basic characteristics of the nation*. So interpreted, *kokutai* forms the foundation of the nation's existence, and its destiny is common with that of the State; so that if this *kokutai* were to suffer change or loss the State would at once lose its existence" (*Kokutai No Hongi*, trans. J. O. Gauntlett [Cambridge, Mass., 1949], Appendix VII, statement by Japanese cabinet, Nov. 1946).

lation, were hardly aware of the emperor's existence. Now both the political oligarchy and the entrenched military turned to the emperor as the supreme symbol of national unity. He was supposed to have blood relationship with the sun goddess Amaterasu Omikami in a direct, unbroken line. He was the "Viceroy of Heaven on Earth," "Heavenly Ruler," "Son of Heaven." "As in the heavens the sun is not double, so on earth there exists but one *Tenno*." [63] His person was sacred and inviolable. Japanese were trained to turn their eyes away from the emperor when in his presence to avoid being shattered by his brilliance. In this special manifestation of Japanese nationalism, loyalty to the emperor was regarded as even more important than loyalty to the state.

The second element of *kokutai* was belief in a mission ordained by heaven. There was a generally accepted view that Japan was bound to follow the path of expansion abroad, and that in doing this she was obeying not only the will of the emperor but also a mandate imposed by heaven.[64] That was the goal of all militant nationalists.

The third pillar of *kokutai* was the concept that the Japanese were unequalled as specimens of humanity by any other people on earth. The reasoning was precise. The nation was a tree. Its trunk was the Imperial House, and its branches the four major family groups—Minamoto, Taira, Jufiwara, and Tachibana. From these ancient familial groups sprang millions of lesser branches and twigs. Through the entire tree ran the same sap, unifying emperor and people. Thus, every single Japanese was a part of the great family, all related by blood, all

[63] Hibino Yutaka, *"Nippon Shindo Ron"* or the *National Ideals of the Japanese People* (Cambridge, England, 1928), p. 92.

[64] Story, *op. cit.*, p. 3. How the sun-myth was translated into Japanese nationalism was explained in this passage by D. C. Holton: "In its actual functional value to modern Japan, the primitive solar mythology has been modified and enlarged by the influence of social and political patterns and impressed by the ulterior motives of tribal, dynastic, and racial aggrandizement, until, reshaped into its modern politico-religious mold, it becomes the symbol of the eternal state. As such, it is the central element of the national spirit, the chief ground of the belief in the one tribe origin of the nation as all descended from a common ancestor, the inspiration of a spiritual mobilization program that is carried in a thousand ways to the length and breadth of the empire, a basis of unity and authority in human affairs that broadens its dominions over men with every success of Japanese arms, and the embodiment of the highest political authority elevated to the position of deity—in a word, the deification of the political might of the military state" (D. C. Holton, *Japan and Shinto Nationalism* [Chicago, 1943], p. 65).

achieving *kiyoki kokoro*, "cleanliness of heart," in a purifying Shinto rite.

The nationalist creed of *kokutai* became the pervasive theme of the Japanese educational system. Both at home and in school the child was inculcated with its basic ideas. First and most important was the concept of *chukun aikoku* (allegiance to the emperor). Stress was also placed on the principles of *bushido*—contempt for death, exaltation of victory, and blind obedience.

Education, religion, and nationalism were all closely combined. In 1868 the emperor promulgated a charter oath, which has since been called "the Magna Carta of Japanese liberalism," authorizing the government to open the nation to Western culture. Christianity flourished in this atmosphere. But nationalists reacted by opposing foreign religions. On August 3, 1899, came the famous Order Number Twelve, which called for instruction of state Shinto religion in all schools.[65] "Shinto," said the Japanese scholar Genchi Kato, "is inseparably connected with the national ideals of the Japanese people." The sacred text of this reassertion of nationalism was the Imperial Rescript on Education issued on October 30, 1890, probably the most influential document in modern Japanese history. It proclaimed Shinto nationalism against Western political and moral ideals. Every Japanese knew its contents, and it was often read in the schools:

Know Ye, Our Subjects:

Our Imperial Ancestors have founded our Empire on a basis broad and everlasting, and have deeply and firmly implanted virtue; Our subjects ever united in loyalty and filial piety have from generation to generation illustrated the beauty thereof. This is the glory of the fundamental character of Our Empire, and herein also lies the source of Our education. Ye, Our subjects, be filial to your parents, affectionate to your brothers and sisters; as husbands and wives be harmonious, as friends true; bear yourselves in modesty and moderation; extend your benevolence to all; pursue learning and cultivate arts; and thereby develop intellectual facilities and perfect moral powers; furthermore, advance public good and promote

[65] The original religion of Japan, Shinto (The Divine Way) is a mixture of nature worship and state worship. It regards humans as descended from the gods, and the dead as ghosts who bring sorrow or joy to the living. There are numerous gods and goddesses. See Genchi Kato, *A Study of Shinto: The Religion of the Japanese Nation* (Tokyo, 1926).

common interests; always respect the Constitution and observe the laws; should emergency arise, offer yourselves courageously to the State; and thus guard and maintain the prosperity of Our Imperial Throne coeval with heaven and earth. So shall ye be not only Our good and faithful subjects but render illustrious the best traditions of your forefathers.

The Way here set forth is indeed the teaching bequeathed by Our Imperial Ancestors, to be observed alike by Their Descendants and the subjects, infallible in all ages and true in all places. It is our wish to lay it to heart in all reverence, in common with you, Our subjects, that we may attain to the same virtue.

The 30th day of the 10th month of the 23rd year of Meiji.

(*October 30, 1890*)
[Imperial Sign Manual, Imperial Seal] [66]

The Japanese educational system was frankly intended for the benefit of the nation rather than merely of the individual. The individual's progress was regarded as advancing the cause of the whole people. The spirit of the system may be judged from this announcement for a teachers' convention in Kyoto:

The sole aim of education is to establish a foundation for the social system by means of the development of the abundance of our national wealth on the one hand and the expansion of the national power abroad. The spirit of patriotism which has been nourished for 2,500 years has at last found an opportunity to exhibit itself, and now there is a chance for the educators to stimulate true nationalism and nourish the national power as a grateful act of appreciation of this glorious period.[67]

Similarly, the first among a series of resolutions adopted by the public school teachers of Tokyo at a convention in 1895 was, "The national idea and patriotism should be stimulated among the pupils of the public schools." [68]

Ultranationalism: Mission and aggression. As we have seen, *kokutai,* the Japanese nationalist polity, was molded by the political oligarchy rather than emerging full-blown from the consciousness of the people. It carried over into the aggressive stage of nationalism that followed.

Japanese ultranationalism was the product of two classes in the social order—the military and the industrialists. The traditions of the

---

[66] From *The Japan Year Book, 1939–1940* (Tokyo, 1939), p. 633.
[67] Alfred Stead, *Japanese Patriotism* (London, 1906), pp. 17–18.   [68] *Ibid.*

samurai [69] warriors carried over into the modern era after the fall of the shogunate and the introduction of the Meiji. The military was convinced that it was Japan's divine mission to bring "the whole world under one roof" (*hakko ichi-u*). To this militarist conviction was added the influence of the *zaibatsu* [70] industrialists. Japanese nationalism was given its direction by these groups with their important control of the military, bureaucracy, police, schools, and means of communication. A second face of Japan began to attract world-wide attention. Alongside its love of beauty, expressed in such arts as flower arrangement (*ikebana*), arrangement of natural stones (*bonseki*), poetry (*tanka* and *haiku*), and social entertainment (*geisha*), was a rising ultranationalism manifested in arrogant militarism and political fanaticism. Assassination was the lot of those politicians who did not move fast enough to satisfy impatient patriots.

Nationalism in both Japan and the Far East was stimulated by a major event in world history—Japan's decisive victory over Russia in 1905. This demonstrated the possibility that a "backward" people utilizing Western technique and organization might triumph over a great military nation which up to that time had conquered more territory in Asia than any other power.[71] Japan's victory made her a world power. In late August of 1914, aware of Germany's possessions in the Far East, Japan joined the Allied powers, but refrained from taking a major part in the war. Meanwhile, she turned her interest to the mainland.[72] During and after World War I, ultranationalist societies began to spring up throughout the country. In 1918 a rightist group called the Rosakai was organized to combat the Reimeikai, a society

---

[69] The *samurai, bushi,* or *buke* caste of feudal Japan, originating in the ninth century when the central government was weakened, rose to power under the shogunate. Its rule lasted for nearly eight hundred years until 1867. Two years later its name was changed to *shizokua* (gentry).

[70] The *zaibatsu* families laid the foundations of great wealth toward the end of the nineteenth century during the era of Japanese industrialization. Dominating heavy industry and the banking system, they also had great influence in political life.

[71] Hans Kohn, *Nationalism: Its Meaning and History* (Princeton, 1965), p. 87.

[72] Japan took advantage of her allies' preoccupation with the war in Europe in 1915 by handing China the notorious Twenty-One Demands, an ultimatum that would have made China a Japanese protectorate. American pressure prevented realization of the Twenty-One Demands, but at Versailles, Japan was permitted to take over Germany's concessions on the Shantung Peninsula.

dedicated to democratic ideals. The next year the Dai Nihon Kokusui-kai (Greater Japan National Essence Society) was initiated under prominent leadership. In 1924 came the Kokuhonsha (National Foundation Society), devoted to the ideology of *kokutai*. There were few prominent politicians, admirals, generals, or businessmen who were not members of this organization.[73] The grass roots of Japanese society were reached by similar organizations such as young men's and young women's associations, which extended into every village. There were even ultranationalist societies among young officers in the army.[74]

In June and July 1927 a conference in Tokyo on foreign affairs was presided over by Prime Minister Gi-ichi Tanaka. The so-called Tanaka Memorial, intended as a summary of this conference, was given to the emperor by Tanaka. Published by the Chinese in 1929, it was denounced by the Japanese as a forgery. Whether this be true or not, the Tanaka Memorial at least has the historical value of summing up Japanese aggressive nationalist ambitions:

After studying the present conditions and possibilities of our country, our best policy lies in the direction of taking positive steps to secure rights and privileges in Manchuria and Mongolia. These will enable us to develop our trade. This will not only forestall China's own industrial development, but also prevent the penetration of European Powers. This is the best policy possible!

The way to gain actual rights in Manchuria and Mongolia is to use this region as a base and under the pretence of trade and commerce penetrate the rest of China. Armed by the rights already secured we shall seize the resources all over the country. Having China's entire resources at our disposal we shall proceed to conquer India, the Archipelago, Asia Minor, Central Asia, and even Europe. But to get control of Manchuria and Mongolia is the first step if the Yamato race wishes to distinguish itself on Continental Asia. Final success belongs to the country having raw materials; the full growth of national strength belongs to the country having extensive territory. If we pursue a positive policy to enlarge our rights in Manchuria and China, all these prerequisites of a powerful nation will constitute no problem. Furthermore our surplus population of 700,000 each year will also be taken care of.[75]

[73] Arthur Tiedemann, *Modern Japan* (Princeton, 1962), pp. 65–66.

[74] For example, the Sakuraki (Cherry Society), composed of young field-grade officers, who conspired to set up a military dictatorship in 1931, but failed to obtain the assistance of their older comrades. Other officers were involved in plots to assassinate the entire cabinet.

[75] *The China Critic* (Shanghai, 1931), IV, 924.

It is still not clear whether the Tanaka Memorial was a Japanese master plan for Asiatic conquest, with Manchuria first and China second, or whether it was a general statement of national aspirations. It was probably not the blueprint of a single grand conspiracy, but it did conform broadly with the general pattern of Japanese ultranationalism.

The course of Japanese expansion after 1931 is well known.[76] In that year the militarists, swamping the liberal government, launched an armed adventure into Manchuria, and the entire province was brought under Japanese control. Every succeeding year was a further milestone in the building of the Japanese empire. Japanese expansionists looked in three directions: in the north to Manchukuo, in the west to China, and in the south to the rich tropical colonies of the European powers. By the time of the attack on Pearl Harbor, Japanese nationalists had outlined the concept of a Greater East Asia Co-Prosperity Sphere, a kind of oriental Monroe Doctrine. The missionary zeal expressed in *kokutai* reached its apotheosis.

Just as Napoleon unwittingly propagated nationalism in early nineteenth-century European countries outside France, so did the Japanese in World War II unconsciously act as the spearhead of nationalism throughout Asia. Japan spread her armies and influence, like a giant octopus, for the purpose of aggrandizement, but the effect was precisely the opposite of what the chauvinists in Tokyo expected. Far from subjugating the occupied areas, the invaders instead accelerated nationalist liberation movements that were already under way.

The Japanese plan was twofold: they would drive out the Western imperialists, and they would use local nationalist leaders to promote Japanese hegemony. The second plan backfired. Though the Westerners were temporarily driven out by a combination of Japanese military strength and local guerrilla forces, the latter gained experience. After the war, when European colonial powers tried to reoccupy their rich Asian provinces, they found rebellious nationalist factions too strong to be pushed aside easily.

The new rational nationalism. Their defeat in World War II left the Japanese stunned and bewildered. Added to their confusion was a clash

[76] See Delmer N. Brown, *Nationalism in Japan* (Berkeley, 1955); Herbert Feis, *The Road to Pearl Harbor* (Princeton, 1950); Ivan I. Morris, *Nationalism and the Right Wing in Japan* (London, 1960); Jerome B. Cohen, *Japan's Economy in War and Reconstruction* (Minneapolis, 1949); and F. C. Jones, *Japan's New Order in East Asia: Its Rise and Fall, 1937–1945* (London, 1954).

between the authoritarianism of their fathers and the democratic principles of the American occupation. The setback was only temporary, for the Japanese people managed to find a balance between the old and the new. There was political stability: democracy functioned with comparatively little friction. There was economic advance: Japanese goods began to appear again in the markets of the world; in addition to such cheap items as toys, pottery, and textiles, there were such solid products as machine tools, optical goods, and electronic equipment. People began to speak of the "Japanese economic miracle" as the nation prospered. Socially, the Japanese faced the dilemma of overpopulation by deliberately lowering their birth rate, a unique accomplishment in Asia.

The Japanese people had enough of ultranationalist fanaticism. On August 15, 1945, the emperor's voice was heard over the radio broadcasting the announcement of surrender. Both the surrender and the broadcast were unprecedented events in Japanese history. One passage of the broadcast was directed specifically at the nationalists who had brought Japan to the verge of destruction:

We are keenly aware of the inmost feelings of all of you, our subjects. However, it is according to the dictates of time and fate that we have resolved to pave the way for a grand peace for all the generations to come, by enduring the unavoidable and suffering what is insufferable. Having been able to safeguard and maintain the structure of the Imperial state we are always with you, our good and loyal subjects, relying upon your sincerity and integrity. Beware most strictly of any outbursts of emotion that may engender needless complications, of any fraternal contention and strife that may create confusion, lead you astray and cause you to lose the confidence of the world.[77]

The words of the emperor made a tremendous impression on a people to whom militarism had brought only misery and humiliation. Having suffered the horrors of an atomic attack, the Japanese inserted a "renunciation of war" clause in their new constitution. The reasoning was precise and simple: ultranationalism with its concomitant militarism had been catastrophic; democratic cultural nationalism had lifted Japan from the ashes and placed her in the forefront of nations.

There were, however, vestigial remains of the older nationalism. A panel of distinguished scholars and civic leaders called for a stronger

[77] Quoted in Story, *op. cit.*, p. 7.

spirit of nationalism to improve and enrich Japan and enable her to play her proper role among the nations. They insisted that the Japanese, fully appreciative of the rich heritage of their ancestors, should also become a "world people," able to bridge the differences between East and West, North and South. The newspaper *Yomiuri*, while approving the purpose, found the recommendations "lacking in persuasive power." [78] When Prime Minister Eisaku Sato urged the restoration of the Kigensetsu (National Foundation Day), the anniversary of the legend of Emperor Jimmu's accession to the throne in 660 B.C., he was criticized by Japanese scholars on the ground that "the move would only distort history and revive old supernationalistic ideas." [79]

For the moment then, Japanese nationalism remains in a quiescent stage, dedicated to respect for the emperor, the national flag, and the national anthem. The people rejected blatant ultranationalism, with its sense of mission and its practice of patriotic assassination. A new pride in achievement took the place of the older need for self-justification and face-saving. Political stability and economic prosperity gave rise to a renewal of national self-confidence. Japanese intellectuals were fascinated by this revival of national consciousness: in their magazines (*Chuo Koron, Jiyu,* and others), many articles were printed evaluating the new Japanese nationalism. Most agreed that Japan could construct her independent greatness not by identifying herself with China, but by emphasizing her own democratic nationalism and taking a position oriented toward neither the East nor the West.

UNFULFILLED GOALS: DISCORDANT
ASIAN NATIONALISM

Asian nationalism originated with anti-imperialism, a sentiment to which it rigidly adhered. For the vast majority of Asians, nationalism meant merely anti-imperialism, clothed in contempt for the European. Asians rejected the European ideas of enlightenment, rationalism, and even the libertarian formula. Except for brief periods in their drive for liberation, most Asians cast aside the liberal-democratic aspects of nineteenth-century European nationalism. They associated anti-imperialist nationalism with Asian progress.

At first the common cause against colonial masters gave most Asians

[78] *The New York Times,* Jan. 17, 1965.   [79] *Newsweek,* Feb. 15, 1965, p. 15.

a sense of solidarity. This was supposed to be a period of transition after which the emergent Asian nations would achieve a sense of unity and politico-economic well-being. The new nationalism, strong and self-reliant, would subdue internal enmities between classes and races. With the spread of industrialization throughout Asia, the old traditional cleavages, based almost entirely on the agricultural pattern of society, would be eliminated. Economic competition would bring a better way of life, and with it a proud sense of national community.

As imperialism abdicated in one Asian country after another, anti-imperialist passion retained its potency. Instead of developing a strong sense of Asian identity, the countries of the Far East went their separate ways. Today nationalism is the most powerful of all forces in Asia. It stands squarely in the way of unitary Communist control or Chinese power.

Asian nationalism was filled with clashing hatreds. It maintained its artificial scorn for European imperialists, long since withdrawn from Asia. Along with Asian nationalism went alarming political tendencies, deteriorating public administration, and worsened economic conditions. Nationalist parties veered toward totalitarianism. The masses remained phlegmatic. Based upon the union of those who had suffered common humiliations, Asian nationalism was dangerous and explosive.

Chapter 8

Politico-religious Nationalism: The Middle East

Nationalism is the force that seeks to raise the Arabs to a rank where they will be totally engaged in universal humanist movements and where their support of internationalist objectives will be more positive and more concrete.

—CLOVIS MAKSOUD

The late Carlton J. H. Hayes, after devoting his academic career to the observation and study of nationalism, came to this conclusion: man's religious sense is exemplified not only in the great surviving religions and in the animism of primitive peoples, but also in contemporary communism and especially in modern nationalism.[1] Hayes described several kinds and degrees of nationalism: some reconciled or allied with historical supernatural religion; others giving quasi-religious sanction to an intrinsically materialist and atheist movement like communism; and still others, themselves religions, jealous and exclusive:

> Since its advent in western Europe, modern nationalism has partaken of the nature of a religion. . . . Nationalism, like any religion, calls into play not simply the will, but the intellect, the imagination, and the emotions. The intellect constructs a speculative theology or mythology of nationalism. The imagination builds an unseen world around the eternal past and the everlasting future of one's nationality. The emotions arouse a joy and ecstasy in the contemplation of the national god who is all-good and all-protecting, a longing for his favors, a thankfulness for his benefits, a fear of offending him, and feelings of awe and reverence at the immensity of his power and wisdom: they express themselves naturally in worship, both private and public. For nationalism, again like any other religion, is social, and its chief rites are public rites performed in the name and for the salvation of a whole community.[2]

Hayes regarded nationalism itself as a religion. Certainly among the many varieties of nationalism is a form in which religious convictions take on special significance. There is an area of the world where two great religions—Islam and Judaism—have tempered sociopolitical nationalism. This is the Middle East, one of the world's strategic crossroads, where Europe and Africa are joined.

There is no unanimous definition of "Middle East," nor is the name universally accepted. Some scholars prefer the term Near East, which dates from the Age of Exploration. Marco Polo and Vasco da Gama, while on their way to the riches of the Far East, looked upon these lands as "nearest" to Europe. Today the Middle East includes countries

[1] Carlton J. H. Hayes, *Nationalism: A Religion* (New York, 1960), p. 18.
[2] *Ibid.*, pp. 164–165.

south of the Soviet Union and west of Pakistan: Turkey, Iran, Egypt, Syria, Lebanon, Israel, Jordan, Saudi Arabia, Yemen, and several smaller territories. Together they cover 2,600,000 square miles on which live about a hundred million people. With the exception of Turkey, Israel, and Iran, these countries belong to the Arab world. "This is the classical land of 'buffer states,' of 'spheres of influence,' of political bribery on a large scale, of industrial 'concessions,' and of 'oil diplomacy.' " [3] It is an area harassed by four major problems: nationalism, oil, lack of water, and the pervading poverty of the masses.

The Biblical cradle of humanity, the Middle East once embraced great civilizations, huge empires, and magnificent cultures. Then followed centuries of stagnation, accompanied by illiteracy, disease, and epidemics, as the area degenerated into one of the most backward regions on earth. In the twentieth century the Middle East, because of its strategic location, became one of the centers of the world stage. The discovery of vast pools of oil, "black gold" for the Western industrial powers, increased the importance of the area. It was subjected to foreign domination, first by the Ottoman Turks and later by Britain, France, and Russia.

Arabs, Turks, Iranians, and Israelis developed an emotional nationalism directed against foreign rule or influence. Nationalists were successful in ending colonial domination in most of the area by the end of World War II, but they achieved this goal only to be faced with continuing problems of hunger, disease, and poverty.

In the Middle East, as elsewhere, nationalism has expressed itself in any number of political, economic, and cultural forms. Western colonialism and local dissensions resulted in a patchwork of states as politically distinct as France, Germany, and Britain. Yet, there is a common denominator to be found in religion. Of the three major groups dominating the Middle East—Semites, Turks, and Iranians—the largest is composed of Semites, including both Arabs and Jews. Among these two peoples, whose languages are closely related, religion has played a decisive role, so much so that it colored the rising nationalism of both peoples.

---

[3] David J. Dallin, *The Big Three: The United States, Britain, Russia* (New Haven, 1945), p. 136. On the critical oil problem, see George Lenczowski, *Oil a State in the Middle East* (Ithaca, N.Y., 1960); Stephen H. Longrigg, *Oil in the Middle East* (New York, 1954); and Benjamin Shwadran, *The Middle East, Oil, and the Great Powers* (New York, 1955).

In this respect the Middle Eastern experience ran counter to that of western Europe, where, after the religious wars of the sixteenth century, rivalries were based first on dynastic and then on national lines. Religion played a progressively lesser role in the development of nationalism in western Europe. This was also true of the new nationalism in Africa, Asia, and South America, where religious aspects were of comparatively little consequence. But the Middle East presented a different pattern.

The Middle East is the center of the world of Islam, the religion of Muhammad. It is the site of Islamic holy places. Its society has been imbued with Muslim culture. Islam was the binding force in the Arab world during the centuries of political and cultural decline, and in modern times, a bulwark in the struggle against European colonialism. "To all Muslim Arabs Islam represents an indissoluble core of identity, a personal possession, and a communal heritage." [4] There have been divisions within Islam (for example the Sunni and Shiite sects), clashes between modernist and fundamentalist viewpoints, and some evidences of retreat among the educated younger generation. But despite such crises, Islamic religious conviction and the sense of religious heritage remain strong.

The relationship between religion and nationalism in the Middle East is exceedingly complex. The idea of brotherhood is mainly Pan-Islamic in orientation and therefore not in harmony with the nationalism related to Pan-Arabism. Yet, politically, the Arabs who traditionally are divided in tribal warfare look to Islam as a common bond.

Added to the complications is the difference between local nationalism, such as Egyptian or Turkish, and regional nationalism, such as Pan-Arab, Fertile Crescent, or Maghribi nationalism. Superimposed on over-all Islamic nationalism is Arab nationalism, which spread throughout the Arab world after World War II. This is not a single political creed but a combination of nationalisms. One form is Nasserism, which holds that Arab nationalism can only be successful under the leaderhsip of the Egyptian Gamal Abdel Nasser. But whether the nationalism is local or regional, the cohesive factor is in large part religious.

Similarly, the Middle East is a focus of aspiration for the Jews. After the Diaspora, the urge to return to the Holy Land of Palestine was held by Jews for centuries. This long-term goal was achieved in 1948 when

[4] Hisham B. Sharabi, *Nationalism and Revolution in the Arab World* (Princeton, 1966), p. 5.

the Jewish state of Israel was proclaimed. Though Israeli nationalism tended to become more and more political in content, its origins were in the religious and cultural traditions of Judaism. On the surface the rivalry between Arabs and Jews had a political complexion; at its root it was patently a religious impulse.

FRAMEWORK: GREAT-POWER ENCOUNTERS

Nationalism in the Middle East was conditioned by the clash of outside interests. For centuries the area was the fulcrum of the Muslim domain, but in the last century and a half it has been subjected to European influence. Europe was the generator of political, military, and intellectual life in the Middle East. The attraction of the Middle East was twofold: its strategic location as a land bridge between Europe and Asia, and its oil. Among the properties of European civilization which were diffused throughout the Middle East was nationalism.

The end of World War II marked a change in foreign pressure on most of the Arabic-speaking areas of the Middle East and North Africa. Until 1945, Europe's two most active colonial powers, Great Britain and France, controlled most Arab countries. Britain dominated the Middle East, while France was more interested in Arab North Africa. Both countries had taken part in two enervating world wars. Though both had been victorious, they were drained of manpower and wealth. Neither was able to reassert its former dominating role in the Middle East.

After 1945 the United States and the Soviet Union emerged as the two most important global powers. In the Middle East this produced a new political climate. As British and French influence receded there, that of the United States and the Soviet Union increased. In the cold war the Middle East became one of the areas of contention: both the United States and the Soviet Union were attracted by the strategic location and oil. This time the interest was more economic than political, although to aggrieved parties economic exploitation (which they called neocolonialism) was considered tantamount to actual imperial rule. Britain and France were by no means completely out of the picture, but they nevertheless found themselves unable to prevent the increasing economic domination of the Middle East by the United States and Soviet Russia.

The fact that the United States and the Soviet Union were anti-imperialist and anticolonial in the older sense was beneficial to the Arabs in the Middle East. Shorn of political and military control by their European masters, the Arabs began to work for independence. The process, which had already begun at the end of World War I when the Turkish Empire disintegrated, was accelerated at the close of World War II. Egyptian nationalism eventually led to the creation of an independent state, the evacuation of British troops, and Egyptian seizure of the Suez Canal. Similar nationalistic impulses brought liberation to other Middle Eastern countries. These successes encouraged the extension of Arab nationalism, or what might more properly be called Pan-Arabism—the desire to include all Arabs in one nation and in one state.

Concurrent with the confrontation of great powers in the Middle East was the division within the Arab world caused by conflicting nationalisms. Local nationalisms proved more powerful than Pan-Arabism. Egypt interpreted Arab nationalism and Arab unity as Egyptian domination of the Middle East. For the Arabs of other Middle Eastern countries, Arab nationalism meant only their own independence, and certainly not control by Cairo. There were continuing rivalries between Arab nationalist leaders, none of whom was willing to entrust the sovereignty of his nation to another state. In this fragmented milieu, Arab unity remained an unattainable goal.

EGYPTIAN STATE NATIONALISM

The opening of Egypt to European influence began in the early nineteenth century under Mehemet Ali (1769–1849), an officer sent by the sultan to repel Napoleon.[5] Mehemet Ali reorganized the army, modernized the economy, and introduced European techniques. He made himself khedive (governor) of Egypt and established a hereditary dynasty which ruled Egypt for more than a century. When Mehemet retired in 1840, he was virtually Egypt's ruler, although the country was nominally still part of the Ottoman Empire.

[5] On Mehemet Ali see Shafik Gorbal, *The Beginnings of the Egyptian Question and the Rise of Mehemet Ali* (London, 1928); Sir George Young, *Egypt* (New York, 1927); and William H. Salmon, *An Account of the Ottoman Conquest of Egypt* (London, 1921).

Mehemet Ali's grandson, Khedive Ismail Pasha (1830–1895), encouraged European penetration of his country, and by senseless extravagance opened the door to European intervention in Egyptian affairs.[6] Because of the American Civil War, demand for Egyptian cotton rose, and it seemed that Egypt was well on the road to prosperity. But Ismail's financial indiscretions drained the treasury. Under his rule Ferdinand de Lesseps, a French engineer, built the Suez Canal, opened in 1869.[7] In 1875, Ismail sold his government's ordinary shares in the Suez Canal Company for £4,000,000. In 1878 he mortgaged about half the state's lands for a loan from the Rothschild family of £8,500,000. Both these deals were made with the prime minister of Britain, Benjamin Disraeli.

This financial improvidence led to Egyptian bankruptcy and Anglo-French financial control. The British and French, dissatisfied with Ismail's failure to make regular payments on his loans, appointed a commission of inquiry, which was transformed into a responsible ministry of the Egyptian government. In 1879 the European powers persuaded the sultan to depose Ismail and to subordinate his son Tewfik to their "dual control." As a result, the British occupied Egypt in 1882. A semblance of Egyptian statehood was preserved, but real control was maintained in London.[8]

These manipulations provoked the first national revolt in the Arab world and the first significant movement against foreign subjugation in the age of imperialism. The British occupation brought Egyptians into contact with European thought, including the growing sentiment of

[6] These extravagances included a parade ground in Alexandria which Ismail Pasha covered with an iron platform so that he would not be annoyed by dust when reviewing his troops. He floated huge financial issues through the exchanges of Europe and borrowed heavily for public works projects. European bankers lent him money at usurious rates of interest.

[7] See Benno Avram, *Evolution of the Suez Canal Status from 1869 up to 1956* (Geneva, 1958); Charles W. Hallberg, *The Suez Canal: Its History and Diplomatic Importance* (New York, 1931); and Sir Arnold T. Wilson, *The Suez Canal* (2nd ed.; London, 1939).

[8] See Evelyn Baring Cromer, *Modern Egypt*, (2 vols.; New York, 1908), for an account of British policy in Egypt; and Wilfrid S. Blunt, *Secret History of the English Occupation of Egypt* (London, 1907), for a highly critical treatment of British administration there. See also Alfred M. Milner, *England in Egypt* (London, 1892); and John Marlowe, *Anglo-Egyptian Relations, 1800–1953* (London, 1954).

nationalism. Because of her already close association with Europe, Egypt became the first country in the Middle East to develop a nationalist movement.[9]

The cry "Egypt for the Egyptians" was heard throughout the period of British management of the country. In 1869, just after the Suez Canal was opened, the first Egyptian nationalist organization, the Party of the Fatherland, was organized. In 1881, Colonel Ahmed Arabi, an officer of peasant origin, led a military revolt against both Turkish control and Anglo-French influence. The British crushed the rebellion and set up an administration ruling the country as a protectorate. They had stumbled into Egypt much against their own will.[10] Though the Egyptian army surrendered, the sentiment of Egyptian nationalism was aroused.

In the period before World War I, Egyptian nationalists called for a new sense of national dignity in the drive for independence. Mohammed Abdu, founder of the Society for the Revival of Arabic Books, urged a transformation in the minds and hearts of his compatriots. Qasim Amin urged his countrymen to learn the ways of industrialization and civic virtue from the West as they anticipated freedom. Ahmed Lufti al-Sayyid recommended that his countrymen absorb the best of European civilization as a means of strengthening their own identity.[11] At the turn of the century Egyptian nationalists were using the phraseology and ideology of European nationalists, as this passage by Mustapha Kamil shows:

[9] For a summary of the background of Egyptian nationalism, see Hans Kohn, *The Age of Nationalism: The First Era of Global History* (New York, 1962), pp. 82–89; and Jamal Mohammed Ahmed, *The Intellectual Origins of Egyptian Nationalism* (New York, 1960).

[10] In 1883 the British appointed the banker Sir Evelyn Baring, who later became Lord Cromer, as administrator to run Egypt's finances and economy. For the next twenty-five years Cromer was in a peculiar position as a representative of Britain who at the same time had to look after the financial interests of other Europeans in Egypt. The French, who regarded the Middle East as their own sphere of influence, bitterly resented this situation. The rivalry almost led to war after the clash at Fashoda in 1898 between the Frenchman Marchand and the Englishman Kitchener. For an official account of the Fashoda incident, see British Foreign Office, *Turkey (Egypt)*, 4960, letter from Rennell Rodd, British representative in Cairo, to the Marquess of Salisbury, British prime minister, Sept. 25, 1898.

[11] "For Lufti national independence was not an end; he was concerned above all with the quality of national life, with the virtues it generated. The first of these virtues was freedom. There is no need to summarize his views on liberty, because they were those of Locke and Mill" (Ahmed, *op. cit.*, p. 112).

Egyptian civilization will last only if it is rooted in the people, if the fellah [peasant], the merchant, the teacher, the student, in short every Egyptian knows that man possesses sacred and inviolable rights, that he was not created to be a tool but to lead an honorable and reasonable life, that no sentiment is more beautiful than the love of our country, that the soul is noble, and a people without independence is a people without existence. Patriotism speedily raises backward people to civilization, greatness and power. Patriotism is the blood that flows in the veins of virile nations and that gives life to all living creatures.[12]

The leading apostle of Egyptian nationalism was the patriot Saad Zaghlul (1860–1927), born of fellahin stock. In 1882 he was involved in the Arab revolt and was detained for a time during the occupation of Egypt by British troops in 1882. After service as a barrister and judge, he became minister of education in 1906 and introduced Western educational reforms. In 1910 he became minister of justice. By 1914, Zaghlul was the leader of the Wafd, the extreme nationalist party, which demanded expulsion of the British from Egypt. Although few Egyptians were involved in the war effort, Egypt became a strategic base for British military operations in the war. As soon as the Armistice was signed, Zaghlul called for recognition of Egyptian independence, basing his demand on President Wilson's policy of self-determination and the British proclamation defining the status of those countries liberated from Turkish rule. He asked for permission to go to London to plead his case. The British refused. Zaghlul's reaction was so hostile that he and several other Wafdist leaders were arrested on March 8, 1919, and deported to Malta. Serious disturbances in Cairo followed. Zaghlul was released in 1923 and returned to Egypt, where he was enthusiastically welcomed. Until his death in 1927 he was Egypt's outstanding personality.

Egyptian nationalism, already strong, was stimulated still further by the presence along the Nile of large numbers of British troops, by economic dislocations, and by Allied propaganda which had promised freedom to the Arabs.[13] When the riots and demonstrations of the early 1920's brought Egypt to the verge of revolution, the British decided to

---

[12] Kohn, *The Age of Nationalism*, p. 86. Mustapha Kamil died in 1908 while still a young man. His funeral in Cairo became a great nationalist demonstration.

[13] From the Allied viewpoint the pledge during wartime for Arab freedom did not apply to Egypt, for it was the only country in the Middle East occupied by a Western power prior to the war.

withdraw. They proclaimed Egyptian independence in 1922, but still controlled foreign affairs, finance, the police, and the Suez Canal. King Fuad I (1868–1936), who ascended the throne on March 16, 1922, showed some sympathy for the British position. However, extreme Wafdist nationalists insisted on unconditional independence and continued to agitate for it. Finally, in 1936, the Anglo-Egyptian Treaty transformed the protectorate into an alliance. British interference in Egypt's internal affairs was ended, but Britain still controlled the Suez Canal. This status was to continue through World War II.

National pride was not appeased by what the Wafdists called halfway measures. The provincial Egyptian nationalism, keyed to continuing struggle with Britain, grew stronger. In World War II the Egyptians adopted a policy of not cooperating with Britain, and even invited Nazis and Fascists as honored guests. The Egyptian government finally did declare war on the Axis on February 24, 1945, but only after the Axis danger to the Middle East had already been removed by Allied victories at El Alamein and elsewhere. When the war was over, nationalism flared up again, promoted this time by groups even more extreme than the Wafdists. On July 8, 1947, Egyptian representatives appeared before the Security Council of the United Nations and accused Britain of maintaining troops on Egyptian territory against the will of the people and endangering Egyptian security by occupation of the Nile Valley. In 1948 came war with Israel and the shocking exposure of Egyptian military weakness. The country was disturbed by a pattern of murderous street riots. King Farouk seemed helpless in this display of national emotion.

By this time Egyptian nationalism was being championed by a new dynamic force—the Committee of Free Officers, organized to rid the country of its king, court aristocracy, and corrupt Cairo politicians. At midnight on July 22, 1952, a group of officers led by Major General Mohammed Naguib and Lieutenant Colonel Gamal Abdel Nasser,[14] seized the army headquarters, captured the national broadcasting station, and took over control of the government. Four days later King Farouk was forced to abdicate in favor of his infant son. At first the

[14] On Nasser see Georgiana Stevens, *Egypt: Yesterday and Today* (New York, 1963); George E. Kirk, *Contemporary Arab Politics* (New York, 1961); Malcolm H. Kerr, *Egypt under Nasser*, "Foreign Policy Association Headline Series," No. 161 (Sept.–Oct. 1963); Wilson Wynn, *Nasser of Egypt* (Cambridge, Mass., 1959); and Keith Wheelock, *Nasser's New Egypt* (New York, 1960).

military junta intended to retain power only temporarily until a responsible civilian government could institute reforms and emancipate Egypt from imperialism and feudalism.[15] When it became impossible to find honest politicians, the officers, although they were inexperienced, decided to retain control. In 1953, Naguib proclaimed Egypt a republic, with himself as president and prime minister, and Colonel Nasser as his deputy.

Soon a rift appeared between the fifty-one-year-old Naguib, who wished to move cautiously toward constitutional government, and the thirty-five-year-old Nasser, a more radical leader who wanted to eliminate old institutions and build a new government. The differences led in 1954 to a clash which resulted in Naguib's fall. Nasser succeeded Naguib as prime minister and later named himself president. He ruled now as the head of the junta.

From this time on Nasser appropriated leadership of the Egyptian national movement. The graduate of a military academy and a veteran of World War II, he had been a fervent revolutionary in his early days.[16] But his youthful idealism began to vanish once he took on the responsibilities of power. He abolished the old political parties and replaced them with a single organization, first called the Liberation Rally, later the National Union, and still later (1962) the Arab Socialist Union. The zealous fighter for liberty soon began to restrict individual Egyptian freedoms and to enhance the power of the central government. Nasser curtailed freedom of speech, press, and assembly on the ground that the Egyptians were not ready for Western democracy. On July 26, 1956, he nationalized the Suez Canal and announced that the revenues would be used to finance the high Nile dam being built at Aswan and due to be completed in 1970. Despite this and other measures, Nasser found it difficult to improve Egypt's sagging economy. Simply dividing and distributing the great estates was no solution for Egypt's economic ills. With severe unemployment, a population growing at the rate of half a million per year, and widespread illiteracy and

[15] In addition to wiping out corruption, the officers' junta aimed to end the power of the pashas. Before the revolution, fewer than twelve thousand pashas, or about ½ per cent of the population, owned a third of the rich farm lands along the Nile. The new government seized all estates larger than 200 acres and divided the land into small plots for distribution among the poor farmers.

[16] See Gamal Abdel Nasser, *The Philosophy of the Revolution* (Buffalo, N.Y., 1959). First published in Cairo in 1953, Nasser's work became a kind of handbook for Egyptian nationalists.

poverty, Nasser was beset by a host of difficulties. Nationalist slogans were just not enough to solve his many problems.

IDEOLOGICAL FOUNDATIONS OF ARAB NATIONALISM

Although he faced grave troubles on the domestic front, Nasser looked beyond the borders of Egypt. An emotional critic of imperialism, he tried to make himself the spokesman of all the non-European African states. Under his opportunistic leadership Egypt became even more the leader of Arab nationalism. His belief was rooted in national pride aroused by the great civilization of ancient Egypt, which was much older than the Arab civilization.[17] In *The Philosophy of the Revolution*, Nasser called upon Egyptians to organize their loyalties in concentric circles. At the heart is the nation—Egypt. Then the continent of Africa is the next circle of loyalty, while circles three and four are the Arab states and the world of Islam respectively.[18]

Because of the complexities involved, it would be best to define terms:

Arab nationalism (al-qawmiyyah al-'arabiyyah). This is not a single political creed, for there is no unanimity on basic principles, goals, and objectives. It is in general a mass nationalist movement attracting the allegiance of Arabs from Morocco to Iraq. Within Arab nationalism there are two common denominators: the concept of Arabism and the idea of unity.

Arabism ('urubah). This is a quasi-mystical term meaning the essence of being an Arab—the sense of belonging to the Arab nation, using Arabic as mother tongue, being born an Arab in an Arab land, being a Muslim.

Unity (wihdah). Implicit in the feeling and awareness of Arabism, this involves political unity, but also the aspiration for a more profound unity beyond the merely political or economic. The roots are to be found in the idea of a Muslim community advanced by Muhammad's early teaching. Arabism means the indivisibility of the Arab nation. Arab nationalists have absolute unanimity on Arabism and unity, but differ on how they are to be implemented. This explains why peoples can struggle for Arab nationalism and still be enemies.

[17] Frederick Hertz, *Nationality in History and Politics* (London, 1944), p. 145.
[18] See Richard M. Fry, "Islam and the Middle East," *Current History* (June 1956), p. 328.

Nasserism (al-Nasiriyyah). The term was originally coined by Nasser's enemies but later came to refer to the movement created by him in the Arab world. It consists of those groups and parties who believe that Arab nationalism can succeed only under Nasser's leadership and hence support his policies and his leadership. Nasserism exists only outside Egypt: it lacks central organization and represents an emotional trend rather than a coordinated movement.[19]

In its propaganda leaflets the Arab Information Center projects this definition:

An Arab is not only a person whose first language is usually Arabic, who has lived in the world or looks forward to participating in Arab aspirations; even more, an Arab is one who believes in a common Arab culture, in a common Arab historical background and social structure, and one who has a feeling of *interdependence* with Arab experiences and traditions. The deciding factor therefore is the *spirit of the Arab community.*[20]

Reduced to its essentials, Arab nationalism thus embodies three main drives:

The urge to freedom and independence. A basic objective is to free Arab territories from foreign oppression. In Nasser's words: "Independence means abolishing the colonial social structure that we inherited from our years of being dominated. . . . It means freedom to make our own decisions, freedom to keep outside anybody's sphere of influence." [21]

The urge for social and economic progress. The Arab National Movement must remove entrenched foreign control which has made Arab society stagnant. In Nasser's words: "For at the heart of the concept of Arab nationalism is the fundamental requirement that it must provide material well-being for its people. Without strong economic sinews, the spiritual, cultural, and political aspirations of Arab nationalism will not endure.[22]

The urge for solidarity. The will and desire for solidarity is ingrained in the minds and hearts of the overwhelming majority of the Arab people. Arab solidarity is an end in itself, for it reflects the community of language, culture, experiences, and aspiration which all

[19] For these definitions I am indebted to Sharabi, *op. cit.*, pp. 96–97.
[20] See *Digest of Major Arab Issues*, Arab Information Center, New York, Sept. 1959, *passim.*
[21] *Ibid.*   [22] *Ibid.*

Arabs share despite political boundaries. It is a positive movement in the sense that it aspires to attain the same norm of life which the Arab people had shared in the past and which was only interrupted after World War I, when Arab lands were divided by European powers against the will of their peoples.[23]

Arab nationalists believe that their spirit of cohesion is not necessarily dependent upon a common religious experience. They say that the Arab world has changed and that they are tired of the pervasiveness of Islam. Some young Arab intellectuals even claim that Islam is an obstacle to progress, or that it is dying. Progress and economic development in the West, they say, came as a result of nationalism. The Arabs, too, must put their loyalty to the state above all else. But the hoped-for Islamic-nationalist ideological split has not been realized.

While the political aims of Arab nationalism are clear, it would be wrong to dismiss the role of religion as negligible. On the contrary it was an essential element of early Arab nationalism and has remained so today despite the development of political overtones. The dominant ideological spirit of the Arab world has been inseparable from its political life. In the pressure for modernization there has been a shift from the older Islamic faith to a newer nationalistic one which advocates politicization of all the important areas of life. The rise of nationalism took place with a diminution, but by no means disappearance, of religious authority. In building the new nation-states, politicians in the Middle East had to deal, often unsuccessfully, with the problem of harmonizing their sense of national consciousness with the persistent relics of Islam. The result was complexity and compounding confusion.

According to a study by Leonard Binder, the uneasy synthesis of religion and politics in Islam is paradoxical: historically religion and politics in the Arab Middle East are one, while theoretically they are dual.[24] Arabs have always thought of themselves first as a religious group and only later as a nation. They tend to deny the existence of an ideological rivalry between Islam and nationalism, or of any tension between religion and politics. To them the possibility of a non-Islamic Arabic government seems somewhat scandalous.

[23] *Ibid.*

[24] Leonard Binder, *The Ideological Revolution in the Middle East* (New York, 1964).

What has emerged from this confrontation, Binder continues, is a kind of coexistence between the Islamic religion and Arab politics. This is expressed in the concept that "Islam is the final and most perfect revelation, and Arab nationalism is the most perfect nationalism." Each contributes in its own way to the glory of God. At the root of this feeling is a recognition by Arabs that the religion of Islam is no longer able to act as a satisfactory base for the new Arab nationalism. But at the same time the Arabs insist on retaining their strong social attachment to Islam. This remains a central problem for nationalists. Political leaders of the past turned to religion to solve all political problems of identity: now the problem has become how much or how little of Islam should be retained in building the new nation-states.

Behind this dilemma is a long historical tradition. When the Arab tribes broke into the Mediterranean and Levantine world some twelve hundred years ago, they brought with them a language (Arabic) and a faith (Islam). Although they separated into kingdoms (Cordova, Tunis, Egypt, and Baghdad), the Arabs maintained linguistic unity as well as the Muslim faith. All believers in the true faith were to be regarded as brothers, and precepts of Islam served to combine all Muslims into a great fraternity.[25] The new religion gave the tribes a national cohesion and intensified their fighting zeal. It was declared the duty of a Muslim ruler to reduce all non-Muslim states to subjection by force of arms.[26] Arab nationalism was stimulated chiefly by common belligerent action against the supplanting of Arab Palestine by the Jewish state of Israel.[27] While politico-economic factors were the contemporary reality, at the base of the differences was the religious and cultural antagonism which colored the pattern of nationalism in the Middle East.

The various nationalist movements in the Arabic-speaking lands gradually fused into a broad, though diversified, front. Like nationalist movements in nineteenth-century Europe, they had to overcome deep-rooted differences in religion, social structure, geographic distance, and vested regional interests.[28] On March 22, 1945, seven Arab states (Egypt, Saudi Arabia, Iraq, Syria, Lebanon, Yemen, and

[25] Cf. Thomas W. Arnold, *The Preaching of Islam: A History of the Propagation of the Muslim Faith* (3rd ed.; London, 1935), p. 416.
[26] Hertz, *op. cit.*, p. 140.   [27] Hayes, *op. cit.*, p. 163.
[28] Kohn, *The Age of Nationalism*, p. 90.

Transjordan) [29] formed the Arab League.[30] The pact had this aim: "The object of the League shall be to strengthen the ties between the participant states, to coordinate their political programs in such a way as to effect real collaboration between them, to preserve their independence and sovereignty, and to consider in general the affairs and interests of the Arab countries." [31]

The idea was to give the Arab people a more spiritually satisfying common national character than that restricted to artificial state boundaries. "It is the form of Arab nationalism which, in spite of dynastic feuds, interstate rivalries, and preoccupation with local interests, gives the Arab League not a little moral strength." [32] A total population of 33,500,000 people in an area of 1,150,000 square miles was to be molded in a vast Arab union. There would be economic cooperation, a new Arab news agency, and an exchange of scholars—all preliminaries to future political unity.

From its beginnings the Arab League was handicapped by looseness of organization and by political fragmentation. High-sounding phrases about Arab unity could not disguise differences. The Egyptians feared the rise of a unified state in northern Arabia which might challenge Egyptian hegemony. Other Arab states resented Egyptian power. The ruler of Saudi Arabia opposed rival Hashimite clans. The Hashimites in the Fertile Crescent (Iraq, Syria, Lebanon, and Transjordan), encouraged by British support, tried to play a central role as unifiers of the Arab world. Politically, Arab union was frustrated by three Arabic nationalisms, each fearing domination by opponents inside the Arab world. Added to political quarrels were continuing religious rivalries, not only between Muslims and assorted religious minorities, but also between individual Muslim sects.[33]

The divergency of interests and policies was revealed in May 1948,

[29] After attaining their independence, Libya, the Sudan, Morocco, Tunisia, and Kuwait joined the Arab League.

[30] On the formation of the Arab League, see Vernon McKay, *The Arab League in World Politics*, Foreign Policy Reports (Nov. 15, 1946). See also B. Y. Boutros-Ghali, *The Arab League, 1945–1955*, International Conciliation No. 498, Carnegie Endowment for International Peace (New York, 1955).

[31] Arabic text in Ahmad Musa, *Mithaq Jami'at al-duwal al-arabiyyah* (Cairo, 1948), p. 1.

[32] Halford L. Hoskins, *The Middle East: Problem Area in World Politics* (New York, 1955), p. 163.

[33] E. A. Speiser, *The United States and the Near East* (Cambridge, Mass., 1947), p. 161.

when all members of the Arab League tried to assist the Palestine Arabs in a critical situation. But only Egypt, Syria, and Jordan were able to provide military help. Later these countries tried to enforce an economic boycott of Israel.

Following his accession of power in 1954, Nasser took over leadership of the Arab nationalist movement. On July 26, 1956, he announced the nationalization of the Suez Canal Company. Though Egypt was badly mauled in a brief war with Israel, France, and Britain, Nasser emerged diplomatically strengthened. He used his increased prestige to advance the cause of Arab nationalism under Egyptian leadership. On February 1, 1958, Egypt and Syria joined to form the United Arab Republic, and on March 8, Yemen associated itself with the union. But in 1961, Syria, annoyed by Egyptian domination, broke with the U.A.R. and returned to its status as a separate country, displaying once again the urge to fragmentation characteristic of Arab nationalism.

Meanwhile, Nasser continued to proclaim himself the leader of Arab nationalism in such speeches as this one, given at Damascus on March 11, 1959:

Fellow Countrymen,

When we took it upon ourselves to raise high the banner of Arab nationalism and defend its call; when we chose the difficult, hard way, the way of defending the whole of the Arab nation, working for it in its entirety, of Arab unity and Arab nationalism, we knew that this way might be a rough one to travel, that it might be easier if we chose one of an isolationist policy, a road with a policy that was indeed selfish, a policy that was based largely on ignoring whatever happened in other Arab countries. We knew that such a policy would be easier at the outset, but that eventually it would hand over one Arab country after another to its enemies, that such a divided Arab country could not achieve solidarity, would inevitably surrender to imperialism; so all of us, each and every one of the sons of this nation, preferred the rough, hard way, the way to Arab unity and solidarity, and resolved to raise the banner of Arab nationalism and exert every effort to consolidate it thoroughly.[34]

Thus Nasser clothed his nationalism in the humanitarian ideals of the early nineteenth-century European nationalism presented by Herder. But while it was conscious of history and cultural identity, Nasserism

[34] The full text is in Muhammad Khalil, *The Arab States and the Arab League* (Beirut, 1962), II, 946.

was activist and pragmatic, socialist in industry and welfare, existential-
ist rather than rational, "democratic" only on the surface.

Opposition to Nasser arose both in and out of the Arab world.
Leaders of other Arab states resented Nasser's assumption of the exclusive right to speak for all Arabs, though they were careful not to
challenge him openly because of his popularity with the Arab masses.
To British journalist Barbara Ward it is yet to be proved that "Arabism" as such can provide the common ground for communities as
diverse in interest as the Arab states:

> But these internal problems are nothing compared with the recklessness of
> Arab nationalism as an international force. No international society can
> survive peacefully if nations organize their energies on the basis of so
> much hatred of other groups. It is hardly a praiseworthy achievement to
> keep the world on the brink of war. No local aim can be worth the risk of
> general destruction. In its blind disregard of other rights and interests, in
> its total absorption in its own ambitions, Arab nationalism may end not by
> recreating the Middle East but by ending the whole human experiment.[35]

TURKEY: FROM RELIGIOUS TO STATE NATIONALISM

After the Crusades, the Seljuk Turks, who had been unable to maintain the integrity of their empire against the crusaders, were supplanted
by the stronger Ottoman Turks.[36] Overrunning the Asiatic provinces
that once had been on the periphery of the Roman Empire, the Ottoman Turks in 1453 took Constantinople and made it the capital of their
empire. Turkish, Byzantine, and Islamic traditions were combined in a
despotic regime that was to last until the end of World War I. The
empire reached its greatest splendor during the regime of Suleiman the
Magnificent (ruled 1520–1566). Thereafter the story is one of decline.

Ottoman rule was based not on a common nationality but on a
dominant religion.[37] The Turkish overlords had little in common with
the Arabic-speaking peoples of their domain other than the Islamic
religion. They reduced the Arabs to the status of provincial vassals

---

[35] Barbara Ward, *Five Ideas That Change the World* (New York, 1959), p. 44.
[36] The Ottoman Turks were named after their outstanding leader, Osman.
[37] See A. Toynbee and K. Kirkwood, *Modern Turkey* (London, 1926); and
Mehmed Pasha, *Ottoman Statecraft*, trans. Walter L. Wright, Jr. (Princeton,
1935).

organized in religious communities called millets, which formed states within the state. They had little use for the Western concept of the national state, but instead insisted upon maintaining the religious character of their empire. The despotism of the sultan was restricted only by the laws of Islam as interpreted by its lawyer-theologians.[38]

The disintegration of the Ottoman Empire may be attributed to a combination of factors, including lack of national unity, misrule, lawlessness, corruption, capitulations,[39] and discontent. Turkish despotism culminated in the long rule from 1876 to 1909 of Sultan Abdul-Hamid II, whose reign included wars with Serbia (1876), Russia (1877–1878), and Greece (1897). Because of the atrocities committed by Turks in Armenia (1894–1896), Gladstone called him "Great Assassin." In fear of the infectious spirit of nationality which he felt was undermining his empire, Abdul-Hamid tried to counter it with more emphasis on religion and by promoting Pan-Islamism. He relied on the religious fanaticism of the Turkish masses to turn back the growing tide of nationalist sentiment.

Abdul-Hamid's task was hopeless, for already during the first half of the nineteenth century the disintegration of the Empire was being hastened by the infiltration of Western nationalist ideas. The spirit of nationalism found ready acceptance among the subject people and led to one independence movement after another. The Russians were delighted by the possibility of collapse of the Turkish Empire, which they styled "the sick man of Europe." What saved the empire from extinction was intervention by the British and the French, who had no intention of allowing the Russians to penetrate to the warm waters of the Mediterranean through Constantinople. But the great powers could only delay the final collapse. The momentum of nationalism throughout the Middle East was too great to be halted.

Turkish intellectuals, in close contact with the West, began to call for reform of the medieval religious despotism by which their country was ruled. They demanded a liberal constitution, parliamentarianism, and Western education. A new nationalist literature appeared. Ibrahim Sinasi, a pioneer in Turkish journalism, was the first to translate French

---

[38] Hertz, *op. cit.*, p. 143.

[39] Capitulations were extraterritorial privileges or immunities enjoyed by foreigners in the Ottoman Empire. They involved immunity from local jurisdiction and resulted in encroachment on Turkish sovereignty.

poetry; Namik Kemal awakened Turkish national consciousness with
his patriotic play, *Vatan* (Fatherland); [40] Mehmed Emin, a religious
poet of lowly stock, became spokesman for the masses; Köpruli Zadé
Mohammed Fūad Bey, a professor at Constantinople University, compiled a history of Ottoman literature. New societies, such as the Turk
Derneyi at Constantinople and the Yeni Lisanjilar at Salonica, were
dedicated to creating a new literature free from foreign influence.
Those nationalist students who were driven from the country continued their agitation from foreign soil in the hope of one day returning
to their homeland and overthrowing the government.

The real founder of the new Turkish nationalist movement was Ziyā
Gök Alp (1875–1924), its most influential apostle. [41] A patriotic poet, he
sang of the new Turkish fatherland:

> A land in which the call to prayer resounds from
>   the mosque in the Turkish tongue,
> Where the peasant understands the meaning of his prayers.
> A land where the schoolboy reads the Koran in
>   his mother tongue,
> O son of the Turk, that is thy Fatherland.

Ziyā Gök Alp sought to educate his people about the idea of the
fatherland in prose as well:

About the concept of "Fatherland." It means a sacred piece of land for
whose sake people shed their blood. Why is it that all other lands are not
sacred, but only that which is called Fatherland? And how does it happen
that those who believe this way do not hesitate to sacrifice their lives, their
families, their most beloved ones? Evidently not because of any utilitarian
value. The sacredness is certainly derived from something sacred. But
what can that sacred thing be?

Is it the state? The state is not a power existing by itself. The state
derives its power from the nation and from the *ümmet: sharaf al-makān
bil-makīn* ["the glory of the residence is with the resident"]! Thus, there
are only two things which are sacred: the nation and the *ümmet* [the
totality of those people who profess the same religion; the state consists of
all those who are administered by the same government; the nation is
composed of all those who speak the same language]. As the objects of

---

[40] Hans Kohn, *Nationalism: Its Meaning and History* (rev. ed.; Princeton, 1965),
p. 62.

[41] See Uriel Heyd, *Foundations of Turkish Nationalism: The Life and Teachings of Ziyā Gök Alp* (London, 1950).

reverence are two, their symbols of the homelands . . . of these two sacred objects should also be two: the homeland of the *ümmet* and the homeland of the nation.[42]

Nationalist opposition to the government crystallized in the Young Turk movement, whose battle cry was "Khalga dogrhu" ("To the people").[43] The Young Turks wanted to blend all the diverse nationalities of the Empire into a common Ottoman nation. They agitated for the use of Turkish as the official language of communication and called for the rejection of Arabic and Persian words. They glorified their Mongolian ancestors and promoted Pan-Turanianism, the national union of all peoples (including those in Russia) of Turanian stock. But above all they demanded an end to the supremacy of Islam and its hierarchy of lawyer-theologians in favor of freedom and equality of all religions. The drift from religious to state nationalism was becoming stronger.

In 1908 the Young Turk movement was successful in overthrowing the old medieval despotism. But the period of their rule (1908–1918) marked a growing estrangement between Turks and Arabs and a series of wars which drained the empire of its strength. The Young Turks were unable to resolve the contradiction between the multinational empire which they wanted to preserve and the modern nation-state which they desired to create.[44]

In 1914 the Ottoman Empire sided with the Central Powers. At the time of the armistice the Ottoman armies were beaten, and Arabia, Syria, Mesopotamia, and Palestine were in the hands of the Allies. The Treaty of Sèvres, signed on August 10, 1920, dismembered the empire and menaced the whole national future of the Turks.[45] Turkish nation-

[42] Ziyā Gök Alp, "Nation and Fatherland" (originally published as "Millet ve Vatan," in *Türk Yurdu*, VI, No. 66; Istanbul, 1914), trans. Niyazi Berkes in *Turkish Nationalism and Western Civilization, Selected Essays of Ziyā Gök Alp* (London, 1959), pp. 78–79.

[43] See the study by Ernest E. Ramsaur, Jr., *The Young Turks: Prelude to the Revolution of 1908* (Princeton, 1957).

[44] Kohn, *Nationalism: Its Meaning and History*, p. 63.

[45] The territorial terms of the Treaty of Sèvres were establishment of mandates in Syria, Mesopotamia, and Palestine; independence for Armenia and the Hedjaz; autonomy for Kurdistan; renunciation by Turkey of all claims on Cyprus, Tripoli, Egypt, Tunis, and Morocco; cession of eastern Thrace to Greece; temporary administration of Smyrna and southwestern Asia Minor by Greece; and cession of the Dodecanese Islands to Italy. The economic terms were payment by Turkey of Allied expenses of occupation; confirmation of prewar concessions to Allies;

alists refused to accept the humiliating treaty. After smashing the Greek invasion of Anatolia, the Turks signed the Treaty of Lausanne, on July 24, 1923, which granted them virtually all they had demanded.[46] Turkey was the only defeated nation of World War I to succeed in negotiating a treaty with the Allies on an equal footing.

The organization of resistance to the Allies and the subsequent Westernization of Turkey was the work of one man, Mustafa Kemal (1880–1938), better known as Kemal Atatürk.[47] If Ziyā Gök Alp was the heart and soul of Turkish nationalism, Kemal was its activist muscle. Born in Salonica, Greece, the son of a timber merchant, he entered the Turkish army as an officer and took part in the Young Turk movement of 1908.[48] After service at Gallipoli and Mesopotamia in World War I, he organized and led the nationalist movement which eventually turned the Greeks out of Smyrna. In 1923 he was elected president and ruled Turkey as an all-powerful but benevolent dictator until his death.

Once in power Kemal set out to create a national state on a new foundation. He expelled what he considered to be alien elements but received immigrants from the Balkans.[49] He replaced the Arabic script by the Latin. He discouraged polygamy and set aside those laws and customs which placed Turkish women in an inferior position. He abolished the fez and introduced the European practice of wearing hats. He also ended the custom that had required women to wear veils. He tried to teach the masses the simple rules of hygiene and health.

Allied supervision of Turkish finances; international control of the Straits; and re-establishment of capitulations for foreign residents in Turkey.

[46] The provisions of the Treaty of Lausanne were relinquishment by Turkey of Mesopotamia, the Hedjaz, Palestine, Syria, the Dodecanese Islands, and other territorial awards of the Treaty of Sèvres; retention by Turkey of Constantinople, Gallipoli, eastern Thrace, Armenia, Smyrna, and Cilicia; exchange of Greek and Turkish subjects; abolition of capitulations; and renunciation of indemnities by the Allies (see Ahmed Emin Yalman, *Turkey in the World War* [New Haven, 1930]).

[47] He earned the name "Kemal" (perfect) for his ability in mathematics as a young student. The designation "Atatürk" (Father of the Turks) came from the Grand National Assembly.

[48] On Mustafa Kemal's life, see Harold C. Armstrong, *Grey Wolf: Mustafa Kemal* (London, 1932); and Dagobert von Mikusch, *Mustapha Kemal* (Garden City, N.Y., 1931).

[49] See Carlile A. Macartney, *National States and National Minorities* (London, 1934), p. 433.

These and other reforms were incompatible with the religion of Islam. Kemal was certain that the Turkish nationality could survive only in an atmosphere of Western ideas and that he must break the ecclesiastical mold. "The good-for-nothing priests," he said, "had in the past decided the form of the constitution, the details of the life of each Turk, his food, his hours of rising and sleep, the shape of his clothes, the routine of the midwife who produced his children, what he learned in schools, his customs, his thoughts, even his most intimate habits." [50] On March 3, 1924, as a first step, Kemal abolished the caliphate as "an antiquated and useless institution." By thus severing the last tie with Pan-Islamism, Kemal turned to his chosen course of state nationalism.[51] He replaced the laws of the Koran with modern civil, penal, and commercial codes. He secularized the state by striking from the constitution the clauses stating that Islam was the established religion.[52] He opposed the doctrine of *kismet* (the will of Allah), a form of fatalism.

In October 1927, Kemal delivered an address at Angora before the deputies and representatives of the Republican Party, of which he was the founder and head. In this unique speech, which lasted four days, from October 15 to October 20, and required 724 pages to print, Kemal reviewed his own role in the transformation of Turkish life. He finished by appealing to his listeners to carry on the work of Turkish national life:

Gentlemen, it was necessary to abolish the fez, which sat on our heads as a sign of ignorance, of fanaticism, of hatred to progress and civilization, and to adopt in its place the hat, the customary headdress of the whole civilized world, showing, among other things, that no difference existed in the manner of thought between the Turkish nation and the whole family of civilized mankind. . . .

Gentlemen, I have taken trouble to show, in these accounts, how a great people, whose national course was considered as ended, reconquered its independence; how it created a national and modern State founded on the results of science.

The result we have attained today is the fruit of teachings which arose

[50] Armstrong, *op. cit.,* p. 241.

[51] Speiser, *op. cit.,* p. 56. This left the Arab world with the choice of turning to a new form of Islamic religious nationalism without Ottoman control, or, like Egypt, turning to a state nationalism of their own.

[52] For the official oath in the name of Allah, the affirmation of an individual's honor was substituted: "I on my honor vow as a Turk."

from centuries of suffering, and the price of streams of blood which have drenched every foot of the ground of our beloved Fatherland.

This holy treasure I lay in the hands of the youth of Turkey. Turkish Youth! Your primary duty is ever to preserve and defend the national independence, the Turkish Republic.[53]

Worn out by his labors, Kemal died in 1938 without having reached his goal of a fully modernized Turkey. There were still many problems. Up to 1945 the Republican Party had tolerated little opposition, but for the next decade other political groups were allowed to be organized. In 1954 the Democratic Party, under Adnan Menderes, set out to obliterate political opposition. This seemed to be a pattern: political parties generally were intolerant of their opponents.

Despite domestic difficulties, the Turks were willing to place their lives and property at stake in order to remain a free people. Turkey's foreign policy remained strictly pro-Western. The country resisted any encroachments by Soviet Russia and maintained friendly relations with the United States in the cold war.

The Turks emerged from a corrupt Ottoman past with a strong state nationalism. Dedicated to the maintenance of national integrity in a dangerous corner of the world, Turkish nationalism was an extension of Kemal's favorite slogan: "Be proud! Work! Be confident!"

ISRAEL: DERIVATIVE NATIONALISM

Nationalism in Africa and Asia was a reaction to colonial exploitation. On the other hand the emergence of Jewish nationalism and the re-creation of the state of Israel were secondary developments provoked by the primary nationalism of western Europe. Return to Palestine had long been a historical ideal, but the impetus came from the coffee shops of anti-Semitic Vienna, the cafes of anti-Dreyfusard Paris, and the cellars of the Jewish Pale in Russia.[54]

[53] *A Speech Delivered by Ghazi Mustapha Kemal, President of the Turkish Republic, October, 1927* (Leipzig, 1929), pp. 721–724.

[54] "Nationalism . . . has been carried to Asia and Africa; and Israel, which to some may seem the return of an ancient people to its long-suspended rights, to others seems—and I believe it to be—the last product of European nationalism: a product which, since it is a national sentiment, not a colonial exploitation, is the more solid and therefore the more formidable. How can we predict the course of the tertiary nationalism which in its turn has sharpened the nationalism of the Arabs?" (H. R. Trevor-Roper, "Jewish and Other Nationalisms," *Commentary*, XXXV [Jan. 1963], 21).

Despite their seclusion in ghettos during the Middle Ages, the Jews never relaxed their yearning for a return to Palestine. Generation after generation of pious Jews made pilgrimages to the Holy Land, some settling there permanently in order to be buried in holy soil.[55] Persecution in Russia and the appearance of anti-Semitism throughout Europe in the late nineteenth century further intensified the yearning for the homeland. Already the idea of Zionism was being preached in western Europe by Moses Hess (1812–1875) and in eastern Europe by Hirsch Kalischer (1795–1874) and Perez Smolenskin (1842–1885). But the two most important names in the history of Jewish nationalism are Leo Pinsker and Theodor Herzl.

Persecution of the Jews in Russia reached a climax in 1882, when murderous assaults were made throughout the Jewish Pale. In that same year Leo Pinsker (1821–1891), a doctor in Odessa, stirred by this manifestation of hatred, wrote his famous book *Auto-emancipation*. Analyzing the effects of anti-Semitism, he concluded that the policy of assimilation, which he had advocated for many years, was ineffective. Jewish dignity and survival, he believed, could be satisfied only by the re-establishment of a Jewish nation somewhere, not necessarily in Palestine. He suggested that the effort was favored by the historical circumstances of the nineteenth century: history was an ally because new states were rising which, at an earlier time, would not have dared to dream of resurrection. The Jews were fortunate that governments were already listening to the clamor of awakening national self-consciousness.[56] Pinsker joined a society called the Chovevei Zion (Lovers of Zion), formed for the purpose of promoting Jewish colonization in Palestine. The first pioneers had already left to settle there and "redeem" (*geulah*) the land.[57]

A new chapter in the history of political Zionism was written by

---

[55] "Diaspora Jewry lavished of its money and learning upon this ever self-rejuvenating remnant in Zion which, largely consisting of scholars and devotees, could not possibly be self-supporting. The *Halukkah* (distribution of Palestine relief) was subject to much abuse and maladministration but it helped maintain a permanently vital link not only between the Holy Land and the community of the Dispersion, but also among the latter in relation to one another" (Salo W. Baron, *Modern Nationalism and Religion* [New York, 1947], p. 227).

[56] See Trevor-Roper, *op. cit.*, p. 15.

[57] Hans Kohn, *Nationalism: Its Meaning and History*, p. 75. The first Zionist colonies, peopled mostly by Jews from Russia and eastern Europe, were established in Palestine in 1882: *Rishon le Zion* in Judea, *Zichron Jakob* in Samaria, and *Rosh Pina* in Galilee. Jewish philanthropists, notably Baron Edmond de Rothschild, contributed generously to these early settlements.

Theodor Herzl (1860–1904), an Austrian journalist, when his classic *The Jewish State* was published in 1896. Embittered by the implications of the Dreyfus affair, Herzl proposed a detailed plan for the establishment of a Jewish commonwealth in Palestine under the suzerainty of the sultan. "The Jewish question," he wrote, "is a national question which can be solved only by making it a political world-question to be discussed and settled by the civilized nations of the world in council." [58] "The distinctive nationality of the Jews neither can, will, nor must be destroyed." [59] And further: "Our national character is too historically famous and in spite of every degradation, too fine to make the annihilation desirable." [60]

In 1897, Herzl founded *Die Welt*, which became the official journal of Zionism.[61] He was astonished when in 1897 some two hundred delegates appeared for the first Zionist Congress at Basel, which demanded a home for the Jews in Palestine secured by public law.[62] The Congress recommended the following means to attain this end: (1) the promotion on suitable lines of the colonization of Palestine by Jewish and agricultural and industrial workers; (2) the organization and binding together of the whole of Jewry by means of appropriate institutions, local and international, in accordance with the laws of each country; (3) the strengthening and fostering of Jewish national settlement and consciousness; and (4) preparatory steps toward obtaining government consent where necessary to the attainment of the aims of Zionism.

As president of the World Zionist Organization, Herzl tried to obtain from Sultan Abdul-Hamid II permission to create a Jewish charter company for settlement in Palestine. But the negotiations were unsuccessful. Similar attempts to obtain assistance from William II, the German emperor, and from other rulers, also ended unfavorably. The lone public offer came in 1903 from the British, when Colonial Minister

[58] Theodor Herzl, *The Jewish State* (New York, 1943), p. 20.

[59] *Ibid.*, p. 24.   [60] *Ibid.*, p. 38.

[61] On the development of Zionism, see Israel Cohen, *The Zionist Movement* (London, 1945); Martin Buber, *Israel and Palestine: The History of an Idea* (London, 1952); and N. Sokolow, *History of Zionism* (London, 1919).

[62] For some time Herzl had wavered between accepting any suitable country and insisting upon the ancient homeland. The strong pro-Palestine sentiment of the delegates to the first Zionist Congress settled the problem. As early as 1891, Baron Maurice de Hirsch had formed a Jewish Colonization Association to transport three million Russian Jews to Argentina, but the movement failed.

Joseph Chamberlain suggested the uninhabited highlands of the East African protectorate of Uganda as a Jewish homeland. Russian Jews, even victims of pogroms, angrily refused the offer. The project was shelved in 1905 by the seventh Zionist Congress. At the same time the British proposal, by officially recognizing the Zionist organization, had the effect of placing the movement on the world's diplomatic map.[63] It also began the long chain of negotiations which eventually resulted in the formation of Israel.

In 1904 the Zionist movement suffered a blow with the death of Herzl. Another setback was the Young Turk revolt of 1908, with its postulation of a united Ottoman nationality. Palestine, populated mostly by Arabs, was then a Turkish province, and the Turks had no intention of awarding it to the Jews.

By this time the Zionist movement, though it was gaining many adherents, had split into political factions: left (Poale Zion), right (Mizrachi), and center (General Zionists). Most of its followers came from the ranks of eastern European Jews living in the United States. Most Spanish Jews (Sephardi) and the prosperous German Jews were either hostile or indifferent to the movement.

Among the world's Jews there was a difference of opinion between those supporting political Zionism and those defending the religious basis of Jewry.[64] The Agudath Israel, the ultraorthodox Jews, objected to political aspects of the movement and insisted that the return to Israel must be made through divine intervention rather than through temporal agencies. The rabbis of reformed synagogues opposed Zionism because of its nationalist character. Anti-Zionism was strong in both Britain and the United States. On May 24, 1917, C. J. Montefiore, president of the Anglo-Jewish Association, attacked political Zionism as incompatible with the religious basis of Jewry. It introduced, he said, "a secular Jewish nationality, recruited on some loose and obscure principle of race and of ethnographic peculiarity." [65] Similar protests were later made in the United States by the American Jewish Committee, headed by Jacob H. Schiff and Louis Marshall. American Jews, it was said, refused to compromise their status as United States citizens with Jewish nationalism. "I believe I am not far wrong," said Schiff, "if

---

[63] Baron, *op. cit.*, p. 231.

[64] For a summary of these differences, see George Lenczowski, *The Middle East in World Affairs* (Ithaca, N.Y., 1952), pp. 314–316.

[65] Quoted in J. M. N. Jeffries, *Palestine: The Reality* (London, 1939), p. 147.

I say that from fifty to seventy per cent of the so-called Jewish Nationalists are either atheists or agnostics and that the great majority of Jewish Nationalist leaders have absolutely no interest in the Jewish religion." [66]

In World War I the Zionist movement was at first divided in its attitude toward the belligerents, but eventually united under Chaim Weizmann (1874–1952), who became the next great apostle of Jewish nationalism. Born in one of the Jewish Pales in Grodno, Russia, Weizmann studied chemistry. In Britain in World War I he was appointed director of the Admiralty laboratories engaged in research work for the War Office. During this period he made an important discovery of a process for the manufacture of acetone, used in high explosives.[67]

On November 2, 1917, the British government announced its sympathy with Zionism in a letter from A. J. Balfour, then foreign secretary, to Lord Rothschild, which became known as the Balfour Declaration. It stated:

His Majesty's Government view with favor the establishment in Palestine of a National Home for the Jewish people, and will use their best endeavours to facilitate the achievement of that object, it being clearly understood that nothing shall be done which may prejudice civil and religious rights of existing non-Jewish communities in Palestine, or the rights and political status enjoyed by the Jews in any other country.[68]

The Balfour Declaration was received with intense criticism by Jews themselves.[69] The British government found it embarrassing to reconcile the declaration with its own commitments to Arab nationalism.[70] An Anglo-French declaration of November 7, 1918, addressed to the

---

[66] *Ibid.*, p. 153.

[67] On Weizmann's life, see his autobiography *Trial and Error* (London, 1949).

[68] Text in L. Stein, *Zionism* (London, 1925). For the story of Zionist negotiations with the British government in World War I and related exchanges with Britain's allies and parallel negotiations with the Central Powers, see Nathan M. Gelber, *Hatsharat-Balfur we-toldoteha* [The Balfour Declaration and Its History] (Jerusalem, 1939).

[69] The declaration was condemned by such diverse elements as the extreme orthodox, the reform and liberal Jews, as well as the Socialist *Bund* in Poland.

[70] A complicating factor was that the British, in mid-1915 and early 1916, had made political promises to the Arabs. To enlist Arab aid in the war, a "Greater Arab Kingdom" was suggested, to consist of the kingdom of the Hedjaz, and, presumably, including Palestine. It was in conformance with this understanding that the Arab revolt, stimulated and led in part by T. E. Lawrence, began in June 1916.

Arabs, supported the enfranchisement of peoples suppressed by the Turks, and in the United States, Wilson's Fourteen Points asserted the principle of self-determination of small nations. The Arabs were delighted by these proposals, but soon were angered by two measures: the French liquidation of the Arab regime set up in Damascus by Prince Faisal, and the British decision to work with the Jewish Agency in Palestine.[71]

On April 25, 1920, the victorious Allies awarded the mandate for Palestine to Great Britain, and on July 22, 1922, Great Britain was confirmed as the mandatory power by the League of Nations. The mandate text explicitly incorporated the Balfour Declaration almost verbatim.[72] Article four provided for a Jewish Agency to cooperate with the mandatory power.[73] Sir Herbert Samuel, a British Jew but not a Zionist, was appointed the first high commissioner of Palestine.

There were only 55,000 Jews in Palestine in 1918. As soon as Jewish immigration began, protesting Arabs rioted. Winston Churchill, the colonial secretary, issued a memorandum on June 3, 1922, in which he restated Britain's aim to create a national Jewish homeland in Palestine, assured the Arabs that all of Palestine would not be converted into a Jewish national state, and then said that the British mandatory power would allow Jewish immigration to the extent dictated by economic conditions in that country. Arabs were not appeased by Churchill's moderate proposals.[74]

With the increase of Jewish immigration and the successful regeneration of the land in Palestine, the Arabs intensified their opposition.[75] There were violent incidents at the Wailing Wall in 1929 and anti-Jewish riots in the early 1930's. In 1935 a group of extremist Jews, calling themselves Revisionists and led by Vladimir Zhabotinsky, opposed

[71] Halford L. Hoskins, *The Middle East* (New York, 1955), p. 101.
[72] For the full text of the mandate, see Royal Institute for International Affairs, *Great Britain and Palestine* (London, 1946), p. 151.
[73] See Lenczowski, *op. cit.*, p. 317.
[74] On British policy in Palestine, see Paul L. Hanna, *British Policy in Palestine* (Washington, D.C., 1942); Esco Foundation for Palestine, *Palestine: A Study of Jewish, Arab, and British Policies* (2 vols.; New Haven, 1947); and Royal Commission on Palestine, *Palestine Royal Commission Report* [Peel Report] (London, 1937). The latter book evaluates the interplay of conflicting forces to the outbreak of the Palestine Arab revolt in 1936.
[75] "To Jews, whether Zionist or non-Zionist, immigration was an urgent human need; to Zionists it was also a potential weapon; but to the Arabs it was a growing menace" (Speiser, *op. cit.*, p. 204).

moderation, seceded from the Zionist organization, and called for the formation of a Jewish state over the whole of Palestine and Transjordan. Another activist party, the Stern Gang, proclaimed a struggle against both Arabs and British. The moderate Zionist community had its own paramilitary Haganah (Defense), which the British branded as subversive. Terrorism mounted, in response to which the British in a kind of Pavlovian reaction sent investigative commissions. Plan after plan was discarded as unworkable.

At a conference arranged in London in February and March of 1939, Arab and Jewish delegations held separate meetings because Palestinian Arabs refused to sit with Jewish representatives. The meeting disbanded without agreement. On May 17, 1939, a final effort to arrive at a compromise solution was embodied in the famous White Paper. Reversing their former policy, the British proposed to create within ten years an independent unitary government for Palestine to be achieved by a gradual devolution of power and to be linked with Britain by a special treaty. The British agreed to limit the number of Jewish immigrants to 75,000 for the next five years, after which immigration was to cease altogether. There were also clauses calling for the discouragement of land transfer from Arabs to Jews. It was a measure of the strength of both Jewish and Arab nationalism that each side contemptuously rejected the White Paper. The Arabs denounced it as condoning Jewish abuses; the Jews attacked it as an intolerable desertion of the Balfour Declaration.

There was a precarious truce among the unreconciled rivals during World War II.[76] The British were more than ever determined to implement their policy in Palestine. The Stern Gang and the Irgun, both terrorist groups, increased their activity against the British.[77] By the end of the war Britain's position in Palestine had become untenable. London turned over the entire problem to the United Nations, which recommended partition of Palestine into Jewish and Arab states. Both sides denounced the proposed solution. On May 15, 1948, Britain abandoned the mandate. That same day the Jewish state of Israel was proclaimed.[78] The Zionist organization ceased its political activity, since

[76] Some thirty thousand Palestinian Jews served in the British war effort in the Near East, while the Palestinian Arabs remained indifferent.

[77] On November 2, 1944, two members of the Stern Gang assassinated Lord Moyne, British minister of state for the Middle East.

[78] See David Ben-Gurion, *Rebirth and Destiny of Israel*, trans. Mordekhai Nurock (New York, 1954), speeches and essays concentrating on the war for independence by Israel's first prime minister.

its goal had been achieved, and confined its work to raising funds for settling immigrants in Israel.

The new state was quickly recognized by both the United States and the Soviet Union. But almost immediately it had to fight for its existence. A combination of Arab League states (Syria, Lebanon, Transjordan, Iraq, and Egypt) launched a war to crush Israel. Prospects for the little state were dim: its army, consisting of the Haganah and some women, numbered 75,000. But the world was astonished by the Israeli performance. With high morale, better equipment, and effective organization, the Jews managed to survive in a cruel war during which atrocities were committed by both sides. Out of the stalemate came a truce, and finally an armistice between Israel and Transjordan was declared on April 3, 1949.[79]

Israel had fought successfully for its existence, but its identity as a state remained precarious. The Arabs, humiliated and angered by the loss of face they had suffered, were determined not to rest until the day they had wiped Israel from the earth. Surrounded by hostile nations growing ever stronger in their desire to destroy her, Israel could count on little support. The Russians, who at first had supported Israel in order to embarrass the British, later encouraged the Arab states in their campaign for revenge. The Western powers, while sympathetic to the little democracy in the Middle East, found it difficult to support her without endangering their access to oil supplies.

Israeli nationalism developed on two fronts. On the domestic scene it took on liberal-democratic and humanitarian qualities. The new na-

---

[79] Among the distressing results of the war was the expulsion of some 700,000 Arabs from their homeland in Palestine. Most lived in poverty in Jordan or at Gaza and were supported by a United Nations relief fund. The return of these refugees remained an article of faith in the speeches of Arab politicians. Ahmed Shukairy, chairman of the Palestine Liberation Organization, declared: "The Arab states will not integrate the Palestine refugees because integration would be a slow process of liquidating the Palestine problem. If there are no Palestinian people, there is no Palestinian cause. We can't conceive of a Babylonian cause today because there are no Babylonians. But we start from the premise that we will achieve the liberation of Palestine soon" (Thomas F. Brady, in *The New York Times*, Apr. 4, 1966). In the eighteen years since Israel came into existence, the Arab refugees increased to 1,300,000 living in four host countries—Jordan, Syria, Lebanon, and the Gaza Strip. The question why the refugees persisted in their hopes when Israel appears to have consolidated her position brought this standard Arab retort: "The Zionists remembered Palestine for two thousand years. Why should we begin to forget in eighteen years?" For an analysis of Israel's policy toward the Arab minority and the Arab refugee problem, see Don Peretz, *Israel and the Palestine Arabs* (Washington, D.C., 1958).

tion-state consisted of three peoples: Palestinian pioneers, orthodox Jews, and refugees. European Jews brought with them the political ideals of the Enlightenment—constitutionalism, parliamentarianism, liberty, equality, and fraternity. Unlike other states in the Middle East, Israel did not develop into a national autocracy; instead she adopted a multiparty system and accepted political freedom as a tradition in the national way of life. Through experience her people had already been conditioned to oppose dictatorship and totalitarianism.

Although the driving force of Israeli nationalism was cultural and religious, it assumed a political aspect as well. The new generation of Israelis paid less attention than its elders to the remains of ancient Judaism. This caused much bitterness among orthodox Jews, an angry minority that retained the old customs and traditions and that predicted disaster for those who wandered from the paths of Judaism. In political conflict the religious parties never polled more than 15 per cent in a general election, yet they represented the majority of the pious Jews in the country. By careful maneuvering they managed to maintain a disproportionately large share of political control and brought about public observance of Judaic customs and traditions.[80] On the other hand, many Israelis, particularly the younger generation, contended that orthodoxy was unable to cope with the complexities of the modern state. Liberal and reform Judaism, popular in the United States, had little impact in Israel.[81]

[80] Although Israel is not formally a theocracy, Judaism is the state religion. Public transportation ceases in Tel Aviv and Jerusalem on the Sabbath; air traffic comes to a halt. Civil marriage is nonexistent. Only the Orthodox interpretation of Judaism is officially recognized. The influence of religious leaders extends far beyond the synagogue.

[81] Most vociferous in its criticism of Israeli "pseudo nationalism" is the American Council for Judaism. According to Rabbi Elmer Berger, executive vice-president: "Judaism is a religion and the sphere of its moral and ethical influence in history has been universal—not tribal or nationalistic. Those who today remain faithful to its spiritual commitments aspire to continue that universalism. Like other historic faiths, Judaism has at various times in history exhibited itself in denominations sharing common fundamentals but displaying varied emphases, reflecting the environment of such a universal faith. It is a perversion of any manifestation of contemporary Judaism to assign its devotees, because they are Jews, any elements of secular nationality relating to national sovereignty, just as any such collective, automatic attribution is in violation of the American constitution principle separating church and state. As Americans of Jewish faith, we have—and we want—not national rights or obligations except as equal, individual citizens of the United States. Israel is the 'homeland' only of its own legal citizens and nationals. The arrogant legal-political claims consistently advanced by both the Israel Govern-

The second face of Israeli nationalism revealed xenophobia coupled with aggressiveness. This was revealed on October 29, 1956, when Israeli troops invaded Egypt and temporarily occupied the Gaza Strip and almost all the Sinai Peninsula up to the Suez Canal. Arnold Toynbee denounced Israeli nationalism, its fanaticism and its Ishmaelitic enmity with its neighbors, as a faithful reproduction of the worst side of European nationalism. He saw it as almost a parody of nineteenth-century nationalism. In his estimation Jewish nationalism, far from being historically justifiable, incorporated the evils of a sentiment that had already caused the Western world much pain, misery, and frustration.

Such Israeli intellectuals as Abba Eban admitted the existence of this other face of nationalism, but they described it as historical necessity. Israel, they said, was an island in a sea of Arab hostility. She could look only to her own strength. Her sharpened sense of nationalism was simply a matter of self-preservation. She could not afford to be weak in the shadow of an irrepressible conflict. As for Toynbee, Israeli nationalists have replied that their consolation lies in the knowledge that Israel is being castigated in the name of all nation-states. The Israeli view is that to denounce all national sovereignty as obsolete, is to confuse historical fact with Toynbee's wish. It is further added that the eclipse of nationalism by some supranational federalism has been predicted so often that it has become one of the platitudes of twentieth-century historiography. In fact, say the defenders of Israeli nationalism, the twentieth century remains the triumphant epoch of the national state as well as the burial ground of all broader associations. For Israel then, they say, the choice is aggressiveness and continued existence, or weakness and oblivion. Criticism is to be expected, but "a Jewish homeland exists; the ideal of freedom to be Jewish has been attained. Israelis are Israelis and Jews. The feat of the Zionists is that they made Judaism and Zionism synonymous." [82]

The argument about Israeli's "aggressiveness" was revived in mid-1967. On May 22, 1967, Nasser declared the Gulf of Aqaba closed to

---

ment and its Zionist appendage that this state, foreign to most Jews of the world, is 'the homeland of the Jewish people' are cut from Zionism's whole cloth fabrication of the 'Jewish people' national entity" (*The New York Times*, May 2, 1965).

[82] Aaron Segal, "Israel and Zionism," *The Nation*, CXCVII (Nov. 9, 1963), 295.

Israeli shipping. On June 3 the Egyptian commander-in-chief, General Mortagi, issued an order of the day to his soldiers in Sinai: "The results of this unique moment are of historic importance for our Arab nation and for the Holy War through which you will restore the rights of the Arabs, which have been stolen in Palestine and reconquer the plundered soil of Palestine." [83]

Within six days the Israeli armed forces smashed the surrounding Arab states in an astounding victory. The cease-fire left Israel in possession of the Gaza Strip, Sharm-el-Sheikh, and the whole of the Sinai Peninsula to the Suez Canal; the old City of Jerusalem; the west bank of the Jordan; and the Syrian heights which had dominated the northern part of Israel. The Israeli victory was not only a defeat for the Arab world but also for the Soviet Union, which had been seeking to extend its prestige in the Middle East by arming the Arabs. Israel became the strongest power in the Middle East.

PROTONATIONALISM VERSUS HETERONATIONALISM:
INTEGRATION AND DIFFERENTIATION

The Arab world encompasses not only the Middle East, running from the Turkish border and the Mediterranean southward to Ethiopia, but also a long line from the Persian border to the Atlantic coast of North Africa. In this great grouping of states, Arabic is the dominant language, and the consciousness of a common nationality is ardently promoted. Nationalist excitement came to the heartland of the Arab world after World War I, when those lands liberated from the Turks were partitioned among the British, French, and Zionists. As a means of weakening the Turks, the British stimulated the revolt of Arab nationalists inside the Turkish empire, where the holy cities of Islam—Mecca and Medina—were located. A nationalist sentiment had already existed among the powerful Arab princes. This sense of national self-consciousness was taken into consideration in the peace settlements during 1919–1920.

The age of conscious nationalism had arrived for the whole Arabic-speaking area. From this point on there occurred a struggle between the new protonationalism of the Pan-Arab world and the heterona-

[83] Randolph S. Churchill and Winston S. Churchill, *The Six Day War* (London, 1967), p. 77.

tional elements among its inhabitants. The terms of the conflict can be expressed as integration versus differentiation.

Arab integration. The Arab world, since decolonization no longer a problem of the great powers, sought a solid framework of its own. Nationalist leaders strove mightily to unite the Arabs across the barriers of religious creeds. They would combine the various nationalist movements in Arabic-speaking lands to produce one broad, though diversified, front. The entire Arab world would be fused into one nationally conscious and politically assertive community, united by a common geographical area, language, religion, and traditions. An Arab cultural renaissance would be the outward signal of this development. All the ruling elites would join in this task, even to the extent of using modern technology to undermine parochial loyalties and to further the cause of Arab integration.

Arab differentiation. Unfortunately for the dreams of Arab nationalists, virtually every Arab people was burdened by heteronational obligations. Throughout the Arab world the self-identification and loyalties of the people remained far beneath the unified national level. Few could see beyond the horizon of the tribe, the religious sect, or the village. It was difficult to overcome deeply rooted differences of social structure and regional interests. Efforts to ensure closer political, economic, military, and cultural cooperation among the Arab states had little success.

Two examples, among many, may be cited. For years the million independent Kurdish tribesmen living in Iraq's mountainous northeastern area have demanded a measure of autonomy from the Baghdad government. After a bloody five-year war, the Iraqi government decided that the rebellious Kurds could be kept happy only by formal recognition of their sense of national consciousness. In July 1966 an agreement was made in which Baghdad promised to observe two nationalisms in Iraq—Arab and Kurdish.

The painful slowness of Pan-Arabism moved Egypt's Nasser to abandon his policy of coexistence with other Arab regimes and to support his ideals by strong-arm methods. In the conflict between Egypt and Saudi Arabia, the atmosphere was poisoned with rumors of plots, counterplots, assassination attempts, and the *coup d'état.*[84] Each side arrested spies and expelled dangerous citizens from the other

---

[84] *The Observer* (London), June 19, 1966.

country. The prospect of a unified or federated Arab state under such circumstances seems slight at the moment.

The nationality problem of the Arab world was summarized by Benjamin Aksin in this passage:

The notable ethnic varieties of the population in question, the still very strong local and tribal identification of many elements within the region, and its division into a large number of states—some traditional, others new—make it more realistic to consider that in this case, too, nationalism, as propagated by the educated élite, is in advance of a socially effective common nationality. Moreover, the impetus of this nationalism is again, as in many other cases, outward-directed, stimulated as it was first by the desire to free the area from European rule and now by common dislike of Israel, and is not free from a xenophobic bias. Whether, if maintained at its present peak, the All-Arab nationalist movement will result in the emergence of a common nationality, even overcoming the divisive effect of separate States, is not yet, certain.[85]

[85] Benjamin Aksin, *States and Nations* (New York, 1964), p. 205.

Chapter 9

Populist Nationalism in Latin America

Happy is the citizen who under the protection of the army of his command has convoked National Sovereignty to exercise its absolute will!

—Simón Bolívar

Nationalism is not so much an exaggerated affirmation of genuine patriotism but rather the incapacity, either through arrogance or resentment, generously and objectively to appreciate other countries or races. . . . Basically, ultranationalism is ignorance.

—A. E. Edwards, publisher
El Mercurio, Santiago, Chile

Latin America is related to Iberia by language, religion, customs, and ethics, all of which influenced the nature of its nationalism. In colonial times the Latin-American peoples received imprint of the conquistadors.[1] A Spanish or Portuguese coloration is reflected in the relics of traditional universalism, individualism, and romanticism. Latin-American history recapitulated to some extent the historical experience of Spain and Portugal. Change seemed fitful and staggering, coming in jolts and starts. Long periods of quiescence were followed by sudden solutions by force. There was a chasm between classes—the wealthy aristocrats on the one side and the landless peasants on the other. Extreme economic contrasts existed not only throughout the colonial period but also in the nineteenth and twentieth centuries. When independence came, many generations were to pass before a middle class could begin to make its presence felt.

Neither the American Revolution, with its ideology of "Life, Liberty, and the Pursuit of Happiness," nor the French Revolution, with its explosive aphorism, "Liberty, Equality, and Fraternity," had much direct effect on Latin America, with the exception of the few isolated intellectuals who were receptive to these new ideas. The most important stimulus to Latin-American nationalism came from Napoleon, though in a way which the dictator hardly expected or wanted. During 1807–1808, French armies invaded Spain, and overthrew the Spanish king. Because Napoleon was making all Europe the private domain of his Corsican family, he presented the Spanish throne to his brother Joseph. In this way Spanish America became a part of the Bonaparte family empire. Spanish Americans reacted strongly against this new situation. They declined to accept Joseph Bonaparte as their ruler,

---

[1] For colonial Latin America, see Bailey W. Diffie, *Latin-American Civilization: Colonial Period* (Harrisburg, Pa., 1945); Lewis Hanke, *The Spanish Struggle for Justice in the Conquest of America* (Philadelphia, 1949); John H. Parry, *The Spanish Theory of Empire in the Sixteenth Century* (Cambridge, England, 1940); Philip W. Powell, *Soldiers, Indians and Silver: The Northward Advance of New Spain, 1550–1600* (Berkeley, 1952); Hubert Herring, *A History of Latin America* (New York, 1961); and Silvio A. Zavala, *New Viewpoints on the Spanish Colonization of America*, trans. Joan Coyne (Philadelphia, 1943).

seized control of their local governments, and at first proclaimed their loyalty to the Spanish House of Bourbon. From rebellion against the French conqueror to calls for independence was a short, logical step.

Soon all of Latin America was embroiled in barracks revolts, politics, and civil wars. Between 1810 [2] and 1825 the Spanish empire in America disintegrated as one Latin-American country after another, except Cuba and Panama, achieved independence. When Ferdinand VII was restored to the Spanish throne in 1815 after the fall of Napoleon, he tried on the basis of legitimacy to restore the old absolutism in his Spanish American possessions. Revolts both inside Spain and in Spanish America in 1820 forced the Spanish ruler to adopt a more liberal regime. In Mexico a republic was set up in 1823, after the Creoles rallied to the cause of independence.[3]

During this era of nationalist fervor there appeared a flood of writing in praise of nationhood.[4] Along with the intellectuals came the activists, Americans of Spanish descent who advocated struggle against Spain as the proper course to independence. Chief among these nationalists were Simón Bolívar and José de San Martín, the two greatest figures of the Latin-American independence movement.

Simón Bolívar (1783–1830) was descended on both sides from noble Venezuelan families.[5] After studying in various European capitals, especially in Madrid, and witnessing the final scenes of the French Revolution, he returned home to join the party of independence in Venezuela. In a series of strategic battles he was able to prove himself a brilliant

---

[2] The dike broke on September 16, 1810, when Father Miguel Hidalgo gathered a force of badly armed Indians while raising the battle cry in the name of the Virgin of Guadalupe, and marched on Mexico City. There the viceroy, supported by Creoles (Spaniards born in America), routed the peasant army and executed its leader. But Hidalgo had succeeded in starting the flood of Latin-American nationalism. Other patriots rose to take his place in the struggle for independence.

[3] See Henry B. Parkes, *A History of Mexico* (Boston, 1938).

[4] John J. Johnson, "The New Latin American Nationalism," *Yale Review*, LV (Winter 1965), 187.

[5] On Bolívar's life, see the most satisfactory single volume, Gerhard Masur, *Simón Bolívar* (Albuquerque, 1948). See also Victor A. Belaúnde, *Bolívar and the Political Thought of the Spanish American Revolution* (Baltimore, 1938); John B. Trend, *Bolívar and the Independence of Spanish America* (New York, 1951); William D. Marsland and Amy L. Marsland, *Venezuela through Its History* (New York, 1954); Guillermo A. Sherwell, *Simón Bolívar* (Washington, D.C., 1921); and John J. Johnson, *Simón Bolívar and Spanish American Independence, 1783–1830* (Princeton, 1968).

tactician. From 1817 to 1821, at the head of an enthusiastic force, he drove the royalists out of New Granada, Venezuela, and Ecuador. On February 15, 1819, the hero of liberation made a speech at Angostura in which he spoke of the idea of national sovereignty:

The declaration of the Republic of Venezuela is the most glorious, most heroic, most worthy act of a free people; it is one that with the greatest satisfaction I have the honor to offer Congress, being already sanctioned by the unanimous will of the free people of Venezuela.

Deign, Legislators, to accept with indulgence the profession of my political faith, the highest wishes of my heart and the fervent prayer which on behalf of the people I dare address you: Deign to grant to Venezuela a government preeminently moral, which will hold in chains oppression, anarchy and guilt. A government which will allow righteousness, tolerance, peace to reign; a government which will cause equality and liberty to triumph under the protection of inexorable laws.

Gentlemen, commence your duties; I have finished mine.[6]

From Bolívar's viewpoint Spain, being unable to attain the submission of Latin Americans, had resorted to devious artfulness in order to bring back "the ignominious yoke." Patriotic Venezuelans had fought against a government whose incentives were "a death-dealing sword and the flames of the Inquisition," "a government that wants not domains, but deserts, not cities but ruins, not vassals but graves." Bolívar's efforts succeeded in creating a new spirit of independence and liberty. His leadership ended forever Spain's domination in the New World.[7]

Three thousand miles away a similar role as national activist was played by José de San Martín (1778–1850), hero of independence movements in Argentina, Chile, and Peru. Born in the Misiones Territory, where his father was a Spanish official, San Martín was educated in Madrid for a military career and served in war against the Moors and against Napoleon.[8] He then dedicated himself to the liberation of the colonies. In 1812 he offered his services to the government of Buenos

---

[6] Simón Bolívar, *An Address at the Congress of Angostura, February 15, 1819* (Washington, D.C., 1819), p. 21.

[7] Bolívar dissipated his entire personal fortune in the cause of revolution. A grateful people hailed him, bestowed on him the title "El Libertador," and twelve years after his death carried his remains to Caracas, where he was buried in the national pantheon.

[8] See the standard biography by Ricardo Rojas, *San Martín, Knight of the Andes,* trans. Herschel Brickell (New York, 1945).

Aires in its war for independence. Convinced that it was necessary to expel Spain from both Chile and Peru, San Martín led an army of three thousand infantry and a thousand cavalry across the Andes in January 1817, a feat comparable to Hannibal's crossing of the Alps. Here he joined forces with Bernardo O'Higgins, the son of an Irish viceroy and a Chilean mother. The two routed the Spanish armies at Chacabuco and Maipú (1817–1818), thereby establishing the independence of Chile. San Martín then pursued his campaign in Peru in 1821 and succeeded in driving out the Spaniards. He assumed the reins of government with the title of protector. However, threatened by jealousy among patriots, royalist intrigue, and the rivalry of Bolívar (whose triumphs had carried him southward to the northern borders of Peru), San Martín voluntarily resigned his authority and left the country.[9] Bolívar's armies finished the task in 1824.

The national enthusiasm stimulated during the wars of independence soon waned. There were barriers to national unity in the independent states. Rigid class distinctions that had plagued the old country carried over into the Latin-American nations. Political and intellectual elites looked down upon their fellow nationals of Amerindian and African origin, and the indigenous Indian population was held in an inferior status.[10] Throughout its history Latin America has been beset by this problem of assimilation.

Most Latin-American states have achieved their independence in the last century and a half. The various moves for freedom were not coordinated, although in most cases they were inspired by the relatively small upper class. The cycle of revolution was long, labored, and complex. During the colonial era, most of the continent was subjected to Spanish absolutism, which unlike British policy in North America, allowed the colonies no experience in self-government. The result was that the Latin-American states, once they had obtained their independence, were badly equipped for the task of governing themselves.

During the nineteenth century, most Latin-American republics oscillated between dictatorship and anarchy. The main conflict was federalism versus centralized government. In several countries led by liberals,

[9] Finding it impossible to live a peaceful life in South America, San Martín left for Europe as an exile and spent the last twenty-five years of his life there. He lived in poverty until his death at Boulogne on August 17, 1850, after vainly offering his services to the nations he had helped to bring into existence.

[10] Johnson, *op. cit.*, p. 187.

the federal form of government was established, as for example in Brazil, with some twenty states at first, three territories, and a federal district. In those countries which fell to dictators, the government was usually centralized. Most Latin Americans remained parochial in their loyalties: they looked to local rather than national leadership. The central governments had little to offer provincial people. During the entire century no national administration in Latin America was able to retain the loyalty of the municipalities and states, as the United States had been able to do successfully.[11]

A major reason for the supplanting of national unity by provincial loyalty was the widespread *caudillo* system, which fostered fragmentation. The *caudillos,* leaders of private armies, first became prominent during the wars of independence, when they acted as front men for the socially powerful, politically oriented landowning class. A landowner would arm a band of his relatives and followers to control a small district. He might join others in order to dominate an entire state or province. Once in possession of a large area, the *caudillo* would march on the national capital, seize the government, and proclaim himself "President of the Republic." His armed followers would be set up as a national army. Rival *caudillos* would then enter into conspiracies to overthrow the incumbent.

OLIGARCHIC CONTRA POPULIST NATIONALISM

The story of nationalism in Latin America revolves around attempts to break traditional molds. The old static nationalism was semifeudal and Church-oriented. Until the late nineteenth century it was the exclusive property of the ruling oligarchy, composed of aristocrats and businessmen. Controlling wealth and income, allied with Church and the military, the ruling few monopolized political and social life. Speaking Spanish and Portuguese, boasting of their European ancestry, nationalists turned east for cultural inspiration and imitated European customs and folkways. Tempered by international interests, dependent upon Europe, oligarchic nationalism was weak and diluted. It was never clear-cut, but rather it was suffused with universalism and localism.

Facing the landed aristocrats and wealthy businessmen were the

[11] *Ibid.*

great masses, including the serfs who worked under conditions of extreme poverty. Excluded from power was the proportionately large Indian population, the mestizos of mixed Spanish and Indian blood, and Negroes. Speaking languages of Indian origin, and mostly pagan or vaguely Christian in religion, the masses gave their loyalty to local community or tribe. They were little impressed by nationalist slogans.

During the last quarter of the nineteenth century a modernizing and secularizing process changed the complexion of Latin-American life. With it came the transformation of nationalism from its oligarchic to a new populist form. Railroads were constructed; ports were improved; cities were modernized; and new manufacturing methods were introduced.[12] Most Latin-American countries, particularly such advanced republics as Chile, Uruguay, and Argentina, turned from feudal agrarianism to urban industrialism.

There also came a change in the social structure which recapitulated the earlier European experience—the emergence of a politically conscious middle class. Behind it was the increasing pace of immigration. Composed of industrialist entrepreneurs, businessmen, professional men, bureaucrats, and white-collar workers, the new bourgeoisie filled the gap between the oligarchy and the masses. Bourgeois spokesmen sought support among those rising from the lower classes, especially workers and miners who had a modicum of literacy and who could satisfy suffrage requirements. The bourgeoisie at first relied on a small but politically wise industrial proletariat, but later sought mass support in their struggle against the traditional oligarchies.

For the new middle class, nationalism was fertile soil. The bourgeoisie did not have the internationalist orientation of the old oligarchies, nor did it possess the parochial loyalties of the Indian and Negro masses. In nationalism it found precisely the right sentiment to believe in and with which to identify itself.[13] Unlike the old nationalism, which lacked political appeal, the new populist nationalism was endowed with political slogans and was then converted into an ideology.[14]

The new middle class, monopolizing access to education and communication, followed the usual procedure of accentuating the elements of nationalism—common traditions, customs, heroes, folklore, music, and art. It was the same pattern, though a century later, that had

[12] See Robert J. Alexander, "Nationalism: Latin America's Predominant Ideology," *Journal of International Affairs*, XV, No. 2 (1961), p. 109.
[13] *Ibid.* [14] Johnson, *op. cit.*, p. 192.

distinguished romanticism in early nineteenth-century Europe. The past was discovered all over again.

An important theme of populist nationalism was *indigenismo*, an identification with the Indian, and to some extent a glorification of him, with particular interest in the Indian past.[15] This followed the new concern of Latin Americans to display their cultural independence from Europe and their determination to color their nationalism with New World conditions. This view was expressed by a Bolivian educator:

We must begin the tasks which we irresponsibly failed to undertake three hundred years ago. . . . A crooked and unsavory way of thinking about the Indian and his meaning with the Bolivian nation must be rectified. We are plagued by anti-scientific prejudices which are basically highly immoral and foreign to the very spirit of nationality. To consider the Indian less than human, ignoring the qualities of his race that are superior to those of the dominant classes, is true inhumanity. . . . This absurd way of thinking was the principal cause of the downfall of Spain in America. . . . But who will undertake this movement which we do not hesitate to call national regeneration? Not the Indian directly, but rather we, the thinkers, the directors, the governors, who are beginning to understand more clearly the whole of our life and the true history of our nature. . . . We will realize that above all we must concede to the Indian respect, justice, dignity, and love, acknowledging that his misery is in many respects our work, and that his resurrection will be our salvation.[16]

Related to *indigenismo*, though in some respects opposed to its extreme form, was a movement to incorporate the Indian into national life. As long as the Indian masses did not participate effectively in everyday affairs, they were regarded as an obstacle to the development of a national culture and a modern state.[17] Nationalist intellectuals sang paeans to the Indian on an abstract level, but in concrete situations most Latin Americans looked down upon the Indian. They regarded him as a sphinx, the inhabitant of a hermetic world that was inaccessible to the white man. "We speak of the Indian as a mass factor in the nation; in

---

[15] Ralph L. Beals and Norman D. Humphrey, *No Frontier to Learning: The Mexican Student in the United States* (Minneapolis, 1957), p. 27.

[16] Franz Tamayo, *La creación de la pedagogía nacional* (La Paz, 1945), pp. 157–158, trans. in Lewis Hanke, *South America* (Princeton, 1959), pp. 135–136.

[17] Beals and Humphrey, *op. cit.*, p. 27.

truth we are ignorant of his individual psyche and his collective drama. The Indian lives. The Indian acts and produces. The Indian does not allow himself to be understood, he doesn't desire communication. Retiring, silent, immutable, he inhabits a closed world. The Indian is an enigma." [18]

The configuration of Latin-American nationalism thus changed in response to the Industrial Revolution and the parallel rise of the bourgeoisie. Unable to cope with new problems, the old oligarchy saw its leadership slip into the hands of the new middle class, composed mostly of naturalized citizens. Strongly nationalistic, the bourgeoisie wanted to be free from foreign economic control and even from cultural influences.

THE WHITAKER PERIODIZATION

The basic trend of Latin-American nationalism was the change from an aristocratic, oligarchic form to the populist character that appeared roughly during the last decade of the nineteenth century. Arthur P. Whitaker has described further changes that have taken place within this general framework.[19] The Whitaker formula lists four important developments in Latin-American nationalism since the late nineteenth century:

Addition of an economic content in the 1890's. The first change was the injection into nationalism of an economic content, partly under socialist influence. This involved a denunciation of imperialism-via-investments, a feat that would have been impossible for armed forces. Subsequently this attitude was broadened to include all "imperialists" as well as the corrupt local oligarchy—*vendepatrias* who had sold out to the imperialists.

Nationalism began to reach full flower about 1910. The narrow nationalism of the anti-imperialist stage was brought into broader focus by the centennial celebrations of independence, particularly in such countries as Argentina, Chile, Colombia, Venezuela, and Mexico. By

[18] Fernando Diez de Medina, Bolivian minister of education, quoted in Robert J. Alexander, *The Bolivian National Revolution* (New Brunswick, N.J., 1958), p. 17.

[19] The précis given here is based on Arthur P. Whitaker, *Nationalism in Latin America: Past and Present* (Gainesville, Fla., 1962), pp. 21–24.

this time the emergent middle class was taking a dominant role in nationalism. Latin-American governments became for the first time practicing members of the family of nations: for most of them the Hague Peace Conference of 1907 was their first top-level international conference. Some clothed themselves in the full panoply of the nation-state, including even an arms race (Argentina, Brazil, and Chile) as well as a power bloc (the ABC bloc). Nationalism in Latin America, which already had political and military overtones, took on cultural and economic aspects. It became outward-looking rather than introspective.

A new type of negative nationalism began in the 1930's. This change was instigated under Communist influence as a weapon of politico-cultural warfare.[20] It was intended primarily to divide Latin America from the United States by creating discord and confusion among Latin Americans. The Communists used Latin-American intellectuals as dupes in propagating divisive ideas, ridiculed everything that tended to unite Latin Americans with one another as well as with the United States and Europe, and emphasized the glory of each national culture in Latin America (such indigenous cultures as the Aztec, Maya, and Inca were praised). This strategy, chauvinistic and isolationist, was quite successful for two decades.

Latin Americans return to the pre-1930 type of nationalism. Starting in the 1950's, Latin-American nationalists, aware now of Communist designs, returned to a positive, humanist form of nationalism. There was also a new interest in Pan-Latin-Americanism.[21]

The Whitaker periodization has the virtue not only of recognizing the major transformations in Latin-American nationalism, but also of defining its trends since the turn of the century. It is difficult to distinguish a clear-cut pattern covering all Latin-American republics, for all have developed at different tempos. The four chronological periods are valuable, however, because they indicate the common denominators in the development of nationalism at differing paces in all the countries, from huge Brazil to tiny Panama.

---

[20] Whitaker credits Víctor Alba for describing this type of nationalism in "La manipulación del nacionalismo en Iberoamérica," *Examen* (Mexico City), May-June 1959, pp. 18–20.

[21] Whitaker suggests that this conclusion, also projected by Alba, has now lost some validity. Though agreeing that Latin-American intellectual nationalists came from the middle class, Whitaker is not at all certain that they shape its opinions, or exercise through this class great influence on public opinion and policy throughout Latin America. (Whitaker, *Nationalism in Latin America*, pp. 23–24.)

CHARACTERISTICS OF LATIN-AMERICAN NATIONALISM

Keeping in mind the fact that nationalism did not develop uniformly throughout the great continent, there are several recognizable patterns:

Latin-American nationalism was derivative. Latin America was no exception to the rule that Europe gave the original stimulus to modern nationalism. The entire continent had long been tied to Europe by language, religion, traditions, customs, and ethical ideals. Latin-American countries borrowed their cultures from those that had evolved in western Europe and the United States in the Enlightenment. There was a connection with the Iberian peninsula, and despite the series of national revolutions against the mother country, Spanish traditions and characteristics persisted. The Latin American found it difficult to rid himself of that traditionalism which burdened Spain and which was in part responsible for its decline. K. H. Silvert recognized this attachment:

The peculiarity of nationalism in Latin America is that nowhere, even in the most advanced countries, has there been an irreparable and hard decision to renounce the advantages of traditionalism and an oversimplified universalism—a renunciation which is in itself the price of social development. The Latin American is taught to jump from loyalty to family and small group to transcendental identifications. He does not recognize the functionalism of an intermediate level of loyalty to impersonal community, and so he makes difficult the establishment of the only processes which can supply the material things for which he is clamoring so loudly.[22]

Apparently the connection was not broken by revolution. Latin Americans assumed a love-hate attitude toward the motherland, somewhat similar to that developed by the peoples of India in their relations with Britain. While romantically praising the indigenous Indian culture, Latin-American intellectuals retained pride in their own Spanish heritage. This oscillation between old and new made the emergence of firm, powerful nation-states a difficult process.

At the same time the tenor of Latin-American nationalism was not always pro-Spanish. Brazil's strong sense of nationalism undoubtedly came in part from her feeling of *not* being Spanish. Here again we see

[22] K. H. Silvert, "Nationalism in Latin America," in Robert N. Burr, ed., "Latin America's Nationalistic Revolutions," *Annals of the American Academy of Political and Social Science*, CCCIV (Mar. 1961), 9.

the two-sided nature of Latin-American nationalism: it both gloried in and resented the Spanish heritage.

Latin-American nationalism was suffused with dignidad. Latin Americans absorbed the Spanish temperament, particularly its accent on pride and dignity. José Figueres, president of Costa Rica (1953–1957), expressed it succinctly: "We have inherited all the defects of the Spanish character, but also some of its virtues. Our poverty does not abate our pride. We have our dignity." [23] The attitude was recognized by James Bruce, the United States ambassador to Argentina during 1947–1949:

The Argentine concept of *dignidad* takes many forms. All Latin Americans share this concept, but the Argentine form is the most acute. To an Argentine, *dignidad* means no man can be criticized in front of his friend. Employees have been known to resign for lesser cause. Even office boys and porters, streetcar conductors and the sanitation men are treated with the same sort of *dignidad*, lest they become enemies. Argentine students must be strictly obedient to teachers, just as the private obeys his officer. Anything less would be *contra la dignidad*.[24]

This sense of dignity produced an intense kind of nationalism sensitive to the slightest criticism. For the Latin American to be connected with the nation was alone a reason for elemental pride. He had a blind faith in the destiny of his country and refused to accept the idea that any other people might be superior to his own. This kind of emotionalism stimulated not only a fanatical patriotism but also an assertive nationalism.

Latin-American nationalism was distinguished by a volatile quality. Added to pride and dignity was a lively desire for quick change and even a certain amount of fickleness. The oversupply of romantic individualism, perhaps a relic of the days of the conquistadors, clashed with the sense of national purpose. There was little understanding that individualism and nationalism must accompany each other if the strength of nationalism were not to be squandered in totalitarian solutions.[25] The result was much unwillingness to await change of regime by the slow-working democratic process. Political succession was often

---

[23] *Hearings before the Subcommittee of Inter-American Affairs of the Committee on Foreign Relations*, 2nd Session (Washington, D.C., 1958), p. 93.

[24] Quoted in James Bruce, *Those Perplexing Argentines* (New York, 1953), p. 7.

[25] Silvert, *op. cit.*, p. 9.

determined by military juntas, or angry university students, or conspirators inside the existing regimes. Government by revolution became almost the traditional standard. Even in the more advanced countries there was a built-in fascination with the idea of solutions by force.

This volatile political temperament was matched by divisions in the social order. The development of national sentiment ordinarily requires a certain amount of common purpose among various strata of the population. But in Latin America that individualism which characterized political life carried over into the class structure in what might be called a kind of class individualism. Relations between wealthy aristocrats, landless peasants, spiritless intellectuals, and selfish businessmen were often hostile. All were equally proficient in uttering patriotic platitudes, but each social group turned to its own interests in times of stress. Certainly this attitude was not characteristic of only Latin America, but it was sufficiently prevalent to render national integration difficult. The sense of national purpose was weakened in Latin America by the fitful oscillation between quiescence and force, between freedom and repression, between humanism and totalitarianism.

Latin-American nationalism was predisposed to statism. In its early stages Latin-American nationalism was nourished in abstract terms by individual intellectuals, much as Herder had laid the cultural foundations for German nationalism. The attitude reflected the liberal nationalism of early nineteenth-century Europe, with its highly romantic content—national flags, national songs, national revival. José Martí, a Cuban patriot, expressed the sentiment in the words: "The person who thinks of himself does not love his country." [26]

This early type of nationalism, however, was superficial. The special property of a small group of intellectual patriots, it scarcely penetrated to the masses. Toward the end of the nineteenth century, with the emergence of a nationalistic middle class and the intensification of economic nationalism, the concept of the state took on reality. No longer was it an abstract ideal vaguely supported by a few intellectuals, but instead it was brought down to the masses in a dynamic and politically charged form.[27] It was this predilection for statism which made the way of democracy so difficult in Latin America.

Latin-American nationalism possessed a common denominator in

[26] José Martí, in *The America of José Martí*, trans. Juan de Onís (New York, 1953), p. 316.
[27] John J. Johnson, *Political Changes in Latin America* (Stanford, 1958), p. 9.

anti–United States sentiment. "What unites us in Spanish America," said a noted Chilean, "is our beautiful language and our distrust of the United States." Throughout its history Latin-American nationalism reflected a desire to be "free" from real or alleged subservience to the powerful northern neighbor.[28] Suspicion ran deep. As the United States blossomed in the second half of the nineteenth century, played a leading role in the New Industrial Revolution, became the financial center of the world, and began to take a major share in Latin-American trade, she displaced France and England as the most influential power in the southern continent. Latin Americans were angered at being drawn into the orbit of the northern neighbor. This resentment took the form of violent verbal attack against the United States.

The pattern was set by one of the most influential writers of Spanish America, José Enrique Rodó, a Uruguayan. In an essay, *Ariel* (1900), Rodó contrasted the United States as a materialistic "Caliban" to Spanish America as "Ariel," the embodiment of man's higher aspirations. He warned the youth of Latin America against being seduced by the materialism of the United States. He tempered his assault by suggesting that in time the United States might become less materialistic, but the message that appealed to his contemporaries was his attack on "the Titan of the North." [29]

Others joined in the attack, including the Venezuelan Rufino Blanco Frombona, who excoriated "the Caliban of the north"; the Chilean Gabriela Mistral, a future Nobel-prize-winning poetess who spoke acidly of "the spike of steel and gold" wielded by the United States; the Argentine Alfredo Palacios, who compared the United States to Faust because it had "sold its soul in exchange for riches and power"; and the Mexican philosopher José Vasconcelos, who cautioned his countrymen against being attracted by the superficial glitter of "Yankee culture." [30]

Latin-American resentment was compounded by United States diplomacy and action,[31] including the war against Spain in 1898, the penetration of Panama, President Theodore Roosevelt's Big Stick di-

[28] Robert J. Alexander, *Communism in Latin America* (New Brunswick, N.J., 1957), p. 6.

[29] Hanke, *op. cit.*, p. 47.

[30] Johnson, "The New Latin American Nationalism," *op. cit.*, p. 189.

[31] See James W. Gantenbein, ed., *The Evolution of Our Latin American Policy: A Documentary Record* (New York, 1950).

plomacy,[32] and President Wilson's intervention in Mexico. Latin-American countries protested against interference in their internal affairs. The efforts of the United States to maintain order by sending marines to Nicaragua,[33] the Dominican Republic, and Haiti were denounced as attempts to dominate the entire continent. Washington's explanation was that these nations had failed to maintain stable governments, avoided the payment of foreign debts, and failed to protect the lives and property of United States citizens. An additional complaint by Latin Americans was directed against United States businessmen and diplomats who refused to accept Latin Americans as equals.

During the administration of President Herbert Hoover (1929–1933), the United States began to abandon its policy of the Big Stick and Dollar Diplomacy.[34] The new American attitude was indicated more fully during the presidency of Franklin D. Roosevelt (1933–1945), who inaugurated the Good Neighbor Policy. Automatic intervention in Latin-American affairs ceased, and revolutionary outbreaks were to be handled by common action.[35] In 1948 the Organization of American States (OAS) was formed at Bogotá to place all the American states on a plane of equality, marking the end of the Monroe Doctrine as a one-sided United States policy.[36]

The OAS failed, however, to stop vocal enmity toward the United States. Latin-American nationalists claimed that while active interven-

[32] The policy of the Big Stick and Dollar Diplomacy grew out of the Roosevelt Corollary to the Monroe Doctrine (1904), which held that since the United States had prohibited European interference in the Western Hemisphere, the United States must at the same time be certain that the Latin-American countries did nothing to provoke such interference. This made the United States "the policeman of the hemisphere."

[33] In 1912, at the invitation of President Adolfo Diáz, American marines were stationed in Nicaragua. Despite revolutionary outbreaks, the presence of American forces undoubtedly helped the maintenance of stability. When the marines withdrew in 1925, revolution broke out again. Marines were sent again to supervise elections in 1928, 1930, and 1932.

[34] See Alexander De Conde, *Herbert Hoover's Latin-American Policy* (Stanford, 1951).

[35] See Gantenbein, *op. cit.*

[36] The Organization of American States was an outgrowth of the Pan American Union, founded in 1910 to deal not only with health and education, but also to intervene in case of threatened conflict in Latin America. The system functioned so well that only one major war, the Chaco War between Paraguay and Bolivia during 1932–1935, took place there in the twentieth century. In 1961, President John F. Kennedy proposed the formation of the Alliance for Progress, dedicated to monetary stability, industrialization, and social change.

tion by United States marines had ceased, *yanqui* imperialism now took the form of aggressive economic penetration by United States business-men. United States petroleum interests in Mexico and Bolivia were expropriated. When Vice-President Richard Nixon made a good-will trip to Peru and Venezuela in 1958, he was insulted and spat upon by young hotheads. José Figueres, former president of Costa Rica, ex-plained this reception in a highly emotional statement that "the act of spitting, vulgar though it is, is without substitute in our language for expressing certain emotions." [37]

CASE HISTORY: FROM LIBERAL TO PERÓNISTA
NATIONALISM IN ARGENTINA

Nationalism unfolded at a varying pace throughout Latin America. Brazil, for example, lagged behind Argentina in the development of national feeling because Brazil's struggle for independence began much later, and because independent Brazil had less need for the cement of nationalism due to the continuity from the colonial period of its gov-erning personnel and institutions.[38] Yet, both countries were to endure fascist nationalism in the form of the Integralistas in Brazil and the Perónistas in Argentina, each of whom fanned the flame of native nationalism in opposition to the liberal and commercial civilization of the United States.[39]

One of the largest and one of the most economically advanced of Latin-American countries, Argentina was weakened by constant politi-cal strife, instability, and military meddling in government. For years she had prided herself on being the richest Latin-American country, the best-educated, and the least burdened by dictatorships,[40] yet she too was destined to undergo a decade of national humiliation under the dictator Perón.

Through the first half of the nineteenth century, Argentina was embroiled in civil and foreign wars.[41] The first stimulus to nationalism

[37] *Hearings before the Subcommittee of Inter-American Affairs of the Commit-tee on Foreign Relations,* 2nd Session (Washington, D.C., 1958), p. 93.
[38] Whitaker, *Nationalism in Latin America,* p. 18.
[39] Kohn, *Nationalism: Its Meaning and History,* p. 80.
[40] Hanke, *op. cit.,* p. 58.
[41] See Ricardo Levene, *A History of Argentina,* trans. and ed. William S. Robertson (Chapel Hill, N.C., 1937); and George Pendle, *Argentina* (London, 1955).

was a result of British attempts to seize the country from the Spaniards. In 1806 a British force temporarily captured Buenos Aires, and the next year again assaulted the town. Both efforts were repelled by the colonists, who were so elated by their victories, unaided by either the Spanish or French, that their thoughts turned to independence. Argentine nationalism was stimulated when Napoleon entered Madrid and proclaimed his brother, Joseph, King of Spain. Just as German national pride flourished in the War of Liberation against Napoleon, so did Argentine patriotism blossom in a four-year war of independence. Ernst Moritz Arndt's "Patriotic Song: The God Who Made Earth's Iron Hoard" was matched by López y Planes' "Patriotic March," which still remains Argentina's national anthem. Slowly and hesitantly, Argentine patriotism was converted into nationalism. The process was similar to European experience, including the familiar romantic creation of myths from the past, discovery of national heroes, national folk songs, stirring patriotic music, accent on the national language, and promotion of national customs and traditions. Politically, this nationalism, in imitation of the European prototype, was liberal in form. The humanitarian ideal was pursued for the next century despite deviations from the democratic way of life.

In 1816 the Argentines formally proclaimed their independence from Spain, but it was not until 1842 that Spain acknowledged it. Meanwhile, when the country was disturbed by continuing civil wars, Juan Manuel de Rosas, a notorious *caudillo*, set up a dictatorship with the help of his *gauchos* (horsemen and herders). Rosas called himself a democrat, but he ruled by terror. Every citizen of Buenos Aires had to wear a red ribbon bearing the inscription "Death to the Savage Unitarians," directed to the opponents of Rosas.[42] The dictator had the same sort of mass following which was later attracted to Perón. Rosas encouraged nationalism by two simple expedients: he attacked the idea of British and French intervention; and he turned the attention of the masses away from their troubles by waging war with Brazil for possession of Uruguay. The consolidation of national sentiment was implemented under dictatorial control.

This temporary setback to liberal nationalism was brought to an end during the administrations of Rosas' former lieutenants Urquiza (1852–1861) and Bartolomé Mitre (1862–1868). But a real step for-

[42] Pendle, *op. cit.*, p. 32.

ward was made during the administration of Domingo F. Sarmiento, a distinguished schoolmaster-statesman. Elected president of the Republic from 1868 to 1874, Sarmiento reorganized the school system according to the ideas of his friend, the American educator Horace Mann. Sarmiento believed that the schoolroom was the most important battlefield in America.[43]

During the remainder of the nineteenth century Argentina took on its modern form.[44] From 1869 to 1914 the population quadrupled.[45] The invention of refrigerated shipping in 1888 enabled Argentina to become the world's greatest exporter of meat as well as one of the largest producers of grain. In this process of conversion from an agrarian to a highly commercialized economy, a small group of two thousand landowners acquired enormous wealth by investing in land and cattle. For two centuries the *gauchos* had ruled the vast *pampas* (grass-covered plains). Now the richest parts of the *pampas* were occupied by the great *estancias* (estates) of the wealthy landowners.[46]

Equally significant was the effect of immigration. Between 1858 and 1930 some six million immigrants poured into Argentina, mostly from Italy and Spain but also from France, Germany, Russia, Switzerland, and Britain.[47] With the railroad as an iron guide, the immigrants gradually pushed the Indians into the hinterland. The nationalization of the immigrants did not proceed with the rapidity which marked melting-pot Americanization in the United States, resulting in what one Argentine called a "social conglomeration."

It was during this transformation from a rural to a modern urbanized economy that Argentine nationalism underwent its most striking change. The old idealized liberal nationalism that had been patronized by aristocrats turned gradually into a populist form. The compelling factors were the rise of a politically conscious middle class and the

[43] Harold Benjamin, "Sarmiento, the Educator," in *Some Educational and Anthropological Aspects in Latin America* (Austin, Tex., 1948), p. 16.

[44] On the Argentine Republic, see Frederick A. Kirkpatrick, *A History of the Argentine Republic* (Cambridge, England, 1931); Ysabel F. Rennie, *The Argentine Republic* (New York, 1945); and Thomas F. McGann, *Argentina, The United States, and the Inter-American System, 1880–1914* (Cambridge, Mass., 1957).

[45] Hanke, *op. cit.*, p. 63.

[46] See Carl C. Taylor, *Rural Life in Argentina* (Baton Rouge, La., 1948).

[47] Hanke, *op. cit.*, p. 65.

appearance of economic nationalism. The middle class was the generator of populist nationalism. A smooth economy became its lifeblood, certainly the most important element in Argentine nationalism. Xenophobia became stronger as Argentines began to demand the end of foreign economic penetration into Argentine financial and industrial life.[48] In 1916 a major political change marked the coming-of-age of the middle class. Hipólito Irigoyen, leader of the Radical Party, which proposed a democratic program, was elected to the presidency. Never had Radicals been able to control so conservative a country. Irigoyen introduced a minimum wage to save the working class from creeping inflation, and raised railway tariffs. But in fourteen years opposition in Congress prevented the Radicals from achieving more than a few important reforms. In 1930 an army junta led by General José Uriburu, in alliance with the conservative aristocracy, overthrew Irigoyen (serving his second term since 1928) in a *coup d'état*. For the next decade Argentina was ruled by thinly veiled dictatorships under military and aristocratic support.

Argentine nationalism turned fascist under Juan Domingo Perón (1895–). The great-grandson of an Italian immigrant, Perón was educated at military schools and became a lieutenant at twenty. On June 4, 1943, in the midst of World War II, he led a party of young nationalist officers in a *coup d'état* against President Ramón Castillo. In 1944 he was appointed war minister and then became vice-president. In February 1946 he was elected president on the Labor Party platform. Assisted by his wife Eva he established himself as a demagogic dictator. In the familiar process he suppressed all political opposition; censored the press (seizing the world-famous Buenos Aires newspaper *La Prensa*); dismissed university professors opposed to his rule; and nationalized banks, railroads, and utilities.[49]

The Perónista dictatorship, similar in form to those established by Mussolini and Hitler, was in the classic fascist mold, combining both nationalism and socialism to achieve power and maintain it. A man of

[48] When oil was discovered in Argentina at the beginning of the twentieth century, the government, with approval of the people, saw to it that the precious product was kept from foreign hands. In 1936 the government nationalized the petroleum fields by forming a monopoly called Yacimientos Petrolíferos Fiscales (YPF).

[49] On the Perón regime, see George I. Blanksten, *Perón's Argentina* (Chicago, 1953); and Robert J. Alexander, *The Perón Era* (New York, 1951).

personal charm, Perón attracted the loyalty of both fellow officers and the masses by appealing to their sense of patriotism. He took into account every possible approach to nationalism:

Political dynamism. Perón worked to establish Argentine primacy over Brazil. In foreign policy he took what he called a "third position" between the United States and the Soviet Union, but which was actually thinly disguised opposition to the United States, always a popular attitude in Argentina. Perón endowed his rule with glamor and mystic appeal. His colorful personality, presented to the public in organized spectacles, gave an illusion of strength, pride, and dignity to a people hungering for recognition.

Cultural ambitions. The Perón regime imitated preceding nationalists by reviving the culture of the Argentine past. In 1952 the government announced a policy to protect the national spirit and to guard it from exotic influences. "We will keep alive our native music and primitive dances, the vivid representatives of our past, reminding us of our native genius, our respect for the family, our cult for courage, the beauty of popular poetry and our vernacular idiom." [50]

Economic goals. Perón's most important objective was to liberate Argentina from foreign influence, particularly that of North America and Britain, by putting into effect economic policies that had already been advocated by his people. In 1947, just a year after assuming the presidency, Perón issued a formal "Declaration of Economic Independence" as the main pillar of his regime.[51] In speech after speech and in published writings he hammered away at this theme. "We have reached our 'coming of age' which enables us, to the same extent as anybody else, to estimate our true value and to govern our country by ourselves. For this reason it is of vital importance that basic industries should be national." [52] Everything should be Argentine: "Those who in previous times commanded here as if they were in their own land, will have to submit and receive our products canned by Argentine hands, transported by Argentine railways and taken to Europe by Argentine ships." [53]

[50] Quoted in Hanke, *op. cit.*, p. 64.

[51] Perón accentuated the impact of this declaration by making it on the anniversary of Argentina's independence in 1816 (see Whitaker, *Nationalism in Latin America*, p. 50).

[52] Juan Domingo Perón, *The Voice of Perón* (Buenos Aires, 1950), p. 132.

[53] Juan Domingo Perón, *Perón Expounds His Doctrine* (Buenos Aires, 1948), p. 149.

Social implications. During his drive to power and in his rule Perón took pains to identify economic nationalism with social revolution. This was the same urge apparent in Hitler's National Socialism,[54] except that Perón was careful to court the favor of labor by leaning ostentatiously in its direction. He identified his opponents as all who were rich, all who did no work, and all those who defended the interests of foreign capitalistic trusts. He won the support of the poor industrial workers, the *descamisados* (the shirtless ones), by enacting legislation favorable to them and by raising wages. At huge Perónista rallies the strong man and his wife [55] made intoxicating promises, many of which they found impossible to carry out.

In the early 1950's the Perón dictatorship ran into increasing trouble. One by one its supporters broke away. The army refused to allow Eva Perón to run for the vice-presidency in 1951. The navy was opposed to army influence in the government. The Roman Catholic Church, which had supported Perón in his earlier drive for power, turned against him because he allowed his wife to assume control of charity organizations previously handled by ecclesiastical officials. The land-owning families disapproved of the man-and-wife team. Worst of all, the economic situation deteriorated. When Perón tried to extricate himself from economic difficulties by seeking help from North American industrialists, he sealed his doom. Argentine nationalism had been constructed with reaction to foreign financial control as its base, and now the dictator was violating his own major principle. After trouble in the provinces, especially in Catholic and conservative Córdoba, armed rebellion broke out in Buenos Aires in June 1955. The revolt was supported not only by large sections of the population but also by business and industrial interests. After a short struggle, Perón fled into exile.

After the expulsion of Perón, efforts were made in succeeding regimes to correct some of the excesses of his nationalism. The Perónista party was outlawed. President Arturo Frondizi tried to heal old political divisions and hostilities, and to have all parties—landowners, labor,

[54] When Roehm and the S.A. (storm troopers) sought to turn the National Socialist movement far to the left, Hitler subjected them to a drastic blood purge.

[55] Eva Duarte, affectionately known by the masses as Evita, was an important part of the man-and-wife team. Snubbed by aristocrats, she organized and ran a huge social service program which made her popular with the *descamisados*. Her death in 1952 was a blow from which Perón did not recover.

army, Church, and industrialists—work together for a new unified Argentina. The retreat from economic nationalism was of critical importance. Frondizi launched a program to attract foreign investment. Ignoring popular sentiment against imperialism, he negotiated contracts with Standard Oil of New Jersey, Royal Dutch Shell, and other foreign companies, enabling them to enter the oil industry in Argentina. Within three years the country was self-sufficient in petroleum.

Frondizi spoke candidly to his people:

These decisions of an economic character point out the end of an era and mark the beginning of what must be a new life for the whole of the nation. . . . The time has come to face facts and adopt heroic measures. . . . The national expansion has already started. . . . Argentina has been living in an economic fiction, the consequences of which are clearly in view. The time has come to end that fiction and to obtain an economy of true costs. . . . Without economic stabilization there will be no material progress, no peace, no quiet, nor any true labor union life. Without stabilization there will be no freedom or democracy in the country. . . . The expansion program we have started . . . shall serve as encouragement to our sister nations and will open the way towards Latin American economic integration.[56]

NATIONAL REVOLUTIONARIES
VERSUS JACOBIN COMMUNISTS

It was predictable that Latin-American Communists would embrace nationalism. It had many advantages for Communists: it permeated all sectors of society and hence tended to give any proponent an aura of respectability; it was directed against the Colossus of the North and thereby provided communism with another weapon in the cold war; it brought to communism the tacit support of nationalists in a kind of popular front directed against capitalist imperialism; and it provided momentum for Communist imperialism.

The issue of communism brought on a struggle for power between the national revolutionaries on the one side and the Jacobin totalitarians on the other. The national revolutionaries, radicals of the democratic left, were a branch of Latin-American nationalists dedicated to the task of bringing about a social revolution. The Jacobin totalitarians, on the other hand, sought to use populist nationalism in the service of either

[56] From President's message of Dec. 29, 1958, in *La Prensa*, Dec. 30, 1958, quoted in Hanke, *op. cit.*, p. 162.

Moscow or Peking. The struggle was not merely a gentlemanly difference of opinion, but a battle to the death.

National revolutionaries. The national revolutionaries, including such parties as the Acción Democratia in Venezuela, the Partido Aprista in Peru, and the Movimiento Nacionalista Revolucionario (MNR) in Bolivia, all stressed economic nationalism. Their aim was to bring economic independence to those Latin-American states which had won political independence from Spain but had become subject to American or British economic influence. They called for limitation or elimination of foreign investments in Latin America and demanded that natural possessions such as oil be nationalized and kept from foreign control. Citing Alexander Hamilton's *Report on Manufactures* and Friedrich List's *National Economy*,[57] they supported positive action to build up their own national economies. The critical factor was always national as opposed to foreign control. Added to this was a belief in political democracy as a way of life. "Democracy, yes; communism, no!"

Jacobin totalitarians. Communists regarded as their most dangerous enemies those elements of the democratic left that sought social reform within the existing framework of society. Both the Soviet Union and Communist China counted on the power vacuum created in Latin America by the advent of populist nationalism. On the assumption that their own ideology thrived best in a climate of political chaos, economic deterioration, and social conflict, they supported the struggle of the "forces of national liberation" for "freedom."[58] They believed that it was impossible to achieve a social revolution in Latin America and to pursue a truly nationalist policy through political democracy. These

---

[57] See Louis L. Snyder, "The Role of Friedrich List in the Establishment of the *Zollverein*," in *German Nationalism: The Tragedy of a People* (Harrisburg, Pa., 1952), pp. 75–101, originally delivered as a paper before the American Historical Association on December 28, 1950.

[58] In Communist jargon, "national liberation" meant freedom from Western imperialism for the peoples of Asia, Africa, the Middle East, and Latin America, with subsequent inclusion in the Communist orbit. Chinese Communists supported revolutionary wars in "underdeveloped" Latin America. The Chinese Communist tactician Lin Piao spoke of the entire globe as divided into cities and rural areas: North America and western Europe were the "cities of the world," while Asia, Africa, and Latin America constituted "the rural areas of the world." Since World War II, he said, the proletarian revolutionary movement for various reasons had been held back temporarily, while the "people's revolutionary movement" was growing vigorously. "We shall fight in ways most advantageous to us to destroy the enemy, and wherever the enemy can be most easily destroyed" (*Jenmin Jih Poh* [organ of the Chinese Communist Party, Peking], Sept. 1964).

goals, they said, could be won only through the challenge of the Jacobin left and a totalitarian dictatorship allied with the Communist motherland.

Latin-American Communists were neither "agrarian reformers" nor "another kind of radical," but part of a global movement.[59] They used democratic slogans and catchwords to lure the masses. The tactics were familiar: in each country Communists acted as if they were the most ardent nationalists of all. They were invariably in the front of anti-*yanqui* demonstrations and riots. They sought recruits among such dissidents as truck and taxi drivers, workers in the tin mines, dissatisfied farmers, and cosmopolitan intellectuals. They saw mass strength throughout the continent in a young generation impatient for change and susceptible to the Marxian vocabulary of revolution. They made a special effort to attract university students in order to influence the next generation of teachers. The task of recruiting was considerably simplified by the disparity that existed between enormous wealth and miserable poverty. In all this activity the Communists shared nationalism with the older Liberals, the Christian Democrats, and sundry other parties. The nationalist movement in Latin America included not only Communists but representatives of every political party.

Cuba became the first and only Communist country in the Western Hemisphere. At first Fidel Castro seemed to be a liberal agrarian reformer,[60] but he eventually cast aside democratic nationalism and associated himself with the world Communist movement.

In 1895 the Cuban people, hoping to free themselves from the repressive rule of Spain, broke into revolt. The leader of the independence movement, José Martí, had spent years in the United States collecting funds from wealthy Cubans in New York and from poor cigar-makers in Tampa and New Orleans. In May 1895, shortly after his return to the island, he was killed in a cavalry skirmish.[61] The brief Spanish-American War stripped Spain of her once mighty American empire. The official United States policy toward Cuba was based now

[59] Robert J. Alexander, *Communism in Latin America*, p. 399.

[60] So observant a journalist as Herbert L. Matthews of *The New York Times*, after interviewing Castro in the mountains of Cuba during his struggle for power, came away with the impression that Castro was a liberal agrarian reformer. It is still not clear whether Castro was a classic hoodwinker or was pushed over the Communist line by the exigencies of politics.

[61] Martí became an honored nationalist hero. See his *The America of José Martí*, trans. Juan de Onís (New York, 1953), pp. 313–316, for a moving letter to a friend explaining why he, a man of peace, was taking up arms against Spain.

on the Platt Amendment, which gave Washington almost unlimited rights to intervene in Cuba.[62] Latin Americans regarded the Platt Amendment as a betrayal of the war aims that had been announced by the United States. It was ended under President Franklin D. Roosevelt in 1934, but North American influence remained strong in the island.

Cuban history in the twentieth century has been a story of turbulence and violence. From 1924 to 1933 the country was ruled by President Gerardo Machado, a strong-armed terrorist. His successor was Colonel Fulgencio Batista, a former sergeant, who for the next twenty-five years made and unmade governments at will. Batista was universally condemned for his tyranny and his tolerance of corruption. Meanwhile, revolution was being planned by Fidel Castro, a young lawyer born into a wealthy family. In 1956, Castro organized the 26th of July Movement, apparently dedicated to democracy and reform. In December, Castro and a dozen companions landed in eastern Cuba from Mexico and launched a sustained guerrilla campaign in the Sierra Maestra Mountains. More and more young Cubans, angered by the brutality of the Batista regime, flocked to Castro. Eventually, in 1958, faced by stubborn and increasing resistance, the government army disintegrated and Batista fled the country. Castro came down from the mountains and entered Havana as a national hero, hailed as the greatest Cuban since the Liberator, José Martí.

Many of those who supported Castro believed that they were fighting for Cuban nationalism, democracy, freedom, and decent government. They split into two groups: moderates who favored democratic government, a supervised capitalist economy, and agrarian reform, and who opposed communism; and extremists who preferred a revolutionary dictatorship, an economy patterned after the Soviet Union, anti-Americanism, and alliance with Communists. For some months Castro seemed to waver between the two groups.

In late 1959, Castro chose communism. Then came the familiar steps of Communist activism: suppression of political opposition, abolition of free elections (on the ground that Castro already had mass support), nationalization of industry, collectivization of agriculture, an intensi-

[62] The important provisions of the Platt Amendment were the following: Cuba must never enter into any treaty with a foreign power impairing Cuban independence; the Cuban government must not contract any public debt in excess of the capacity of its ordinary revenues to discharge; the United States was authorized to intervene to preserve Cuban independence and maintain law and order; and Cuba agreed to sell or lease to the United States lands necessary for naval or coaling stations.

fied propaganda campaign against the United States, and close relations with Moscow. Firing squads went to work to purge "opponents of the revolution." [63]

Castro was supposed to make agricultural Cuba a Caribbean paradise, but within a few years the economy slid toward bankruptcy. He was able to survive only because of a military machine worth $500,000,000 supplied by the Soviet Union and a subsistence-level dole amounting to about a million dollars a day.[64] The physical plant disintegrated, with no way to replace it. The sugar crop, representing 90 per cent of the country's foreign exchange, dropped from 6,800,000 tons in 1961 to 3,800,000 in 1963.[65]

For the first time communism became a serious challenge in Latin America. Castro described his rule as "the first Socialist revolutionary regime." Cuba became not only the prototype but also the preceptor of incipient Communist revolutions throughout the continent. After 1960, gangs sponsored and armed by Castro were trained in Cuba to create as much chaos as possible elsewhere. Guerrillas came to Cuban camps from Colombia, Haiti, Venezuela, and the Dominican Republic. Radio stations in Havana broadcast propaganda throughout Latin America. The goal was to create ripe revolutionary conditions for "national liberation struggles." The technique was largely unsuccessful.[66]

The story of Castroism is not yet finished. It aims to demonstrate to all Latin America that the best road to nationalist regeneration lies through communism blended with opposition to the United States. Whether or not this goal will be achieved remains to be seen.

PAN-AMERICANISM VERSUS
PAN-LATIN-AMERICAN CONTINENTALISM

Parallel to the conventional nationalism of individual countries was that variety of supranationalism designated as "pan" movements.[67] This

[63] From January 1, 1959, more than 335,000 Cubans—one out of every twenty-one persons on the island—went into exile. First were the landowners and businessmen, followed by the middle class, and then the farmers and laborers whom Castro had promised to save from exploitation by the United States.

[64] *Time*, Oct. 8, 1965, p. 26.   [65] *Ibid.*

[66] In July 1964 the Organization of American States, by a vote of fifteen against four (Bolivia, Chile, Mexico, and Uruguay), denounced Communist Cuba as an aggressor because of its efforts to undermine the Venezuelan government. All OAS members were ordered to break diplomatic ties with and to suspend trade with Cuba. Only Mexico continued to maintain relations with Castro.

[67] See Chapter 12.

represented a synthesis of individual nationalisms, a kind of larger nationalism among closely related peoples. The idea penetrated Latin America, as elsewhere.

A distinction must be made between Pan-Americanism and Pan-Latin-American continentalism. Pan-Americanism, fostered by the United States,[68] was intended to bring all the American republics into closer association for the promotion of common economic and cultural interests, peace, and security.[69] The first International American Conference, inspired by U.S. Secretary of State James G. Blaine, was held in Washington during 1889–1890. Created at this time was the Bureau of American Republics, which became the nucleus of the Pan-American Union, later the Organization of American States (1948), and still later the Alliance for Progress (1961).

Pan-Americanism was not an extended nationalism but rather an attempt by the United States to assure hemispheric solidarity.[70] It was based on the idea that the peoples of the Western Hemisphere were bound together in a relationship that set them apart from the rest of the world. Several serious obstacles slowed down its progress:

Political barriers. It became increasingly difficult for the United States and Latin-American nations to discuss their political aims from a common standpoint. Latin Americans distrusted Washington's foreign policy.

Social differences. North Americans were convinced of the value of their democracy and looked with disdain upon dictatorship. Many Latin Americans apparently accepted dictatorship as suited to their needs.

Economic clashes. Latin Americans believed that Pan-Americanism

[68] The first Pan-American conference, called the Panama Congress, was called as early as 1826 by Simón Bolívar, but the attendance was poor and there were no significant results.

[69] On the history of Pan-Americanism, see Joseph B. Lockey, *Pan-Americanism: Its Beginnings* (New York, 1920); Laurence Duggan, *The Americans: A Search for Hemisphere Security* (New York, 1949); Richard F. W. Behrendt, *Inter-American Economic Relations: Problems and Prospects* (New York, 1948); Paul R. Olson and C. Addison Hickman, *Pan-American Economics* (New York, 1943); Thomas F. McGann, *Argentina, the United States, and the Inter-American System, 1880–1914* (Cambridge, Mass., 1957); and Arthur P. Whitaker, *The Western Hemisphere Idea: Its Rise and Decline* (Ithaca, N.Y., 1954).

[70] The Pan-American movement had no necessary nexus with the Monroe Doctrine, but in effect its decisions involved the application of that doctrine on a wider, more modern scale. In recent years the United States has favored the inclusion of Canada in the Pan-American system.

should devote itself to the problem of economic equality instead of expressing material power and international influence. North Americans attributed this attitude to simple envy.

Cultural divergencies. Latin America always had closer cultural and moral ties with Europe, especially with Spain and Portugal, than with the United States. The dominant language was Spanish, the secondary tongue was Portuguese, and English was a poor third.

Psychological blocks. Another obstacle was the difference in temperament between North and South Americans. In the clash of stereotypes, North Americans thought Latin Americans were lazy, fickle, and unprogressive, while the latter looked upon their neighbors to the north as aggressive, materialistic, and uncultured.

Arthur P. Whitaker concluded that the Pan-American movement, with its mystique and supposedly strong bonds, was virtually moribund:

After 1940 the substance of the Western Hemisphere idea was lost, and its place was taken first and briefly by globalism and then by new twofold divisions of the globe, not into the traditional Eastern and Western hemispheres, but into Northern and Southern hemispheres, or, more frequently, into the Communist and non-Communist worlds. Both of these new-style divisions of the world grouped Western Europe with all or most of America, and thus they were in headlong conflict with the classic Western Hemisphere idea, an essential component of which was the separation of Europe from America. . . .

Despite several centuries of the common experience of development in a New World environment, the history of the Americas has so far successfully resisted the efforts of American historians to integrate it in accordance with the Western Hemisphere ideas.[71]

The analogue of Pan-Americanism was Pan-Latin-American continentalism, also known as *Hispanidad.*[72] This form of continental nationalism was by no means peculiar to Latin America: there were continental implications in Pan-Africanism and Pan-Asianism, as well as in the Pan-European idea inherent in the concept of a United States of Europe. There were two lesser movements within Pan-Latin-American continentalism. The broader, but less influential, included some

---

[71] Whitaker, *The Western Hemisphere Idea*, pp. 154, 157.

[72] By far the best treatment is Arthur P. Whitaker, "Continental Nationalism and the United States," in *Nationalism in Latin America*, pp. 55–77. See also Santiago Magariños and Ramón Puigdollers, *Panhispanismo, su transcendencia histórica, política y social* (Barcelona, 1926).

twenty-six Latin-American states; *Hispanidad,* the more important, was limited to eighteen Spanish-speaking states.[73]

Since the Age of Exploration, in which Spaniards took a leading role, and the struggle for independence in the early nineteenth century, attempts were made to assure Spanish American solidarity. As each Spanish American nation assumed national identity, it looked with sympathy upon the similar experiences of its continental neighbors. In 1811, when the Chilean Juan Egaña was charged with the task of drafting a constitution by the patriots' first National Congress, he wrote a document in which he called Chile a "people" and reserved the designation "nation" for a union of Chile with the other free peoples of Spanish America.[74] This was conterminous with the liberal nationalism then prevailing in Europe that had provided the guidelines for the development of early nationalism in South America. For the rest of the century this idea of a community of Spanish American interests persisted, though on a small scale.

The broader Pan-Latin-American continentalism, which included the non-Spanish-speaking states of Latin America, begun to assume shape in the first decade of the twentieth century. It was associated with such factors as the rise of the middle class, the new industrialism, and the transformation from aristocratic to populist nationalism. However, the gap between Spanish-American *Hispanidad* and Pan-Latin-American continentalism was never breached: Brazil and Haiti, especially, leaned away from the idea of Spanish unity.

Neither form made much progress. Militating against a broader nationalism of either Spanish American or Latin-American variety was the pattern of oscillating between anarchy and dictatorship. The South American continent thus went the way of fragmentation rather than union. The major note of unity was dislike for North America, expressed by a preference either for *Hispanidad* or Pan-Latin-American continentalism over Pan-Americanism.[75] The Communist attempt to

[73] The Spanish-speaking states: Argentina, Bolivia, Chile, Colombia, Costa Rica, Cuba, Dominican Republic, Ecuador, El Salvador, Guatemala, Honduras, Mexico, Nicaragua, Panama, Paraguay, Peru, Uruguay, and Venezuela. The non-Spanish-speaking states: Brazil (Portuguese); British Guiana, British Honduras, Jamaica, and Trinidad-Tobago (English); French Guiana and Haiti (French); and Surinam (Dutch). (Cf. *Statistical Papers,* United Nations, 1964.)

[74] Whitaker, *Nationalism in Latin America,* p. 57.

[75] See Jorge Castañeda, *Mexico and the United Nations* (New York, 1958), especially ch. vii.

steer both movements to the extreme left did not have much success.

Nationalism of the conventional type, limited to individual countries, remained the dominant ideology of Latin America. It was the cement which held together the smaller as well as the larger, more advanced industrial nations. Most Latin-American countries provided too small a market to support an advanced modern industry, and in effect became economic colonies of the more successful industrial nations. It would have been to their advantage perhaps to have joined the larger units. But the sense of nationalism was so strong that fragmentation continued in spite of the danger that because of it the entire Latin-American fabric would unravel.

CONTINENT IN FERMENT

Latin-American history was distinguished by complexity and mystery, as much by its diversity as by its common character.[76] It was in part receptive to European forms, but at the same time it had distinct elements of its own—the mystique of a spiritual affinity with Spain, a quality of accommodation between ethnic groups, internecine rivalries, and crises resulting from confusing national identifications. Here, as well as elsewhere, nationalism proved a force for fragmentation: none of the major Latin-American countries gave any indication of being willing to yield its national individualism to continental nationalism.

Latin-American nationalism meant change, both revolutionary and evolutionary, with emphasis upon revolution. The pattern was variegated. Brazil directed its nationalism to the evolutionary goal of modernization. Argentina, always hovering on the brink of change, sought a balance between bourgeois and populist nationalism. Cuba and Bolivia dedicated themselves to progress through revolution. The nationalist leaders of Chile and Venezuela spoke the language of revolution, but were willing to adopt the strategy of evolutionary means. Peru and Colombia sought change but also tried to retain what they deemed best and most useful from the past. In all these objectives nationalism was regarded as the most convenient tool and as a kind of starting point.

For the United States, the powerful neighbor to the north, Latin-

[76] "Despite the similarity of language, origin and religion, Bolivia is more different from Chile than Sweden is from Italy. Paraguay is more different from Venezuela than France from Greece" (Charles W. Cole, in *The New York Times Book Review*, Jan. 29, 1967, p. 1).

American nationalism remained a problem of the utmost importance. Since 1823 the United States, by the Monroe Doctrine, had staked out limits for the American mission—the Western Hemisphere rather than merely North America. Reaffirming its repugnance for foreign interference, the United States told European countries plainly that it possessed vital interests in the entire hemisphere. This policy reduced the possibility of European expansion in Latin America, and even today it is an obstacle to penetration by Communist countries. However, the Monroe Doctrine proved to be a two-edged sword: it also served to stimulate Latin-American nationalism and Latin-American resentment against the United States. Politically, despite the cautious language of diplomacy, Latin-American countries rejected North American interference in their affairs. Economically, Latin-American nationalism acted as a barrier to United States investment. Culturally, anti-*yanqui* sentiment was a bar to communication between North and South. A diminution of the anti-United-States element of Latin-American nationalism is scarcely to be expected under such circumstances.

It is always inadvisable to predict the future of nationalism anywhere. But based on current trends, it is probable that most Latin-American nations are headed for the establishment of some kind of nationalist authoritarian socialism.

Chapter 10

Melting-Pot Nationalism: The United States

We had invited the oppressed of all nations to find
shelter here, and to enjoy with us the blessings of free
institutions. They came by the millions. Some were
not so welcome as others, but under the assimilating
force of American life in our temperate climate,
which stimulates the working energies, the spirit
of orderly freedom, and thus favors the growth of
democracies, they became good Americans, most in the
first, all in the following generations. And so with all
the blood-crossings caused by the motley immigration,
we became a substantially homogeneous people, united
by common political beliefs and ideals, by common
interests, laws, and aspirations,—in one word—a nation.

—CARL SCHURZ
Convocation Address on the 20th Anniversary of
the University of Chicago, January 4, 1899

The American nation was born in the Age of Reason with its emphasis on liberty, constitutionalism, and parliamentarianism. The United States housed a society which had little use for medieval feudal and manorial practices and valued the right of every individual to life, liberty, and the pursuit of happiness. The poor, the weak, and the miserable of Europe, burdened by political and religious oppressions, flocked to the New World. Infused with a spirit of sturdy individualism, they enthusiastically entered the rough frontier life. They abolished monarchy and aristocracy, separated church and state, and forged a nation. They were blessed with great leaders. John Adams, in a letter written to Thomas Jefferson in 1813, expressed this exuberant thought: "Our sure, virtuous, public-spirited federative republic will last forever, govern the globe, and introduce the perfection of man." It should be added that on other occasions Adams was less optimistic.

The United States began its life not as a nationalist undertaking but as a new political experiment dedicated to the principles of federation and free government. In the New World, as in the Old, nationalism succeeded in overcoming every movement designed to limit it. Nationalism revealed itself as vital and energetic—a most dynamic force in American history.[1]

The history of the American republic runs parallel to the history of modern nationalism. Yet, nationalism in the United States is different from the nationalisms in Europe. America, a new nation, was created out of the most miscellaneous materials. Its languages, law, and culture were inherited from the Old World. The Founding Fathers were determined that their new country would differ profoundly from the nations of Europe. "From John Crèvecoeur and Condorcet to Tocque-

---

[1] It is strange that among American historians, who have written on every conceivable phase of American history, few have indicated an interest in the special meaning and development of American nationalism. There is no extensive history on the subject. The most valuable book is Hans Kohn, *American Nationalism* (New York, 1957), a volume of five essays delivered in 1956 at Northwestern University. Among the best treatments on the periphery of nationalism are Merle Curti, *The Roots of American Loyalty* (New York, 1946); Max Savelle, *Seeds of Liberty: The Genesis of American Politics* (Chicago, 1953); and Henry Steele Commager, *The American Mind* (New Haven, 1950).

ville and Grattan, from Bryce and Münsterberg to Brogan and Myrdal, foreign observers drew confidently on the lineaments of 'that new man, the American.' " [2] What took place in the New World was a great experiment along new lines, and the nationalism that evolved was itself a product of the new mold.

In the American experience many of the elements which had contributed to nationalism in other countries were lacking. There was initially no common defined territory: America was a huge land separated by seas from the rest of the world, but diverse peoples flocked to different areas, a tendency that at first fostered sectionalism rather than nationalism. There was no common religion: Puritans, Anglicans, Calvinists, Catholics, and others came to the New World. There were few common historical traditions: the early immigrants to America came from lands of varying backgrounds and traditions. There were originally no common myths connected with the past, or linked, as in England, to such legendary figures as King Arthur and his Knights of the Round Table. There was in early America no common cultural pattern. Above all, there was no common descent, or lineage stretching backward in time to an *Urvolk:* it was necessary to displace the Indian. Yet, out of all this emerged "a nation of many nations."

Hans Kohn has presented the thesis that the United States, despite its size, should be compared not with Europe as a whole but rather with certain individual nations which sought federation:

The American sections did not resemble European nations: otherwise the United States would not have survived all the trials and tests since the Civil War with the force of cohesion which it has shown throughout and with a conformity in loyalty which by far surpasses all the divisions of ethnic origin, economic interests and sectional allegiance. Instead of comparing the United States with Europe as a whole, as Turner [3] and his followers did, we shall gain a better understanding if we view the United States against the background of other nations or national groupings in Western Europe—Switzerland, Scandinavia, Germany, Italy, the Habsburg monarchy—which in the middle of the nineteenth century sought a way to unite various sectional interests and traditions within a national whole that

[2] Henry Steele Commager, "The Ambiguous American," *The New York Times Magazine,* May 3, 1964, p. 16.

[3] Frederick Jackson Turner (1861–1932). In 1893, Turner launched a new school of historical interpretation by emphasizing the influence that the frontier, then vanishing rapidly, had exerted on American development from its early days.

would allow liberty of development to all its parts without imposing the hegemony of one of them.[4]

Kohn suggested that many European nations sought a federative solution to their political problems, but that after the middle of the nineteenth century this federative polity declined almost to the point of extinction. It persisted and survived in the United States. Here again American nationalism differed from its European counterparts.

American nationalism repeated the European experience, however, in one respect—the gradual displacement of early nineteenth-century humanitarian nationalism by an integral form, rigid in structure and expansionist in tendency. American nationalists, like their European counterparts, developed what Merle Curti has called "incipient organic theory."[5] American nationalists, too, began to see their nation as if it were a living organism, possessing a personality, a body and soul.

The characteristics of American nationalism may be summarized as follows: a libertarian and egalitarian quality based on British and French experience; an accent on materialistic factors; a multiethnic character, assimilatory in nature, and respecting diversity; and a moralistic tone extending in a kind of missionary zeal to spread the American image. After a brief résumé of the origins and development of American nationalism, we shall return to an examination of these characteristics.

FROM COLONIAL SOCIETY TO NATIONAL FOCUS

The beginnings of American nationality may be traced back as far as 1648, the time of the English Civil War, when the Massachusetts General Court rejected Parliament's authority over internal affairs.[6] An

---

[4] Kohn, *American Nationalism*, pp. 99–100.

[5] "The most self-conscious nationalists did, to be sure, now and then look upon the nation as if it were a living organism, an actual personality, endowed with a body and a soul that transcended the aggregate of individual bodies and souls. . . . During and after the Civil War, Northern intellectuals developed the incipient organic theory, which at first did not reach the rank and file in the North. In the Old World the organic theory was likewise serving the integral type of nationalism that had largely replaced the older, humanitarian variety of the early nineteenth century. In time the newer conception of nationalism tended, in the United States as in Europe, to overshadow the older, humanitarian kind" (Curti, *op. cit.*, p. 175).

[6] The reason was because "our allegiance binds us not to the laws of England any longer than we live in England."

incipient sense of national loyalty became evident by about 1740, although insularity and provincialism continued to exist in colonial America.[7] There emerged a growing self-consciousness, a sense of restlessness, and a desire for independence, all noted by travelers from Europe in the latter part of the eighteenth century. By 1763 the colonies were determined to employ freedom in self-government and demanded full equality with the peoples of England.[8]

The American Revolution (1775–1783) marked the coming-of-age of American national consciousness. At this time the image of America as a British colony was replaced in the minds of Americans by the idea of a genuine American nation. The Revolution constituted the gestation period of the American national image, and the end of the war, its birth.[9]

A characteristic sense of loyalty was expressed by Timothy Dwight, a chaplain of the revolutionary army, in his poem "Columbia" (1777):

> Columbia, Columbia to glory arise,
> The queen of the world, and child of the skies!

[7] See Savelle, *Seeds of Liberty*, pp. 556ff.; and Curti, *op. cit.*, pp. 3–29.

American historians differ in judging at what point the colonists stopped considering themselves Englishmen and began to think of themselves as Americans. For example, James Truslow Adams, Michael Kraus, Oscar Handlin, and others see Americanization of the colonists as a slow, almost imperceptible process that took place throughout the colonial period. Max Savelle places the date somewhere between 1748 and the outbreak of the French and Indian War, while Allan Nevins sees the critical decade as extending from the passage of the Stamp Act to the creation of the First Continental Congress. Kenneth C. Wheare recognizes no American sense of nationalism until long after the formal ties were broken with England. This variety of opinions is described in an excellent study by Richard L. Merritt, who, utilizing Karl W. Deutsch's quantitative approach to the study of nationalism, examined symbolic identifications in the colonial period. His conclusion: "The changing processes of symbolic identification in the American colonies seem to have been neither revolutionary or evolutionary in the strictest sense of these terms. Rather, like other learning situations, they were both gradual and fitful, with a few periods of extremely rapid advances (or breakthroughs) interposed with other periods of more or less mild relapses" (Richard L. Merritt, "The Emergence of American Nationalism: A Quantitative Approach," *American Quarterly*, XVII [Summer 1965], 334).

[8] Apparently, the English authorities, failing to realize that the Americans were developing a passion to manage their own affairs, chose just the wrong moment to enforce mercantile regulations that had been long neglected and tried to impose new taxes.

[9] Max Savelle, "Nationalism and Other Loyalties in the American Revolution," *American Historical Review*, LXVII (July 1962), 923.

The genius commands thee; with rapture behold,
While ages on ages thy splendors unfold. . . .

To conquest, and slaughter, let Europe aspire;
Whelm nations in blood, and wrap cities in fire;
Thy heroes the rights of mankind shall defend,
And triumph pursue them, and glory attend.

A world is thy realm: for a world be thy laws,
Enlarg'd as thine empire, and just as thy cause;
On freedom's broad base, that empire shall rise,
Extend with the main, and dissolve with the skies.[10]

The vision was caught and by the end of the war in 1783 there was a recognizable trend in the direction of American nationalism. But the United States was not yet by any modern standards a nation. Though materials of nationhood were present, cohesive force was lacking. Most citizens in 1790 retained a sense of loyalty to county, province, or section, or to state or party.[11] A political nexus had been discovered, but unless a national tradition was soon established the states would develop rivalries similar to those existing in Latin America.[12] Immigrants felt little or no attachment to the nation; they had been attracted chiefly by the prospect of cheap land. The frontier drew thousands away from the settlements of the East, where they might have favored the development of national rather than provincial institutions.[13] The decisive fact, however, was that a constitutional republic was created in 1787. From that time, the national will, though often shaken, always remained supreme.[14]

The War of 1812, a turning point in American history, stimulated the rise of nationalism. "We are going to fight for the re-establishment of our national character," wrote Andrew Jackson.[15] Despite the opposition of the New England states to the war against the British, hostili-

---

[10] Timothy Dwight, "Columbia," in Elihu Hubbard Smith, ed., *American Poems, Selected and Original* (Litchfield, 1793), pp. 62–63.

[11] C. H. Van Tyne, *The War of Independence: American Phase* (Boston, 1929), p. 271.

[12] See Chapter 9.

[13] Boyd C. Shafer, *Nationalism: Myth and Reality* (New York, 1955), p. 157.

[14] *Ibid.*, p. 114.

[15] Note this early use of the term "national character." On national character, see Louis L. Snyder, *The Dynamics of Nationalism* (Princeton, 1964), pp. 55–75.

ties began after the failure of diplomacy. President Madison and his party appealed to nationalism, and the people, although still influenced by sectionalism, concurred.

The nationalistic impulse provided by the War of 1812 brings to mind a general tendency in nationalism. Nationalism is always invigorated by concentration on an enemy, real or imagined. For decades before 1812, Britain was the enemy: politicians as well as the public made it a point to twist the lion's tail. Americans felt that European powers in general and Britain in particular were seeking to hem them in. In much the same way, German nationalism before 1914 was in part a reaction to the feeling that other nations were setting up barriers against German expansion. William II complained that the great powers were closing all doors to the German people.

American nationalism developed rapidly after the War of 1812. Chief Justice Marshall, in *Cohens v. Virginia* (1821), expressed the new mood in forceful terms:

That the United States form, for many, and for most important purposes, a single nation, has not yet been denied. In war, we are one people. In making peace, we are one people. In all commercial relations, we are one and the same people.

In many other respects, the American people are one; and the government which is alone capable of controlling and managing their interests, in all these respects, is the government of the Union. It is their government, and in that character they have no other. America has chosen to be, in many respects, and to many purposes, a nation.[16]

This judicial expression of nationalism was followed on January 26 and 27, 1830, by Daniel Webster's statement of nationalist theory during an emotional peroration depicting what would happen if South Carolina should refuse to recognize a ruling of the Supreme Court:

I have not allowed myself, Sir, to look beyond the Union, to see what might lie hidden in the dark recess behind. I have not coolly weighed the chances of preserving liberty when the bonds that unite us shall be broken asunder. I have not accustomed myself to hang over the precipice of disunion, to see whether, with my short sight, I can fathom the depth of the abyss below; nor could I regard him as a safe counsellor in the affairs of the government, whose thoughts should be mainly bent on considering, not

---

[16] Quoted in Samuel Eliot Morison and Henry Steele Commager, *The Growth of the American Republic*, I (New York, 1962), 477.

how the union may be preserved, but how tolerable might be the condition of the people when it should be broken up and destroyed. While the Union lasts, we have high, exciting, gratifying prospects before us, for us and our children. Beyond that I seek not to penetrate the veil. God grant that in my day, at least, that curtain may not rise! . . . God grant that on my vision never may be opened what lies behind! When my eyes shall be turned to behold for the last time the sun in heaven, may I not see him shining on the broken and dishonored fragments of a once glorious Union; on States dissevered, discordant, belligerent; on a land rent with civil feuds, or drenched, it may be, in fraternal blood! Let their last feeble and lingering glance rather behold the gorgeous ensign of the republic, now known and honored throughout the earth, still full high advanced, its arms and trophies streaming in their original lustre, not a stripe erased or polluted, not a single star obscured, bearing for its motto, no such miserable interrogatory as "What is all this worth?" not those other words of delusion and folly, "Liberty first and Union afterwards"; but everywhere, spread over in characters of living light, blazing on all its ample folds, as they float over the sea and over the land, and in every wind under the whole heavens, that other sentiment, dear to every true American heart— Liberty *and* Union, now and for ever, one and inseparable! [17]

By 1835 nationalism became a concern for union above claims of state and party. A Cincinnati editor observed in that year, "Necessity compels us to lay aside sectional, political, and religious differences— and to unite as brothers." [18] By the middle of the nineteenth century American nationalism had come of age. It was the outcome of the emergence of national feeling, national pride, and the stimulation of westward expansion. There was no longer any doubt that a sovereign American people existed.[19]

In the 1840's few Southerners would have followed their states out of the Union. In fact, the strongest claims for American nationalism had been asserted by such presidents as Washington, Madison, Monroe, Jackson, and Polk. But the growth of Southern sectionalism and con-comitant rise in popularity of States' rights led to a clash between the principles of national union and self-determination. For some time before the conflict broke out, prominent Southerners voiced an emo-

[17] Quoted in Richard Hofstadter, William Miller, and Daniel Aron, *The American Republic*, I (Englewood Cliffs, N.J., 1959), 149.

[18] *Ibid.*, I, 497.

[19] It was obvious that in 1861 the American people cared enough about nationalism to maintain it by force of arms. The Civil War marked the collapse of the sovereignty of separate states.

tional attitude on sectionalism, praising the South as "my native land," or as "my home, my fatherland." This Southern sectionalism was expressed by a young jurist and poet, Alexander Beaufort Meek, who was born in South Carolina and died in 1861:

> Land of the South! Imperial Land!
> How proud thy mountains rise!
> How sweet thy scenes on every hand!
> How fair thy covering skies!
> But not for this,—oh, not for these,
> I love thy fields to roam,—
> Thou hast a dearer spell to me,
> Thou art my native home! [20]

The issue of "native home" was solved on the battlefields of the fratricidal Civil War, one of the more important landmarks in the development of American nationalism. James Russell Lowell regarded the war as a climactic boundary in American nationalism: "[The people] have not been involved in war by the passions or interests of their rulers, but deliberately accepted the ordeal of battle in defence of institutions which were the work of their own hands and of whose beneficence experience had satisfied them." [21] The triumph of Northern arms established a national state, indivisible and indissoluble. The Civil War tested the respective strengths of a society that was still agricultural and of a society increasingly industrialized. It examined the viability of two constitutions under critical conditions. [22]

The course of American unity confirmed Montesquieu's hope that in a large territory, unity and liberty could be merged in a federation. The federal structure was one of the most characteristic elements of American unity. Here again the United States departed from the European mold, for Europe was consumed by ancient rivalries. [23]

[20] Quoted in Henry C. Carrington, *Patriotic Reader* (Philadelphia, 1887), p. 451.

[21] James Russell Lowell, *Collected Works*, VI (New York, 1890), 214.

[22] Above all the Civil War tested the strength and determined the future of the federal union. The majority of American historians feel that this great trial of the United States was the crucible from which the mature nation emerged.

[23] Here, too, American historians generally agree that the case of America can in no way be compared to conditions in Europe. The original federation of states was much smaller than the present one. All were weak and found it necessary to join together in order to hold their own against England and the other countries which had colonies in the vicinity. Most American states later developed in the empty land held by the Union.

The United States had been an expansionist nation. Before the Civil War it had acquired no territory beyond the continental limits. For about two decades after the war the American people seemed to have forgotten the earlier expansionist impulse. Toward the end of the century the sense of manifest destiny that had led Americans to seize an empire from Mexico was revived. A new national psychology, nourished by industrialization, demanded overseas expansion. The new nation became a world power.[24]

LIBERTARIAN AND EGALITARIAN NATIONALISM

From its beginnings American nationalism stressed the desirability and the necessity of individual liberty. Liberty and equality became the watchwords of the new nation. The ideal was expressed by many Americans, but with particular cogency by Carl Schurz on April 18, 1859, in a speech on "True Americanism" in which he described the principles against which illiberal movements such as Know-Nothingism foundered. Schurz later recalled his speech:

I then described . . . my ideal conception of the American republic as the hope and guide of liberty-loving mankind developed itself, how peoples struggling for liberty and hampered in that struggle by old inherited institutions and customs and habits of thinking were wistfully looking to the new world for the realization of that ideal; how this new world, by the evolutions of history, appeared predestined and wonderfully fitted for that realization; how, by the assembling and intermingling of the most vigorous elements of all civilized nations, a new and youthful nation was created; how that new nation asserted and maintained its rightful independent existence upon the principle that all men are created equal and are endowed with certain inalienable rights among which are life, liberty, and the pursuit of happiness; how this basic principle indicated the great historic mission of the American republic, and how the best hopes of mankind were bound up in the fulfillment of this mission, for which we were responsible to the world.[25]

[24] Frederick Hertz, *Nationality in History and Politics* (London, 1951), p. 187.
[25] *The Reminiscences of Carl Schurz*, II (New York, 1907), 121. The Know-Nothings were a secret political organization, flourishing from 1853 to 1856, whose object it was to keep foreign-born Americans powerless by strict naturalization laws and exclusive choice of native-born Americans for political office. The name was popularly applied because members of the party replied: "I don't know," to all questions about the party.

The tie which united the new nation—and at the same time separated it from other nations—was not based on the usual attributes of nationhood, such as common language, territory, descent, or cultural traditions, but on the idea of liberty expressed in the Constitution and in the Bill of Rights.[26] Libertarianism was an English, not an American invention. It evolved in a long development from the Magna Carta to the revolutions of the seventeenth century.[27] Carl Becker has written, "The philosophy of the Declaration was not new, but good old English doctrine newly formulated to meet a present emergency." [28] There was some rivalry: Americans imagined that their liberties were of a higher degree than those of the English. James Truslow Adams believed that "Americans probably had far more liberty than the English at home, and they revolted probably because they were the freest of all people." [29] Whatever the degree of liberty, the Americans did absorb the English idea of constitutional liberty and on the basis of their own experience broadened it into a highly successful political and social formula. The Founding Fathers, inspired by an enthusiasm for freedom, wished to break away from "the pernicious labyrinth of European politics," and create a new and better world, thus "vindicating the honor of the human race." [30]

If the general inspiration of American libertarian nationalism came from England, its specific forerunner was the English philosopher John Locke.[31] The Resolve at New London on December 10, 1765, that "the People have a Right to reassume the exercise of that Authority which by Nature they had, before they delegated it to Individuals," was purely Lockean, and Jefferson's Declaration of Independence was an eloquent application of the ideas made familiar by Locke by a century and a half of American experience.[32] Jefferson himself admitted that when he set to work to draft the Declaration, he turned to neither

[26] Kohn, *American Nationalism*, pp. 8–9.   [27] *Ibid.*, p. 28.

[28] Carl Becker, *The Declaration of Independence* (New York, 1922), p. 231.

[29] James Truslow Adams, *Revolutionary New England, 1691–1776* (Boston, 1923), pp. 14 ff.

[30] Hertz, *op. cit.*, p. 184.

[31] See Louis Hartz, *The Liberal Tradition in America* (New York, 1955); and "The Great Mr. Locke, America's Philosopher, 1783–1861," in Merle Curti, *Probing Our Past* (New York, 1955), pp. 69–118.

[32] "Once Whiggery 'discovered' America, the whole of American thought shook down almost automatically into a kind of nationalism found nowhere else on earth, exploding the familiar category of Carlton Hayes: a 'traditionalist nationalism' that was liberal, a Burkean nationalism that was Lockean" (Hartz, *op. cit.*, p. 207).

book nor pamphlet: "All its authority rests on the harmonizing sentiments of the day, whether expressed in conversation, in letters, printed essays, or the elementary books of public right, as Aristotle, Cicero, Locke, Sidney, etc." [33] Certainly Locke's empirical epistemology provided not only a logical basis for faith in human reason but also a rational basis for the principle of individual liberty.[34] By setting limits to the power of any government over men's lives and property, and by insisting that government must observe the natural laws guaranteeing freedom and security, Locke not only rationalized the long struggle of the English people against the Stuarts but also gave the American colonists their own justification for freedom. They were fully accustomed, under pioneer conditions, to a large measure of actual liberty and freedom from interference: Locke's conception of the social contract solidified their views.[35]

This extraordinary concern for personal liberty, which in the United States was regarded as the natural right of man, became axiomatic throughout the course of American historical development. Alexander Meiklejohn expressed it in this passage:

America has an ideal. It is Liberty. That is, I am sure, our deepest commitment. No one who reads our national literature, who listens to our daily speech, who mingles in the common course of our living, can fail to hear the note rising above all the others in which we express ourselves. The man who fails to find in us a deep, consuming passion for freedom does not know what we are.[36]

Americans deferred to Europeans in art or in science, but they felt themselves masters in political life. They were quite certain that their belief in individual liberty and social mobility was the way to a better future. Indeed, American fulfillment of common ideals strongly affected the European mind. In the words of Michael Kraus, "The community of interest that was created in the last third of the eighteenth century among liberals everywhere in the Atlantic civilization

[33] Thomas Jefferson, *Writings*, VI (New York, 1869), 407.
[34] Max Savelle, *The Colonial Origins of American Thought* (Princeton, 1964), p. 53.
[35] John Herman Randall, Jr., *The Making of the Modern Mind* (Boston, 1940), pp. 344–345.
[36] Alexander Meiklejohn, *What Does America Mean?* (New York, 1935), p. 71.

has been an enduring factor in the life of western society to our own time." [37]

Throughout American history attacks on the libertarian formula were made by a host of movements ranging from Know-Nothingism to McCarthyism.[38] But the zeal for freedom did not diminish.[39] The libertarian nexus of American nationalism was retained even through the two world wars. In times of stress the Americans temporarily relinquished their cherished liberties; but after each conflict, when the emergency had ended, sovereignty was automatically returned to the people and their rights reaffirmed.

The libertarian aspect of American nationalism was closely associated with egalitarianism. Throughout its history the United States, in comparison with European countries, was egalitarian in temper, and it remains so today.[40] As early as 1835, Tocqueville stated in his book *De la démocratie en Amérique* that this was the most pervasive of all American traits.

Among the novel objects that attracted my attention during my stay in the United States, nothing struck me more forcibly than the general equality of conditions. I readily discovered the prodigious influence which this primary fact exercises on the whole course of society, by giving a certain direction to public opinion, and a certain tenor to the laws; by imparting new maxims to the governing powers, and peculiar habits to the governed. I speedily perceived that the influence of this fact extends far beyond the political character and the laws of the country, and that it has no less empire over civil society than over the Government; it creates opinions, engenders sentiments, suggests the ordinary practices of life, and modifies whatever it does not produce. The more I advanced in the study of American society, the more I perceived that the equality of conditions is

[37] Michael Kraus, *The Atlantic Civilization: Eighteenth-Century Origins* (Ithaca, N.Y., 1949), p. 313.

[38] "Conservative Americans and Englishmen have been worried about possible excesses of liberty, and throughout the history of the United States voices have been raised against dangers of corruption and demogogy, allegedly inherent in mass democracy" (Hans Kohn, *Democracy and Liberty: The Swiss Example* [New York, 1956], pp. 78–84).

[39] "The loss of Liberty, the rise of anarchy and despotism as a result of corruption and immorality, of demagogues and mass pressures, have been predicted by critics of American life throughout its history. All these predictions have turned out to be unfounded" (Kohn, *American Nationalism*, p. 19).

[40] D. W. Brogan, in *Saturday Review*, Jan. 2, 1965, p. 35.

the fundamental fact from which all others seem to be derived, and the central point at which all my observations constantly terminated.[41]

Those Americans who came from the Old World believed that there was greater equality in the new homeland. In Europe the individual's social position was fixed, and he could do little to improve it. In the New World, on the other hand, where equality and social mobility were stressed, it was possible to travel the road from poverty to riches, and back again. There were class distinctions, but they were temporary and indeterminate. Equality became the common denominator of American life. Henry Steele Commager described the leveling process as follows: "The American has scholars and scientists but no intelligentsia; he has ministers and priests but no ecclesiastical class; he has soldiers and sailors, but no military class. For that matter America has no aristocracy, no bourgeoisie, no proletariat and no peasantry: it just has people." [42]

The blending of libertarianism and egalitarianism gave American nationalism many of the qualities that have persisted to the present day. Both libertarianism and egalitarianism were essential to melting-pot nationalism. Along with these factors was the impetus of American economic nationalism, to which we now turn.

MATERIALISTIC HALLMARK:
AMERICAN ECONOMIC NATIONALISM

The American experiment was a blend of individual liberty, social equality, and unlimited economic opportunity. It combined idealism with materialism, manifested in a pattern set in colonial days and continuing through the period of American leadership in the Second Industrial Revolution. Parrington described a clash on the American scene between the idealism of the French Enlightenment and the English philosophy of *laissez faire*.[43] The juxtaposition was maintained

---

[41] Alexis de Tocqueville, *Democracy in America*, trans. Henry Reeve, I (New York, 1904), xxix.

[42] Henry Steele Commager, "The Ambiguous American," p. 114.

[43] "At the beginning of our national existence two rival philosophies contended for supremacy in America: the humanitarian philosophy of the French Enlightenment, based on the conception of human perfectibility and postulating as its objective an equalitarian democracy in which the political state should function as the servant to the common well-being; and the English philosophy of *laissez faire*, based on the assumed universality of the acquisitive instinct and postulating a

throughout the course of American history. The Founding Fathers expressed the Lockean ideology of "life, liberty, and property" in the more euphonious "life, liberty, and the pursuit of happiness." Calvin Coolidge made it clear that "the business of America is business," to which he added, "The chief ideal of the American people is idealism. I cannot repeat too often that America is a nation of idealists." [44]

From its earliest days the American colonial population was recruited mainly from the working classes of Britain and Europe.[45] The materialist urge was strengthened in a society where careers were open to talent. One of the more important motivations originated in Calvinism. The Puritans and those of Calvinist leanings, including Presbyterians and Quakers, regarded worldly success as a sign of God's grace. Business was a good thing: in the Puritan view personal gain, social good, and God's will became one and the same thing. This doctrine was almost perfectly attuned to the needs of young expanding capitalism.[46]

As the infant nation grew it placed major emphasis on its economic life. Despite periods of recession, the people enjoyed the fruits of material well-being. National aims became closely bound with material achievement. Americans began to interpret their productivity and wealth as a sign of greatness. David M. Potter described the Americans as a people of plenty. Abundance, he said, exercised a pervasive influence on the shaping of the American character.[47]

---

social order answering the needs of the abstract 'common man,' in which the state should function on in the interest of trade" (Vernon L. Parrington, *Main Currents in American Thought* [New York, 1930], Book III, p. xxiii).

[44] Quoted in Arthur M. Schlesinger, *Paths to the Present* (New York, 1949), p. 16.

[45] "From the beginning America was made up of what they call in England the middle and laboring classes, and it has always remained so. This is, in fact, one of the most important things about it" (James Truslow Adams, *The American: The Making of a New Man* [New York, 1943], p. 49).

[46] Thomas C. Cochran, *Basic History of American Business* (Princeton, 1959), p. 10. This was the view presented by Max Weber in describing the Protestant ethic in the genesis of capitalism.

[47] David M. Potter, *People of Plenty: Economic Abundance and the American Character* (Chicago, 1954), p. 208. According to Potter, the study of national character should not stand apart from the study of character formation in the individual. He described economic abundance as a factor whose presence and force could be recognized clearly and precisely in the development of the personality of the American child. He saw the same factor as recognizable with equal certainty in the broad range of American experience, ideals, and institutions.

The economy that had already been expanding before the Civil War grew with explosive force after that conflict. The spectacular economic development from 1865 to 1890 was almost without parallel in modern times.[48] From 1870 to 1890—the span of a single generation—the federal system grew from thirty-eight to forty-five states, and the population nearly doubled, from 38,558,000 to 75,995,000. In 1860 the United States was a second-rate industrial country, lagging behind England, France, and Germany, but by 1890 the value of her economic goods almost equaled the combined production of the other three countries.[49] From 1860 to 1917, American manufacturing activity multiplied twelve times over.[50] By the 1870's technological advance and mechanization made it possible to produce more of everything than the American market could absorb at profitable prices.[51] Because of rapid industrialization and urbanization, the United States was no longer merely a farming country. Inside its borders was the greatest free-trade market in the world. The height of economic acquisition was reached in the "business baroque period" from 1890 to 1912, when the leaders of business exulted in the power and riches won by national centralization.[52]

National centralization was the key to this success. During these rapid developments the bonds of nationality became stronger rather than weaker. Industrialization knitted the country together with bonds of steel. The defeat of the Confederacy in the Civil War infused the concept of nationality with a kind of mystical quality, and the sense of

[48] "With a stride that astonished statisticians, the conquering hosts of business enterprise swept over the continent; twenty five years after the death of Lincoln, America had become in the quantity and value of her products, the first manufacturing nation in the world. What England had once accomplished in one hundred years, the United States had achieved in half that time" (Charles A. and Mary Beard, *The Rise of American Civilization*, II [New York, 1939], 176). See also on the growth of American industrialization, Samuel P. Hays, *The Response to Industrialism, 1885–1914* (Chicago, 1957); Edward C. Kirkland, *Industry Comes of Age: Business, Labor, and Public Policy, 1860–1897* (New York, 1961); Ida M. Tarbell, *The Nationalizing of Business, 1878–1898* (New York, 1936); and Thomas C. Cochran and William Miller, *The Age of Enterprise* (New York, 1942).

[49] England, the homeland of the First Industrial Revolution, was displaced by the United States and Germany in the Second Industrial Revolution.

[50] This enormous increase in economic power turned out to be a decisive factor in the outcome of World War I.

[51] Ray Ginger, *The Nationalizing of American Life, 1877–1900* (New York, 1965), p. 4.

[52] Miriam Beard, *A History of the Business Man* (New York, 1938), p. 641.

national accomplishment was heightened by the adventure of settling the West.[53] American nationalism became imbued with economic considerations.

Sociologists differ in their analysis of the effects of industrialization and urbanization on the American social character. David Riesman has adhered to a materialistic interpretation of changes in values. He explained American character and values by relating them to the supposed demands of a certain type of economy and its unique organization. The American economy, in order to be productive, needed certain types of individuals and required that they held certain values. This was a materialistic interpretation of social phenomena.[54]

Seymour Martin Lipset challenged this concept as inadequate. America, he said, had no monopoly of entrepreneurs or bureaucrats. The British and Swedish societies for decades possessed occupational structures similar to that of the United States. To Lipset the derivation of social character almost exclusively from traits associated with occupational or population profiles was incorrect. Riesman's materialistic interpretation, said Lipset, underestimated the extent to which basic American national values, once institutionalized, affected the consequences of technological and economic change.[55]

THE MULTIETHNIC CHARACTER
OF AMERICAN NATIONALISM

Oliver Wendell Holmes called Americans "the Romans of the modern world—the great assimilating people." The amalgamation of peoples appeared early in American history; it was retained thereafter as a highly desirable characteristic of the American society. America was a new nation forged out of the most miscellaneous human materials. Although Americans inherited their language, laws, and culture from the Old World, they were determined that their nation would differ from the mother countries of the European continent.[56]

The multiethnic character of the new nation was recognized early

[53] Arthur M. Schlesinger, *The Rise of Modern America, 1865–1951* (New York, 1951), p. 162.

[54] See David Riesman, *The Lonely Crowd* (New Haven, 1950).

[55] See Seymour Martin Lipset, *Culture and Social Character: The Work of David Riesman Reviewed,* ed. Seymour Lipset and Les Lowenthal (New York, 1961).

[56] See Henry Steele Commager, "The Ambiguous American," p. 16.

(1782) by J. Hector St. John de Crèvecoeur, a transplanted Frenchman who became famous as the author of *Letters from an American Farmer*. Whence came all these people? Crèvecoeur saw them as a mixture of English, Scotch, Irish, French, Dutch, Germans, and Swedes, a promiscuous breed which produced "that race now called American." The poor of Europe flocked to this great American asylum:

What then is the American, this new man? He is either an European, or the descendant of an European, hence that strange mixture of blood, which you will find in no other country. I could point out to you a family whose grandfather was an Englishman, whose wife was Dutch, whose son married a French woman, and whose present four sons have now four wives of different nations. *He* is an American, who leaving behind him all his ancient prejudices and manners, receives new ones from the new mode of life he has embraced, the new government he obeys, and the new rank he holds. He becomes an American by being received in the broad lap of our great *Alma Mater*. Here individuals of all nations are melted into a new race of men whose labors and posterity will one day cause great changes in the world.[57]

This concept of social fluidity persisted during the subsequent development of the nation. America's history was largely the result of a vast folk migration, a society created by the intermingling of migrants. On they came, the people of many nations—English, Germans, Swedes, Dutch, French, Scotch-Irish, Highland Scots, Italians, and Jews.[58] "You cannot spill a drop of American blood," wrote Herman Melville, "without spilling the blood of the whole world. . . . We are not a nation so much as a world. . . . We are the heirs of all time and with all nations we divide our inheritance." [59]

By the middle of the nineteenth century the poet Walt Whitman, who regarded himself as a kind of high priest of American democracy, was writing paeans to his country, "center of equal daughters, equal sons." America, he said, was not merely a nation, but a teeming nation of nations. This was a new breed of men with a new national consciousness. Other states, he said, indicate themselves in their deputies, but the genius of the United States was not to be found in its executives

[57] J. Hector St. John de Crèvecoeur, *Letters from an American Farmer* (Dublin, 1782), pp. 37 ff.
[58] See Michael Kraus, *Immigration: The American Mosaic* (Princeton, 1966).
[59] Quoted in *ibid.*, p. 10.

and legislatures, nor in its ambassadors, or authors, or colleges, but always most in the common people:

Their manners, dress, friendships—the freshness and candor of their physiognomy—the picturesque looseness of their carriage . . . their deathless attachment to freedom—their aversion to anything decorous or soft or mean—the practical acknowledgement of the citizens of one state by the citizens of all the other states—the fierceness of their reused resentment—their curiosity and welcome of novelty—their self-esteem and wonderful sympathy—their susceptibility to a slight—the air they have of persons who never knew how it felt to stand in the presence of superiors—the fluency of their speech—their delight in music, the sure symptom of manly tenderness and native elegance of soul . . . their good temper and open-handedness—the terrible significance of their elections—the President's taking off his hat to them not they to him—these too are unrhymed poetry.[60]

Toward the end of the century further recognition of the American mixture of people and mores came—without Walt Whitman's glowing exaggeration—from James Bryce, English historian and diplomat. An entranced observer of the American scene, Bryce doubted whether differences of blood had the importance which they had assumed, and he was skeptical of claims of racial superiority for Anglo-Saxons. "What strikes the traveler," he wrote in *The American Commonwealth* in 1888, "and what the Americans themselves delight to point out to him, is the amazing solvent power which American institutions, habits, and ideas exercise upon new-comers of all races. The children of Irishmen, Germans, and Scandinavians are far more like native Americans than prevalent views of heredity would have led us to expect; nor is it without interest to observe that Nature has here repeated on the Western continent that process of mixing Celtic with Germanic and Norse blood which she began in Britain more than a thousand years ago." [61] Bryce further believed that the intellectual and moral atmosphere into which the settlers from Europe came had more power to assimilate them than their racial qualities had power to change it. The future of America, he said, would be less affected by the influx of new

[60] From the preface to *Leaves of Grass* (New York, 1855).
[61] James Bryce, *The American Commonwealth*, II (London, 1888), 709. Bryce's "solvent power" later became the "melting pot," a phrase coined by Israel Zangwill as the title of a play in 1908 concerning immigration problems.

blood than anyone who had not studied the American democracy could realize.

Soon there was a mounting debate over the desirability of immigration. How effective was it? Did the immigrants who came to the United States really become Americans or did they remain attached to the lands of their origin? As immigration increased, a number of American historians, influenced by training in Germany, sought the origin of American libertarianism not in English experience but in the old Teutonic ideals which supposedly united Germany, England, and the United States.[62] Edward Augustus Freeman attributed the beginning of the idea of liberty to Arminius, who freed the Germans from the Romans in the German forests: "We gave our part in the great deliverance by the wood of Teutoburg; Arminius, *liberator Germaniae,* is but the first of a roll which goes on to Hampden and to Washington." [63]

Others tended to discount the Teutonic role and to praise the role of the Anglo-Saxon "race" as standing for individual liberty and democracy. In an article titled "Manifest Destiny," published in 1885, John Fiske prophesied that one day "four-fifths of the human race will trace its pedigree to English forefathers, as four-fifths of the white people of the United States trace their pedigree today." [64] He was certain that the Anglo-Saxons originated the political institution of federalism, "the fittest of all political institutions," which would eventually be accepted throughout the world.[65]

Josiah Strong, a Congregationalist minister, believed it was the historic mission of the Anglo-Saxons to bring the ideals of civil liberty and spiritual Christianity to peoples in the remote areas of the world. "If I read not amiss, this powerful race will move down upon Mexico, down upon Central and South America, out upon the islands on the sea, over upon Africa and beyond. And can anyone doubt that the result of this

[62] See Edward N. Saveth, "Race and Nationalism in American Historiography: The Late Nineteenth Century," *Political Science Quarterly,* LIV (Sept. 1939), 421 ff.

[63] Edward Augustus Freeman, *The Chief Periods of European History* (London, 1886), p. 64.

[64] John Fiske, "Manifest Destiny," *Harper's New Monthly Magazine,* LXX (Mar. 1888), 588.

[65] In 1901, Fiske was asked to be the American representative at the millennial celebration in King Alfred's honor. His topic was "The Beginnings of Federalism in New England, as Related to the Expansion of Alfred's World." See Michael Kraus, *A History of American History* (New York, 1937), p. 378.

competition of races will be 'the survival of the fittest'?" [66] Strong was not opposed to immigrants: they would be welcomed as Americans if they wished to become Americans.

There is among our population of alien birth an unhappy tendency toward aggregation, which concentrates the strain upon a portion of our social and political fabric. . . . Our safety demands the assimilation of these strange populations, and the process of assimilation will become slower and slower and more difficult as the proportion of foreigners increases. . . . We may well ask whether this in-sweeping immigration is to foreignize us or we are to Americanize it.[67]

Thus, Strong did not reject the nation of many nations: he accepted the intermingling of ethnic stocks and its enhancement by immigration. However, he warned against the overflow of immigrants living under conditions which made their assimilation almost impossible and thereby creating an obstacle to the fulfillment of America's destiny.[68]

The melting-pot issue was accentuated in the difficult years of World War I. Theodore Roosevelt, a proponent of intervention long before 1917, proclaimed that there was "no room for the hyphen in our citizenship." "We must shun as we would shun the plague all efforts to make us separate in groups of separate nationalities. We must all of us be Americans, and nothing but Americans; and all good Americans must stand on an equality of consideration and respect, without regard to their creed or to the land from which their forbears came." [69] The most popular war poster, by Howard Chandler Christy, depicted a young girl appealing to Americans to buy Liberty Loans and pointing with pride to a list of names, saying "Americans All!: Du Bois, Smith, O'Brien, Knutson, Cejka, Haucke, Pappandeikopolous, Gonzales, Andrassi, Villoto, Levy, Turovich, Kowalski, Chiczanevicz." [70]

Beginning in 1924, when the first law limiting immigration was

---

[66] See Josiah Strong, *Our Country: Its Possible Future and Its Present Crisis* (New York, 1891), pp. 222–223.

[67] *Ibid.*, pp. 59, 61.   [68] Kohn, *American Nationalism*, p. 160.

[69] *The Works of Theodore Roosevelt*, XIX (New York, 1928), 301 ff.

[70] The racialist Madison Grant was appalled by this poster, which he attributed to "some misguided enthusiast" in the Treasury Department. He was angered by the use of a girl of "pure Nordic type." "The one native American," he complained, "is hidden under the sobriquet of Smith, and there is an implied suggestion that the very beautiful lady is a product of this melting pot." (Madison Grant, "The Racial Transformation of America," *North American Review*, CCXIX, [Mar. 1924], 343).

passed, curtailment of immigration accelerated, or made possible, the incorporation and assimilation of foreign groups.[71] In World War II the various immigrant strains were even more united than they had been in the earlier war. "In the American army for the liberation of Europe, men of German, Polish, Italian, Croat, and a dozen other national origins have marched side by side; in the presidential election of 1940 one candidate could speak with pride of his Dutch, the other of his German ancestry." [72]

The debate over the success of the melting pot continued. On one side was the contention that immigration was slowly and insidiously eating away at the heart of the United States, and that what was being melted was the American nationality itself.[73] It was charged that the melting pot was "a crime against nature"; that New York City was "a *cloaca gentium* which will produce many amazing racial hybrids and some ethnic horrors that will be beyond the powers of future anthropologists to unravel"; that if the melting pot was allowed to boil over without control "the type of native American of Colonial descent will become as extinct as the Athenian of the Age of Pericles, and the Viking of the Age of Rollo." [74]

On the other side was the case for cultural pluralism which described America as "a democracy of nationalities," "a multiplicity in a unity," "an orchestration of mankind." [75] It was predicted that in times of stress American unity would collapse because of domestic racial antagonisms, a prophecy that continues to be projected. There was diversity, but there was also cohesion under stress. When, after World War II, American isolation evaporated and the United States took its place as a global power, the melting pot withstood the strain of world responsibilities.

Despite the difficulties of a pluralistic society, America tended to become more and more homogeneous. The more the Americans were different, the more they became alike. American Jews contributed heavily to Israel, but few were willing to return to the land of their ancestors. They would not leave the United States. American Negroes,

[71] Kohn, *American Nationalism*, p. 167.

[72] Edward H. Carr, *Nationalism and After* (London, 1945), p. 35.

[73] See Henry Pratt Fairchild, *The Melting Pot Mistake* (Boston, 1926).

[74] For these and similar views, see Madison Grant, *The Passing of the Great Race* (New York, 1918), *passim*.

[75] Horace M. Kallen, *Culture and Democracy in the United States* (New York, 1924), pp. 123 ff.

even though there was increasing friction with their fellow white citizens, did not dream of migrating to the newly independent African states.[76] What took place was the molding of a nation of many peoples, certainly imperfect in many ways but nevertheless a striking achievement in the history of Western civilization.

MORALISTIC NATIONALISM AND MISSIONARY ZEAL

From its earliest days American nationalism exhibited a moralistic quality along with the urges of money and power. For Americans the idea of national destiny was always related to the betterment of mankind. The Founding Fathers, products of the Enlightenment, were dedicated to the principles of liberty and equality, concepts reaffirmed by Lincoln and most of his successors. Americans remained convinced that their way of life was virtuous and a decided contribution to the perfection of mankind. "We air a great people, and bound to be tolerable troublesome to them kings," boasted one early American.

The central theme of morality in American life was derived from Judaic-Christian ethics, and especially from the Puritan ethic. A curious mixture of religious and political feelings was characteristic of American society.[77] Originally a theocratic society, it went through drastic modification and turned to a morality in which economic success became evidence of moral correctness.

What begins as a theocratic principle ends by becoming a tradition that it is not very easy to distinguish from utilitarianism. . . . To work hard, to lead an orderly life, to have a name for integrity and fair-dealing, not to spend one's substance in reckless display, to have the resolution to carry out the purposes you undertake—it is, roughly, an ethic such as this that the religion of America had shaped when the basic tradition was formed.[78]

Although there is no necessary connection between success and moral virtue, Americans throughout their history associated the success-pat-

[76] American Negroes made this clear in many letters-to-the-editor: "I am an American who happens to be a Negro, and I am proud of both facts" (John M. Driver, Sunnyvale, California, in *Time*, Nov. 11, 1966, p. 18).

[77] "In more theologically minded countries, sharp theological doctrines actually helped define the boundaries of *religious* sentiment; similarly in such countries the definitions of political theory help separate a special field of *political* doctrine. But in the United States religious and political thought overflow into each other" (Daniel J. Boorstin, *The Genius of American Politics* [Chicago, 1953], p. 158).

[78] Harold Laski, *The American Democracy* (New York, 1948), p. 27.

tern with achievement, linked achievement with work, and endowed work with almost mystical ethical values.

Observers of the American scene from Tocqueville to Siegfried and Brogan agreed on one point: Americans "tend to see the world in moral terms." In the 1880's, James Bryce wrote:

They are a moral and well-conducted people. . . . The average of temperance, chastity, truthfulness, and general probity is somewhat higher than in any of the great nations of Europe. The instincts of the native farmer or artisan are almost invariably kindly and charitable. He respects the law; he is deferential to women and indulgent to children; he attaches an almost excessive value to the possession of a genial manner and the observance of domestic duties.

. . . They have an intelligent interest in the form of faith they profess, are pious without superstition and zealous without bigotry. The importance which some still, though all much less than formerly, attach to dogmatic propositions, does not prevent them from feeling the moral side of their theology. Christianity influences conduct, not indeed half as much as in theory it ought, but probably more than it does in any other modern country, and far more than it did in the so-called ages of faith.[79]

Though national characteristics are subject to change, the moralistic tinge of American nationalism proved to be remarkably enduring. Americans thought in terms of right and wrong, good and bad, ethical and unethical. When the thirteen colonies declared their independence on July 4, 1776, they did so in a document that placed their cause on a high ethical plane, endowing all men with the rights of life, liberty and the pursuit of happiness. The moral strain showed in a series of slogans: In April 1898 it was "Liberate Cuba!" In April 1917 it was "Make the world safe for democracy!" In April 1941 it was "Rid the world of Hitler!" Throughout the social structure there was evidence of a strain of morality. American heroes were not successful merely within a certain ethical framework. They had to be, or appear to be, "self-respecting, decent, honorable, with a sense of fair play." [80]

[79] James Bryce, *The American Commonwealth*, II (3rd ed.; New York, 1900), 285–286. The way in which Americans identified the nation with moral principles is of endless fascination for American historians. "The identification of the nation with moral principle, moral will, moral struggle and regeneration, led to the conviction that only through the nation can the individual realize his own moral freedom" (Curti, *op. cit.*, p. 177).

[80] Dixon Wecter, *The Hero in America* (New York, 1941), p. 482. "The American character, whatever its shortcomings, abounds in courage, creative

Early American moral and religious impulses did not remain enveloped in complacent sentiment, but were transformed from moralistic to missionary nationalism. Following the enthusiasm of the Revolution and the creation of the new nation came the nationalistic surge. The Americans purchased Louisiana, claimed Oregon, and conquered California. They were attracted by great areas of unsettled or sparsely settled land lying beyond the frontiers. This continental expansion differed from the European variety in that it was a drive into contiguous territory.

The shift from moralistic to expansionist nationalism was expressed vividly by John L. O'Sullivan, a Jacksonian Democrat, who in 1839 predicted that the United States was destined to be a great nation:

Yes, we are the nation of progress, of individual freedom, of universal enfranchisement. Equality of rights is the cynosure of our union of states, the grand exemplar of the correlative equality of individuals; and, while truth sheds its effulgence, we cannot retrogade without dissolving the one and subverting the other. We must go onward to the fulfillment of our mission—to the entire development of the principle of our organization—freedom of conscience, freedom of person, freedom of trade and business pursuits, universality of freedom and equality. This is our high destiny, and in nature's eternal, inevitable decree of cause and effect we must accomplish it. All this will be our future history, to establish on earth the moral dignity and salvation of man—the immutable truth and beneficence of God. For this blessed mission to the nations of the world, which are shut out from the lifegiving light of truth, has America been chosen; and her high example shall smite unto death the tyranny of kings, hierarchs, and oligarchs and carry the glad tidings of peace and good will where myriads now endure an existence scarcely more enviable than beasts in the field. Who, then, can doubt that our country is destined to be *the great nation* of futurity? [81]

In the July-August 1845 issue of his magazine, *The United States Magazine and Democratic Review,* O'Sullivan first used the term "manifest destiny." [82] Foreign governments, he wrote, were seeking to ob-

---

energy, and resourcefulness, and is bottomed upon the conviction that nothing in the world is beyond its power to accomplish" (Schlesinger, *Paths to the Present*, p. 22).

[81] John L. O'Sullivan, "The Great Nation of Futurity," *The United States Magazine and Democratic Review,* VI (Nov. 1839), 6.

[82] On manifest destiny, see Albert K. Weinberg, *Manifest Destiny* (Baltimore, 1935); Bernard A. De Voto, *The Year of Decision, 1846* (Boston, 1943); Francis

struct the annexation of Texas in order to check "the fulfillment of our manifest destiny to overspread the continent alloted by providence for the free development of our yearly multiplying millions." It was only just, he said, that Americans spread the ideals of their great experiment —liberty and federated self-government.

The doctrine was quickly taken up by press, politicians, and nationalists who wanted an excuse for national expansion. The settlement of the frontier had entered its last phase and now Americans were ready to wrest an empire from Mexico. The immediate cause of the Mexican War of 1846–1848 was a dispute over the boundaries of Texas. After a quick campaign, the United States acquired not only California, but also New Mexico.[83] American nationalists insisted that their conquest was merely the fulfillment of a divine mission instigated by a force beyond human control. Americans would extend "the area of freedom." It was their destiny not merely to teach by precept but also to gather more land and peoples into the American fold. This thread of idealism ran through a speech given by Commodore Robert F. Stockton on December 30, 1847:

No thoughtful observer of the progress of the United States can fail to be impressed with the conviction that we enjoy a degree of happiness and prosperity never before vouchsafed to the nations of mankind. With an unexampled measure of political liberty; unbroken social order; extraordinary growth of the arts and sciences—philanthropic and benevolent institutions, the fair offspring of the Christian faith, extending their blessed agency, in all directions—unbounded, religious toleration, heaven's best gift; for which our fathers risked and suffered most—with all these rich endowments, do we not indeed present an example of the beneficent care of Providence for which we can find no parallel in the history of man? . . .

We have vanquished Mexico. She is prostrate at our feet—we can afford to be magnanimous. Let us act so that we need not fear the strictest

Parkman, *The Oregon Trail* (New York, 1949); and Norman A. Graebner, *Empire on the Pacific* (New York, 1955).

"A special variety of nationalism—resentment in the nation over interference by Europe in the affairs of Texas—is credited in some accounts with having generated Manifest Destiny. . . . That a national spirit so strong and unified as to generate Manifest Destiny could have emerged from such a composite of disharmonies is inconceivable" (Frederick Merk, *Manifest Destiny and Mission in American History* [New York, 1963], pp. 59–60).

[83] On the Mexican War, see Justin H. Smith, *The War with Mexico* (2 vols.; New York, 1919); and *The Annexation of Texas* (2 vols.; New York, 1911).

scrutiny of the Christian and civilized world. I would with a magnanimous and kindly hand gather these wretched people within the fold of republicanism.[84]

The Civil War, fought in part to maintain the unity of the nation against disintegrative Southern nationalism, marked a temporary decline in American expansionism. In the 1880's expansionism was revived. The older form of manifest destiny had been based on a simple faith in the superiority of the American people and the desirability of their political institutions, both lauded to the skies in Fourth of July oratory. The new manifest destiny was armed with the supposedly scientific racial doctrines so popular in Europe. Darwinism was translated into "domination of the fittest"; advocates of national expansion used Darwinism to rationalize the domination of backward peoples. A blend of racialism, the sense of national mission, and interest in foreign markets was used to justify the task of bestowing the blessings of benevolent rule on less fortunate peoples. Americans took seriously the mission of conducting the political civilization of the modern world. All sections of the population, whether militaristic or pacifistic, educated or uneducated, shared in these enhanced nationalistic beliefs.

Ardent moralistic nationalism was at the root of America's war with Spain in 1898. Senator Albert J. Beveridge of Indiana presented the case for annexation of the Philippines in a highly emotional address to Congress. The United States, he said, had rescued the Filipinos from a "savage and bloody rule," and it was plain that they preferred "the just, humane, and civilizing government of the United States" to that of Spain. One passage especially deserves mention as a classic expression of missionary nationalism:

God has not been preparing the English-speaking and Teutonic peoples for a thousand years for nothing but vain and idle self-contemplation and self-admiration. No! He has made us the master organizers of the world to establish system where chaos reigns. He has given us the spirit of progress to overwhelm the forces of reaction throughout the earth. He has made us adept in government that we may administer government among savage and senile peoples. Were it not for such a force as this the world would relapse into barbarism and night. And of all our race He has marked the American people as His chosen nation to finally lead in the regeneration of the world. This is the divine mission of America, and it holds for us all the

[84] Robert F. Stockton, in *Niles' National Register*, Jan. 22, 1848.

profit, all the glory, all the happiness possible to man. We are trustees of the world's progress, guardians of its righteous peace.[85]

While this type of aggressive nationalism received support among the people, not all Americans accepted it. In an angry letter to the editor of the Boston *Evening Transcript,* the psychologist William James denounced the conduct of the United States government in the Philippines as "a national infamy" and as "infamous callousness and insult":

Shall [American conduct] be execrated by ourselves? Shall the unsophisticated verdict upon its hideousness which the plain moral sense pronounces avail nothing to stem the torrent of mere empty 'bigness' in our destiny, before which it is said that we must all knock under, swallowing such higher sentiments with a gulp? The issue is perfectly plain at last. We are cold-bloodedly, wantonly and abominably destroying the soul of a people which never did us an atom of harm in their lives. It is bald, brutal piracy.[86]

Carl Schurz also asked whether it was wise to become entangled in the contest for territorial aggrandizement that distracted other nations and drove them far beyond their original designs. "If this democracy, after all the intoxication of triumph in war, conscientiously remembers its professions and pledges, and soberly reflects on its duties to itself and others, and then deliberately resists the temptation to conquest, it will achieve the greatest triumph of the democratic idea that history knows." [87]

Schurz and other Americans were troubled by the contrasts they saw between earlier American expansion on contiguous territory and the global growth that followed the Spanish American War. They recognized dangers that overseas expansion presented to democracy at home. The American people, they believed, had already given proof of their strength, honesty, and wisdom, and would stand infinitely mightier before the world than any number of subjugated vassals could make them. The best interests of America, both moral and material, lay, they said, in a nationalism which recognized the right of all peoples, including those backward in civilization, to their own development. America,

---

[85] *Congressional Record,* XXXIII, part 1 (Jan. 9, 1900), 707.

[86] Boston *Evening Transcript,* Mar. 1, 1899, p. 16.

[87] Carl Schurz, *American Imperialism: The Convocation Address Delivered on the Occasion of the Twenty-seventh Convocation of the University of Chicago, January 4, 1899* (Chicago?, 1899?), p. 31.

they charged, had fallen in martial excitement to the false idol of national destiny.

THE NEW AMERICAN NATIONALISM
IN THE GLOBAL AGE

American nationalism after 1945 underwent a transformation as a result of such technological achievements as increasing industrialization, urbanization, and population growth, and the new role of the United States in world affairs. However, the change did not alter radically those basic characteritsics of the older form of nationalism—libertarianism, egalitarianism, idealism, materialism, and multiethnicism. Recent studies dealing with American values present arguments for the continuity of the fundamental ideals of the American society, all of which were reflected in the new nationalism.[88]

The libertarian formula was retained as zealously as ever. Democratic egalitarianism, which had been proclaimed in the American Revolution, remained the proud banner of Americans despite their emphasis upon competition, success, and status. More than ever Americans regarded their nation as representing the apotheosis of political democracy, liberty, and equality.[89]

American nationalism acquired several new characteristics: it functioned in a global milieu; the melting pot assumed a new form; there was a transition from provincialism to regionalism to nationalism; there was a retreat from autarchic isolationism; and nationalism took on a strongly anticommunist quality.

The global milieu. Americans did not consciously strive for world power, but it came and along with it was the problem of world responsibility. The nation which had but recently arrived at the level of leadership in international affairs suddenly found itself confronted with enormous and unaccustomed obligations. Americans were now faced with the necessity of holding to their own national interests while seeking to solve urgent political, economic, and moral problems throughout the world.

[88] See Daniel J. Boorstin, *The Genius of American Politics* (Chicago, 1953); Louis Hartz, *The Liberal Tradition in America* (New York, 1955); Ralph H. Gabriel, *The Course of American Democratic Thought* (New York, 1956); and Elting E. Morison, *The American Style* (New York, 1958).

[89] See Curti, *op. cit.*, pp. 48 ff.

American nationalism was a source of inspiration for the emergent new nations. The United States had been the first of the modern countries to break the bonds of European imperialism. The message of independence and freedom was attractive to the neophyte nations. Created out of old empires or colonies, they set about the business of forming a state in the American fashion, and emulated, at least on the surface, American libertarianism, idealism, and materialism. "Of all the major older nations, the United States should be the most sympathetic to new nations struggling to establish independence, to attain self-sufficiency, to create a national consciousness; of all the major older nations, the United States is the one best equipped to counsel and guide this process." [90]

The Founding Fathers were certain that Americans had been called by Providence to fight for the dignity and happiness of mankind. George Washington urged his people to "preserve the sacred fire of liberty" as well as "the republican model of government" for the world, and Tom Paine saw it "in our power to make the world happy." This optimistic prescription was renewed after World War II, when every global event became of prime importance to the American people—from the failure of the Hungarian rebellion to war in South Vietnam. Senator William Fulbright, a critic of American foreign affairs, saw the nation moving in the direction of a policy of manifest destiny in Asia in seeking to establish an "Asian Doctrine" comparable to the Monroe Doctrine in the Western Hemisphere.[91] But according to the Johnson administration, it was necessary to pursue not only a Great Society on the domestic scene but a great world society in which the United States would act as leader and prototype.

Thus, American missionary nationalism became a world-wide influence. It justified and encouraged the stirring of new life among the undeveloped nations. The taint of materialism was small: American nationalism stayed with the ideal of independence and freedom.

Changing melting-pot nationalism. The American melting pot functioned since the early days of the republic and remained a distinguishing factor in American nationalism. Each of the minorities in the crucible contributed in its own way to the formation and development of the nation, yet each managed to maintain its cultural distinctiveness.

[90] Henry Steele Commager, in his introduction to *American Civilization* (New York, 1961), p. 3.
[91] See *Time*, July 29, 1966, p. 17.

In the last decade there has been a change in the way the melting pot functions. Ethnic groups left the old neighborhoods and scattered through the cities. The old enclaves disappeared. In the age of affluence, minority groups took leave of the proletariat and assumed a place in the burgeoning middle class. The new generation turned away from the foreign-language press; minority cultures merged into the American culture. No matter what their former homeland—Ireland, Hungary, Italy, or elsewhere—Americans took pride in the American image.

Within this extraordinary leveling process, the American Negro experienced special problems. Making less economic and social progress than other minorities, the Negro, according to many of his leaders, had to fight for a place in the American power structure. The struggle degenerated into chaos: there was confusion between the identification of the Negroes as an ethnic and cultural group and the problem of political autonomy. One group of Negro activists demanded Black Power. Insisting that they had waited too long for an equality consistently denied them, they proclaimed their lack of interest in the common venture of building the American nation. They would turn to Negro nationalism rather than the American nationalism that cast them aside from the common experience of other minorities.

From provincialism to regionalism to nationalism. The new American nationalism witnessed the culmination of a process of nationhood. The United States had been founded by provincials from European soil. European provincials were products of conquest; American provincials were conquerors themselves who pushed the nation westward. For generations provincialism was expressed in such stereotypes as hayseeds, country hicks, bumpkins, Mencken's booboisie and Sinclair Lewis' Babbitt. Provincials remained suspicious of outsiders: they would have as little as possible to do with the power that emanated from Washington.

Provincialism retained its hold as regional diversity developed.[92] Each major area of the country endowed its own subculture with distinctive values, habits, and prides. The East, culturally and financially dominant, was internationally minded, still looking to Europe, and blending European values into its system. The South continued to respect Protestant morality, strong family relations, idealization of women, and

[92] See John Gillin, "National and Regional Cultural Values in the United States," *Social Forces,* XXXIV (Dec. 1955), 107–113.

white supremacy. The Midwest, heart of American society, emphasized democratic leveling, isolationism, and material values. The Southwest was motivated by the romantic values of Spain. The Northwest, influenced by the harshness of nature, stressed frugality, hard work, and down-to-earth values. The Far West, housing refugees from other areas of the United States rather than the Old World, was a land of change and novelty, high social mobility, and optimism expressed in hope for "progress unlimited." Stereotypes these were, but behind them was a modicum of fact.

Yet, these regional diversities were superimposed on national standards which made the United States the most culturally homogeneous nation of its size in history. Slowly, however reluctantly, all regions of the country were forced into the national stream. Provincialism changed into local diversity, regionalism into nationalism. Americans retained their subcultures but at the same time lost their old sense of separateness. In the global age the whole world became the province of Americans, and the old spirit of separateness remained only as a curiosity.

Retreat from isolationism. American isolationism can be traced to the beginning of the republic. The feeling of alienation from Europe was bolstered by the belief that the Old World was falling apart, leaving America as the hope of the future. George Washington's Farewell Address advised the nation to steer clear of permanent alliances with foreign nations and trust to "temporary alliances for extraordinary emergencies." Although this address nowhere contained the phrase "entangling alliances" (used by Jefferson in his First Inaugural Address), Washington's counsel was interpreted as a plea for isolation, which for the better part of the nineteenth century became a positive virtue.

There was also a conflict between expansionism on one hand and national autarchy on the other. In its early phases American expansionism, led by the trader, speculator, and missionary, aimed to acquire land through purchase, not conquest. Only toward the close of the nineteenth century, when the economic exploitation of the backwoods neared completion, did national expansion become widespread.[93] American hermitlike seclusion was ended as the nation entered the stream of

[93] Curti, *op. cit.*, p. 93.

imperialism.[94] The two world wars made isolation objectively impossible, even though some of its values persisted. The plea for isolation generally was based on American indignation in response to the wickedness and injustice of foreigners.[95]

Some American historians see isolationism as an expression of unhealthy nationalism. This point of view was expressed by Tremaine McDowell, who saw two main currents in American life: one moved historically from sectionalism to isolationism to imperialism; and the other moved from nationalism to cultural pluralism to One World.[96] McDowell found a community of interest between diseased nationalism and isolationism:

The events of American history indicate that nationality becomes dangerous when it is the tool of diseased nationalism, and that the latter becomes diseased when economic and political pressures become too powerful. Symptomatic of disease in American nationalism have been excessive concern with the acquisition of land, an inclination to make the state all-powerful, national egocentricity, in relation to our regions or to the world as a whole, and self-glorification either through romantic inflation of the past or braggart glorification of the present. In its final state unhealthy nationalism takes the form of isolationism. The best corrective to these abnormalities is the subordination of economic and political activities to cultural nationality.[97]

There was little isolationist sentiment in the new American nationalism. The majority of the American public did not regard involvement in Vietnam as expansionism, but rather as a necessary task to maintain order in a disorderly world. The feeling was that the United States,

[94] In 1897 the Bureau of Foreign Commerce stated: "The 'international isolation' of the United States so far as industry and commerce are concerned has, in fact, been made a thing of the past by the logic of the change in our economic requirements . . . now that we ourselves have become a competitor in the worldwide struggle for trade" (quoted in Schlesinger, *The Rise of Modern America, 1865–1951*, p. 171).

[95] Before World War II, the extreme isolationists in the United States, believing that national security was not involved, ridiculed the possibility of Hitler's designs on the United States and urged that entrance into the war be avoided. Among isolationist spokesmen were Charles A. Lindbergh, the former transatlantic aviator, senators Gerald P. Nye of North Dakota and Robert A. Taft of Ohio, the Hearst press, and the Chicago *Tribune*. Interventionists, on the other hand, saw the struggle as a world revolution of totalitarianism against the free way of life.

[96] Tremaine McDowell, *American Studies* (Minneapolis, 1948), pp. 82–96.

[97] *Ibid.*, p. 89.

much against its will, had been forced into the role of global policeman.

Anticommunist cast. Finally, American nationalism took on a strongly anticommunist tinge, just as Russian nationalism was stimulated by anti-Americanism. The United States created its own mixture of anticommunism and nationalism. American and Russian interests collided throughout the world. The rivalry was expressed in the subtleties of the cold war, in which each side adamantly maintained its own position but stopped short of actual war. The Khrushchev-Kennedy confrontation in 1962 nearly resulted in conflict. American U-2 flights had revealed evidence of forty intermediate-range Russian missile sites in Cuba that would be capable of hitting targets as far away as northern Georgia. When the United States decided to blockade all offensive Russian weapons destined for Cuba, both NATO and the OAS rallied to the defense of the American action. The crisis was eased when the Russians capitulated: Khurshchev ordered twelve of twenty-five ships, presumably carrying offensive arms, bound for Cuba, to reverse direction, and decided to dismantle Cuban missile bases, while Kennedy agreed to lift the blockade and not stage an invasion of Cuba.

Chapter 11

Messianic Nationalism: The Soviet Dilemma

[The] new Soviet nationalism is often a bewildering combination of traditional Great Russian nationalism, elements of Western universalist Marxism, and, most important of all, a system of rationalizations of the political order which has taken shape in the Soviet Union since 1917.

—FREDERICK C. BARGHOORN

Absolutism in eighteenth-century Russia recognized few if any elements of nationalism. The entire social order, from absolute monarch to ignorant peasant, knew little and cared less about nationality or nationalism. Catherine II (1729–1796) was a German princess who had married the crown prince, later Czar Peter III. Catherine, suspicious of anything concerned with the French Revolution, had no use for democratic principles. Her court, army, and bureaucrats turned out to be more German than Russian. Aristocrats took pride in their ability to speak French. The intelligentsia was inclined to substitute the Orthodox creed for nationality, while the masses had only the vaguest understanding of the meaning of nationhood.

All this was altered by the current of nationalism which flowed eastward from Paris in the late eighteenth century. Napoleon's aim was to acquire glory for himself, his family, and France, in that order; but instead he implanted the seeds of nationalism in the countries he conquered. Russia was no exception. Here, too, a sense of nationalism was solidified in an atmosphere of hatred. The Russians regarded Napoleon as an antichrist who had tried to lead the Roman Catholic West against Moscow, citadel of the true faith. They were motivated by two emotions: contempt for the French dictator and uncompromising love for the Mother Russia that he attacked.

Nationalism was expressed as early as 1802 by Nikolai Mikhailovich Karamzin (1766–1826), an historian, critic, and poet who built his reputation as a eulogist of Russian autocracy. An enthusiastic Francophile in his youth, Karamzin journeyed to western Europe during 1789–1790. What he observed in the West made him more devoted to his homeland. The concluding entry in his *Letters of a Russian Traveler* revealed the type of emotional patriotism later to be seen in the works of Dostoevsky: "Kronstadt Coast! Motherland! I bless you! I am in Russia and in a few days I shall be with you, my friends! I stop everyone I meet, I ask questions only to speak Russian and to hear Russian people. You know that it would be difficult to find a more miserable town than Kronstadt, yet to me it is a dear! The inn here might be called the 'inn of beggars,' yet I am happy in it." [1]

---

[1] Nikolai Mikhailovich Karamzin, *Letters of a Russian Traveler, 1789–1790,* trans. Florence Jonas (New York, 1940), p. 340.

When Karamzin pointed with pride to language, he was directing attention to one of the main props of modern nationalism. Language, he said, was important for the patriot. He urged his countrymen to disregard those who looked upon their own speech as coarse and disagreeable. "Our language is capable not only of lofty eloquence, sonorous, picturesque poetry, but also of tender simplicity, and sounds of feelings and sensibility." [2] Moreover, he was certain that Russia had her own special national traditions, different from revolutionary France. Russians, he said, were altogether too humble to realize the existence of their national values: "Let us grant that some nations surpass us altogether in enlightenment, having enjoyed more favorable conditions; but let us also not ignore all the blessings of fate when we consider the Russian nation. Let us assume our place by the side of other nations. Let us clearly pronounce our name, and repeat it with noble pride." [3]

Russian nationalism emerged in the early nineteenth century as a concomitant of romanticism.[4] From its beginnings it was compounded of two seemingly diverse elements: the desire of the Westerners—those Russian intellectuals who looked to the West for inspiration—to emulate all aspects of Western society including its breakdown into fractious national states; and a violent compensatory Slavic nationalism characterized by a belief in Russia's mission to rule the world.

The Westerners, impressed by the Enlightenment and the ideals of liberty, equality, and fraternity, hoped to turn Russian sentiment in the direction of Herder's cultural nationalism. Dissatisfied young nobles and officers, called Decembrists after the date of their ill-destined action in 1825, were influenced by Western ideas during the Napoleonic campaigns. They urged either a constitutional monarchy or a republic, and got neither. Wanted by the police, they were harried out of their hiding places and either shot down or exiled to Siberia.[5] The

[2] Nikolai Mikhailovich Karamzin, "On the Love of the Fatherland and on National Pride, 1802" (quoted in Karamzin's *Memoir on Ancient and Modern Russia*, ed. and trans. Richard Pipes [Cambridge, Mass., 1959], p. 58).

[3] *Ibid.*, p. 57.

[4] For an excellent treatment of the rise of early Russian nationalism, see Anatole G. Mazour, *Russia: Past and Present* (New York, 1955), pp. 30–36.

[5] On the Decembrists, see Mikhail Osipovich Zetlin, *The Decembrists*, trans. George Panin (New York, 1958); and Anatole G. Mazour, *The First Russian Revolution, 1825: The Decembrist Movement, Its Origins, Development, and Significance* (Berkeley, 1937). See also *Cambridge Modern History*, X (London, 1907), ch. xiii, 441 ff.

collapse of the Decembrist movement marked the triumph of Slavophilism.

Slavophilism gave early Russian nationalism its character. The term itself eventually became synonymous with Russian nationalism. In their Russianized version of Hegelianism, the Slavophils took from Hegel everything connected with "national predestination," or the mission of world leadership. In this respect Slavophilism resembled Germanophilism.[6] It feared revolutionary contagion from the West. The deeper this fear penetrated, the coarser and more offensive Slavophilic nationalism became. The West had failed, said the Slavophils, because its body had been devoured by the cancer of rationalism. Russia, to be sure, had been spared the disease.[7] The Slavs were young, virile, promising; the West was decadent and senile. Prince Odoevsky expressed it this way: "Western Europe is on the high road to ruin! We Russians on the contrary are young and fresh and have taken no part in the crimes of Europe. We have a great mission to fulfill. Our name is already inscribed on the tablets of victory: the victory of science, art, and faith await us on the ruins of tottering Europe."[8]

Under the influence of intensified Slavophilism, Russian nationalism assumed a blind, ugly form. During the long reactionary reign (1825–1855) of Nicholas I,[9] Slavophilic nationalism crystallized into messianic form. The glory of Russia became a new trinity: dynasty, Orthodox Church, and the village commune. Poets sang of the Russian as "the most perfect citizen on earth" and of Holy Russia as "the first state of the world." "Europe is pagan, Russia is holy Christian." Moscow would succeed Rome and Byzantium as the central city of a new world empire, a third Rome. Minorities, especially Ukrainians and Jews, were brutally persecuted under the policy of Russification.

The sense of messianic mission granted by Providence began to take hold and grow rapidly. Messianic nationalism was stimulated by Russia's many talented poets and novelists. The first Russian poet well known to the outside world was Alexander Sergeyvich Pushkin

---

[6] Mazour, *Russia: Past and Present*, p. 36.   [7] *Ibid.*

[8] Quoted in Mazour, *Russia: Past and Present*, p. 33.

[9] On Nicholas I, see Fanny Mayne, *The Life of Nicholas I* (London, 1855); Edward Henry Michelson, *The Life of Nicholas I* (London, 1854); Louis Thouneval, *Nicholas 1ᵉʳ et Napoleon III* (Paris, 1891); Sidney Monas, *The Third Section: Police and Society under Nicholas I* (Cambridge, Mass., 1961); and T. Schliemann, *Geschichte Russlands unter Kaiser Nicholas I* (Berlin, 1904–1908). See also *Cambridge Modern History*, X, 413 ff.

(1799–1837), one of whose great-grandfathers had served as a general under Peter the Great.[10] In his early career Pushkin was a romantic, influenced, like many Europeans of his time, by Byron. At first he felt sympathy for the rebellious Decembrists and their Western orientation, but later he denounced the West for its sympathy toward the Polish uprising of 1830.[11] Pushkin was regarded in the West as a great international poet ranking with Shakespeare, Racine, and Goethe, but inside Russia he was adopted by Slavophilic nationalists as their supreme spokesman—as a great poet who expressed the strength and spirit of Russian nationalism.

Other representatives of the golden age of Russian writers took up the cause of Russian messianic nationalism. In 1842, Nikolai Gogol (1809–1852),[12] at the end of his *Dead Souls*, compared Russia to a troika, a small sleigh drawn by three horses, rushing over the hard snows toward the goal of world leadership. "Whither are you speeding, Russia of mine? . . . Rent into a thousand shreds, the air roars past you, as you are overtaking the whole world, and shall one day force all nations, all empires, to stand aside, to give way to you!" [13]

Feodor Mikhailovich Dostoevsky (1821–1881) proposed a democratic Christian nationalism.[14] A famous conversation on Slavophilism takes place in Dostoevsky's novel *The Possessed* (1873) between the student Shatov, a former serf, and Nikolai Stavrogin, a brilliant aristocrat. " 'I believe in Russia,' said Shatov. 'I believe in her orthodoxy. . . . I believe in the body of Christ. . . . I believe that the new advent will take place in Russia.' "

On June 8, 1880, at a Moscow meeting of the Society of Lovers of Russian Literature, Dostoevsky delivered a passionate eulogy on Push-

[10] On Pushkin, see E. J. Simmons, *Pushkin* (New York, 1937); and Abraham Yarmolinsky, *Pushkin in English* (New York, 1937).

[11] See, for example, Pushkin's poem, "To the Slanderers of Russia," which Russian nationalists regarded as his supreme achievement.

[12] On Gogol, see David Magarshack, *Gogol: A Life* (London, 1957); and B. L. Brazol, *The Mighty Three: Pushkin, Gogol, Dostoevsky* (New York, 1934).

[13] Quoted in Hans Kohn, *Basic History of Modern Russia* (Princeton, 1957), p. 130.

[14] On Dostoevsky, see Brazol, *op. cit.;* David Magarshack, *Dostoevsky* (London, 1962); Ronald Kingsley, *The Undiscovered Dostoevsky* (London, 1962); G. Brandes, *Dostojewsky* (Berlin, 1899); Abraham Yarmolinsky, *Dostoevsky, A Life* (New York, 1934); E. J. Simmons, *Dostoevsky: The Making of a Novelist* (New York, 1940); J. Lavrin, *Dostoevsky* (New York, 1943); and J. A. T. Lloyd, *Fyodor Dostoevsky* (New York, 1947).

kin as a great national poet.[15] Pushkin, he said, possessed the peculiarly Russian gift of universal comprehension. And Russia, he added, was the only nation qualified to understand, to reconcile, and to inspire the rest of Europe. In the process of making herself most essentially Russian, Russia would become more completely European.

[Pushkin] was the first—precisely the first, and there was no one prior to him—to discern and give us the artistic types of Russian beauty directly emerging from the Russian spirit, beauty which resides in the people's truth, in our soil. . . . I merely say that among all nations the Russian soul, the genius of the Russian people is, perhaps, more apt to embrace the idea of the universal fellowship of man, of brotherly love—that sober point of view which forgives all that is hostile; which distinguishes and excuses that which is desperate; which removes contradictions.[16]

Slavophilic nationalism's most fervent apostle was Nikolai Danilevsky (1822–1885), an anti-Darwinist scientist and thinker.[17] In Danilevsky's view, Russia was different from Europe because God had willed it so. The Slavs formed a special species, he said, one family led by "Big Brother" Russia. Russia was not Europe and Europe was not Russia. The new culture from the West destroyed the very heart and soul of Russia, which had its own national mode of life, language, songs, attire, customs, and traditions. The main stream of world history had begun with two sources on the banks of the old Nile. One, the heavenly and godly, went over Jerusalem and the city of the czars and, in serene purity, reached Kiev and Moscow; the other, earthly and human, divided into two main streams—culture and politics, flowing over Athens, Alexandria, and Rome into Europe. "On Russian soil there arises a new spring: a socio-economic stream, which satisfies the masses of

[15] On the day before, Turgenev had delivered a speech in which he admitted that he was unable to decide the question whether or not Pushkin was the Russian national poet, in the sense that Shakespeare, Racine, and Goethe were the national poets of their respective countries. It was in response to this address that Dostoevsky delivered his impassioned address.

[16] F. M. Dostoevsky, *The Diary of a Writer,* trans. Boris Brasol (New York, 1949), II 960–961. These excerpts are from Dostoevsky's "Explanatory Word Concerning the Address on Pushkin," which he used as an introduction for the printed version of the speech.

[17] On Danilevsky, see K. Pfalzgraf, *Die politisierung und Radikalisierung Problems: Russland und Europa bei N. J. Danilevsky,* Forschungen zur osteuropäischen Geschichte, Vol. I (1954).

people in exactly the right way. On the wide stream of Slavicdom all these streams will join together to form a mighty stream." [18]

Few Russian intellectuals dared to attack Slavophilic nationalism and its cult. One of the rare critics was Vladimir Sergeyevich Solovyev (1853–1900), philosopher and poet, son of the historian Sergi Solovyev. In his book *Against Extreme Nationalism* (1889), Solovyev described three successive stages of Russian nationalism: first, the cult of the Russian people as the privileged bearers of universal truth; second, the veneration of this people as an elemental force irrespective of all truth; and third, the cult of its exclusive cultural and historical character—a negation of the very idea of universal truth. In its latest stages, Russian nationalism had lost intellectual content and had become insensitive to every rational objection. It was impossible, Solovyev said, to enter into direct discussions with the supporters of extreme Russian nationalism because to them the violent contradiction between their views and human reason or conscience was a matter of pride rather than something problematical.

Solovyev doubted that this extreme nationalism expressed the Russian mind. One could not solve the problem, he said, by questioning the Russian masses directly. But one could search Russian history and literature. Here Solovyev concluded that the greatest representatives of Russian literature showed themselves to be free of all national exclusivism. They were affected by all that was good among other peoples, and they condemned all that was bad among the Russians. The obscurantists, said Solovyev, took certain passages out of context which seemed to coincide with their views and thus claimed for their own defense the greatest Russian authors. They used reactionary romanticism to bolster their own concept of nationalism.

As to Pushkin, nobody can prevent our nationalists from closing their eyes to the Byronism of his youth and the great universality of his maturity. . . . Gogol's great Russian satire, the last judgment on Russia before Sevastopol [the Crimean War] is abandoned in favor of the superficial and abstract sermons of that author's *Correspondence*. The nationalists prefer certain general passages of Goncharov about nihilism to his Oblomov, an essential type of Russian impotence, masterfully represented and denounced. As regards the European liberal Turgenev, and Saltykov, the

---

[18] Nikolai Yabolevich Danilevsky, *Russland und Europa: Eine Untersuchung über die kulturellen und politischen Beziehungen der slawischen zur germanisch-romanischen Welt*, trans. Karl Notzel (Stuttgart, 1920), pp. 278–279, 326.

nationalists ignore them and declare their work devoid of all interest. They discover in Dostoevsky a firmer nihilist who never fully repented for his Western-inspired universal Christian ideas. . . . Finally, while bowing to Tolstoy's popularity, they simultaneously praise the artistic value of his novels and obscure the humanitarian principles which inspired them (they came partly from Rousseau) and which smothered all incipient nationalism.[19]

In denouncing Slavophilic nationalism Solovyev was moved by what he deemed the necessity for Russian universalism. An admirer of the Christian humanism of Erasmus and Thomas More, he believed that reconciliation of the Eastern and Western churches was extremely important for European civilization. He pointed to the influence of the West in the formation of Russian universalism. He denied that the only important truths in the life and work of the Russian people were those of exclusively national origin. But his was a lone voice speaking in a nationalist wilderness. Despite Solovyev's strictures, the messianic quality of Russian nationalism was retained. Russian nationalists opposed their values to those of others as the criterion of all ethical and social judgments. Solovyev may have regarded Russian nationalism as false and immoral, but to deny its existence was specious and historically inaccurate.

MARXISM-LENINISM AND BOURGEOIS NATIONALISM

One of the principles announced by the *Communist Manifesto* in 1848 was internationalism. The call was made in the cry: "Workingmen of the world, unite! You have nothing to lose but your chains." This ideology was closely bound up with the history of nationalism. From its beginning, Marxism was placed between two revolutions: the national—a democratic overthrow of feudalism, and the social—a Communist revolt against capitalism.[20] The interrelationship between the two marked the development of both nationalism and socialism for a century after 1848.

Marx and Engels, founders of modern socialism, believed that the national bourgeois-democratic revolution had to take place in order to

[19] Vladimir Solovyev, "Against Extreme Nationalism," quoted in Hans Kohn, ed., *The Mind of Modern Russia* (New Brunswick, N.J., 1955), p. 225.
[20] Cf. Demetrio Boersner, *The Bolsheviks and the National and Colonial Question, 1917–1928* (Geneva, 1957), p. 269.

enlarge the base of eventual socialist upheaval. Marx saw the government of the national state as nothing more than a committee for the administration of the consolidated affairs of the bourgeois class as a whole. Nationalism in his view was normal for the ruling bourgeoisie in Europe. He regarded national states as an indispensable step in the establishment of a harmonious cooperation of peoples, without which the rule of the proletariat was not possible. Though conscious of its force, he saw no reason to believe that in the end nationalism could prevent the proletarian socialist movement from taking its inevitable course. Nationalism, he said, might hamper the growth of class consciousness, perhaps delay it, but eventually it had to lead to the international unity of the proletariat.[21]

Convinced that national and democratic tasks must precede the socialist revolution, Marx and Engels had to struggle against their own comrades who turned their eyes westward and looked for an immediate revolution which would usher in world socialism. The result was a long series of ideological clashes from 1848 to 1928 between those who were certain that the socialist West would liberate the feudal East, and those who held that the national-revolutionary East would assist the liberation of the capitalist West.[22] Marx and Engels predicted the development in two stages: there would be national revolutions in central and eastern Europe which would presuppose and stimulate the development of socialism in the West; and the socialist revolution of the Western capitalists would then follow. In presenting this view Marx and Engels limited their consideration to Europe.

Unfortunately for Marxian ideologists, the course of history refused to follow the "scientific" pattern so carefully constructed by Marx and Engels. First, when the great revolutionary explosion came, it appeared not in highly industrialized Britain or Germany but in relatively backward, almost feudal, Russia. Second, revolution broke out not only on the continent itself, but in Europe's overseas colonies as well—in Asia, Africa, the Middle East, and Latin America. Early Marxian theories required revision. This was the task of Nikolai Lenin, who had to mold the ideology to fit a new set of circumstances but also had to maintain a semblance of Marxian orthodoxy.

Lenin, like Marx and Engels, looked upon nationalism as essentially a

[21] Cf. Richard Pipes, *The Formation of the Soviet Union: Communism and Nationalism, 1917–1923* (Cambridge, Mass., 1954), pp. 21–22.

[22] Boersner, *op. cit.*, p. 269.

phenomenon of the capitalist era, destined to disappear eventually with the end of capitalism itself. He saw bellicose bourgeois nationalism as fooling and disuniting the workers in order that the bourgeoisie might lead them by the halter. Those who wanted to serve the proletariat must unite the workers of all nations and fight bourgeois nationalism. According to Lenin, bourgeois nationalism and proletarian internationalism were irreconcilably hostile and expressed two different outlooks on the national question. Lenin said that by championing the slogan of national culture, building on it an entire plan and practical program of "cultural-autonomy," his opponents the Bundists were actually serving as the vehicle of bourgeois nationalism among the workers.

While thus excoriating nationalism as a bourgeois phenomenon, Lenin also used it for his own purposes. In the infighting which followed the Russian Revolution of November 1917, he waged an ideological battle against the "Westernizers" in the Marxian camp, who believed that a proletarian uprising was imminent throughout western Europe and that world socialism would be realized quickly as a result of the Bolshevik example. Such opponents as Rosa Luxemburg, Nikolai Bukharin, Karl Radek, and most of all Leon Trotsky, certain of the world-wide nature of the revolution, rejected any concern with national problems inside Russia. They believed that the imminent world revolution would make such problems superfluous.

Against this view of the Westerners, Lenin adopted the Eastern position: he would concentrate on the problem of nationalities inside Russia. The capitalist world, he said, had solved the problem because there each nationality had its own state. Eastern Europe, and especially Russia, had large, multinational empires which of necessity had to transform themselves into national states before international socialism could develop. It was important, Lenin believed, for the minor nationalities to lose their identities in the more advanced nationalities. As eastern Europe and Russia reached the economic status of the West, they could lose their multinational character. All national groups would then have equal opportunities. Once local national hostilities and rivalries were removed, the way to a supranational world system of socialist government would open. The local nationalities, in Lenin's view, must be exploited for the common socialist good.

At first Lenin spoke in terms encouraging to the nationalities in Russia. The Bolsheviks would respect the right of national self-determination. But, as on other occasions in history, theory clashed with practice. No sooner was the Revolution won by the Bolsheviks than Lenin was faced with annoying claims from the nationalities. In Byelorussia, the Ukraine, and elsewhere there were attempts to form independent national republics. Lenin quickly dropped his slogan of national self-determination and sent troops, mostly controlled by Bolsheviks, to smash any attempt to take him at his word. He had no more respect for the wishes of minority nationalities than he had for the popularly elected Russian Constituent Assembly. Nationalism was just, pure, refined, and civilized only when it was utilized in the service of the Bolshevik Party. The supranational Union of Soviet Socialist Republics was achieved not by the principle of national self-determination but by compulsion. Lenin suppressed all uprisings and plots and disseminated propaganda claiming that freedom and equality were endemic to the Bolshevik system. In fact, no nationality in the Soviet Union could dare to deny Marxism and its interpretation by Lenin as the supreme law, unless it wished to commit collective suicide.

Lenin's viewpoint prevailed and the Third International accepted his ideological victory. But he recognized complicating factors. There was just enough truth in the views of his opponents to make it necessary to play both ends against the middle. A shrewd tactician, he evolved an ingenious formula. From the beginning of the Revolution, communism had appealed to the new national movements in Asia, Africa, the Middle East, and Latin America for assistance in the common struggle against capitalism. Lenin, in turn, wanted their support. He began to teach that the national and the colonial problem were the same thing. Inside Russia the revolt of the subject nationalities must be utilized to serve the cause of the proletariat now in power. In the same way, the colonies outside Russia were the subject nationalities of the Western capitalist order; the colonies would join the rebellious workers to break down the citadel of capitalism. The subject nationalities inside Russia would be used for solidifying the Russian Bolshevik Revolution; the subject colonies of the Western capitalist world would be used to bring about the eventual world revolution.[23]

At the Second Congress of the Comintern in 1920, Lenin proposed a

---

[23] In Lenin's eyes this was merely an extension of the Marx-Engels position which supported only those national liberation movements which served the cause of socialism. Both Marx and Lenin contemptuously dismissed any uncontrollable emancipation movements which came at an inconvenient time and which tended to veer away from socialist control.

special handling of the colonial question. He presented two alternatives. First, if the West became socialist at once, it could guide the colonies toward socialism without requiring them to go through the intervening capitalist phase. Second, if the West failed to produce the required revolution in short order, then the colonial countries themselves, with Russian support, would achieve their bourgeois-democratic revolutions against the great capitalist powers. The body of Mother Russia would stretch like a bridge between East and West. Her companion, the Comintern, would stand between the two, between the workers of England, Germany, and France, and the peasants and soldiers of China, India, Indonesia, and Iran.[24]

The struggle between Western and Eastern tendencies survived Lenin and carried over into the Stalinist period. Lenin's contribution was an enormous one: he had proclaimed the Russians the truly socialist people and the guardians of Marxism, the true faith. In providing strong leadership during the shift from Czarism to Bolshevism, he had left unbroken the Russian tradition of autocracy. He called on Russians to spread the socialist gospel to all nations. It was his successor Stalin, however, who was responsible for the revival of messianic Russian nationalism in its most fanatical form.

JOSEPH STALIN AND THE PURGE
OF THE NATIONALITIES

The blending of communism and Russian nationalism was the life-work of Joseph Stalin, Lenin's successor. It was Stalin who connected Russian nationalism organically with the Communist program. Ironically, he was not a Great Russian but a Georgian. This was not unusual in the history of nationalism—the Corsican Napoleon adopted France as an object of his affections, and Hitler, the fanatical German nationalist, was born an Austrian.

Lenin, disturbed by talk among his colleagues about "the free development of every nationality," commissioned the young Stalin to write an article on "Marxism and the National Question." [25] In his much-publicized essay Stalin discussed the concept of the nation as well as the theory of cultural autonomy in the Russian socialist movement. He

[24] Boersner, *op. cit.*, p. 271.
[25] See the English translation of J. Stalin, *Marxism and the National Question* (New York, 1942).

denounced extraterritorial national-cultural autonomy because it led to a split of the Social Democratic Party along national lines. As proof he pointed to the Austrian experience, where the idea of national-cultural autonomy had led to a division of the Austrian Social Democrats into national components. This divisive tendency, warned Stalin, was dangerous for the entire socialist movement.

For the remainder of his career Stalin consistently denounced local nationalisms. He believed that the very idea of national self-determination was simply a "cloak for counterrevolution." It could always lead to civil war. But as he cautiously made his way to power, Stalin took a position between the two extreme views, emphasizing simultaneously the dangers of Great Russian nationalism and the necessity for strong centralization.[26] He would turn on the nationalities later, in his own good time.

Two of the major problems which Stalin faced in his political career were closely connected with the development of nationalism in the Soviet Union. The first was his quarrel with Leon Trotsky on the direction of the revolution. The second revolved around the issue of nationalities in the Soviet Union.

Lenin, Father of the Revolution, died on January 21, 1924. Stalin and two other Old Bolsheviks, Gregori Zinoviev and Lev Kamenev, took the reins, although Lenin in his testament called Stalin "too cruel and too brutal" to wield supreme power. Stalin had little difficulty in shunting Zinoviev and Kamenev aside, but the struggle with Leon Trotsky became a deadly one. Trotsky, without previous military experience, had recruited, trained, and commanded the Red Army through three years of civil war. A skillful orator, he thundered that communism could succeed in Russia if the rest of the world were Communist. An advocate of permanent revolution, he denounced Stalin for deserting "true Communist principles," favoring the peasants over factory workers, and failing to arouse the world to revolution.[27]

[26] Basic Communist assumptions worked to the advantage of Stalin's opposition to the nationalities. The unity, centralization, and omnipotence of the Communist Party, the hegemony of the industrial proletariat over the peasantry, the subordination of the national principle to the class principle—all these Communist doctrines were in fact responsible for the plight of the minorities (Pipes, *op. cit.*, p. 280).

[27] On the Stalin-Trotsky quarrel, see Bertram D. Wolfe, *Three Who Made a Revolution* (New York, 1948); Isaac Deutscher, *The Prophet Unarmed* (New York, 1959); and Leon Trotsky, *My Life* (New York, 1930).

In May 1925, Stalin made a crucial statement which gave direction to the concept of "Socialism in One Country." [28] "Is it possible," he asked, "to build socialism by our own efforts in our country, technically and economically backward, if capitalism persists in other countries and for a more or less considerable period?" He replied to his own question: "Leninism answers this question in the affirmative." In Stalin's view it would be possible to construct "a fully Socialist party" under the leadership of the working class and on the basis of an alliance between workers and peasants. But the final victory of socialism, its assurance against the attempts at intervention and the restoration of capitalism, presupposed the final victory of socialism on a world scale.

Stalin regretted that the Western proletariat had failed to see what was good for it and had been unsuccessful in its efforts to seize power. The Soviet Union would proceed alone, without any help from the West, to build socialism inside her own borders and on her own terms. On the other hand Trotsky, who saw revolutions as permanent and unable to stop their momentum at any given point, believed himself to be faithful to the tenets of classical Marxism. Stalin was the victor in the struggle: he expelled Trotsky from the Communist Party, banished him from Russia in 1929, and may have engineered his execution in Mexico in 1940.

Once rid of his most dangerous opponent, Stalin became the strong man of the new Soviet government. He regarded himself as the carrier of the Revolution and as indispensable in the task of solidifying socialism in one country. This task required effort, achievement, and suffering far surpassing in scale that of the original Bolshevik revolution of 1917–1921.[29] The goal was to bring all areas of the U.S.S.R. under the hegemony of Great Russia, an aim fraught with major difficulties.[30] The policy varied from indecision, to temporary concessions, to crushing military force. But there was never a doubt of Stalin's intention— he pursued his goal with the single-minded determination of a fanatic.

The great reversal came in the decade from 1929 to 1939. At the Sixteenth Party Congress (April 23–29, 1929), Stalin, not yet sure of

[28] Speech to the leaders of the Moscow party organization: "On the Results of the Work of the 14th Conference of the Russian Communist Party."

[29] Cf. Frederick C. Barghoorn, *Soviet Russian Nationalism* (New York, 1956), pp. 12–17.

[30] Cf. John S. Reshetar and Michael Luther, *Aspects of the Nationality Problem in the U.S.S.R.*, Harvard Project, Human Resource Research Institute Technical Research Report, No. 3 (Dec. 1952); and Pipes, *op. cit.*, pp. 241–282.

his ground, warned against Great Russian chauvinism, "the main danger on the national front." Then, a decade later, the Eighteenth Party Congress (March 1939) began to report great victories, not over "Great Russian chauvinism" but over various "nationalist deviations." This shift in emphasis was parallel to the growing conflict between the gradually developing national consciousness of the nationalities and the increasing centralization of the Soviet state.[31] It was not a mere contest between federalism and particularism, but rather a major shift in political emphasis, a deliberate policy designed to maintain the strength of the Communist Party and the position of Stalin as dictator. This was totalitarianism in action with no concessions to local nationalism of any kind.

In building a spirit of revolutionary fervor the Bolsheviks had denounced the old Czarist regime as hopelessly reactionary and backward. Now Stalin decreed an about-face. The Czarist regime and the old army were painted as "civilizing forces" in their policy of Russification. They had brought to the minority nationalities the benefits of association with the Great Russian people.[32] Nationalism was an acceptable notion for the centralized Bolshevik state, but certainly not for the nationalist minorities inside the Soviet Union. Soviet nationalism was good; local nationalism was an archaic notion that had to be swept away by triumphant Russian workers.

In Soviet semantics every assertion of national individuality was defined as evil "local nationalism." Whether linguistic, political, economic, or religious in nature, the right of self-determination was suppressed. To Stalin the very existence of non-Russian languages was dangerous. Such terms as "Soviet" or "dictatorship of the proletariat" or "people's democracy" might lose their significance if incorrectly translated. The government, therefore, insisted on introducing into each local language a large number of Russian and Russianized "international terms." The aim was to make all languages conform to the Slavic tongue.[33]

Politically, Stalin was determined to achieve centralization at any

[31] Zbigniew K. Brzezinski, *The Permanent Purge: Politics in Soviet Totalitarianism* (Cambridge, Mass., 1956), p. 77.

[32] Raymond A. Bauer, Alex Inkeles, and Clyde Kluckhohn, *How the Soviet System Works* (Cambridge, Mass., 1956), p. 199.

[33] Walter Kolarz, *Russia and Her Colonies* (New York, 1953), p. 18. A Stalin-supported decree, dated March 13, 1938, made the teaching of the Russian language obligatory in all schools of the national minorities.

cost. Because each local nationalism was too weak by itself to oppose centralized rule at Moscow, some sought to extend their power and prestige by closer relations with other non-Russian local states. To Stalin this was "treasonable counterrevolutionary activity." He accepted Pan-Slavism because it was regionalism devoted to Great Russian interests, but any other kind of "pan" movement was not to be tolerated.

Stalin was equally adamant in centralizing all economic activities in Moscow. He also moved to counter what he called the disintegrative tendency of religion. Because traditionally the Russian Orthodox Church identified religion with nationality, this proved to be a major task. Moreover, the struggle against "bourgeois cosmopolitanism" was accompanied by a revival of anti-Semitism. Stalin discouraged both Judaism and Islam as foreign ideologies in the Soviet body politic.

Between 1936 and 1938 came Stalin's purge of the nationalities, which surpassed in brutality the excesses of Russification in imperial Russia. Stalin wanted to destroy rival leadership at the provincial level. His elimination of nationality leaders went hand-in-hand with terror against possible rivals at his own level in both government and army.

The purge followed a set form. The timing was coordinated in Moscow for the entire Soviet Union. First came the preliminaries: criticism in the local press followed by denunciation of sabotage, wrecking, and cooperation with foreign agents. The dictator's propaganda attacked "nationalist deviators," "nationalist infiltrators," "bourgeois nationalists," "counterrevolutionary-Trotskyite-diversionist-espionage-terrorist-organizations," and "wrecking rightists," all key terms in Stalin's special purge vocabulary. The intelligentsia, professionals, and administrators in the nationalities were regarded as the most dangerous agents of bourgeois nationalism. Once the proper tone of hysteria was created, there followed expulsion of party members, imprisonment, and even execution. Thousands were dragged out of their homes at night and sent to unknown parts of the Soviet Union, there to languish or die as victims of Stalin's Russification program.

From Moscow, Stalin personally directed the purge. He sent Nikita Khrushchev to the Ukraine, where resistance had been strong since the civil war, with the special task of destroying the leaders of the Ukrainian Communist Party.[34] He dispatched other emissaries to Tashkent in

[34] Brzezinski, *op. cit.*, p. 78. National aspirations were promoted strongly by émigré Ukrainians, especially in the United States. On Ukrainian nationalism, see

Uzbekistan to remove "the nationalist-Trotskyite-Bukharinite-gang and all their supporters." [35] In Byelorussia, "wreckers, saboteurs, and nationalists," accused of plotting to sell the area to the Poles and of having instigated a nationalist conspiracy against the Soviet Union, were brought to trial and purged. In March 1938, V. F. Sharandovich admitted that he had been a Polish intellectual for eighteen years and that he had directed a "nationalist conspiracy against the Soviet Union." [36] Similarly, in Azerbaijan, Armenia, Georgia, the North Caucasus, and elsewhere, secret organizations, "separatist and nationalist in culture," were uncovered and purged in swift blows.[37]

By terror, Stalin crushed the century-old national movement among the minorities. There would be no local nationalisms, only the nationalism of the Soviet Union. Nor could there be any national parties formed among the nationalities: the Communist Party in Moscow was to be the only centralized political organization.

STALIN'S OPTION FOR NATIONALISM

Stalin's purge of the nationalities was a major phase of his drift to centralized nationalism. In the middle of the 1930's, at a time when his supreme power was unchallenged, he turned the Soviet state to the path of nationalism. In 1919 he had kept to the line that "proletarians have no motherland," that nationalism was obviously a bourgeois prejudice and a capitalistic anachronism. The Stalin of 1935 departed from his earlier views. Now he restored the army ranks of lieutenant-general and major-general which had been abolished in the November revolution. Suddenly, with encouragement from the dictator, books, magazines, plays, and movies began to glorify the personalities of Russian history, including Ivan the Terrible and Peter the Great.

To provide the Russian people with a national hero around whom they could build and maintain their sense of nationalism, Stalin inter-

---

John S. Reshetar, *The Ukrainian Revolution: A Study in Nationalism* (Princeton, 1952); and John A. Armstrong, *Ukrainian Nationalism, 1939–1945* (New York, 1955).

[35] See Brzezinski, *op. cit.*, pp. 79–80.   [36] *Ibid.*, pp. 181, 247.

[37] Although the purge of nationalities reached its peak during 1936–1938, it was continued after World War II. During 1946–1947 came a further cleansing of the Ukrainian and Byelorussian party cadres. In the fall of 1953 the Georgian, Azerbaijan, and other republican Communist parties were purged.

jected his presence into every part of Russian life.[38] His portraits, busts, and monuments appeared throughout the country. His picture was placed not only in every school house but in every room in every school building. Streets and cities (Stalino, Stalinsk) were named for him, as well as factories and farms. The tallest mountain in the Soviet Union was named for Stalin (Lenin Peak, nearby, was slightly lower in altitude). Newspapers praised "The Great Teacher of the Toiling Masses" and toasted "The Age of Stalin." Behind this saccharine adulation was Stalin's awareness that one of the most appealing elements of nationalism was veneration of heroes. He awkwardly nominated himself an object for national worship.[39]

Stalin's shift to nationalism necessitated the rewriting of history. Mikhail Nikolayevich Pokrovsky (1868–1932), a Marxist historian who had denounced nationalism and patriotism as bourgeois sentiments, was discredited and his disciples purged. Historians, Stalin said, must show a greater reverence for the Russian past. This attitude was equivalent to an order. On August 22, 1937, a government commission announced an award to Professor A. V. Shestakov of the second prize of 75,000 rubles for the most satisfactory textbook on the history of the U.S.S.R. (there was no first prize). Designed specifically for the third and fourth grades, this textbook, with Stalin's approval, was written to inculcate the young student with the spirit of nationalism. The following is from the Introduction:

[38] On Stalin as national hero, see Isaac Deutscher, *Stalin—A Political Biography* (New York, 1961); Eugene Lyons, *Stalin: Czar of All the Russias* (New York, 1940); and Walter Duranty, *Stalin and Company* (New York, 1949).

[39] Stalin's successor, Khrushchev, accused him not only of monstrous crimes but also of supporting a "cult of personality," exaggerated worship of his person. See Nikita S. Khrushchev, *Special Report to the 20th Congress of the Communist Party of the Soviet Union* (New York, 1956), a pamphlet annotated by Boris I. Nicolaevsky and published by *The New Leader* under the title *The Crimes of the Stalin Era*. A typical passage reads as follows (p. 17): "Stalin, on the other hand, used extreme methods and mass repressions at a time when the Revolution was already victorious, when the Soviet state was strengthened, when the exploiting classes were already liquidated and Socialist relations were rooted solidly in all phases of national economy, when our party was politically consolidated and had strengthened itself both numerically and ideologically. It is clear that here Stalin showed in a whole series of cases his intolerance, his brutality and his abuse of power. Instead of proving his political correctness and mobilizing the masses, he often chose the path of repression and physical annihilation, not only against actual enemies, but also against individuals who had not committed any crimes against the party and the Soviet Government. Here we see no wisdom but only a demonstration of the brutal force which had once so alarmed V. I. Lenin."

OUR COUNTRY

The U.S.S.R.—The Land of Socialism. There is only one Socialist country in the world. That country is our country.

Our country is the largest in the world. To the north, it is bounded by eternal ice; and in the south it is so hot in the summer that oranges and lemons ripen, and tea and cotton grow.

Our country is the richest in the world in natural resources. Everything needed for existence is found in our country.

Year after year, there is more of grain and other wealth in this country.

Year after year, the number of factories, schools, theaters and cinemas increases.

Its old cities are growing at an unusually rapid pace, and new cities are being built.

The working people of the U.S.S.R. are becoming more prosperous all the time, and their life is becoming better and happier.

In no other country in the world is there such friendship among the various peoples as in the U.S.S.R. In the 11 Constituent Republics of the Soviet Union there are 50 nationalities, making a total of 170,000,000 inhabitants. All are united in one fraternal union, which we call the Union of Soviet Socialist Republics, or U.S.S.R. for short. All the peoples of the U.S.S.R. work for the common good. In the U.S.S.R. there are no parasites, capitalists and landlords, as there are in other countries. In the U.S.S.R. there is no exploitation of man by man. All of us work for ourselves, and not for parasites.

In the past, our country was a backward country; now it has become the most advanced and mighty country in the world.

That is why we love our country so much; that is why we are so proud of our U.S.S.R.—the Land of Socialism.

The Road to Socialism was mapped out for us by the great Party of the Communists, the Bolsheviks. This Party led the struggle of our fathers and mothers, the struggle of the workers and peasants, when they overthrew the rule of the tsar, of the landlords and capitalists. Under the leadership of the Communist Party we created a workers' and peasants' government, and built Socialism.

What This Book Teaches. It tells you how people lived in the past; how the peoples of the U.S.S.R. fought their oppressors and enemies; how they succeeded in making our country the Land of Socialism. From this book you will also learn about the life and struggle of the people in other countries.

All this is called *history*.

We love our country and we know its wonderful history. Those who know history understand present-day life better, are better able to fight the enemies of our country, and make Socialism stronger.[40]

Stalin's national Bolshevism won its way to acceptance in World War II. When on June 22, 1941, Hitler's armies invaded the Soviet Union, Stalin urged the defense of Russia in what he now termed the Great Patriotic War. Curiously, the Nazi Fuehrer unwittingly helped Stalin in one of the key blunders of the war. So strong was Ukrainian nationalist sentiment that Hitler was welcomed at first as a liberator from Stalinist oppression.[41] The German leader made a crucial mistake: he was so carried away by his hatred for Russia and by joy in conquering the Ukrainian breadbasket that he immediately set up an iron Nazi rule.[42] Instead of taking advantage of Ukrainian separatism and using it in his war against Stalin, he treated the subjugated Ukrainians as conquered members of a lower order. For the bewildered Ukrainians there was little choice between two dictators. When it became obvious that the invading Germans intended to wage a war of enslavement and extermination against all Russians, including Ukrainians, the latter turned to their Russian heritage.

In the Nazi-Bolshevik struggle there was savage brutality on both sides. Russian nationalism was solidified in the harsh campaign against the Germans. Again and again Stalin proclaimed that the Great Russians were the driving force in the Soviet Union, not merely one of the 180 peoples of the U.S.S.R. in the war against the "fascist beast Hitler." Russian journalists habitually mixed straight reporting with nationalistic propaganda. The Russians were always heroes, the Germans villains. The most popular advocate of this highly tendentious reporting, de-

[40] A. V. Shestakov, *A Short History of the U.S.S.R.* (Moscow, 1938), pp. 7–8. The title page notes: "Indorsed by the All-Union Government Commission."

[41] The Ukraine was the most sensitive area in the U.S.S.R. from the viewpoint of the Russian nationality problem. Ukrainian nationalism had manifested itself early in the civil war in the effort to set up an independent republic. Stalin gave high priority to the area in his drive for Russification; he made it a point to purge local nationalist leadership. Ukrainian nationalism was inflamed by émigrés operating from Poland.

[42] In his harsh subjugation of the Ukrainians, Hitler was undoubtedly motivated by anxiety to implement the geopolitics of Karl Haushofer. According to Haushofer, industrialized Germany was potentially a great heartland (*Herzland*), which, bolstered by the agricultural breadbasket of the Ukraine, would be unconquerable in the future. Hitler had no intention of granting freedom to the Ukrainians once his armies penetrated the area.

signed to strengthen Russian patriotism, was Ilya Ehrenburg.[43] In October 1942, *Pravda* declared that the Great Russians formed the "vast majority" in the army, a remarkable claim in view of the fact that they constituted less than half the population of the U.S.S.R.[44] Efforts were made to include the sacred name of Lenin as an apostle of Russian nationalism. The army newspaper *Red Star* printed an article titled "Lenin and Stalin on Soviet Patriotism," which asserted that Lenin in exile on the island of Capri had reproached Maxim Gorki for having "forgotten Russia." [45]

Typical of the patriotic style of Russian war journalism was this passage from a report by journalist Konstantin Simonov on the battle for Moscow (October-November 1943):

Moscow! Millions of Soviet fighters, from the snow-covered peaks of the Caucasus to the leaden waves of the Barents Sea, dream of you today. They see you before them—proud and invincible, having thrown back from your ancient walls the alien, iron-clad hordes.

Moscow—to the Russian people you have ever been a symbol of their Native Land, the symbol of life. And henceforward you have also become for them the symbol of victory, a victory which does not come of itself, but which must be won, as you won it under your ancient walls.[46]

Symptomatic of Stalin's nationalism was a change in the national anthem. In December 1943 the "Internationale," the rallying song of Communism, was abandoned in Soviet Russia. Instead, there was a new fiery patriotic anthem, "Motherland," beginning with these lines:

> Unbreakable Union of freeborn Republics,
> Great Russia has welded forever to stand;
> Created in struggle by will of the peoples,
> United and mighty, our Soviet Land!
>
> Sing to our Motherland, glory undying,
> Bulwark of peoples in brotherhood strong!

[43] See, for example, Ehrenburg's report on the situation on the Mozaisk front near Moscow in *Soviet War News Weekly* (London), Jan. 29, 1942.

[44] *Soviet War News Weekly* (London), Oct. 16, 1942. Russian is the language of about half the people of the U.S.S.R. They are called Great Russians to distinguish them from two other major Slavic groups, the Byelorussians and the Ukrainians. All speak Slavonic tongues derived from an older Indo-European language.

[45] *Red Star*, July 1, 1943.

[46] Konstantin Simonov, *Moscow* (Moscow, 1943), p. 23.

Flag of the Soviets, peoples' flag flying,
Lead us from vict'ry to victory on! [47]

For Stalin the issue was simple: Soviet Russia was threatened with annihilation by a deadly enemy, and the only way to cope with him was to forge Russian national life as a mighty weapon of vengeance. This was no time to depend upon the good will of the international proletariat. The view was presented dutifully in 1944 by Nikolai Tikhonov, one of the most popular Soviet poets: "National pride, hitherto buried in the hearts of the Soviet people, burst forth in a bright flame before the threat of enslavement and in the face of deadly danger." [48]

On the eve of victory Stalin was still ordering greater emphasis on the leading role of the Great Russians in the war. Addressing Red Army commanders on May 24, 1945, he praised the Russian people "as the most outstanding in the U.S.S.R." He paid tribute to their "clear minds, steadfast character, and patience." [49]

SOVIET NATIONALISM AFTER 1945

Russian nationalism after World War II remained within the mold set by Stalin before the outbreak of the conflict. Several phases may be noted: Stalinist nationalism was retained inside Russia; the purge of nationality deviations in the republics was continued; there was a revival of messianic expansionism; and the international Communist community was split into fragments.

Retention of nationalism inside Stalin's Russia. Instead of retreating from the path he had inaugurated before the war, Stalin in the immediate postwar years continued his drive to construct an impregnable Soviet nationalism. He was concerned about Russian fraternization with Westerners during the war. In the common effort to destroy Hitlerism, Soviet troops, scientists, artists, and writers had drawn closer to their Allied counterparts in the West. These Russian citizens began to see that the anti-Western propaganda they had heard for years was exaggerated. Far from being pitiful slaves of harsh capitalism, the Westerners seemed quite human, and their standard of living was much higher than that of the Soviet Union.

[47] Quoted in Mazour, *Russia: Past and Present,* p. 643. For another version see Grayson Kirk, "Nationalism, Internationalism, and War," in Ralph Linton, ed., *The Science of Man in the World Crisis* (New York, 1945), p. 503.
[48] Quoted in Barghoorn, *op. cit.,* p. 239.   [49] See Kolarz, *op. cit.,* p. 19.

To counter any pro-Western trend in his monolithic state, Stalin began a campaign against "rootless cosmopolitanism" and "servile adulation of things foreign." Beginning in August 1946 a new ideological offensive penetrated every corner of Soviet life. Russians were told that they had little or nothing to learn from the West. They were a nation of workers and peasants who, having constructed the first successful socialist state in history, were the proper leaders of the world. At Stalin's instigation the Soviet government began to take credit for all the achievements of Imperial Russia. Explorers who had been either Russian aristocrats or foreign navigators in czarist service suddenly became national heroes. In September 1947 the eight hundredth anniversary of the founding of Moscow was celebrated in a great public demonstration sponsored by the government. During this ceremony Stalin pronounced Moscow both the initiator of a centralized Russian state and the center of world communism. In May 1950, celebrations were held throughout Russia to commemorate the one hundred fiftieth anniversary of the death of Field Marshal Alexander Suvorov, who had distinguished himself in the Seven Years' War.[50]

Stalin's campaign to raise the self-confidence of his people credited Russians with virtually every invention and discovery known to man. It was claimed that Russians had invented the steam engine, telegraph, telephone, radio, dynamite, the motion-picture camera, synthetic rubber, the automobile, the streetcar, the airplane, even baseball. Russian military leaders claimed credit for such advances in their profession as the first submarine and tank, and asserted that Russian explorers had discovered one-third of the world.[51]

These claims were greeted with derision in the rest of the world, but inside the Soviet Union they were taken with utmost seriousness. Performance in the Olympic Games became for the Russians a serious test of national prestige; seldom in the history of the games did any nation prepare its athletes as carefully as did the sensitive Russians. Young Russians were especially influenced by the romantic appeal of Soviet world leadership. All this signified intense love for the motherland, a sentiment strong in Great Russia and, less markedly, among a surprising number of non-Russians in the U.S.S.R.[52]

Continued purge of the nationalities. During the war Stalin took no chances on the allegiance of the nationalities. To counter their sus-

[50] Kolarz, *op. cit.*, pp. 166–167.   [51] *Ibid.*, pp. 169–170.
[52] Bauer, Inkeles, Kluckhohn, *op. cit.*, p. 226.

pected disloyalty, he dissolved the Volga German, Kaymyck, Chechen-Ingush, Crimea, and Kabardino-Balkarian republics.[53] After the war he continued to exterminate the more vigorous nationalists in these areas or deported them elsewhere. He was concerned above all with such major nationalities as the Ukrainians, Byelorussians, and Georgians, but he was just as careful in watching the high party commands of such small nationalities as the Azerbaijani, Moldavians, Karelo-Finns, Estonians, and Latvians.[54]

The most sensitive area was the Ukrainian Soviet Socialist Republic, whose population of approximately forty million was about a third as large as that of the Russian Soviet Socialist Republic. The eastern Ukraine had already been Russified, but the western part, which contained a quarter of the Ukrainian population, still presented problems for Stalin. As late as 1947 the Ukrainian Insurrectionary Army was fighting Soviet and Polish troops in the Carpathian Mountains of the western Ukraine. At the sixteenth Congress of the Ukrainian Communist Party in 1949, Nikita Khrushchev, who had been sent by Stalin to purge the party, denounced "bourgeois nationalist errors and distortions" and excoriated nationality deviation as "the most harmful and one of the most living residues of capitalism." [55]

Stalin paid equal attention to Byelorussia and its nationality sentiment. Byelorussians avoided use of their own language in the streets lest they be suspected of bourgeois nationalism.[56] Stalin insisted that the people of his own mountain region of Georgia use the Russian language.

During World War II, Stalin eased the official attitude toward religion on the ground that religon might be a factor in strengthening nationalism. But this did not include the Jews, whom both the Imperial and Soviet regimes traditionally defined as a major national minority. After the war Stalin continued a policy of repression and charged that Jews were more loyal to Zionism than to the Soviet regime.[57] In the

[53] The regime later announced that these minority nationals had been disloyal (*Pravda*, June 28, 1946).

[54] See Merle Fainsod, *How Russia Is Ruled* (Cambridge, Mass., 1953), p. 495.

[55] Bauer, Inkeles, Kluckhohn, *op. cit.*, p. 201.

[56] *Ibid.* See also Nicholas Vakar, *Byelorussia: The Making of a Nation* (Cambridge, Mass., 1956).

[57] In the 1920's the new Soviet government created a "Jewish Autonomous Region" in Birobidzhan in eastern Siberia. Jewish settlers were promised greater freedom if they would cultivate the area successfully. The experiment was not

middle and late 1930's he drastically reduced the role of Jews in top Soviet leadership, including Jewish Bolsheviks of the early Communist days. He denounced Jews as "homeless cosmopolitans" who understood nothing about Russian nationalism. He was about to purge a number of Jewish doctors for plotting to take his life when he died in 1953.

The problem of nationalities survived Stalin. Despite continuing efforts at Russification, the lines separating the Russians from the nationalities, particularly in language, became sharper. The process was recorded by Richard Pipes:

What is occurring may be described as a process of the emergence of modern nations within the Soviet Union. The smaller nationalities are slowly giving ground by dissolving either among the Russians or among the ethnic groups whose language and culture are most closely related to their own. The major nationalities, on the other hand, . . . are gaining in cohesion.

Language, of course, is only one of several criteria of national viability. . . . But it is a most important criterion. The transition from one language to another is, perhaps, the single most dramatic manifestation of a shift in national allegiance. The fact that it is not occurring among the major peripheral nationalities gives some ground for arguing that the burden of proof in discussing the fate of Soviet nationalities lies on those who foresee their imminent dissolution in a single Soviet nationality.[58]

Revival of messianic nationalism. Although Soviet propaganda continued to appeal to "proletarian internationalism," it revived messianic Great Russian nationalism. Russian imperial messianism, supported by Gogol, Pushkin, and Dostoevsky, believed that world society could be saved only by conforming to superior Russian ways. This sense of mission reappeared after World War II under Stalin's direction. It exalted the Russian system into a universal gift for mankind.[59] Communism would eventually take over the entire world. The paradise of socialism would be directed from Moscow, its invigorating center.

---

successful: neither the Russian regime nor the Jews found it satisfactory. The government later replaced Yiddish with Russian in the schools and flooded the area with other national groups. To the regime the Jews remained a nationality problem.

[58] Richard Pipes, "Soviet Colonialism: Does it Exist?" *Problems of Communism,* XIII (Jan.–Feb. 1964), 6. See also Barbara Ward, *Faith and Freedom* (London, 1954), p. 176.

[59] Barghoorn, *op. cit.,* p. 231.

Soviet nationalism, far from being a divisive factor in modern times, would be Russia's contribution to the world.

The theory was bolstered by Russian expansion both during and after the war. After the triumph at Stalingrad in early 1943, the Russians pushed the invading Germans westward and reached Poland, where the war had begun. Here the Russians created the first satellite state. Gradually they set up a belt of Communist countries from the Baltic to the Mediterranean. In the final year of the war, Stalin agreed with Roosevelt and Churchill at Yalta to conduct free democratic elections for postwar governments in the liberated countries of eastern Europe. As soon as the war ended, Stalin forgot his pledge. Eliminating the opposition one at a time, Soviet Russia took over Poland, Rumania, Hungary, East Germany, Bulgaria, and Czechoslovakia.[60]

Thus began the construction of a new Communist community of nations. The power of the Soviet Union at this time was so great that she well might have absorbed the new satellites into the Soviet federated structure. But there were many practical considerations working against this course of action. It would have antagonized the Allies, already angered by Stalin's violation of his pledges. It would have weakened the international Communist movement. It might have provoked the peoples of eastern Europe to revolt against their new Communist governments. National differences in the relatively large states of eastern Europe were too great to be ignored.[61]

The contiguous Baltic states, occupied by the Russians, presented a different situation. Lithuania (26,173 square miles), Latvia (24,695

[60] The Soviet technique in setting up satellite regimes included three steps: support of coalition governments with the key ministries of police and defense held by Communists; elimination of non-Communist officials; and seizure of power by local Communists as Soviet troops stood by. The new Soviet bloc in eastern Europe was then separated from the Western world in what Winston Churchill called an "iron curtain" extending from the Baltic to the Adriatic Sea.

[61] Paul Shoup, "Communism, Nationalism and the Growth of the Community of Nations after World War II," *American Political Science Review*, LVI (Oct. 1962), 889.

"Despite the international images in its ideology, Communism has not abolished any major nation-state. The only exceptions, the three small Baltic states of Estonia, Latvia, and Lithuania, were parts of the Russian Tsarist Empire before 1914. Generally, nation-states have proved remarkably durable even under Communism, and they have given rise, in time, to different varieties of Communist doctrine, as in the cases of Russia, Yugoslavia, and mainland China" (Karl W. Deutsch, *Nationalism and Social Communication* [rev. ed.; Cambridge, Mass., 1966], p. 3).

square miles), and Estonia (17,413 square miles) were set up as constituent republics of the U.S.S.R. on the ground that "they had always
been linked with Russia." There were also acquisitions in the Far East.
The Kurile Islands, held by Japan, were annexed as "genuine Russian
land," and Japanese southern Sakhalin was acquired as compensation
for its loss by czarist Russia in 1905.

From this point on, Russian foreign policy was dedicated to expansion. As Western colonialism receded in Africa, Asia, and the Middle
East, the Russians tried to fill the resulting vacuum with Communist
regimes. Moscow exploited every "national liberation movement" as a
blow against Western capitalism. By 1948 the cold war had begun—a
war of nerves, propaganda, and a possible prelude to actual war. While
Soviet Russia embarked assiduously on her own version of imperialistic
expansion, Russian schools were flooded with pamphlets denouncing
"United States Imperialism in the Philippines." [62]

From a psychological point of view, the new Soviet nationalism was
compensatory and projective in nature.[63] There are those who contend
that the national group is the totality of individuals comprising it, and
that the Adlerian concept of inferiority complex can therefore be
applied to nations. Soviet leadership, they say, compensated for a
feeling of inferiority by creating a self-image which exaggerated Russian virtues while depreciating those of other peoples in capitalist

[62] See Louis L. Snyder, *The Imperialism Reader: Documents and Readings on
Modern Expansionism* (Princeton, 1962), pp. 547–617.

[63] Here is an example of the necessity for a multidisciplinary approach to the
study of nationalism. Because nationalism is a group sentiment, it lends itself to
investigation not only by social psychologists but also by psychiatrists and
psychoanalysts. Any study of motivation behind Soviet messianic nationalism
needs the expert assistance of psychologists and neighboring disciplines. Historians
of nationalism, although aware of psychological implications, are untrained in
the study of group psychology and need help from other disciplines. Regrettably,
although the field is wide open, psychologists have devoted comparatively little
attention to national group behavior. See, for example, the review by Boyd C.
Shafer of Leonard Doob, *Patriotism and Nationalism: Their Psychological Foundations* (New Haven, 1964) in *Journal of Modern History*, XXXVII (June, 1965),
274. "The author," wrote Shafer, "does not go beyond what is generally known.
. . . For the most part [the book] elaborates upon the findings of other scholars,
historians as well as psychologists. . . . The general subject of the book still needs
much investigation. The researches of Otto Klineberg, Jean Piaget, Gordon
Allport, and others deserve to be carried further, and the political and scholarly
world would profit much." It should be added that hopefully Doob, a distinguished psychologist, will continue to apply the tools of his discipline to the study
of nationalism.

countries. The sentiment was easily exploited by a totalitarian government. In theory a dictatorship of the proletariat, the Russian regime was actually a dictatorship in the hands of the executive leadership of the Communist Party. The latter could turn to propaganda to elaborate Russian qualities and denigrate foreign peoples.

A distinction must be made here between the Russian government and the Russian people. The regime was faced with the critical dual problem of maintaining its existence against a hostile capitalist world as well as against domestic discontent. Hence it adopted an official policy of nationalism, chauvinism, and xenophobia. In the words of Frederick Barghoorn:

Chauvinism regarding Soviet achievements has been accompanied in Soviet thought by utopian-messianic pretensions with regard to the part of the world which has not yet experienced the blessings of "socialism." Moscow believes, or pretends to believe, that communism will inherit the earth. It holds out to mankind the vision of the harmonious society without coercion and inequality. But Soviet messianism justifies a plan for a Russian communist world organized and directed from Moscow.[64]

Official Russian xenophobia differed from that of other peoples. Throughout its existence the Soviet regime had to contend with cosmopolitan sentiments among the intelligentsia, which it unfailingly condemned as bourgeois cosmopolitanism. Equally as difficult for the government was the predisposition of ordinary Russians to show a curiosity and even a friendly regard for foreigners and their customs. Soviet youth regularly went through phases imitating foreign models —from the Italian *dolce vita* to American dancing to British music. To the shocked elders of the Russian world this was simply "hooliganism."

Fragmentation: Strains in the Communist bloc. Stalin thought it was essential to exploit Russian nationalism as a shield against dangers from the capitalist world. While continuing to denounce nationalism as an outmoded bourgeois concept, he replaced Marxian internationalism with a national conception of Soviet citizenship, in order to develop a centralized Soviet nationalism. We have seen that preliminary steps were Russification of the nationalities inside the Soviet Union and construction of a totalitarian system in eastern Europe under Moscow's control. The ultimate goal, still far away, was to destroy all differences among nations. But until then Stalin would make use of nationalism in

---

[64] Barghoorn, *op. cit.,* p. 232.

his own way—Soviet Russian nationalism would precede Communist supranational integration. Moscow was the fulcrum of world communism. Stalin was its high priest: from him emanated the authoritative interpretation of Communist gospel, and Communist parties the world over would conform to the line set by the master. Even if a new policy required taking an opposing viewpoint, the subsidiary Communist parties were expected to remain in the center of the speeding train of history and not lose their balance even on an abrupt turn.

The Communist bloc split into two parts: the belt of Communist nations in eastern Europe, and the Communist countries which broke away from Russian control, especially Yugoslavia and Communist China.[65]

Domesticism. National Communist parties existed in Poland, Rumania, Hungary, East Germany, Bulgaria, and Czechoslovakia before they were taken over as Soviet satellites.[66] Their party leaders, selected and trained in Moscow long before the war, were convinced of the necessity for unity among the Communist parties and were anxious to place their national states under the aegis of the new supranational Communist order. When they came to power, they unhesitatingly recognized not only the priority of Moscow but its role as final source of power. Each country would develop its own domestic nationalism by adapting Soviet conditions to its own needs. But centralized Communist power was never in doubt—it emanated from Moscow.

National communism among equals. The second development—the split of the Communist bloc into national fragments—became one of the most important trends of the postwar world. There was a strong and successful demand for the duplication of Communist institutions

---

[65] Paul Shoup noted three possible alternatives for the Communist bloc system in Eastern Europe: "(1) the nation in question might develop a form of Communist rule somewhat different from that in the Soviet Union but adapted to her own conditions; (2) the nation might adopt Soviet institutions and practices in their entirety but remain so independent of the Soviet Union that any form of integration would only make permanent the inferior status of the satellite nation and its party; and (3) the nation might pattern herself after the Soviet Union in the belief that the successful construction of a totalitarian state required (and would lead to) the duplication not only of Soviet institutions, but also of Soviet power" (Shoup, *op. cit.*, p. 892). As examples, Shoup pointed to Poland for the first alternative (where the national party was weak), and to Yugoslavia for the second (where the national Communist party was strong and dominant).

[66] The term "domesticism" was coined by Zbigniew K. Brzezinski, in his book *The Soviet Bloc: Unity and Conflict* (Cambridge, Mass., 1960), p. 52.

and Soviet power on a national scale. This view held that the only correct method of achieving a Communist world was to build communism in each country separately. Stalin's theory of a Communist orbit around the Soviet Russian motherland was challenged by the demand of other Communist states to pursue their own national versions of communism before the world was ready for true internationalism. Faced with increasing determination of Communist states to reassert old nationalisms, the Kremlin was gradually forced to shift its ground and concede that Moscow was not the only place where communism could be defined. Communist nationalism, as shown in Rumania and other satellites in recent years, is likely to remain a long-range force in the Communist camp. Thus far, the two main defectors have been Yugoslavia and Communist China.

TITOISM AND THE ISSUE OF EQUAL
NATIONAL COMMUNISM

In 1947 the Russians set up a new propaganda machine, the Communist Information Bureau (Cominform), to coordinate the activities of Communist parties throughout the world. At the same time it sought to impose the Stalinist view of nationalism on all the satellites. Its headquarters were in Belgrade, Yugoslavia. The Yugoslav regime was headed by Marshal Tito, alias Josip Broz, metalworker, leader of the Yugoslav partisans against the Germans in World War II, president of the National Committee of Liberation, and head of the Yugoslav regime. Tito was both a Communist and a Yugoslav nationalist, a combination which soon led to difficulties with Moscow.[67]

In other satellite countries the Communist Party leaders looked eagerly to Stalin for guidance. But the situation was quite different in Yugoslavia. The Slavic Serbs, indigenous inhabitants of the Yugoslavic state created after World War I, had always been fiercely independent mountaineers who resented any outside influence in their affairs.[68] The

[67] On the conflict between Stalinist nationalism and Titoism, see Royal Institute of International Affairs, *The Soviet-Yugoslav Dispute* (London, 1948); and R. Conquest, *Power and Policy in the U.S.S.R.* (New York, 1961).

[68] When, on June 28, 1914, the Archduke Francis-Ferdinand of Austria-Hungary came to Sarajevo to review troops, Serbian nationalists were angered because the date was the 525th anniversary of the Battle of Kossovo Field ("field of the blackbirds"), at which, in 1389, the Turks had broken the power of the great Serb empire. Serbian nationalists were known for their excitable sense of patriotism.

Yugoslav Communist partisans, led by Tito in World War II, had a sense of independence which made it difficult for Stalin to fit them into his private mold of national communism. Yugoslav "partisan chauvinism" regarded the Communist Party as the dominant political organization in the Balkans. It had no intention of taking orders from Stalin or anyone else. Tito and his followers decided from the very beginning that they would duplicate Soviet institutions in their own way.

Stalin's reaction was one of scarcely suppressed fury. He accused the Yugoslavs of moving too fast down the road to socialism. He denounced Tito in a formidable warning: "We think Trotsky's career is sufficiently instructive."

On April 12, 1948, Tito opened an historic session of the Yugoslav Central Committee. After a brief introduction and the reading of Stalin's letter, Tito read the draft of his reply, which included these remarks:

What exactly is the issue? It appears to us that we differ on how relations should stand between our two countries. There is no doubt we share the view that they should be the very best and friendliest relations; but how to clear them up—there lies the difference of opinion.

What are the elements we consider indispensable to the firmness of our relations and to indestructible friendship? First, absolute respect for the principle of national and State independence, as expounded by Lenin and Stalin in their works; second, absolute trust, without which relations cannot be lasting and firm. The Soviet people and above all their leaders must believe that the new Yugoslavia under her present leadership is moving irresistibly to socialism. . . .

The experiences of successful revolutionary development in every people's democracy should be considered a continuation and addition to the experiences of the great October Revolution, as something new in revolutionary practice, and wholly in the spirit of the science of Marxism and Leninism.

The role of the Soviet Union should consist in extending the full and comprehensive support of her authority to the new democracies, making special use in propaganda of the successes achieved in these new democracies in the realization of socialism.[69]

In the summer of 1948, Stalin displayed his impatience with this heresy by ordering the Cominform to denounce Tito and his regime in Yugoslavia for gross deviations from the international party line. Rus-

[69] Quoted in Vladimir Dedijer, *Tito Speaks* (London, 1953), pp. 346–347.

sian propaganda excoriated Tito for the benefit of Communist parties everywhere. A new term, "Titoism," was added to "Trotskyism" as a curse in the Russian lexicon of political vituperation. Tito was thus censured because Stalin was worried that leaders in other satellites might follow his example and threaten Russian control of the Communist bloc.[70] Stalin called on the entire Communist world to isolate the Yugoslav heretic. Tito was not impressed.

Politically, the issue had little to do with communism, for Tito at the time was among the most active Communists of eastern Europe. The two countries fell apart on the straight issue of irate nationalism, as indicated in this passage by Barbara Ward:

> With that division—which, had it not been for Russia's fear of Western military action, would doubtless have led to a Russian occupation of Yugoslavia as swift if not as painless as the Communist seizure of Czecho-slovakia—the pretense that Russia had any new principle to offer in international relations was finally exploded. The new communism was the old imperialism writ large. Nationalism merely appeared with more total pretensions by reason of its vestigial link with the idea of a world crusade.[71]

Tito and the Yugoslavs were opposed to Moscow's attempt to direct the Yugoslav economy. In Yugoslavia socialization of industry and collectivization of agriculture were more advanced than in any eastern European satellite. But Yugoslavia needed manufactured goods from the West, and inside the country the peasants insisted upon independent ownership of small plots of land.[72] To meet these demands, Tito preferred to run his country's affairs in his own way without interference from abroad, even from Moscow.

Culturally, the split was sharpened by Yugoslavia's partly Western orientation. Psychologically, the independent and confident Yugoslavs had no taste for a position as "little Slav brother" to the Russian "big Slav."

This combination of factors led Tito to defy openly Stalin's politi-

[70] For example, the Gomulka Communists in Poland and the Kostov Communists in Bulgaria revealed similar nationalist ideas that motivated Tito. Stalin feared that Communists in the satellite countries, encouraged by Tito, might divide into national and international wings, suggesting the earlier division of western European socialists into revisionist and orthodox Marxists.

[71] Ward, *op. cit.*, p. 177.

[72] William G. Carleton, "Is Communism Going National?" *Virginia Quarterly Review*, XXV (Summer 1949), 328.

cal, military, and ideological pressures. The idea of a Yugoslav David hurling stones at the Russian Goliath seemed laughable at the time, but Tito's nationalism showed surprising strength. Despite denunciations from Moscow, he was firm and persisted in his course. The result was a deathblow for Russian Soviet monolithic supranationalism. It never recovered from the Yugoslav heresy.[73] Rumania, Albania, and other countries formerly in the Russian sphere of influence caught the fever, until the satellite system began to break down. This astonishing change was wrought by nationalism.

THE SPLIT WITH COMMUNIST CHINA

After overrunning the mainland, the Chinese Communists established the People's Republic of China on October 1, 1949. At first the Chinese obediently followed the Soviet pattern because they needed money, equipment, and technicians. It was soon evident, however, that the Chinese were becoming impatient with control from Moscow. Stalin, remembering his difficulties with Tito in 1948, decided that force would not work in handling the problem of national communism.[74] The differences developed into a quarrel along nationalistic lines.

At the Twentieth Party Congress, held in Moscow in 1956, Russia and China began to drift apart. Khrushchev not only denounced Stalin in an emotional outburst, but also urged peaceful coexistence with the capitalist nations. The Chinese Communists were angry on both counts. They admired Stalin's aggressive policies, and they opposed peaceful coexistence. Russian leadership could not do otherwise, be-

[73] After Stalin's death in 1953, Khrushchev tried to bring Yugoslavia back into the Russian orbit. In August 1963 he visited Yugoslavia to greet Tito and to praise Yugoslav socialism. But he feared a spread of heresy. In 1953, Soviet tanks smashed a spontaneous revolt in East Germany. In 1956, when Hungarian students rose against their Communist masters, and together with other rebels, turned on the police, Khrushchev sent Russian troops and tanks to crush the rebellion before it could set off a chain reaction in the Soviet empire. The victory was at best a Pyrrhic one: the subtle process of national communism continued.

Tito's national communism and the increasing nationalization of the old satellites in eastern Europe encouraged the West in its efforts to wean them further away from Soviet Russia. A West German magazine, *Der Volkswirt*, spoke of a "national renaissance" in eastern Europe and urged increasing contacts from the West to promote national communism against what it called "integral communism." (*The New York Times,* May 9, 1965, p. 12.)

[74] Zbigniew K. Brzezinski, "Deviation Control," *American Political Science Review,* LVI (Mar. 1962), 5–22.

cause revolution by the working class could not be expected to take place in highly industrialized and prosperous capitalist nations. Although the Russians would not admit it, history was not following the pattern of *Das Kapital* and the *Communist Manifesto,* and Marxism was becoming less and less relevant to socioeconomic realities in the modern world. Russian leaders began to inquire and to think in terms of necessary adjustments.

Mao Tse-tung and the Chinese Communists identified the Russian stand as clearly revisionism, and no word could have a more contemptuous ring. Peking would remain true to the gospel of Marx and Lenin. She would follow the letter and spirit of Leninist belligerence; she would remain distrustful of capitalism; she would continue the holy war.

The ideological clash was only one element of this internecine quarrel. The issue of national communism, as in the case of Yugoslavia, was decisive. The Chinese, refusing to remain subservient to Moscow, decided to take their own path. In Communist theory, historical national boundaries should have been only incidental factors in plans for a future world society, but instead they came to represent critical dividing lines between separate concentrations of power.[75] There were many points of conflict, including Russian-Chinese rivalry in influencing the new nations of Asia and Africa, and differences in policy toward India, Korea, and Vietnam.

The differences developed into a contest between the two giants. Of the world's 105 Communist parties in 1965, Moscow won control of 72, compared to only 21 for Peking. Twelve others, mainly in western Europe, remained vaguely independent.[76] Tension reached a serious point as early as October 1961 at the Twenty-second Congress of the Russian Communist Party. Khrushchev denounced tiny Albania but offered her economic assistance. Subsequent meetings between leaders of the two Communist nations ended in quarrels and mutual abuse. Russian leaders were infuriated by the fact that the growing Sino-Soviet split made possible a new assertion of nationalism by the smaller Communist parties in Europe and elsewhere. Clearly, the proposed

[75] Shoup, *op. cit.,* p. 894.

[76] *Time,* international ed., Aug. 6, 1965, p. 28. In such countries as France and Italy, where Communist Party strength was large, the national parties exercised a veto power over decisions from Moscow.

supranational union of the Communist bloc had been shattered by virulent nationalism.

SOCIALIST SUPRANATIONALISM VERSUS COMMUNIST NATIONALISM

Historically, every great movement of modern times—the Commercial Revolution, the Protestant Reformation, the Catholic Counter Reformation, the French Revolution, the Napoleonic Era, the Industrial Revolutions—contributed to the intensification of nationalism. Such collectivist movements as socialism and communism proved to be no exception. Nationalism originally appeared in the modern state, with its middle-class orientation. Now Socialist and Communist movements began to provide education, work, jobs, promotions, insurance, and increased social services for the mass of citizens.[77] Anything which appeared to help the collectivist state also seemed to enrich the mass of its citizens. As the masses looked more and more to their national governments for their livelihood, they became more and more nationalistic. This heightened nationalism occurred among the masses despite the dialectic arguments of Marxian prophets who predicted exactly the opposite course.

Friedrich A. Hayek, in his book *The Road to Serfdom*, described the paradox:

One of the inherent contradictions of the collectivist philosophy is that, while basing itself on the humanistic morals which individualism has developed, it is practicable only within a relatively small group. That socialism so long as it remains theoretical is internationalist, while as soon as it is put into practice, whether in Russia or in Germany, it becomes violently nationalist, is one of the reasons why "liberal socialism" as most people in the Western world imagine it is purely theoretical, while the practice of socialism is everywhere totalitarian. Collectivism has no room for the wide humanitarianism of liberalism but only for the narrow particularism of the totalitarian.[78]

[77] Carleton, *op. cit.*, p. 330.
[78] Friedrich A. Hayek, *The Road to Serfdom* (Chicago, 1944), p. 141. "That communism withered to the same concept of social organization is characteristic of its common roots in social aberration. Both nationalism and communism . . . found their characteristic form in barracks society" (Robert Strausz-Hupé, *The Estrangement of Western Man* [London, 1953], p. 217).

In his testimony before the Committee on Foreign Relations of the United States Senate on February 20, 1967, Henry Steele Commager spoke of the metamorphosis of communism. When Senator Claiborne Pell asked whether communism itself contains the seed of its own destruction, Commager replied:

Self-destruction? I would say metamorphosis, sir, rather than self-destruction. But it is fascinating to see that the elements of nationalism are stronger than communist ideology. There is a Polish communism, a Hungarian communism, a Yugoslav communism, an Albanian communism, and I am quite sure that there will be as many different communisms throughout the globe as there are Western nationalities with their separate cultures and philosophies and separate animosities. And there is another form of change which we have seen very markedly in some of the European communist countries; namely, that as they achieve their goals they do not so much destroy communism as transform it into a quasi-socialistic communism, far less belligerent and far less ideologically motivated than at the beginning.

This was true of the French Revolution as well and it is clearly happening in Russia and the satellite countries.[79]

Thus, while Soviet ideology and vocabulary remain Marxist-Leninist and internationalist, the reality is a triumph of nationalism. Both Russians and satellites value the nationalism which ties them to their predecessors.

The Communist revolutions that took place in Europe and Asia turned out to be more nation-conscious than class-conscious. Organized and consolidated along national lines, they were not so much international as they were national. In both bourgeois and Communist states the individual merged his personality into that of the group. This was true of the Western democratic states as well as both Communist Russia and Communist China: the individual felt that the violent instincts he had to curb within the in-group could be given a wider range when absorbed in collective action toward the outsider. Thus, an element of early middle-class nationalism was carried over into the collective state, with similar motivations. Reinhold Niebuhr recognized the phenomenon: "There is an increasing tendency among modern men to imagine themselves ethical because they have delegated their vices to larger and

[79] "Changing American Attitudes toward Foreign Policy," *Hearing before the Committee on Foreign Relations,* United States Senate, 90th Congress, 1st Session (Washington, D.C., 1967), p. 36.

larger groups." [80] Neither the bourgeois state nor the collective community was free from this dominant nationalistic urge.

Soviet communism became a strange mixture of Marxian remnants, state socialism with leanings toward free enterprise, and above all, nationalism. In the ensuing struggle of these three trends for ascendancy, nationalism proved more durable than collectivism or internationalism. Russian leaders, of course, deny it. On July 19, 1965, Soviet Premier Aleksei N. Kosygin stated: "For our society, nationalistic survivals in any form, whether they be nationalism, great-power chauvinism, racism, or anti-Semitism, are naturally alien and contradictory to our outlook." [81] This claim may be interpreted in several ways: It may be a tactical device to redefine nationalism ("Communist nationalism is a blessing; bourgeois nationalism is a curse"); it may be sheer perversity; or it may be a special kind of obtuseness.

That national sentiment remained strong in contemporary Russia was indicated by the tendency to glorify traditional Russia. The popular young poet Eugeny Vinokurov recently paid tribute to "Holy Russia" in these lines:

> There is a ferment in Russia,
> Like a bread-bin filled with yeast.
> I want, O Holy Russia, that in me
> Your very soul should ring and cry. [82]

---

[80] Quoted in Edward H. Carr, *The Twenty Years' Crisis* (London, 1941), p. 203.
[81] Paris edition of the New York *Herald-Tribune*, July 20, 1965.
[82] Eugeny Vinokurov, in *Literaturnaya Rossiya*, May 1, 1964.

Chapter 12

Nationalism and Supranationalism

*Only when man succeeds in developing his
reason and love further than he has done so
far, only when he can build a world based
on human solidarity and justice, only
when he can feel rooted in the experience
of universal brotherliness, will he have
found a new, human form of rootedness,
will he have transformed his world into a
truly human home.*

—ERICH FROMM

Advocates of a world order regard nationalism as an artificial sentiment, obviously an inappropriate basis for a world society, and mostly evil in its effects. They say that the deep-rooted prejudices of nineteenth-century nationalism can be transcended only by a supranationalistic global government and society. They admit that nationalism was a political response to the needs of the nineteenth century. But the twentieth-century world, they say, has become much smaller as a consequence of advances in communication and transportation, and it is now necessary to adapt political theory to these new conditions. In this context, they reason, the old nationalism, with its localized economics, has become outmoded and unnecessary. "If a society becomes a nation when it thinks it is one, a supranational consciousness can arise in the same way, particularly when promoted by the trend of economic and technological change and the menace of tyrannical aggression." [1]

To supporters of the One World idea, supranationalism is the only way to end the centuries-old blight of war. They recommend that the methods by which citizens of any one country have lived in peace among themselves should be applied to international relations. Nationalism should be extended to its next logical step—a United States of the World. Just as the people of one nation accept the fact that their problems can be solved only by common laws, traditions, and institutions, so should the peoples of the world act together for their common good.

How can this supranational society be attained? First, say its advocates, by promoting a voluntary pool of nationalities in regional form. Then world regional organization would be established in which each part owed its ultimate loyalty to the world society. Where the Italian liberal nationalist Giuseppe Mazzini had projected the idea of a sisterhood of nations within the framework of the old nationalism, those supporting the One World idea favor a combination of regions within a world context. The many evils of nationalism would be dissolved by supranationalism. As political friction is removed, as industrial, technological, and scientific revolutions bring greater prosperity to peoples

[1] John Boule, *The Nationalist Idea* (London, 1955), p. 64.

everywhere, as the social order becomes more urban and cosmopolitan, as cultural barriers are broken down, and as people become psychologically prepared for a new form of global organization, a workable and peaceful world order becomes possible. Just as western Europe's medieval society turned into an organization of states in the early modern period, so would the present system of national states be succeeded by a new type of world organization. If representatives of more than a dozen nations could work together in harmony in Antarctica, why could there not be a working supranationalism elsewhere?

Advocates of a world federation say that it would eliminate international anarchy and provide a rational basis for international relations. They would adapt the ideas of the American Founding Fathers to current world problems. A distinction is made between two kinds of sovereignty: a legitimate form that takes jurisdiction over a nation's institutions and culture; and an illegitimate form—by which one people may endanger another—that takes the way of unilateral action in the world community. World federalism, say its proponents, would distinguish between these two forms. It would enact clear laws defining the nation's sovereignty, the limits of its freedom of movement, and its place in global society. It would prevent nations from arbitrarily pursuing their own interests. The old disputes and conflicts would disappear as men outgrew their political adolescence.

On paper the idea seems logical and unassailable. But history is distinguished by a wide gap between theory and practice. Supranationalism has tended to remain stubbornly within the realm of ideas and ideals. Nationalism, intense and persistent, remains the reality. This is more than merely an interesting phenomenon in world history: it is of crucial importance in the tenor and development of contemporary society.

NATIONALISM WRIT LARGE: THE "PAN" MOVEMENTS

Carlton J. H. Hayes regarded cultural nationalism, with its limited objectives, as a blessing, and has suggested that integral nationalism, because of its aggressive tendencies, could be a curse.[2] Nationalism in its aggressive form was a mania, a kind of exaggerated egoism. It reflected "an intolerant attitude and behavior towards one's fellows: a

[2] See Carlton J. H. Hayes, *Essays on Nationalism* (New York, 1926), pp. 245–250.

belief in the imperial mission of one's own nationality at the expense of others, particularly at the expense of backward people; a habit of carrying a chip on one's national shoulder and defying another nationality to knock if off; . . . a spirit of exclusiveness and narrowness which feeds on gross ignorance of others and on inordinate pride in one's self and one's nationality." [3]

The effort of aggressive nationalism to expand into supranational form may be seen in the formation of the "pan" movements.[4] They may be defined as political or cultural trends that promote the solidarity of peoples bound to each other by common or kindred language, race, or traditions, or some other tie such as geographical proximity.[5] They may be either spontaneous or planned. They may arise in smaller states seeking to increase their prestige by linking themselves with larger and more powerful states. In most cases, however, they appear when aggressive national states take the initiative in seeking to extend their power over contiguous or noncontiguous countries of similar background. The national state which considers itself superior in power and culture will seek to dominate closely related political and cultural entities.

The protoype of modern "pan" movements was the Roman Empire, which combined the political, economic, and cultural life of all western Europe in a Latin nationality. In this broader sense, too, the British Empire in the nineteenth century and Soviet Russia in the twentieth were both "pan" movements aiming to incorporate peoples of varied culture in either an empire, a commonwealth, or an economic bloc. In the narrow sense, however, modern "pan" movements represented an extension of nationalism beyond national frontiers.

The "pan" movements were vague and ill-defined. Each was distinguished by a different set of characteristics and each was a combination of several factors related to nationalism. The one common characteristic was that "pan" movements arose most often among peoples who spoke the same or similar tongues. To this common linguistic quality was added usually one other dominating element, for example: messianic zeal (Pan-Slavism); territorial expansionism (Pan-Germanism); religion (Pan-Islamism); race (Pan-Africanism); anticolonialism

[3] *Ibid.*, p. 250.
[4] For the best brief treatment, see Hans Kohn, "Pan-Movements," in *Encyclopedia of the Social Sciences*, XI (New York, 1935), 544–553.
[5] *Ibid.*, p. 544.

(Pan-Asianism); culture (Pan-Celtism); or geography (Pan-American-ism).

As a matter of convenience the "pan" movements may be divided into three groups: national "pan" movements, religious "pan" movements, and continental "pan" movements.

National "pan" movements. Originating in the nineteenth century, this category was simply an extension of nationalism. It covered a variety of states, some seeking national unification and expansion (Pan-Germanism), some calling for "racial" emancipation (Pan-Slavism, Pan-Turanianism), and some devoted merely to cultural kinship (Pan-Hispanism and its relatives, Pan-Lusitanism and Pan-Iberianism). The linguistic factor was strong in some cases (Pan-Germanism), somewhat weaker in other (Pan-Slavism). In all these movements, political motivations were active and influential, though at times combined with cultural patterns.

Pan-Germanism was essentially a movement for the expansion of Prusso-German power by the union of all German-speaking people in one political body.[6] It aimed to include not only the German-speaking population of Germany itself, but also the German-speaking people of the Hapsburg monarchy, Switzerland (the Zürich area), France (Alsace), the Low Countries (Dutch and Flemish were regarded as Germanic dialects), and later even all German-Americans in North and South America. Pan-German ideas were inspired by apostles of nationalism who pointed to the civilizing mission and colonizing efforts of the medieval German empire in eastern Europe and who proclaimed the desirability of German world leadership. Among them were Ernst Moritz Arndt, poet of the War of Liberation; Friedrich List, founder of the *Zollverein;* Heinrich von Treitschke, zealous nationalist historian; Richard Wagner, glorifier of the German Spirit; and Houston Stewart Chamberlain, theoretician of Nordic supremacy.[7]

Pan-Germanism was given a strong impetus by the Franco-Prussian War of 1870–1871. After the Prussian victory and the unification of Germany, two nationalist movements, Einiges Deutschland (Unified

---

[6] On Pan-Germanism, see Mildred Wertheimer, *The Pan-German League, 1890–1914* (New York, 1924); R. Usher, *Pan-Germanism* (Boston, 1913); and Alfred Kruck, *Geschichte des Alldeutschen Verbandes, 1890–1939* (Wiesbaden, 1954).

[7] On these and other apostles of German nationalism, see Louis L. Snyder, *German Nationalism: The Tragedy of a People* (Harrisburg, Pa., 1952), *passim.*

Germany) and Grossdeutschland (Greater Germany), were formed.
In 1891 these two organizations were combined in one society called
the Alldeutscher Verband (Pan-German League) under the leadership
of Professor Ernst Hasse of Leipsig, a fanatical imperialist. A product
of the nationalist temper of the day, the Pan-German League had three
main aims: strengthening of national consciousness, support of Germans abroad, and promotion of German power in Europe and overseas.
It worked closely with other nationalistic societies, such as the East
Mark Association and the Navy League.[8]

During the Wilhelminian era, the Pan-Germans supported William
II in his policies of colonial expansion and a big navy. Their sense of
national egoism and desire for expansionism influenced Germans who
were not members of the League itself but who were concerned about
the fate of their "racial brethren" in Austria-Hungary and elsewhere.
Pan-German propaganda had a growing influence not only upon public
opinion in Germany but also upon the government itself.[9] In World
War I, Pan-Germanism was a consideration in the alliance with Turkey
aimed at the extension of Mittel-europa (Germany, Austria-Hungary,
Turkey, and Bulgaria) to include Constantinople. There was also a
Pan-German motivation in the occupation of Belgium and the attempt
to disassociate Flemish Belgium from the remainder of the country and
to bring it under German influence. There were Pan-German overtones in the policy *vis-à-vis* Poland, which allowed it autonomy, but
only under German supervision.

The Pan-German movement declined temporarily in 1918 after the
defeat of Germany. Along with it went the dissolution of the Austro-
Hungarian Empire and the whole scheme of Mittel-europa, as well as
the *Drang nach Osten,* German expansion eastward. With Germany
deprived of border territories and colonies, Pan-Germans began to
revive the worst features of their movement. The German National
Party was led by Alfred Hugenberg, a dedicated Pan-German. Hitler
adopted Pan-Germanism as a basic political principle for his Third
Reich. However, his success in absorbing one European country after
another led him to abandon the Pan-German idea and substitute for it a

---

[8] On German nationalistic societies, see Louis L. Snyder, *From Bismarck to
Hitler: The Background of German Nationalism* (Williamsport, Pa., 1935), pp.
110–136.
[9] Hans Kohn, *Nationalism: Its Meaning and History* (rev. ed.; Princeton, 1965),
pp. 70–71.

goal of Napoleonic grandeur—control of all Europe. His annexation of Austria and parts of Czechoslovakia in 1938 and his designs on Danzig and Poland in 1939 helped to precipitate World War II.

Similarly, Pan-Slavism was intended to promote the political and cultural unity of all Slavs, even against their will, into a greater Russia which would dominate the world.[10] Pan-Slavism should be distinguished from Slavophilism, an early nineteenth-century movement which arose in Russia as a reaction against wholesale adoption of Western ideas and reforms.[11] The idea of Slav affinity was first broached in the seventeenth century by Jurij Križanić, a Catholic priest. In the early nineteenth century, Slav intellectuals, influenced by the rise of romanticism and nationalism, particularly in the work of Johann Gottfried von Herder, began to speak of a Slavic national consciousness and a unified Slav cult to replace the "declining Latin-German culture."

On June 1, 1848, the first Pan-Slav Congress was held at Prague. Under the presidency of František Palacký (1798–1876), the congress, anti-Russian in tone, called for a union of the Western Slavs (Czechs, Moravians, Silesians, and Slovaks), Eastern Slavs (Poles and Ukrainians), and Southern Slavs (Croatians, Slovenes, Serbians, and Dalmatians). The defeat of Russia in the Crimean War (1853–1856) led to the transformation of vague Slavophilism into a militant and nationalistic Russian Pan-Slavism. The initiative for Pan-Slavism now came from Russia rather than from the minor Slav states. The Slav minorities in the Austro-Hungarian Empire became known as the Little Slavs, while Russia became the "Big Slav Brother." The Little Slavs were critical of Russian influence, but this attitude changed after the Hungarian *Ausgleich* (compromise) of 1867. (The *Ausgleich* referred to the Dual Monarchy, the name given to the Austro-Hungarian Empire.) The Czech demand for a trialism was brusquely rejected. Angered, the Czechs began to support Russian Pan-Slavism. When in 1867, the

[10] On Pan-Slavism, see Hans Kohn, *Pan-Slavism: Its History and Ideology* (Notre Dame, Ind., 1953); Michael B. Petrovich, *The Emergence of Russian Pan-Slavism, 1856–1870* (New York, 1956); Paul Rankor Rado, *Who Are the Slavs?* (Boston, 1919); Albert Mousset, *Le monde Slave* (Paris, 1946); Rudolf Vrba, *Russland unter der Panslawismus* (2 vols.; Prague, 1913); and A. Fischel, *Der Panslawismus bis zum Weltkrieg* (Stuttgart, 1919).

[11] See Chapter 11.

Second Pan-Slav Congress met in Moscow, the minor Slavs supported Russian leadership of the Slav world.

The chief apostle of Russian Pan-Slavism was Nikolai Danilevsky (1822–1885), whose book *Russia and Europe: An Inquiry into the Cultural and Political Relations of the Slav World and the Germano-Latin World* (1869) urged Russians to liberate and unite all the Slavs.[12] Danilevsky feared European hostility toward Russia and the Slav world. The inevitable struggle, he said, would result in full political liberation of all the Slav peoples and formation of a Pan-Slav union under the hegemony of Russia. The Slav type, he said, was superior and would be the first to embody four cultural activities—religious, political, esthetic-scientific, and socioeconomic. Western Europe, said Danilevksy, had degenerated into religious anarchy, characterized by the political despotism of Catholicism and the foolish Protestant idea of basing religious truth on personal authority; on the other hand, the majority of the Slav people became the chief guardians of religious truth in Orthodoxy. Politically, the Slavs were among the most gifted families of the human race; unlike the English, Russia did not send out colonists to build new political societies, but instead expanded gradually and irresistibly on all sides, assimilating foreign populations. In the socioeconomic sphere, Danilevsky said, Russia was the only large state with the unshakable stability provided by peasant ownership of land. The Slavs would combine to eradicate imitativeness and servility to the West. But first Russia would have to face the task of liberating her racial brothers by instilling in them the spirit of independence and Pan-Slav consciousness.[13]

The pressure of Pan-Slavism helped provoke the Russo-Turkish War of 1877–1878. Additional Pan-Slav congresses were held at Prague (1908), St. Petersburg (1909), and Sofia (1910). Pan-Slavism played a role in the events leading up to the outbreak of World War I, especially in the Balkans where the Slavic Serbs opposed Austrian domination. The Soviet government renounced Pan-Slavism in 1917, but gradually revived Pan-Slav slogans as a means of facilitating Communist control of eastern European countries. A new Pan-Slav Congress met in Belgrade on December 8, 1946. At that time Tito seemed to be a firm supporter of Stalinist communism and Pan-Slavism, but eighteen

[12] See Chapter 11.
[13] See Hans Kohn, *The Mind of Modern Russia* (New Brunswick, N.J., 1955), pp. 195–210.

months later, in June 1948, came the open break between Soviet Russia and Yugoslavia. Less and less was heard of Pan-Slavism as the movement was absorbed in the rising Pan-Russianism.

Religious "pan" movements. The second category stressed not political unity but religious attitudes. Less tangible than national "pan" movements, religious "pan" movements tried to combine the peoples of one religious faith in a supranational state. The lines of combination were generally vague and more theoretical than actual. The most striking feature was the zeal, sometimes the fanaticism, of the believer who was convinced of the superiority and his own religion and its mission to expand throughout the world. Among such movements were Pan-Islamism, Pan-Christianity, and Pan-Anglicanism.

Pan-Islamism, once the most active of the religious "pan" movements, called for a union of all Muslim countries on the bases of common religion (Islam), a common religious book (the Koran), and a common language (Arabic).[14] Because in Islam all believers were considered equal, there could be no inequality in the sight of God. All Muslims would unite in a religious community under God's law.

Rapid advances in transportation and communication in the nineteenth century brought Muslims more closely together. Those in the Middle East and North Africa began to regard the subjugation of their brethren in Europe as a personal degradation. The feeling of unity was so strong that it broke through the traditional enmity of the Sunnite and Shiite sects. A new emphasis was placed on the cult of classical Arabic, the sacred tongue of all Muslims. The major apostle of the new Pan-Islamism was Sayyid Jamal ud-din al Afghani (1838–1896), who hated the British and was the the first to preach Muslim resistance in Europe.

The Ottoman Empire, the most powerful Muslim state, exploited the Pan-Islamic spirit, although it was incompatible with the Pan-Turanianism (union of all Turks) preached by the Young Turks. Turkish Muslims made contact with Muslims in other countries, encouraged the *hadj* (pilgrimage to Mecca) and presented the sultan as the caliph for all believers. Pan-Islamism supported a *jihad* (holy war) against the Allies during 1914–1918.

When religious and national "pan" movements conflicted, the latter invariably won. The ambition of individual Muslim rulers was far

[14] On Pan-Islamism, see Lothrop Stoddard, *The New World of Islam* (New York, 1921).

stronger than the internationalism of religion. After World War I, Pan-Islamism was succeeded by Pan-Arabism. Though Pan-Arabism retained a religious connotation, it was essentially a political movement.[15]

Pan-Arabism is the general term for unification of the Arab-speaking peoples.[16] Arabia proper is only a small part of the Arab world. There are Arabic-speaking countries in North Africa to the west of Egypt (Libya, Tunisia, Algeria, and Morocco). In the Middle East there are many peoples not of Arab origin who over the course of the centuries have become thoroughly Arabian, speaking Arabic and regarding themselves as Arabs. Yet, these peoples are torn by jealousies among themselves and resist efforts to impose an Arab supranationalism on their own strong sense of nationalism.

Since the thirteenth century, when the Ottoman Turks rose to power, Arabs sought reunification and a return to their former pre-eminent position. The growing aversion to Turkish domination, culminating in the twentieth century, was stimulated by the increasing tempo of European nationalism. Another factor was the attempt made by the Turks to appropriate leadership of the Pan-Islamic movement, an effort which led to the strengthening of Pan-Arab sentiment.

The ineffectiveness of Pan-Islamism was revealed in World War I. In 1914 the Turkish caliph called for a holy war against the Allies. The move failed. The Allies, especially Britain, encouraged Arab nationalism under Ibn Ali Husain (*c.* 1854–1930), a descendant of Muhammad. Ruler of Mecca and a powerful religious leader, Husain had great influence in the Arab world, a position passed on later to his sons, Abdullah, Amir of Transjordan, and Faisal.

Pan-Arabism was excited by the Balfour Declaration of 1917. The idea of Palestine as a national homeland for the Jews was totally unacceptable to Arab leaders. From this time on, hostility to Zionism became the hallmark of Pan-Arabism. After World War II the Arab League was formed with the admitted goal of crushing the new state of Israel.[17]

[15] See Chapter 8.

[16] On Pan-Arabism, see Eugene Jung, *La revolte Arabe* (2 vols.; Paris, 1924–1925); George Antonius, *The Arab Awakening: The Story of the Arab National Movement* (Philadelphia, 1939); F. A. Sayegh, *Arab Unity: Hope and Fulfillment* (New York, 1958); and Morroe Berger, *The Arab World Today* (London, 1962).

[17] The main instrument of Pan-Arabism became a political party called the Baath (Renaissance), whose platform included *Wahadi Arabiya* (oneness) and

In the conflict between religious Pan-Islamism under Turkish auspices and supranational Pan-Arabism, the latter turned out to be the hardier movement. Despite its political orientation Pan-Arabism retained a strong religious quality. It defended Islam zealously; it rejected Turkish domination fanatically.

Continental "pan" movements. The third type of "pan" movement was geographically oriented and predominantly continental in scope.[18] This category tried to overcome national particularism and to arrive instead at a supranational order based on common continental territory. But here again there is a confused and imperfect picture because of varying degrees among movements of linguistic, racial, and cultural similarities. Pan-Americanism stressed language and culture.[19] Pan-Asianism interpreted continental unity as anticolonialism and a continued struggle against imperialism.[20] Pan-Africanism, lacking the bond of linguistic unity, based its appeal on common racial stocks.[21] Its aim was to unify all the countries of Africa in a black supranationalism and to eliminate colonialism and white supremacy on the continent. It was stimulated by European colonization of Africa in the late nineteenth century. An added factor in its development was the education of future African leaders in the United States and Europe in the early twentieth century.[22]

---

socialism. It was active in most Arab states, including Egypt, Jordan, Saudi Arabia, Lebanon, Syria, and Yemen.

[18] See Karl Haushofer, *Geopolitik der Pan-Ideen* (Berlin, 1931).

[19] See Chapter 9. On Pan-Americanism, see also Joseph B. Lockey, *Pan-Americanism: Its Beginnings* (New York, 1920); Laurence Duggan, *The Americas: The Search for Hemisphere Security* (New York, 1949); John T. Humphrey, *The Inter-American System: A Canadian View* (Toronto, 1942); W. S. Robertson, *Hispanic-American Relations with the United States* (New York, 1923); Richard F. W. Berendt, *Inter-American Economic Relations: Problems and Prospects* (New York, 1948); Paul R. Olsen and C. Addison Hickman, *Pan-American Economics* (New York, 1943); Arthur P. Whitaker, *The Western Hemisphere Idea: Its Rise and Decline* (Ithaca, N.Y., 1954); Thomas F. McGann, *Argentina, the United States, and the Inter-American System, 1880–1904* (Cambridge, Mass., 1957); Helio Lobo, *O Pan-Americanismo e o Brasil* (São Paolo, 1939); and Jesús M. Yepes, *Philosophie du Panaméricanisme et organisation de la paix* (Neuchâtel, Switzerland, 1945).

[20] On Pan-Asianism, see Shao-ch'i Liu, *Internationalism and Nationalism* (4th ed.; Peiping, 1954).

[21] A degree of repetition is necessary here to show the place of Pan-Africanism among the general "pan" movements. See Chapter 6. On Pan-Africanism, see also R. L. Buell, *The Native Problem in Africa* (New York, 1928), and Colin Legum, *Pan-Africanism* (London, 1962).

[22] See Marcus Garvey, *Philosophical Opinions* (2 vols.; New York, 1923–1926).

The early Pan-African movement did not propose immediate independence of the African states or black supremacy, but instead favored gradual self-government and interracialism. The Pan-African Congress, which convened at Manchester, England, in 1945, included such future African leaders as Kwame Nkrumah (Gold Coast) and Jomo Kenyatta (Kenya). Nkrumah later founded the West African National Secretariat to promote a United States of Africa, and became the self-appointed leader of Pan-Africanism. The First Congress of Independent African States convened in Accra, Ghana, in 1958.[23] In the early 1960's the Pan-African movement split into three groups: the Union of African states and Madagascar (Brazzaville states)—a loose economic association of twelve former French colonies;[24] the Casablanca group (Morocco, Ghana, Guinea, Mali, United Arab Republic, and Libya);[25] and the Pan-African Movement of East, Central, and South Africa (PAFMECSA), founded by political leaders in Nyasaland, Kenya, Uganda, Tanganyika, Zanzibar, Rhodesia, Mozambique, Rwanda, and Burundi.

Throughout its existence the Pan-African movement was burdened by differences in leadership, political orientation, and national aims. There was little agreement among its supporters on its scope and meaning. National differences conflicted with regional goals; regional interests collided with the supranational aims of the wider Pan-African movement.

In this respect Pan-Africanism was typical of all the "pan" movements. Most were lacking in clarity, and were abused by self-seeking manipulators. A basis for supranational unity could be found in theory, for it was always easy to invoke common ideals and sympathies. But in practice there was too much dissension among peoples who were supposed to provide the common base. Slavs often felt greater hostility among themselves (Poles versus Russians, Ukrainians versus Poles, Serbs versus Bulgarians) than against others.[26] Attempts at linguistic union ran into difficulties: Pan-Celtists were unsuccessful in their attempts to unite Gaelic, Welsh, and Breton dialects; the Irish preferred to speak English. Despite common interests, Pan-Americanism re-

[23] Liberia and Ghana were the only African states represented at the First Congress of Independent African States. The others (Egypt, Tunisia, Libya, Morocco, and the Sudan) were Arab and Muslim.

[24] See Chapter 6.   [25] *Ibid.*

[26] Kohn, *Nationalism: Its Meaning and History*, p. 71.

mained weak and ineffective. Its analogue, *Hispanidad*, accenting the international mission of a nonexistent Spanish race, made little or no progress.[27]

Nationalism proved to be the stronger sentiment. Grandiloquent speeches, manifestations of harmony, the gaudy show of unity at international congresses—all these practices of the supranational "pan" movements were compensatory gestures. There was little indication that the force of nationalism was weakened by the "pan" movements.

SUPRANATIONAL PARLIAMENTS: THE LEAGUE OF
NATIONS AND THE UNITED NATIONS

Equally unsuccessful in overcoming the strength of nationalism were two supranational parliaments—the League of Nations and the United Nations. In both cases members refused to sacrifice even a small part of national sovereignty to world government. It is a melancholy story.

Nationalism, in the form of political rivalry and aggression, was one of the causes of World War I.[28] Appalled by that bloodbath, men of good will tried to avoid another global cataclysm by setting up the League of Nations.[29] Behind the League was a long history of projects for international organization to maintain the peace.[30] Woodrow Wilson predicted that another world conflict would break out within twenty years if some international authority were not devised to prevent it.[31]

[27] See José P. lá Cárcales, *La misión internacional de la raza hispánica* (Madrid, 1928). See also Chapter 9.

[28] In addition to nationalism, the basic causes of World War I may be summarized as economic conflict, international anarchy, militarism, and psychological acceptance of war as a solution for national rivalries.

[29] On the League of Nations, see Viscount Cecil, *The Great Experiment* (London, 1941); H. E. Davis, ed., *Pioneers of World Order* (New York, 1944): T. Marburg, *Development of the League of Nations Idea* (New York, 1932); D. Hunter Miller, *The Drafting of the Covenant* (New York, 1928); Felix Morley, *The Society of Nations* (Washington, D.C., 1932); Alfred E. Zimmern, *The League of Nations and the Rule of Law* (2nd rev. ed., 2 vols.; London, 1939); F. P. Walters, *History of the League of Nations* (London, 1952); T. P. Conwell, *The League Council in Action* (London, 1929); and M. E. Burton, *The Assembly of the League of Nations* (New York, 1945).

[30] See Chapter 12.

[31] This prophecy may be compared with that of a German delegate to the Versailles Peace Conference, who, after the signing of the peace pact, said to a French observer: "We shall see you again in twenty years!"

A combination of related factors was responsible for the failure of the League of Nations. While it was able to solve such minor quarrels as the dispute between Finland and Sweden over the Aaland Islands, and the differences between Greece and Italy over Corfu, the League revealed itself to be woefully weak when major crises arose in Manchuria (1931), in Spain (1936), and in Czechoslovakia (1938). Two articles of the League's Covenant turned out to be handicaps: Article X, which guaranteed territorial sovereignty, froze the system of Versailles and gave the League the reputation of being a club of victors; and Article XVI, which provided for economic but not military sanctions against aggressors. Added to these hindrances was the failure of the United States to join the League.

By far the most damaging handicap of the League was the unwillingness of its members to sacrifice even a small part of their sovereign interests for the sake of international cooperation. The great powers preferred to reserve important matters for their own decision. Winston Churchill said in 1946: "The League of Nations did not fail because of its principles and conceptions. It failed because these principles were deserted by those states which had brought it into being. It failed because the governments of those states feared to face the facts and act while time remained. This disaster must not be repeated." [32]

The principal success of the League lay in providing the first workable design for a permanent international organization, a pattern on which the United Nations was later modeled. The hope for a supranational organization was inherited by the founders of United Nations.

The statesmen who were invited by President Roosevelt to meet at San Francisco in 1945, before the end of World War II, wanted to avoid the danger of postwar reaction. The charter of the United Nations made commitments against war and called upon the nations of the world to build a dynamic international society that would advance human rights and fundamental freedoms, as well as economic and social justice. The statesmen wrote a document sufficiently flexible to enable the organization to adjust itself to unanticipated postwar problems. Those problems came: the revolt of the colonial peoples, the threat of nuclear warfare, the political tensions related to exploration of outer space, and the global demand for economic equality.[33] Hans Kohn has

[32] Quoted by U Thant in "New Ideas for a New World," *Saturday Review*, July 24, 1965, p. 24.
[33] Clark M. Eichelberger, "Alternative to Anarchy," *Saturday Review*, July 24, 1965, p. 35.

written: "The United Nations represents the realization of the entirely new situation which has emerged from World War II, where nationalism has become world-wide but where the deadly destructiveness of total weapons and, thanks to the new means of communication, the neighborly independence of all peoples on this shrinking earth demand a new and less bellicose attitude." [34]

In its existence the United Nations has shown greater vitality and staying power than the League of Nations. It has some impressive assets: it is more universal than the League of Nations; [35] it has kept alive the dream of world order; it has acted as an occasional peacemaker in small disputes; it has provided a decompression chamber for larger quarrels; it has given representatives of new nations an important education in the ways of international cooperation; and its specialized agencies, such as the World Health Organization (WHO), have performed valuable work.

When the United Nations was founded in 1945, it represented an older world of big-power politics. The United States, western Europe, and Latin America comprised 65 per cent of the original membership. There were only four African states. During the postwar years, however, the character of the membership underwent a transformation. With the decline of colonialism, new states sprouted up rapidly. By 1966 there were 36 African states in a total of 114 members. The new Afro-Asian group held 55 per cent of the membership. In theory a two-thirds majority in the General Assembly could now be formed by countries representing only 10 per cent of the world's population. [36]

It was a revolutionary development. In the tradition of Western parliamentarianism, small nations began to be heard on equal terms with the larger ones. The small countries were unified on one big issue—opposition to colonialism. Although colonialism had been liquidated, they insisted that it still existed in the form of "neocolonialism." The new nations were committed to the United Nations because it gave them a sense of security and importance. Most called themselves "unaligned countries," but were in fact aligned against the West, and some regarded Communist aggression as merely "national liberation movements."

[34] Kohn, *Nationalism: Its Meaning and History*, p. 91.
[35] Of the 114 members of the United Nations, only Indonesia withdrew its membership, after denunciation by Sukarno. But after Sukarno's fall, the new Indonesian leadership brought the country back into the United Nations.
[36] *Time*, Apr. 2, 1965, p. 27.

Supporters of the United Nations believed that military sanctions made the new organization more effective than the old League of Nations with its ineffectual Article XVI. But a new weakness appeared when the Russians virtually paralyzed the work of the Security Council by indiscriminate use of the veto.[37] The United States countered by pushing through the Assembly a resolution calling for "uniting for peace," which gave the Assembly power to take peace-keeping action when the Security Council was prevented from doing so by the veto.

The United Nations was fortunate in having a series of distinguished secretaries-general, including Trygve Lie (Norway), Dag Hammarskjöld (Sweden), and U Thant (Burma). All were devoted advocates of world organization. In Dag Hammarskjöld's United Nations Day statement, October 24, 1960, which became his last testament, he said:

No matter how deep the shadows may be, how sharp the conflicts, how tense the mistrust reflected in what is said and done in our world of today, . . . we are not permitted to forget that we have too much in common, too great a sharing of interests, and too much that we might lose together for ourselves and for succeeding generations ever to weaken in our efforts to surmount the difficulties and not to turn the simple human values, which are our common heritage, into the firm foundation on which we may unite our strength and live together in peace.[38]

U Thant spoke in similar fashion in 1965:

We have a basic problem in our varied heritage of prejudice, resentment, and nationalistic feelings. These are relics from a slower, more isolated, less populated age. They have no place in a liberal and dynamic world of change and progress. Nonetheless they are frequently exploited or artificially preserved to sustain other struggles. At our best, we know how outmoded and irrelevant these national and racial prejudices are, but we still need a strong and conscious effort to overcome them.[39]

These were glowing words, but unfortunately the United Nations became an instrument representing a consensus of national states, rather than defining and enforcing strict supranational principles. True, it made inroads into the realm of international anarchy, but it was not

[37] When the United Nations Charter was originally written, both the United States and Russia supported the veto clause. Russia used the veto more than a hundred times, while the United States refrained from invoking it.

[38] Quoted by Andrew W. Cordier, *Saturday Review*, July 24, 1965, p. 28.

[39] U Thant, *op. cit.*, p. 25.

able to resolve the chaos. In times of stress, nations turned away from it, seeking instead settlement of their disputes by their own devices. They were reluctant to bring to the world organization, as they were obligated to do, those situations which threatened world peace. Both the Russians and the French, along with several smaller nations, refused to pay their shares of the assessment for peace-keeping operations in the Congo and the Middle East. Yet, according to Article XIX of the United Nations Charter, any member more than two years in arrears with its financial contributions loses its vote in the General Assembly. Although these debts were relatively small, both the Russians and the French maintained that the United Nations was conceived as a loose association of federated states each of which maintains its sovereignty, and that they as sovereign states did not have to support military interventions of which they did not approve.

This unwillingness to relinquish even a small portion of national sovereignty in favor of world organization was further evidence of the strength of nationalism. Nationalism was neither bankrupt nor outmoded.

REGIONALISM AND SUPRANATIONALISM

The sovereign nation-state remains the basic politico-economic and military unit of world society. Supranationalism is still a dream. Between the sovereign nation and world federation is the middle ground of regional groups.

Regionalism, like any other "ism," is difficult to define. It may be described as a bloc of peoples held together primarily by geographical ties but in combination with one or more historical, economic, ideological, ethnic, or religious factors. According to Hedwig Hintze, "regionalism must be distinguished from nationalism in that it recognizes a higher unity and superior national interests transcending the attachment to the local region." [40] Joseph C. Roucek takes the opposite view, holding that "regionalism can hardly be distinguished from nationalism, for the most troublesome difficulties of regionalism and separatism have been caused . . . not so much by economic or class interests as by the nationalistic agitation." [41]

[40] Hedwig Hintze, "Regionalism," in *Encyclopedia of the Social Sciences*, XIII (New York, 1935), 208.
[41] Joseph C. Roucek, "Regionalism and Separatism," in Feliks Gross, *European Ideologies* (New York, 1948), p. 588.

Regionalism may be either centrifugal or separatist. Centrifugal regionalism may be seen in the cantons of the Swiss Republic, which had different languages and cultural conditions, but which managed to represent and maintain a unity. Separatist regionalism is advocated by Irish, Welsh, and Scottish nationalists in Great Britain, the Basques in Spain and France, the Flemings in Belgium, and the Ukrainians in Russia.

Regionalism refers to a supranational bloc characterized by uneven internal structures based on geography and on common cluster patterns of language and culture. An example is the region of Scandinavia, which is politically more unified today than at any other time in its history. Geographical, linguistic, cultural, and economic cooperation cuts across the national boundaries of Norway, Sweden, and Denmark.[42] A composite Dano-Norwegian literary language closely approaches Old Norse forms and has proved itself to be a literary vehicle of great power.[43] According to Gerald M. Spring, this language was more than a mere linguistic or literary phenomenon. It stimulated a kind of popular renascence, and by restoring the culture as well as the language of the peasant, enriched national life.[44]

A valuable contribution toward understanding the nature of regionalism within world organization was made in 1944 by Arnold Brecht, who presented four main categories of supranational organization: the proposal of universalists; of major-regionalists; of minor regionalists; and of ideological unionists.[45] The univeralists supported a world-wide organization. The major-regionalists recommended federations of continental scope. Minor regionalists proposed federal groupings of smaller countries. The ideological unionists advocated a confederation of democracies or a league of united nations.

Brecht saw these ideas as not mutually exclusive. All four, he said, were needed. Whichever was realized first should be established in such a way as not to preclude the other three. Because of his own back-

[42] Gerald M. Spring, *Nationalism on the Defensive* (Glendale, Calif., 1937), p. 18.
[43] Oscar J. Falnes, *National Romanticism in Norway* (New York, 1933), p. 354.
[44] Spring, *op. cit.,* p. 19.
[45] In 1944, Arnold Brecht was Professor of Political Science of the Graduate Faculty of the New School for Social Research. Prior to 1933 he was Director of the Division for Constitution and Administration in the German Ministry of the Interior. His classification was presented in *Regionalism and World Organization* (Washington, D.C., 1944), pp. 11 ff.

ground in European politics, Brecht was interested in the problem of
European federalism and world organization. He granted that some
functions, as for example preservation of peace among nations, could
not be performed by regional groupings alone but required an over-all
world organization. Other functions, he predicted, could be carried out
through regional arrangements. This was the experience of the United
States, which was a regional grouping of states of "quasi-continental"
scope:

I propose to discuss the need for a *"quasi*-continental" or "major" region.
This type of organization does not necessarily coincide with continental
boundaries, geographically speaking. The traditional boundaries of Europe, Asia and Africa are arbitrary, and, as for the Western Hemisphere,
we hardly know whether the Americas constitute one or two continents.
Quasi-continental organization will be used here to mean a formation of
such scope that it is substantially continental and not merely a group of
some of many states situated within a continent.

The need for quasi-continental organization derives from territorial
contiguity or neighborhood proximity. This creates some special problems, particularly if there is a considerable density of population, but it
also facilitates their solution—technologically speaking—through the
agency of an over-all organization.

Neighborhood is, of course, a relative concept. Nevertheless, however
defined, it obviously cannot embrace the antipodes. Nor can it describe
the relationship between Europe and the Americas or between Europe and
Asia. Where the boundaries are drawn is a matter of political expediency
and necessity rather than of doctrine.

Every quasi-continental region is, of course, a major region. But a major
region is not necessarily limited to a particular continent. It may combine
countries that are grouped around a sea, in which a major region may
assume the character of a fifth type of organization, cutting across quasi-
continental regions.[46]

Brecht saw the most pressing need for quasi-continental organization
in Europe. Europe was densely populated, and some thirty sovereign
states laid claim to its limited space. Europe, he said, was quasi-continental, whether or not Soviet Russia, Spain, or the southeastern regions
be included. He warned that no quasi-continental organization could
be formed in Europe without Great Britain or central Europe. The
idea was to bring together some four hundred million people, as well as

[46] *Ibid.*, pp. 12–13.

a third of the world's food supply, trade, and industry. To Brecht this amounted to a protest against archaic nationalism.

Brecht and other observers believed that the expansion of regionalism as a counterforce to nationalism should take place in large areas. Karl W. Deutsch shared this view: "The larger the area in which *genuine* integration and development can be carried on successfully, the greater will become the probability that eventually the challenge of world order and world government will be mastered.[47]

Proponents of regional groupings describe them as islands of hope in a world of sovereign states. Regional combinations, they say, are eminently sensible and logical. They point to cooperation among countries that had once been divided by old animosities. For example, in Asia the Colombo Plan mingled aid from six donor nations (Australia, Canada, Japan, New Zealand, the United Kingdom, and the United States) with mutual help among eighteen countries in a loose cooperative system. The Association of Southeast Asia (ASA) brought Malaysia, Thailand, and the Philippines together for socioeconomic cooperation. Nine Far Eastern nations started the Asian and Pacific Council (ASPAC). Similar organizations were created in Africa—the 38-member Organization of African Unity (OAU), and in Latin America—the Organization of American States (OAS).

Despite this activity, most new countries remained too sensitive about their national sovereignty to allow development of the regional idea. They generally agreed that regional integration was advisable. But in practice regionalism could not overcome the handicaps of European divisiveness, Asian jealousy, African sensitivity, and South American pride.

THE CALL FOR EUROPEAN UNION

This noble continent . . . is the origin of most of the culture, arts, philosophy, and science of both ancient and modern times. If Europe were once united in the sharing of its common inheritance there would be no limit to the happiness, to the prosperity, and glory which its three to four hundred million people would enjoy.[48]

These words spoken by Winston Churchill in 1946 were followed by his proposal "to create the European family" and "to build a kind of

[47] Karl W. Deutsch, *Nationalism and Social Communication* (New York, 1953), p. 167.
[48] Winston Churchill, speech at Zürich, Sept. 19, 1946.

United States of Europe." The suggestion was by no means new; it was even older than the idea of a United States of America. Roman imperialism had arranged the units of Europe into an orderly system, but the Roman complex eventually broke down and was succeeded by individual states. There was temporary unity again under Charlemagne, but after his death his empire fell apart. In 962, Otto I set up the Holy Roman Empire of the German Nations as the heir, though not the successor, of the Roman Empire. Throughout the Middle Ages this ideal of a universal empire persisted despite localism and particularism. "Modern Europe gloried in its divisions. Yet the essential unity of Europe . . . could not be ignored."[49]

The urge for European unity has been revealed again and again in modern times. Either Pan-European continentalism (west of Russia), western European regionalism, or European federalism seemed to be indicated.

The idea of European union had both theoretical and practical implications. Its theory ran parallel to that on which the League of Nations was founded.[50] The original forerunner was Pierre Dubois, who suggested a union of Christian states in his *De recuperatione terrae sanctae* (*c.* 1306).[51] This was followed by a variety of schemes for European union, which were proposed during the era of dynastic nationalism when the new doctrine of national sovereignty was being solidified. The Duc de Sully (1560–1641) urged a "Grand Design" involving the creation of a united Europe of fifteen countries, nearly equal in strength, all to be constitutionally integrated in a permanent league. Behind the suggestion was neither altruism nor peace: Sully wanted to prevent the extension of Hapsburg power. In 1693, William Penn, the founder of Pennsylvania, published his "Essay Toward the Present and Future Peace in Europe," in which he proposed a parliament for the "State of Europe." In 1712, the Abbé St. Pierre proposed a European confederation, "a permanent league of European states on the basis of the *status quo*," with one international army to enforce submission to its will. In 1795, Immanuel Kant suggested a European confederation under a republican form of government. In 1796, Edmund Burke spoke of Europe as "virtually one great state having the same basis of general law, with some diversity of provincial customs

---

[49] Reginald D. Lang, "European Federalism," in Gross, *op. cit.*, p. 961.

[50] See Chapter 12.

[51] On proposals for European unity, see S. J. Hemleben, *Plans for World Peace through Six Centuries* (Chicago, 1943).

and local establishment." [52] In 1814, Claude Henri Saint-Simon called for a European union governed by a parliament fashioned on the English model. For the remainder of the nineteenth and during the twentieth century, the theory of European union attracted a host of supporters.

Not only theoreticians but men of action sought the same goal. The unification of Europe was attempted by Charles V (1500–1558), the last Holy Roman emperor to be crowned by the pope. Charles V was frustrated by a combination of French, Turks, and German Lutherans; in 1556 the disgusted emperor abdicated and turned over his vast possessions to his son. Philip II (1527–1598) also had European ambitions, although he, like his father, regarded Europe as an extension of Spain. Louis XIV (1638–1715) similarly sought to unify Europe after a French pattern. Napoleon Bonaparte (1769–1821), after centralizing France, tried to extend his idea to all Europe: until his death he insisted that his only goal was to settle Europe's problems by creating a United States of Europe under his own benevolent leadership. Instead his conquests led to the rise of counter nationalisms throughout the Continent.

The nineteenth century emerged as an age of strongly assertive nationalism within the European system of pluralistic states. European nations all tried to nurture and enjoy their diversities. The vision of international organization was stimulated by the formation of the International Telegraphic Union (1865), the Universal Postal Union (1874), and the Hague Conferences (1899 and 1907). An attempt was made to achieve a balance of power by the formation of the Triple Alliance and the Triple Entente. Failure led directly to World War I. The League of Nations, fostered by Britain and France, was designed to safeguard national sovereignty. In 1929, Aristide Briand, worried about German resurgence, proposed a United States of Europe. He regarded economic union as useless because it would lead to domination by the stronger powers, and therefore proposed immediate political federation.[53]

[52] Edmund Burke, *Letters on a Regicide Peace* (London, 1796).

[53] The problem was the difficulty of reconciling a real national autonomy with the needs of a larger society. "There is no hope at all in creating a world society whose unity is to be bought at the cost of sacrificing what the nations (the only communities that now exist) have painfully learned about themselves. Each nation will have its own handicaps to overcome, but that is given by the nature of the case" (D. W. Brogan, *The American Character* [New York, 1944], p. 169).

Adolf Hitler wanted a United States of Europe, too, but under Nazi control. His "Thousand-Year Reich" was intended to envelop all Europe. In twelve short years he turned the dream into a nightmare. The Hitler regime fulfilled the forecast of Austrian poet Franz Grillparzer that "the road leads from humanity through nationalism to bestiality."

THE URGE FOR POLITICAL FEDERATION

The impact of World War II led to a revival of the idea of European union. "Great Britain was exhausted and impoverished. Germany did not exist; France was barely alive; defeated Italy did not count; and the smaller countries were not important." [54] Europe seemed to collapse from delayed shock. What could be done about the national state and its recurrent frictions? Perhaps there would grow out of the ruins a new European community which could survive in a multinational commonwealth, sharing cultural values as well as politico-economic institutions. The idea of European union took three forms: political (Parliament of Europe), economic (Common Market and European Free Trade Community), and military (NATO and Warsaw Pact).[55]

The desire for political union was weakest of all, precisely because no nation, large or small, despite the lessons of global war, was willing to sacrifice a portion of its sovereignty. On November 17, 1948, Winston Churchill opened a United Europe Exhibition with a speech in which he discussed the constitutional form which United Europe should take. To imagine that Europe was ready for either a political federation or customs union, he warned, was wholly unrealistic. But under mounting pressure of danger and necessity, he said, conceptions which might seem impracticable today might quite possibly be thought obvious and inevitable in a few years' time.

My advice is not to attempt at this stage to define too precisely the exact constitutional form which will ultimately emerge. We would do better to concentrate our united efforts on immediately practicable steps. . . .

It may, of course, be argued that a purely deliberative Assembly would develop into an irresponsible talking-shop, that it would be better to leave the work of European unification to be achieved through inter-governmental negotiations. That is not true. The assembly will perform an

---

[54] Joseph M. Jones, *The Fifteen Weeks* (New York, 1955), p. 41.
[55] For an excellent survey of the idea of European union, see Hans A. Schmitt, *The Path to European Union* (Baton Rouge, La., 1962).

essential task and one which cannot be performed by governments; the task of creating a European public opinion and sense of solidarity among the peoples of Europe.

The creation of a deliberative European Assembly naturally involves no transfer of sovereignty and raises no constitutional problems whatsoever. If the British Government decides to give its support to the proposal which has been put forward by the governments of France and Belgium, the European Assembly will assuredly become an accomplished reality. It is therefore to be hoped that our government, which has publicly proclaimed its belief in the principle of European unity, will not hesitate.[56]

In 1949 the Council of Europe was organized, with a charter proclaiming the aim "to achieve a greater unity between its members for the purpose of safeguarding and realizing the ideals and principles which are their common heritage and facilitating their economic and social progress." The Council consisted of a Committee of Ministers, a Consultative Assembly, and a Secretariat.[57] Powers of decision were vested in the Committee of Ministers, composed of the foreign minister of each participating country. The Consultative Assembly, the Parliament of Europe, consisted of 144 members who met at Strasbourg. Never before had parliamentarians from different European countries met in a joint assembly to debate their common problems.

Those who created the Council of Europe believed that they were establishing a supranational authority with real powers, but from its very beginning the organization was handicapped by rules which limited its authority. The Committee could act only by unanimous vote, another concession to national sensitiveness. Because each member nation feared "dictation by foreigners," the Consultative Assembly could only "recommend" to the Committee of Ministers. Assembly deputies could debate as much as they wished, but they could not take action.

In its early days the Council of Europe was attended by the most distinguished Continental statesmen, but gradually its parliamentary sessions took on the character of a debating society. Because its political status was uncertain, the Council turned its attention to cultural and legal matters. Its cultural coordinators worked to promote European unity by encouraging exchanges of teachers, research fellowships, art

[56] Winston Churchill, quoted in Lionel Curtis, *World Revolution in the Cause of Peace* (Oxford, 1949), pp. 95–96.
[57] See Russell Hill, "The Organization of Europe," in *Foundations of World Organization* (New York, 1952), pp. 73 ff.

exhibitions, and translation services. In the legal area the Council tried to bind its members together in a human rights convention. Citizens inside each member nation could appeal in some cases beyond the highest courts of their own countries to the European Human Rights Court in Strasbourg, which would investigate each claim.[58]

Although Churchill supported European union, he made it clear that the creation of a deliberative European assembly "naturally involves no transfer of sovereignty." Yet, European authority meant that each government would have to relinquish a portion of its national sovereignty to the international body. The tantalizing questions remained: How far, if at all, could any one country go to merge into the common whole? To what extent was it willing to surrender its sovereignty?

Neither political leadership nor public opinion in Europe was convinced that national sovereignty should be sacrificed to the common good. Most Europeans found it difficult to conceive of common governmental institutions. When they thought of a "Europe of States" they visualized a Napoleonic or Hitlerian imperium in which one powerful state would dominate the rest. To be part of an entity in which political decisions were made beyond the national borders seemed fantastic and dangerous to most Europeans.

The painful lack of progress toward political union did not discourage its supporters, who insisted that the idea must not die. Antoine Pinay, a former French premier, represented the attitude of political integrationists: "I believe that, without offending national sensibilities, it is possible to 'make Europe.' And the world scene shows that the need for a politically united Europe is as great as ever." [59] Jean Monnet, president of the Action Committee for United Europe, believed unity would bring an end to centuries of bloodshed: "If this trend to unity . . . were to be lastingly interrupted, the creation of Europe and . . . the organization of world peace would be endangered." [60] Addressing a symposium in Vienna on June 15, 1965, George F. Kennan, former American ambassador to the Soviet Union and to Yugoslavia, spoke of the dangers of the German problem, especially the "arbitrary borders which plunged millions of people into unhappiness." "There is no

[58] By September 1965 the screening commission of the European Human Rights Court in Strasbourg resolved more than 2,200 complaints and passed only two on to the Court (*Time*, international ed., Sept. 24, 1965, p. 61).

[59] *Daily Telegraph Magazine* (London), No. 55 (Oct. 8, 1965), p. 27.

[60] *Ibid.*

better solution," he said, "than the creation of a United States of Europe, a supranational federative political system." The unity of Europe within her natural units, Kennan added, would require inclusion of the Communist states.[61]

ECONOMIC INTEGRATION: COMMON MARKET

Considerably more encouraging than the Parliament of Europe was the progress of economic integration. In the dark days of World War II, Allied leaders, planning for the peace that lay ahead, foresaw a massive drive for reconstruction of the Continent. At the same time they dreamed of the day in western Europe when all nations would work for economic unity. The handicaps resulting from national fragmentation would be overcome; trade barriers would be lowered; uniform codes regulating industry and labor would be introduced; communication between nations would be harmonized.

The immediate postwar problem was reconstruction. The assistance needed by western Europe was supplied by the United States. On June 5, 1947, Secretary of State George C. Marshall made a speech at Harvard in which he launched the European Recovery Plan (ERP). It provided that those countries receiving aid would remove obstacles to trade with one another. On April 16, 1948, two weeks after Congress voted an appropriation of five billion dollars, European recipients of aid signed a multilateral convention which marked the birth of the Organization for European Economic Cooperation (OEEC). Each member recognized the interdependence of prosperity: all would work together to achieve a maximum exchange of goods, services,

---

[61] *The New York Times*, June 16, 1965. Among other Eurocrats, Lord Gladwyn condemned nationalism as "the suicidal instinct in Europe's blood," and insisted that "archaic nationalism . . . in an Age of Super Powers and Super Bombs is about as relevant to modern problems as the arquebus for the First Crusade" (Lord Gladwyn, *The European Idea* [London, 1966], pp. x, 150). "If the Community now set up in Western Europe is to continue, if it is going to be a hopeful experiment favoring world peace, if it is to be able in its component parts, namely the ancient nation-states of Europe, to fulfill their real destiny and not to lapse gradually into sheer provincialism or satellization, it must possess certain supranational powers. It can have no such powers, and it will therefore fairly soon join the limbo of fine projects and frustrated hopes, unless the present and chauvinistic mood of France changes and unless both she and Britain can come together in accordance with a genuine economic and political supranational plane" (*ibid.*, p. 129).

and capital; all agreed to stabilize their currencies and to use their manpower resources efficiently.[62] On July 1, 1950, sixteen European countries launched an attack on currency problems by forming the European Payments Union (EPU). Payments between the members, instead of being bilateral, were to be made multilaterally through the EPU.

The Soviet Union, which had worked closely with the Allies in destroying Hitler, refused to participate in these plans for the recovery of Europe and would not allow the countries under her control to take part in them. Europe was thus divided economically. Yet, the Marshall Plan was phenomenally successful in accelerating western European recovery. Under the stimulus of the OEEC there was gratifying progress. Industrial quotas were ended within a decade. The OEEC was so successful that it extended its aims, changing its name to Organization for Economic Cooperation and Development and coordinating Western aid to the developing world.

On May 9, 1950, a step was taken toward economic integration of western Europe which marked a new epoch in European history. In a momentous press conference, Robert Schuman, former French foreign minister, made the startling proposal of a "limited but decisive plan" to place French and German coal and steel production under a common authority, within the framework of an organization open to the participation of the other European countries. Schuman believed that pooling the production of coal and steel would ensure the establishment of common bases for economic development—the first stage toward European federation—and would change the fate of those regions so long devoted to the manufacture of arms.[63] The basic features of his plan were as follows: there would be free competition in the production and sale of coal and steel in the participating countries; there would be no customs barriers, no import quotas, no currency restrictions; there would be conditions for fair competition—abolition of double pricing (one for internal and one for external markets), a halt to discriminatory rail rates, and equalization of cost factors by common wage policy and similar investment plans. All this, Schuman was certain, would eliminate the threat of future conflict between the two arch rivals, France and Germany, and would constitute the first concrete founda-

[62] See *OEEC, The Organization for European Economic Recovery: History and Structure* (Paris, 1953), pp. 9–12.

[63] Hill, *op. cit.*, pp. 75–76.

tion for the European federation that was indispensable to the preservation of peace. On April 18, 1951, West Germany, France, Belgium, Italy, Luxembourg, and Holland signed a treaty establishing the European Coal and Steel Community (ECSC).

Behind Schuman's proposal was an urge to prevent a return to old-fashioned nationalism. Each country would be prepared to relinquish a portion of its sovereignty in favor of the stability, prosperity, and common good of the whole. The program was to be administered by a High Authority composed of men appointed jointly by the governments but not answerable to the governments. In practice, however, the ECSC demonstrated in its first seven years that partial integration could bring only limited success. The High Authority and the national governments began to tread on one another's toes, and accomplishment was spotty.[64]

Nevertheless, the six nations of ECSC resolved to form even closer economic ties. On March 25, 1957, the foreign ministers, all ardent Europeans, of the countries concerned (West Germany, France, Belgium, Italy, Luxembourg, and Holland) met in Rome to sign a treaty creating the European Economic Community (EEC), commonly called the Common Market, or Inner Six, or the Six.[65] A program was set up for achieving a customs and economic union over a twelve-year period. Each participating country agreed to abolish barriers to the free movement of goods, labor, capital, and services. Each would work to unify economic policies and to achieve social improvement.

The accomplishments of the Common Market were formidable. Since 1957 it has slashed tariffs on industrial goods by 60 per cent; cut customs duties by 45 per cent on certain agricultural products; eliminated the former quotas which limited the amount of goods that could be exported from one country to another within the Community; and called for eventual elimination of tariffs on all goods. As a result the EEC nations experienced significant growths in both trade and national output. From 1958 to 1962 their total external trade increased more than 50 per cent, while national production, measured in constant prices, rose an average of 5.4 per cent a year. Even more important was the increase in trade among the six EEC nations themselves. It rose

[64] Schmitt, *op. cit.*, p. 203.
[65] Greece and Turkey became associate members.

about 98 per cent from 1958 to 1962, at a time when world trade rose only about 20 per cent.[66]

Provision was made that other nations could join the Common Market only with the unanimous consent of the current members.[67] In 1959 at a meeting in Stockholm, seven nations outside the EEC formed a grouping of their own, the European Free Trade Association (EFTA), known as the Outer Seven. Full members were the United Kingdom, Sweden, Denmark, Norway, Switzerland, Austria, and Portugal, while Finland was an associate member. Composed of the peripheral countries of western Europe, the EFTA proposed to face the Common Market with a united program in the hope that its members could get better terms as a group.[68] There were four differences between the ways the EFTA and the Common Market functioned: EFTA as a free-trade area had no common external tariff with other nations; each member of the EFTA continued to maintain its own independent foreign trade policy with nations outside the association; the EFTA limited its tariff cuts and other measures easing trade barriers to industrial products; and there was little unified administrative structure in the EFTA, and almost no effort was made to harmonize laws and regulations.[69]

There was little hope that western Europe could do anything decisive about political union until it healed the EEC-EFTA split. Whether or not there can be an outright merger is not clear at this time.

Economic integration of Europe, including Soviet Russia and her satellites, would include an area of two million square miles and unite more than a third of the world's food supply, trade, income, and coal

[66] These figures are from Arnold B. Barach, *The New Europe and Its Economic Future* (New York, 1964), pp. 108–110.

[67] The United Kingdom could have entered the Common Market when it was established but she did not become a member. Her later efforts to join were frustrated by the opposition of General de Gaulle.

[68] The so-called Eurocrats worked to heal the trade split between the Common Market Six and the European Free Trade Association Seven. The idea was to bring about complete economic integration of western Europe and then link up with the Communist countries. A complicating factor was that Russians regarded both the EEC and the EFTA as villains in a capitalistic plot. Moscow subsequently organized a counterunion called Comecon, consisting of the satellite states of Poland, Czechoslovakia, East Germany, Hungary, Bulgaria, and Rumania.

[69] Barach, *op. cit.*, p. 110. On January 1, 1967, the EFTA countries completed the elimination of all industrial tariffs.

and steel. This, said the Eurocrats, must be achieved in a slow, continuing process, starting in a few countries and then expanding.

The urge to integration was by no means unanimous. Although he wanted France to remain in the Common Market, President de Gaulle jealously guarded his country's sovereignty. In early 1965 he withdrew French representatives from the Council of Ministers of the Inner Six. His specific objection was the proposal of other members that the agricultural levy by the Common Market, even though it benefitted France, might ultimately pass out of the control of individual nations and be placed at the disposal of the Community. To de Gaulle this was unacceptable: he would not allow France's independent budget to be placed in the hands of supranational authority. In his estimation the integration of Europe had gone far enough.[70] This point of view was opposed by other members of the Common Market, notably the Netherlands.[71]

There was some support for de Gaulle's position even among members of the European Free Trade Association. In each case it was feared that economic union might lead to political integration. Prime Minister Tage Erlander of Sweden stated bluntly: "In our eyes Sweden could only join the Common Market if the Six were to drop their goal of a politically federated Europe, which we do not regard as feasible." [72] The Swedish people, he said, considered themselves a part of European civilization and had a very deep stake in Europe's economic growth, but they drew the line at political federation. Sweden, he continued, was willing to cooperate with the Common Market, even if the goal was eventual political federation, but she was not prepared to go further than economic integration.[73]

This point of view was also expressed by Emanuel Shinwell, Labor member of Parliament for Durham (Easington): "If the members of

[70] De Gaulle particularly resented the fact that in 1966 most Common Market decisions were to be taken by qualified majority vote, instead of allowing a veto power for individual nations. He called for "intergovernmental cooperation," while the Eurocrats wanted a federation dominated by a supranational parliament.

[71] In interviews at The Hague on October 4, 1965, with staff members of the Netherlands Foreign Office working on European integration, I was assured that the Netherlands "is quite willing to sacrifice all or a part of its sovereignty in a federal union of Europe." Further: "The Netherlands has taken the lead in the business of transferring economic into political regionalism." And: "The Netherlands as a small country has little to lose by federalism."

[72] *Daily Telegraph Magazine* (London), No. 55 (Oct. 8, 1965), p. 27.

[73] *Ibid.*

the EEC can solve their economic problems, and display a reasonable measure of unity, it would seem feasible that Britain would be ready to enter an economic agreement. But as long as the concept of a supranational government and a European Parliament exists there will be strong opposition to British entry into the Common Market." [74]

The Eurocrats insisted that the powers of western Europe must join together if they were to keep from disappearing. Europe would rise to a new grandeur only by forming a supranational union and surrendering the most conspicuous luxuries of independence.[75] Had not the Common Market revived Europe, revealed the power of modified free enterprise in the face of socialist theory, and contributed to changing the balance of economic power in the world? The case for union was expressed eloquently by Paul-Henri Spaak, foreign minister of Belgium:

Fifteen years after the Schuman declaration Europe has, in one respect, gone a great deal further than we had hoped it would. In another respect it has lagged far behind.

We had anticipated great obstacles in the path of economic integration but our forecasts were wrong. Progress has been faster than we had hoped and smoother than we believed possible. But the signatories of the Common Market Treaty in 1957 were all statesman with a common conception of what Europe should be: they believed that a politically united Europe would be the logical sequence to an economically integrated Europe. Today, however, we are compelled to recognize that the political unification of Europe has not taken place. There has been the much publicized Franco-German *rapprochement,* but it does not seem to have had much effect. All attempts to get Europe going again on the political front have failed.

Where there is a political will there is a way through technical difficulties, however big. But when the political will is lacking, even minor technical difficulties block all progress. And today among the Six the political will to "make Europe" is much weaker than it was.

There are several reasons for this: the first, of course, is the return to power of General de Gaulle, who is fundamentally opposed to the concept of supranationality, while steadfastly proclaiming his support of the Com-

---

[74] *Ibid.,* p. 28. Although Mr. Shinwell was speaking for himself and not for the Labor government, and although the Labor government wanted membership in the Common Market, the reservation regarding political integration seemed implicit in British policy.

[75] Schmitt, *op. cit.,* p. 245.

mon Market. Then there is the very success of the Common Market in the economic field, which has led some people to believe that there is no sense in going any further for the time being. Then there is the fact that, perhaps inevitably, the building of a politically united Europe has become an inner, domestic issue among the rival political parties of the Six, with a weakening effect on an ideal which should be above party politics. . . .

I still believe that if an economically united Europe is to grow, some form of political organization is necessary, indeed inevitable. Whatever happens, France's partners will not accept that the Common Market Treaty be tampered with or watered down. Our aims have not changed, and we are more than ever convinced that the method set forth in the Common Market Treaty is the right one, and indeed the only possible one for Europe, if it is to play a part among the giants of the nuclear age.[76]

MILITARY UNION: NATO

The cement binding the Western Allies and the Soviet Union in World War II was the common threat posed by Hitler. The partners began to drift apart in the late days of the war. Stalin, excessively suspicious, had no intention of implementing his promise made at Yalta that the nations of eastern Europe would be free to determine their futures. Churchill, always the *Realpolitiker*, distrusted the Russians and urged that Allied armies penetrate as far eastward as possible. Roosevelt, believing that "Uncle Joe" was susceptible to Rooseveltian charm, was just beginning to realize his error when he died.

The Soviet threat to Berlin in 1948 and the conquest of Czechoslovakia made it clear to western Europeans that they needed military as well as economic support. This led to the formation of the North Atlantic Treaty Organization (NATO) in 1949. Its purpose was to construct a barrier against Soviet imperialism after the many evidences of its expansionist policy in the immediate postwar years. The treaty was also intended to guarantee peace in Europe by establishing a balance of power between East and West. Eventually there were fifteen members. West Germany was brought in and rearmed as a result of continued Communist pressure, notably the Korean War, which began in 1950.

Soviet Russia made many complaints about NATO and uttered threats against it. But she never translated denunciation into action. NATO grew steadily stronger: there were no further penetrations of

[76] *Daily Telegraph Magazine, op. cit.,* p. 28.

western Europe after the fall of Prague. Western European countries were freed from the nightmare of Soviet attack. Of all the continents, Europe became the calmest—a rare development in its history. This tranquillity was due in large measure to the protective shield supplied by NATO.

NATO had guaranteed peace in western Europe. Why should it be dismantled or destroyed? The membership in 1965 was shocked by de Gaulle's decision to denounce NATO and to intimate that France might withdraw altogether from the organization in 1969, when it was due for renewal. He requested that the alliance's international headquarters as well as the American forces in France leave French territory by April 1, 1967. At the same time he indicated that France would remain allied to Britain, Germany, Italy, and the Benelux countries through Western European Union. If France left NATO's organization, she would still be directly bound to a mutual defense network, although not integrated into it.[77]

Behind de Gaulle's action were many considerations: France, he said, wanted to retain her national integrity, while NATO was fundamentally an American apparatus; France preferred to substitute bilateral alliance ties for NATO membership; France wanted no part of allied political integration and did not desire to be "integrated into wars" against her own interest; and France differed with her NATO partners over nuclear strategy, particularly with West Germany's claims for the complete range of atomic weapons.[78]

Not the least important factor in de Gaulle's opposition to an organization which guaranteed security for France was his continuing resentment of American power. The complete egoist, de Gaulle never forgot or forgave real or fancied insults. Leader of the Free French during World War II, he had expected a responsible position at the Allied summit, though his country had been beaten by the Germans. When Roosevelt and Churchill agreed that de Gaulle was a frustrated Joan of Arc, the Frenchman reacted with an angry *revanche* which survived Roosevelt's death for more than two decades.

De Gaulle's attitude toward NATO provoked a fierce controversy. Paul-Henri Spaak made a blistering attack: "If each country in Europe and North America withdrew into its own shell this would undoubtedly cause complete disorder and permanently hinder political unifica-

[77] C. L. Sulzberger, in *The New York Times*, international ed., Nov. 19, 1965.
[78] Paul-Henri Spaak, in the *Sunday Times* (London), May 8, 1966.

tion of Europe. Does France want to drive us into repeating all the mistakes we committed between the wars?" [79] Sicco Mansholt, a Dutch vice-president of Euromart, berated de Gaulle for "inadmissible methods" and declared: "If Europe breaks down, French grandeur will be just a balloon that will collapse with the first pinprick." [80] Dean Acheson, a former American secretary of state, who had helped draft the Atlantic Pact, spoke angrily: "It is a curious situation of a recovered patient—a convalescent who has been weak, who has been ill and has finally been built up and has good food and good care, been in a warm house and warm bed and suddenly he says: 'I'm a great big man, I don't need any more food, no more doctors, no more house. I want to get out in the wind and the rain, the ice and the snow. I don't need any of this protection.' " [81]

De Gaulle's attitude represented essentially the triumph of national egoism in its struggle with the Eurocrats. Neither de Gaulle, France, nor Europe was ready to abandon nationalism in favor of an enveloping supranationalism.[82]

The military army of NATO moved to a village in southern Belgium, and the civil arm was transferred to new headquarters near Brussels. To repair the damage, the fourteen NATO military members set up a Defense Planning Committee to study the new defense system. They also formed a Nuclear Planning Group, consisting of seven nations including West Germany, to select targets and deploy NATO's nuclear force of seven thousand warheads. Apparently there was still fear of Soviet aggression, despite the blow dealt to NATO by de Gaulle.

NATO had owed its origin to the threat of Communist aggression. In part because of its success, it seemed to lose its *raison d'être*, and began to search for new functions, possibly diplomatic rather than military.

[79] *Ibid.*

[80] *Newsweek*, international ed., July 26, 1965, p. 27.

[81] *The New York Times*, Apr. 5, 1966.

[82] As NATO lost its French geographical base, its opposing monolith, the Soviet bloc, also began to dissolve into a loose group of Communist nations.

Chapter 13

Retrospect and Prospect

*In this time of mental and verbal confusion
when general political terms have become so
emotionally fraught that they cover disparate
realities, we have to start rethinking many
concepts in their historical context and in
their concrete application. One of the chief
concepts about which this rethinking has to
be done in the interest of human freedom and
of the possibility of cultural intercourse
and universal rationality is the concept
of nationalism.*

—HANS KOHN

Perhaps we can best judge the role of nationalism today by pinpointing it within the framework of world revolution. There are three powerful revolutionary drives in contemporary society—communism, nationalism, and humanitarianism.[1] These three "isms" have independent qualities, although on occasion they are intermingled. Communism and nationalism, for example, are being woven to form the same fabric.

The Communist world revolution tried to achieve its goal by taking advantage of other revolutionary trends. Lenin identified communism with global anticolonialism. But communism failed in its attempt to move into the vacuum left by decolonization, and both Soviet Russia and Communist China have themselves retreated from internationalism toward nationalism.

The nationalist world revolution has not yet been completed. At the present moment it remains the primary revolutionary force. Old established states hold on to their national sovereignty, while the emergent nation-states think exclusively in terms of national political independence. Nationalism was the agent which helped to deliver them from colonialism.

The third drive operating in contemporary society is the revolution for human rights. Undeveloped countries of Asia and Africa, having successfully completed their national revolutions, turn to this tremendous problem of human rights. The continuing struggle may be seen in Latin-American countries, which, having long since won their nationhood, seek to narrow the gap between wealth and poverty. We see fleeting evidences of this demand in even the nations of the Near and Middle East. Despite the cold war the revolution for human rights goes on. The Russians, inhibited by Communist dogma, are beginning to think in terms of "thaw" and freedom. In the United States many who had long been convinced that their country was a homeland for the free individual, suddenly felt the impact of racial revolution, in part a reflection of the global demand for human rights.

---

[1] For a stimulating discussion of this idea, see Arthur Larson, "The Real Nature of the World Revolution," *Saturday Review*, June 3, 1967, pp. 15-18. I am indebted to Mr. Larson for the conclusions expressed in this section.

On the assumption that vestiges of the past carry over into the future, reasonable men hope that there will be greater progress in human rights when the national revolution is completed. There are as yet, however, few signs that nationalism has spent its force.

NATIONALISM AS AN "OBSOLETE" PHENOMENON

Some observers regard nationalism not only as a logical absurdity but as a sentiment that has already outlived its usefulness. Harold J. Laski saw nationalism as an obstinate virus or disease germ infecting the body politic of mankind:

You cannot heal so deep-seated a disease with an incantation. . . . Nationalism breeds imperialism, and . . . the latter, at long last, breeds nationalism in the peoples whom it subjects to its control. . . . Have we not, if we would escape the immense conflict that such a sequence portends, to think in different terms? Having tried the world of sovereign states, each looking to its own interests, each unlimited in law in the will it may seek to operate, each competing with its rivals in terms of force, and force alone, as the ultimate arbiter between different wants, can we really be content with the results? Does not the mere selfishness of ensuring our own survival compel us to think in different terms? [2]

Where Laski denounced nationalism in political terms, Erich Fromm excoriated it as our incest, our idolatry, and our insanity. In Fromm's view the average man obtains his sense of identity from belonging to a nation, rather than from being a "son of man." Man's objectivity, that is, his reason, has been warped by a fixation. He uses different criteria in judging the members of his own clan and the "stranger." Paranoid delusions about the stranger can spring up at the slightest provocation. "This incestuous fixation not only poisons the relationship of the individual to the stranger, but to the members of his own clan and to himself. The person who has not freed himself from the ties to blood and soil is not yet fully born as a human being; his capacity for love and reason are crippled; he does not experience himself nor his fellow man in their—and his own—human reality." [3]

Added to these denunciations was the viewpoint of Bertrand Russell: "Nationalism is in our day the chief obstacle to the extension of social

[2] Harold J. Laski, *Nationalism and the Future of Civilization* (London, 1932), p. 43.
[3] Erich Fromm, *The Sane Society* (New York, 1955), p. 58.

cohesion beyond national boundaries. It is therefore the chief force making for the extermination of the human race. Everybody is agreed that the nationalism of other countries is absurd, but the nationalism of one's own country is noble and splendid, and any one who does not uphold it is a lily-livered cur." [4]

Some scholars view nationalism, originally a progressive movement, as a replacement for the old bonds of feudalism and religion. According to Hans J. Morgenthau, "the nation-state has been rendered obsolete to the nuclear revolution in the same way in which feudalism was made obsolete 200 years ago by the first industrial revolution of the steam engine." [5] Recent history has shown the growing inadequacy of the national state as the limit of political, military, and economic sovereignty.

Religion also provides a parallel. The same emotional intensity and mental distortion that characterize integral nationalism accompanied the religious wars of the sixteenth and seventeenth centuries. Both Protestants and Catholics believed in the sanctity of their religions and went to war to defend them. Heretics were sought out, put to the rack to elicit confessions of guilt, and on occasion turned over to civil authorities to be burned at the stake. Today these religious excesses are regarded as strange and archaic characteristics of a less civilized age. [6] In the second half of the twentieth century, religious tolerance is not regarded as a sin or a crime but as a very desirable attitude in civilized societies. The great religions are beginning to coexist peacefully. [7]

In times of nationalistic fervor, religion was succeeded by the state —the recipient of obedience—and the dissenter became the traitor. Those who regard nationalism as a curse believe that it is as subject to change as religion. They say that there is no necessity for maintaining it as a way of life in modern times. National emotion, they insist, need not be overpowering. Future generations might consider misuse of national emotion to be as inconceivable as perversion of religion seems to us today. [8]

Those who are convinced that nationalism is obsolete regard it as

[4] Bertrand Russell, *New Hopes for a Changing World* (London, 1951), p. 69.

[5] Hans J. Morgenthau, at *Pacem in Terris* convocation, Feb. 1965, quoted in *Saturday Review*, May 1, 1965, p. 26.

[6] Julius Braunthal, *The Paradox of Nationalism* (London, 1946), p. 15.

[7] U Thant, in *The New York Times*, Jan. 4, 1966.

[8] Braunthal, *op. cit.*, p. 15.

absurd in an age of atomic, biological, and chemical weapons. Atomic weapons can be hurled at enemies across frontiers which are little wider in time than a village street.

We cannot escape from this foreshortening of our world, for every month, our test pilots with all the resources of science behind them are achieving fresh velocities beyond the speed of sound and the designers of armament are plotting the parabolas along which rockets with atomic war heads may one day pass at the speed of light. This is our world, . . . its sovereignties almost as laughable as the old family feuds, its killings as fratricidal, its warfare as likely to destroy in one holocaust family and neighbor and town.[9]

Hans J. Morgenthau charges that any national government pursuing pre–atomic age foreign policies with the support of atomic weapons becomes the enemy of its own people.[10]

Edward H. Carr holds the viewpoint that nations and international relations are in process of undergoing another subtle, though not yet clearly definable, change. According to Carr, a first look suggests beyond doubt that nationalism has never been stronger than at this moment, yet closer analysis reveals certain opposing trends. World War II seemed to mark a retrogression from the unqualified nationalism of the preceding period. There is a contrast between the patriotic fervor of 1914 and the absence of national exaltation at the outbreak of World War II—not least in Germany. National hatreds, losing their old spontaneity, masked themselves in ideological trappings. "In Germany the 'hymn of hate' has not reappeared; in Great Britain what is called 'Vansittartism' is the rather shamefaced rationalization of a frank popular emotion of the last war. Even the 'nationalism' of Hitler became, as time went on, less and less specifically German. It was 'Aryan' and 'Nordic.' "[11] Carr further noted that quislingism could not be explained wholly in terms of brute force and was difficult to reconcile with the picture of an age of unbridled and militant nationalism. Further, none of the main forces that was victorious in World War II was nationalistic in the older sense. Neither Great Britain nor

[9] Barbara Ward, *Truth and Freedom* (London, 1954), p. 209. In a more recent book, Miss Ward claims that as the old nationalisms recede, new planetary loyalties may help us achieve world amity in the atomic age. See Barbara Ward, *Space Ship Earth* (London, 1966).

[10] Morgenthau, *op. cit.*

[11] Edward H. Carr, *Nationalism and After* (London, 1945), pp. 34–35.

the British Commonwealth was ever finally overwhelmed by the nationalist tide. And the two giants of world politics, the United States and the Soviet Union, bore nonnational names and multinational status —the United States by its melting pot, and the Soviet Union by its comprehensive Soviet allegiance embracing a multiplicity of nations. Finally, Carr saw in Europe some small units of the past continuing for a few generations longer to eke out a precariously independent existence, but surviving only as anomalies and anachronisms in a world which had moved on to other forms of organization.[12]

Writing at the end of World War II, Carr was unable to foresee the extent of the demand for self-determination that would come in Asia and Africa. The surge to independence was invariably followed by an intensification of nationalism, and nationalism in the emergent countries took on the quality not of a cultural blessing but of a political curse. The statesmen of new nations did not agree that the nation-state was obsolete. They regarded their own nationalism as less dangerous than that of the powerful nations. This point of view was presented by S. O. Adebo, Nigeria's representative in the United Nations: "If nationalism is a danger to international interdependence, as I think it is, the greater danger comes from the nationalism of the older and major powers rather than from the nationalism of the new nations. The examples of the great developed countries, and particularly the major powers of the world, to the new nations are—if I may put it bluntly, with all respect to their great wisdom—simply deplorable." [13]

CONTINUITY: NATIONALISM PERSISTENT

Far from retreating, nationalism retains its vigor in the atomic age as a basic form of human association. It has become no less urgent than in the past, and certainly has not disappeared. This is the situation despite the fact that nationalism runs contrary to the needs of economic development which exert such powerful influence on contemporary life.[14] Cultural diversities have lessened, but not cultural nationalism.

World War II, a boundary mark in the history of nationalism, was

[12] *Ibid.*

[13] Chief S. O. Adebo, at *Pacem in Terris* convocation, Feb. 1965, quoted in *Saturday Review,* May 1, 1965, p. 26.

[14] Richard Pipes, "The Forces of Nationalism," *Problems of Communism,* XIII (Jan.–Feb. 1964), 2.

an explosive period in which nationalism was regarded as having saved the Western powers and their way of life from destruction. Attempts made after the war to reject nationalism in all its forms as an unmitigated evil impressed neither the established powers nor the new nations. The older powers automatically placed their national interests first and ethics a poor second. Since 1945 the nations of the world have doubled in number from 68 to 127, and each new country promotes its own self-interest, power of decision, and armed forces. Each has pledged to defend its sovereign independence.

In 1944, before the end of World War II, the observant historian Carl Becker pointed out the trend:

After the war is over, nationalism, whatever its defects, will remain for any foreseeable future what it has been for a long time past—the strongest political force in the modern world; and this force will be exerted in the form of many sovereign independent states.

This sentiment cannot be abated or the power curbed except in the sense that the people of any country can, if they have sufficient intelligence and moral sense, use the power for purposes more enlightened and ends more desirable because they take into account the rights and interests of other nations.[15]

Today nationalism still reveals itself in the belief that progress can be made only through the nation-state, as well as through the impulse of its growth, regardless of the narrow aims of class or party (Soviet Union) or universal interest (United Nations). Whether we like it or not, we must accept the fact that this revival of the multiple-power system continues to emphasize the sovereign state rather than the peoples and groups inside states or humanity. The game of international power politics continues. Nationalistic movements and practices are still growing.[16]

The evidence is overwhelming. Despite oratory on the ideals of international brotherhood, the great powers resist encroachment on their right to act independently. In stirring nineteenth-century tones, President de Gaulle argues that each country must enjoy unrestricted nationalism in order to be, and to feel, strong. Europe, he insists, must remain a loose aggregation of sovereign states.

[15] Carl Becker, *How New Will the Better World Be?* (New York, 1944), p. 74.

[16] Karl W. Deutsch, *Nationalism and Social Communication* (New York, 1953), p. 164.

Trouble spots throughout the world testify to the potency of the continuing nationalism. A few examples indicate the trend. Kashmir remained of national interest to both India and Pakistan. Driven by nationalistic zeal, Indians were certain that the loss of Kashmir would endanger hundreds of other princely states and work to the disadvantage of Indian unity. At the same time it was to the national interest of Muslim Pakistan that Kashmir, with a population that was more than 85 per cent Muslim, be retained within the framework of political Islam.

This clash of opposing nationalisms on the subcontinent was one of many throughout the world, each recapitulating in some way the experiences of the nineteenth century. The rivalry between Dutch-speaking Flemings and French-speaking Walloons in Belgium was generated by linguistic nationalism. Celebrating its centennial of nationhood, Canada stressed the blessings of nationalism, as the socialist New Democratic Party turned nationalism against "United States capitalist domination." In the era of decolonization Spain suddenly laid claim to Gibraltar as a matter of "national honor." The Greeks demanded the return of the Elgin Marbles from the British Museum because they were "national property." On May 8, 1965, Shalva Sanokoyev contributed an article to the Russian magazine *International Affairs* in which he denounced the West for supporting "a national renaissance in Eastern Europe" and for promoting national communism against what he called "integral communism." [17] On May 22, 1965, the Portuguese Ministry of Education accused the Portuguese Writers Association of "deeply offending national sentiment" by having awarded a prize to a white Portuguese writer who sympathized with African nationalism.[18] The publication of Yale's Vinland map in October 1965 proved how an ostensibly innocent piece of historical research could arouse the most violent passions.[19]

No nation was immune. In June 1966 some 46,000 members attended the annual congress at Karlsruhe of Germany's neo-Nazi party, the National Democrats (NPD). The NPD platform was a compendium of jumbled nationalistic edicts. Delegates cheered speakers who called for the withdrawal of foreign troops and the return of Germany's lost

[17] *The New York Times,* May 9, 1965.   [18] *Ibid.,* May 23, 1965.
[19] See Raleigh Ashlin Skelton, Thomas E. Marston, and George D. Painter, *The Vinland Map and the "Tartar Relation"* (New Haven, 1965). The publication of the map angered Italian nationalists, who resented the implication that Norsemen had come to the New World before Columbus.

lands in the East. With tears in their eyes, the neo-Nazis stood up and sang the national anthem "Deutschland über Alles," including the first verse, disapproved in West Germany since the war.[20] The NPD gathered strength in Hesse and Bavaria, at a time when West German leaders hastened to assure the world that the movement was innocuous and that the German people had had enough of extreme nationalism. When the Erhard government fell in late November 1966, a black-red coalition came to power (black for the conservative Christian Democratic Party, red for the Social Democratic Party) with a new chancellor, Kurt Georg Kiesinger, a former member of the Nazi Party who had obtained a clearance from Allied and German authorities. In late April 1967, 6.9 per cent of the voters in the Rhineland Palatinate and 5.8 per cent in Schleswig-Holstein cast their ballots for the NPD. Some 200,000 West German votes enabled the party that is run by former Nazis to win four seats in each of the two state parliaments.

Not even England was spared the contagion. Already troubled by Scottish nationalism, it encountered further difficulties in Wales. A by-election held on July 14, 1966, at Carmarthen won the Welsh Nationalists a seat in the House of Commons. When the result was announced in Carmarthen, hundreds of cheering men and women, crying openly and hugging each other, began to sing "Land of My Fathers" in Welsh. The victorious candidate, president of the Nationalist Welsh Party, spoke in Welsh: "You cannot set a limit to the march of a nation. I don't think a Parliament for Wales can be very long delayed." [21] This was familiar language in the history of nationalism.

The symbols and techniques of nationalism not only continued to be used by the old established countries but also by the emergent nation-states. The latest revised collection of the world's national anthems lists more than 150, hailing the glories of every nation from Communist China ("Build anew the Great Wall from flesh and blood, arise!") to Tunisia, whose anthem paid tribute to "the spirit of our Habib, the great leader." [22] The national anthem of Western Samoa faithfully copied older European models:

> Oh! see and behold the stars
> On the waving banner;

[20] *Daily Express* (London), June 20, 1966.
[21] *Daily Telegraph* (London), July 15, 1966.
[22] *The National Anthems of the World* (Stuttgart, 1965), published by Stuttgart's Institut für Auslandsbeziehungen.

They are a sign that Samoa
Is able to lead. Oh!

Most new nation-states rejected their own rich supply of music and
instead copied the marches and hymns of Europe. The Brazzaville
Congo's "La Congolaise" ("Congolese, arise!") owed its inspiration to
"La Marseillaise." But Kenya's proposed anthem grafted its words
("Oh God of all creation / Bless this our land and nation") to the
music of a tribal lullaby. The new hymn of Cameroon was refreshingly
modest: "In barbaric times you lived your early days / But bit by bit
you are now leaving savage ways."

There was no perceptible change in the practice of inculcating
nationalism on children in school. The emotional patriotism which lies
at the root of nationalism starts inside the family and carries over into
the history classroom.[23] At school the child absorbs prejudices about his
own and other people and learns to place high value on his nation.
Teachers customarily are not inclined to remove the child's national
and racial bias. The immediate aim of education in such a system is to
lay a psychological foundation for a determined resistance to attack.[24]

A report on nationalism in current education was made by two
psychologists at a recent meeting of the British Association for the
Advancement of Science.[25] Basing their conclusions on a survey made
among children from six to eight years old in Austria, Belgium, Greece,
the Netherlands, and Britain, the psychologists reported that the first
thing most children learned about the people of other nations was to
dislike them. In general the children said that they liked the United

[23] The evidence of nationalism in education is overwhelming. In the appendix of
his *France, A Nation of Patriots*, Carlton J. H. Hayes presented a digest of French
textbooks in history used in the 1920's in French schools at the 7–9-year age level.
The following passage, titled "Moral of History," can be matched by excerpts
from history textbooks in virtually all countries: "Children, you have read the
history of your country, the recital of its victories and defeats, its prosperity and
adversity. Love your country as citizens and soldiers. As citizens you will fulfill all
your duties and remain attached to the institutions which the Republic has
founded. As soldiers you will perform with zeal your military service and, if the
Fatherland appeals to your devotion, you will be ready to shed your blood for it.
Thus France will follow the path of its glorious destiny if all citizens are united in
the same sentiment, love of the Fatherland" (Carlton J. H. Hayes, *France, A
Nation of Patriots* [New York, 1930], p. 346).

[24] Jonathan F. Scott, *Patriots in the Making* (New York, 1916), p. 251.

[25] Gustav Jahoda, professor of psychology at the University of Strathclyde in
Glasgow, and Henry Taifel, a social psychologist at Oxford. The meeting was
held in Cambridge, England, on September 3, 1965.

States and France better than they did Germany and the Soviet Union, even though they could not locate the four countries on a map of the globe. "Emotional attitudes toward various foreign countries are, as it were, built into small children before they have assimilated even the most elementary factual information about them." In experiments the children were asked to arrange photographs of people identified by nationality according to whether they liked or disliked them. Generally, the researchers reported, the children said that the people they liked belonged to their own nationality. This was especially true of English children. "One could almost say that among young children in England the word 'English' is equivalent to 'nice' and 'not English' to 'not nice.' " [26]

By preference the leaders of contemporary nations urged their young people to retain their "noble inheritance." In 1949, Vincent Massey, a Canadian educator and statesman, projected a credo "for young Canadians conscious of their country and with convictions about its life." With slight variations this credo could be utilized for the young people of every nation:

I believe in Canada with pride in her past, belief in her present, and faith in her future.

I believe in the quality of Canadian life, and in the character of Canadian institutions.

I believe in the Commonwealth of Nations within whose bounds we have found freedom, and outside which our national life would lose its independent being.

I believe in our abiding friendship with our nearest neighbors; an honest friendship without either the subservience or the mimicry which must impair true partnership.

I believe that Canada is one, and that if our minds dwell on those things which its parts have in common, we can find the unity of the whole.

I believe that with sound work, the spirit of a team, and an awareness of ourselves, we can look forward to achievements beyond our imagining.[27]

For the patriot these are fair words spoken by Massey in reverence for his country. For the internationalist this credo is obsolescent and dangerous. For the historian of nationalism it stands as another example of the most powerful political sentiment of our day.

[26] New York *Herald-Tribune*, Paris ed., Sept. 4–5, 1965.
[27] Vincent Massey, *On Being Canadian* (Toronto, 1949), p. 184.

INTENSIFICATION OF COLLECTIVIST NATIONALISM

To the old bourgeois nationalism was added an intensified socialist or collectivist nationalism, a development that was parallel to the emergence of collectivism in the twentieth century. With the age of bourgeois control and *laissez faire* well beyond its prime, nationalism was adopted in both the older countries and the new nation-states by societies which boasted of their large proletarian population. Collectivism was a new element in the history of nationalism.

This does not mean the triumph of a socialist or Communist way of life. Actually the dream of international proletarian revolution has faded.[28] The key factor was the failure of world revolution after the Russian Revolution of November 1917. Russian internationalism, as we have seen, eventually changed into Soviet nationalism, "a blend of Great Russian imperialism . . . and of Marxist determinism, monism, and universalism." [29] Lenin regarded the Soviet state as merely a temporary bastion until the highly industrialized West should turn Communist and thus fulfill Marx's prophecy. The world simply refused to adhere to Marx's formulas and Lenin's activism. Individual nations, instead of joining a vague global community, became the battlefields of the collectivist struggle. Russian leaders established the Comintern as the central organization to fight the battle for communism on many fronts. Instead of granting national autonomy, the Kremlin came to regard the Comintern—the supreme carrier of the revolution—as its special property. The process reached its culmination in Stalin's decision to seek socialism in one country.

There is a distinction between Marxian socialism and socialist collectivism. Today socialism throughout the West has more or less abandoned Marxism as its theoretical foundation and its practical guide.[30] Nineteenth-century Marxism has not fared well when applied to the realities of the twentieth century. "Only in the lands outside the Western historical community has Marxism tremendously gained in influence and prestige, a process which no Marxist at the end of the last century would have thought possible. . . . Nowhere is the emphasis on

[28] Carr, *op. cit.*, p. 51.

[29] Frederick C. Barghoorn, *Soviet Russian Nationalism* (New York, 1956), p. 255. See Chapter 11.

[30] Hans Kohn, "A New Look at Nationalism," *Virginia Quarterly Review* XXXII (Summer 1956), 332.

national sovereignty and its sanctity today as strong as in Communist society." [31] Marxian socialism was always defeated in its attempts to be international.[32] Labor internationalism proved to be a futile ideology: the real trend went exactly counter to it, for the labor movement again and again had to bow to nationalist sentiment not only because it was not strong enough to counter it, but because it coincided with the urgent interests of labor.[33] In virtually every crisis nationalism proved to be stronger and more resistant than class feeling.

Yet, despite the difficulties of Marxian socialism, there is a trend toward collectivism of one form or another. Perhaps the term "collectivist" should be used instead of "socialist," or "collectivist-socialist." No matter what the name, the society in which we live turns more and more in this direction. The process is twofold: as the nations of the world become more collectivist, they at the same time become more nationalist, and the more nationalist they become, the more collectivist they remain.

There appears to be a universal tendency of collectivist policy to become nationalistic. Workers everywhere identify themselves with the cause of nationalism. They find security in its strength. Their interests are common: they may not know all the members of their own community but at least they think and talk the same way.

What socialists seriously contemplate the equal division of existing capital resources among the peoples of the world? They all regard the capital as belonging not to humanity but to the nation—though within the nation few would dare to advocate that the richer regions should be deprived of some of "their" capital equipment in order to help the poorer regions. What socialists proclaim as a duty toward the fellow-members of the existing states they are not prepared to grant to the foreigner.[34]

Marxist theoreticians have a set reply to the contention that collectivist programs tend to become nationalistic. In Marxian dialectics, nationalism (bourgeoisie) and socialism (proletariat) are thesis and antithesis, which under historical impact are combined in a synthesis called "national socialism." This synthesis, then acts as a new thesis (national socialism), opposed to another synthesis (communism). Out

---

[31] *Ibid.*

[32] Franz Borkenau, *Socialism: National or International* (London, 1942), p. 158.

[33] *Ibid.*

[34] Friedrich A. Hayek, *The Road to Serfdom* (Chicago, 1944), pp. 140–141.

of this conflict, say the theoreticians, will emerge the "truly socialist state," just and humane, the social paradise for which men have awaited patiently through the centuries. Unfortunately, this explanation fails to conform to realities of the twentieth century. Marxian collectivism on a world scale has shown itself to be unattainable, except in the service of a small elite.

NATIONALISM AND WORLD ORDER

Carlton J. H. Hayes called the "new trinity" of nationalism—the combination of nationality, the national state, and national patriotism —the "most powerful political sentiment of the contemporary world." [35] The uncompromising sovereign national state continues to be the master institution of modern times. Nationalism remains a tough fact of life, "fed by roots that are sunk deep in man's need to hold on to the values deemed good." [36] It still excels other appeals to human emotions—social or religious appeals—by its impact on masses and individuals alike.[37]

For the achievement of needs and desires, for order and safety, the nation seems to be the modern means. Everything the citizen hears and sees seems to re-enforce this observation. The radio is national, television is national. The schools teach national citizenship. The historians chiefly teach and write national histories. Literature and cooking and sports are judged on national criteria. Even science and music, written in international notation and symbol, becomes Russian, German, French, or American, rather than just science and music. To make certain that national values rather than others prevail, patriotic societies in every country demand with some success that foreign influences be rooted out, that only good national or "one hundred per cent" ideas be encouraged.[38]

We have seen that nationalism was originally a sentiment devoted to individual liberty. It attracted men concerned with the problem of protecting themselves against both internal and external enemies: they

[35] See Carlton J. H. Hayes, *Essays on Nationalism* (New York, 1926), pp. 245–250.

[36] Henry C. Dillard, "Nationalism: Mid-Century Puzzle," *Virginia Quarterly Review*, XXVIII (Oct. 1952), 546.

[37] Kohn, *op. cit.*, p. 321.

[38] Boyd C. Shafer, *Nationalism: Interpreters and Interpretation*, Publication No. 20: Service Center for Teachers of History, American Historical Association (Washington, D.C., 1959), p. 12.

were certain that it was a means by which they could find security in uncertain times. Since then virtually every political idea and activity of men has worked to promote nationalism. The sentiment became suffused with romantic idealization of the past, exaggerated and oversentimentalized. In both its older and its newer patterns it tended to become the opposite of what it set out to be. First it stressed universal freedom and the universality of culture; later it assumed an arrogant, aggressive, integral form.

A dangerous gap remains. In this day of advanced communication, when the peoples of the world are closer together than ever before, virtually every important influence on the lives of men is international. Yet, man's loyalty remains with the national state. The more closely people become interdependent, the more they react by turning to their national traditions.

This chasm between nationalism and internationalism remains a central problem of mankind. The survival of man may well depend on whether or not the gap is bridged. Harold J. Laski put it bluntly: "Nationalism emerging into statehood results, in a word, in an egoism which we discover to be intolerable. Either we must curb its excesses —which mean the end of the sovereign state—or they will destroy civilization." [39] In an age of hydrogen bombs there is always the possibility that an atomic holocaust induced by extreme nationalism might mean the end, or the near end, of the human race.

Many historians, although aware of the risks of prophecy, remain pessimistic. They find it problematical whether or not in the long run all the nations of the world, including the liberal democratic, the communist, and the primitively tribal, can compose their respective nationalisms and learn to live together in peace. They believe that the world is farther removed from the goal of peace than a half century ago. Peace, they say, would require a far better understanding of the complicated psychology of nations than has yet been attained. If nationalism is to be succeeded by some other kind of loyalty, perhaps to a world religion or to a world state, then other realities and other myths will have to provide as much and to affect the peoples of the current nations as deeply as nationalism.[40]

The British historian Hugh Seton-Watson expresses no doubts about

[39] Harold J. Laski, *Nationalism and the Future of Civilization* (London, 1932), p. 26.
[40] Shafer, *op. cit.*, p. 12.

the future of nationalism. In the first issue of the *Journal of Contemporary History*,[41] he predicts an intensification of nationalism, the emergence of more "monsters" like Hitler and Stalin, and an increasing resemblance of the new African dictatorships to the Third Reich, rather than to Russia or China. He believes that the new Hitler or Stalin would probably come from the "uprooted, classless, faceless hordes" of the big cities of Europe and America. More significant than Hitler's petty bourgeois background was his experience in the "morally and culturally uprooted population of the great city," while Stalin, the other great mass exterminator of our age, was also "a half-educated, classless, uprooted figure." Seton-Watson describes the nationalist regime built up by Nasser in the last ten years as similar to fascist totalitarianism. There is danger in the proliferation of nationalist regimes: "Revolutionary nationalist regimes, applying techniques of mass mobilization, injecting their quasi-socialist ideologies, and moving from simple dictatorship ever farther towards totalitarianism, may end up nearer to the Third Reich than to the Soviet or Chinese model." Seton-Watson sees little sign of fascism in Western democracies, but detects such trends in Argentina, the Muslim Brotherhood, and Japan. While the Spanish and Portuguese regimes retain undoubted elements of fascism, both appear to be in decline. Potentially more dangerous than passing trends in western Europe might be some form of Negro fascism in the northern United States or a totalitarian trend in Quebec nationalism.

Against pessimistic views of the future of nationalism may be balanced the claim that, although the new nationalism retains the same characteristics as the old, it is likely to be only a phase of political development. This interpretation holds that nationalism should be judged as a comparatively recent phenomenon in the course of history: possibly it may subside before too long. In the words of John Bowle, "All ideologies shift and change, and all societies develop. We may yet witness the development of the nationalist idea into a world view, in spite of the frightful catastrophes its debasement may still bring about." [42] Karl W. Deutsch describes a double action: "Thus far, the age of nationalism has grouped people apart from each other, and may for a time continue to do so. But at the same time it is preparing them,

---

[41] Hugh Seton-Watson, "Fascism, Right and Left," *Journal of Contemporary History*, I, No. 1 (1966), pp. 183–197.

[42] John Bowle, *The Nationalist Idea* (London, 1955), p. 64.

and perhaps in part has already prepared them, for a more thorough-going world-wide unity than has ever been seen in human history." [43] Deutsch believes that even the growth of national consciousness may contribute to this end. "To reveal what is, to show the true state of affairs for part of the political problems of a part of mankind may serve as a preparation for teaching men to be aware of the whole pattern of their affairs, and of the single problem of mankind on its painful way to unity. As men attain this insight into the essential unity of their fate on this planet, the age of nationalism and of the growth of nations may recede into its proper historical perspective." [44]

It would seem that a remedy for the excesses of nationalism would be an international reign of law, based on conviction and agreement. Global federation and the sovereign national state are incompatible. In the present situation the nations jockey for position to enhance their national power. In a world community, on the other hand, no part would have the power or the right to act as its own will deemed best, without regard to the will of the other parts. Each member would be bound by the combined will of the constituent members. "We must choose between the one and the other; we cannot have both. We must recognize that international law has a claim superior to municipal. We must admit that there are things a state is not entitled to will—fields of decision in which its choice is one term only in an equation of forces. Little by little there must grow [in a world community] the author-ity to determine all questions." [45]

It is agreed generally that the key to effective world cooperation is education. It will be necessary for schools to teach not the narrow national history which has been thought desirable and sufficient, but world history from an unbiased point of view. Children from an early age would be made aware of the quality of men and of the interde-pendence of mankind. Textbooks would be made as free as possible from national prejudice. All history texts used in schools would be written by scholars dedicated to the progress of the human race rather than to any special nation. "The books to be used in teaching would have to be free from national bias, as far as humanly possible. There would have to be devices to secure impartiality. I should like to have the parts dealing with South America written by Norwegians, but the

---

[43] Karl W. Deutsch, *Nationalism and Social Communication* (New York, 1953), p. 167.
[44] *Ibid.*   [45] Laski, *op. cit.*, p. 29.

parts dealing with the Vikings should be written by Italians, and the parts dealing with medieval Italy by Americans." [46]

Merely to state the problem is to indicate its immensity. The idolatrous character of nationalism in schools throughout the world can be seen in the reaction to violations of its symbols. Erich Fromm pictures a child who refuses to take an oath of allegiance in the classroom, or who says specifically: "I do not love my country." Furious contempt would automatically be poured upon this youngster by both teachers and other students. If the child went further and trampled upon his country's flag, he would have done something unspeakable. "He would have committed a crime which is not *one* crime among others, but *the* crime, the one unforgivable and unpardonable." [47]

A clue to the difficulty of modifying nationalist teaching may be found in the example of a project sponsored by the United Nations Educational and Scientific Organization (UNESCO). In 1962, UNESCO organized the International Commission for a History of the Scientific and Cultural Development of Mankind, under the chairmanship of Professor Paulo E. de Barrêdo of Brazil, and composed of a group of distinguished contributors from all over the world. Their purpose was to publish a "strictly scientific" history, departing from the traditional approach, with particular importance attached to "political, economic, and even military factors," and offering as a corrective the story of how men, individually and collectively, conceived of their common humanity. The aim was to show the fundamental unity of the various groups of mankind and at the same time to strike a blow at biased national history. The contributors would subjugate their feelings of nationalism in favor of a world view. The first volume, which appeared in 1963, was entitled *Prehistory and the Beginnings of Civilization*.[48] There were immediate differences of opinion even on an

---

[46] Russell, *op. cit,* pp. 146–147. According to the Swiss psychologist Jean Piaget, neither patriotism nor even the idea of a homeland comes naturally to a child. The child assumes that his surroundings and his way of life are the only possible ones in existence. Otto Klineberg and Wallace E. Lambert add that the process of stereotyping begins at home, often unwittingly, as parents try to give their children a sense of national identity. Children refer to foreign groups as "people who are not like us"—an attitude they maintain for the rest of their lives. See Maya Pines, "How Different is Foreign?" *The New York Times Magazine,* May 21, 1967, pp. 70–79.

[47] Fromm, *op. cit.,* p. 59.

[48] Jacquetta Hawkes and Leonard Woolley, *Prehistory and the Beginnings of Civilization* (London, 1963).

innocuous subject unrelated to national states. At the end of those chapters for which he was responsible, coauthor Sir Leonard Woolley was forced to add extensive footnotes giving space to Professor I. M. Diakanoff, a Soviet historian who lectured the author on his misinterpretation of "the laws of social development in history." Undoubtedly succeeding volumes, especially those dealing with national history, will encounter even more difficulties.[49] The limited success of the project indicates the extent of the task facing those who would purge textbooks of national bias.

Of necessity then we must return to our persistent theme: the nation-state remains the chief political instrument of the world; nation-preserving and nation-building remain the major political pursuits of man. Karl W. Deutsch suggests that we are faced with three alternatives: a world of nationalist conflicts; a world of international political and legal conformity; or a pluralistic world of sovereign nations and diverse social systems striving to avoid fatal collisions and to respect their currently irreducible diversity.[50] Human beings must learn nonnational ways of doing things. Our task is to create a world community, and in the process avoid the dangers of nationalism without sacrificing our rich national cultures.

[49] Volume II appeared in 1965: Luigi Pareti, *The Ancient World* (New York, 1965).

[50] Karl W. Deutsch, *Nationalism and Social Communication* (rev. ed.; Cambridge, Mass., 1966), p. 4.

Index